Teacher and Education in a Developing Society

By the Same Author

- *Data Communication and Computer Networks*
- *Development and Planning of Modern Education* (9th Edition)
- *Essentials of Educational Psychology* (2nd Edition)
- *Essentials of Educational Technology* (2nd Edition)
- *Essentials of Examination System: Evaluation, Tests and Measurement*
- *Landmarks in the History of Modern Indian Education* (7th Edition)
- *Principles, Methods and Techniques of Teaching* (2nd Edition)
- *Teacher and Education in a Developing Society* (5th Edition)
- *Teaching of Commerce: A Practical Approach* (2nd Edition)
- *Teaching of History: A Practical Approach* (4th Edition)
- *Teaching of Social Studies: A Practical Approach* (4th Edition)
- *Theory and Principles of Education*
  (*Philosophical and Sociological Bases of Education*) (13th Edition)

Teacher and Education in a Developing Society

Fifth Edition

J C Aggarwal
Deputy Director of Education (Retd.)
Directorate of Education, Delhi

VIKAS®
VIKAS® PUBLISHING HOUSE PVT LTD

VIKAS® PUBLISHING HOUSE PRIVATE LIMITED
E-28, Sector-8, Noida-201301 (UP), India
Phone: +91-120-4078900 • Fax: +91-120-4078999
Registered Office: A-27, 2nd Floor, Mohan Co-operative Industrial Estate, New Delhi-110044
E-mail: helpline@vikaspublishing.com • Website: www.vikaspublishing.com

SALES AND BRANCH OFFICES OF VIKAS® AND S CHAND AND COMPANY LIMITED

Chennai : Ph: 044-2363 2120, chennai@schandpublishing.com
Guwahati : Ph: 0361-2738 811, 2735 640, guwahati@schandpublishing.com
Hyderabad : Ph: 040-4018 6018, hyderabad@schandpublishing.com
Jalandhar : Ph: 0181-4645 630, jalandhar@schandpublishing.com
Kolkata : Ph: 033-2335 7458, 2335 3914, kolkata@schandpublishing.com
Lucknow : Ph: 0522-4003 633, lucknow@schandpublishing.com
Mumbai : Ph: 022-2500 0297, mumbai@schandpublishing.com
Patna : Ph: 0612-2260 011, patna@schandpublishing.com

Teacher and Education in a Developing Society
ISBN: 978-81259-3846-0 Product Code: V7TED69TEDU10ENAE10O

Fifth Edition 2010
Reprint 2022 (Twice)

PRINTED IN INDIA
By Vikas Publishing House Private Limited, Plot 20/4, Site-IV, Industrial Area Sahibabad, Ghaziabad-201010 and Published by Vikas Publishing House Private Limited, E-28, Sector-8, Noida-201301

Preface to the Fifth Edition

The author is grateful to the readers for their positive response to this book.

The book has been thoroughly revised in the light of the facts and figures contained in the following publications:

1. *'Annual Report 2006-2007'*, Ministry of Human Resource Development, Government of India.
2. *'Annual Report 2007-2008'*, U.G.C.
3. *'Census of India 2001'*, Registrar General and Census Commissioner, India.
4. *'Economic Survey 2008-2009'*, Ministry of Finance and Company Affairs, Government of India.
5. *'Selected Educational Statistics 2000-2001'*, Ministry of Human Resource Development, Government of India.
6. *'Eleventh Five Year Plan 2007-2012'*, Planning Commission.
7. *'The State of the World's Children 2009'*, UNICEF.
8. *'India 2008'*, Ministry of Information and Broadcasting, Government of India.

It is hoped that the Fifth edition of this book would prove all the more useful to the readers.

J C Aggarwal

Preface to the First Edition

This book is essentially 'student-centred' and 'examination-centred'. It is designed to fulfil the examination needs of the B.Ed. students of various universities in India. All possible efforts have been made to provide an exhaustive treatment of all the topics in a cogent, lucid and simple manner so that the students can grasp the subject matter clearly and completely and are able to give suitable answers with full confidence.

The book is divided into five parts: Part 1: Education: Philosophical and Sociological Basis of Education; Part II: Education in a Developing (Emerging) Society: Part III: Teacher's Role, Education, skills, Competencies and Status; Part IV: Diverse Issues covering eleven Contemporary Educational Topics; Part V: Recent Development in Education and Statistics.

Facts and figures in the book are based on the publications of the Ministry of Human Resource Development, Department of Education, Government of India; National Council of Educational Research and Training (NCERT); National Institute of Educational Planning and Administration (N1EPA); University Grants Commission (UGC); Association of Indian Universities (A1U); United Nations Educational Scientific and Cultural Organisation (UNESCO); United Nations Children's emergency Fund (UN1CEF) and the World Bank.

The author is grateful to all the authors and the publishers whose books he has made use of in the preparation of this publication.

J C Aggarwal

Contents

Part V:
RECENT DEVELOPMENTS IN EDUCATION

List of Illustrations

List of Tables

Part I

Education: Philosophical and Sociological Basis

1 Definition, Meaning and Function of Education

Different Interpretations of Education

Philosophers and thinkers from Yajnavalkya (about 600 BC) to Gandhi (1869-1948 AD) in the east and Socrates (469-399 BC) to Dewey (1859-1952 AD) in the west have defined education in accordance with their philosophy of life. The result is that different concepts and definitions of education have emerged.

The concept of education is like a diamond which appears to be of a different colour (nature) when seen from different angles (Point of view or philosophy of life).

There are four important reasons for different interpretations and definitions of education.

1. Complex nature of human personality.
2. Complex nature of environment.
3. Different philosophies of life.
4. Different educational theories and practices.

Significance of Education

Nevertheless, in spite of these difference, one thing seems to be certain Education plays an important role in moulding the character and personality of an individual.

It is on account of this reason that J.B. Watson (1878-1958) a great behavourist psychologist, once observed "Give me a dozen healthy infants, well-formed and my own specified world to bring them up in and I'll guarantee to take anyone at random and train him to become any type of specialist I might select—doctor, lawyer, artist, merchant chief and yes, even beggarman and thief, regardless of his talents, penchants, tendencies, abilities, vocations and race of his ancestors." We may not entirely agree with this statement but certainly there is a great truth in it and on account of this, educational institutions are set up for the education and training of youth.

Joseph Addison (1672-1719) believed, "what sculpture is to a block of marble, education is to a human soul."

The Education Commission 1964-66, the first commission in independent India which examined all the facts of education at all levels very aptly began its report with these words, "The destiny of India is now being shaped in her classrooms. This we believe, is no mere rhetoric. In a world based on science and technology, it is education that determines the level of prosperity, welfare, and security of the people. On the quality and number of persons coming out of our school and colleges will depend our success in the great enterprise of national reconstruction whose principle objective is to raise the standard of living of our people."

The National Policy on Education 1986 and as slightly modified in 1992 has also observed, "The country has reached a stage in its economic and technical development when a major effort must be made to derive the maximum benefit from the assets already created and to ensure that the fruits of change reach all sections. Education is the high way to that goal" Again it states, "In our national perception education is essentially for all. This is fundamental to our all-round development, material and spiritual. In sum education is a unique investment in the present and the future."

According to thinkers in ancient India, Vidya or knowledge or learning or education was considered the 'third eye' of man, which gives him on insight into all affairs and teaches him how to act; it leads us to our salvation: in the mundane sphere it leads us to all round progress and prosperity. The illumination given to us by Vidya shatters illusion, removes difficulties and enables us to realise the true value of life. A person who does not possess the light of education, may be really described as blind. The correct insight, which men and women get from Vidya, naturally increases their intelligence, power and efficiency. The uses of Vidya are too diverse to be enumerated exhaustively; it nourishes us like the mother; directs us to the proper path like the father; and gives us delight and comfort like the wife. It increases our fame; and makes us pure and more cultured. When we are in the solitude of a journey, or of a foreign country, it serves us as a valued companion. It is thus a veritable desire-yielding tree.

The following verse is a common saying in India.

Swadesh pujyate raja,
Vidvan sarvatra pujyata

A king is respected in his own kingdom while a learned man is worshipped every where. The Hindu law-givers even go further and lay down that the very sight of a learned man is sacred.

Education in ancient India aimed at the following:

Sarve bhavantu sukhinah, Sarve santu niramaya, Sarve bhadrani pashyahtu, Ma Kaschit dukhabhay bhavet.

Let all be happy and healthy,
Let all be courteous and gentle, and
Let nobody feel the pinch of sorrow.

Definitions of Education

Thoughts of some great eastern especially Indian thinkers on education

1. *Aurobindo, Sri* (1872-1950)—Building of the human mind and spirit.
2. *Confucius* (551 - 478 B.C.) A Chinese Scholar—Development of the whole man.
3. *Dayananda, Swami* (1824-1883)—Formation of Character.
4. *Gandhi, M.K.* (1869-1948)—All round drawing out of the best.
5. *Krishnamurti, J*—Helping the individual to flower greatly in love and wisdom.
6 *Munshi, Jawahar Lal* (1887-1974)—Making a youngman an embodiment of the finest in his culture.

7. *Nanak, Guru* (1469-1539)—Enabling an individual to win victory over the five enemies—lust, anger, greed, infatuation and ego. (Kam, Korodh, Lobh, Moh, Ahankar)
8. *Nehru, Jawahar Lal* (1889-1964)—Enabling the individual to be a producer as well as a good citizen.
9. *Radha Krishnan, Sarvapalli* (1888-1975)—Training the intellect, refinement of the heart and discipline of the spirit.
10 *Rama Krishna Parmahansa* (1836-1886)—Purification of the mind and the heart.
11. *Rigveda* (3000 B.C.)—Noble thoughts coming from every side.
12 *Sankaracharya* (788-820)—Realisation of the self and attainment of '*Mokisha*' (Salvation).
13. *Tagore, Rabindranath* (1861-1941)—Making life in harmony with existence.
14. *Upanishad, Brihadarsa Nayak* (1000 BC)—Leading from the unreal to the real, from darkness to light, from death to immortality.
15. *Vivikananda, Swami* (1863-1902)—Manifestation of the perfection already in man.
16. *Zakir Husain* (1897-1969)—Helping the mind of the educand to realise absolute moral and intellectual value.

Some Great Western Thinkers on Education

17. *Aristotle* (384-322 B.C.)—Creation of a sound mind in a sound body.
18. *Comenius, John Amos* (1592-1670)—Development of the whole man.
19. *Dewey, John* (1859-1952)—Increasing social efficiency.
20. *Emerson, Ralph Waldo* (1803-1882)—Controlling the mind.
21. *Erasmus, Desiderius* (1466-1536)—Developing real wisdom.
22. *Froebel, Friedrich* (1782-1852)—Leading and guiding for peace and unity with God.
23. *Harris, T. William* (1835-1928)—Preparing the individual for the reciprocal union with society.
24. *Herbart, Johann Friedrich* (1776-1841)—Developing morality.
25. *Horne, H.H.* (1874-1946)—Adjusting with the ultimate nature of the cosmos.

26. *Huxley, Thomas Henry* (1825-1895)—Fashioning the will of the individual to enable him to move in harmony with nature
27. *Jacks, M.L.*—Enabling the child to sense eternal realities.
28. *Kilpatrick, William Heard* (1871-1925)—Enabling the child full participation in the richest available group life.
29 *Locke, John* (1632-1704)—Attainment of a sound mind in a sound body.
30. *Mann, Horace* (1796-1859)—Educating children in the great eternal principle of justice and might which underline the entire length of human existence.
31. *Milton, John* (1608-1674)—Fitting a man to perform justly, skillful, and magnanimously all the official, both private and public, of peace and war.
32. *Montaigne, Michel Eyquem De* (1533-1592)—Cultivating manners, behaviour, and judgement than bare and mere liberal learning.
33. *Montessori, Maria* (1870-1952)—Helping in the complete unfolding of the child's individuality.
34. *Sunn, T. Percy* (1870-1944)—Complete development of the individuality of the child so that he can make an original contribution to human life according to the best of his capacity.
    Parker, Francis Wayland (1837-1902)—Realisation of all the possibilities of human growth.
35. *Pestalozzi, Johann Heinrich* (1746-1827)—Natural, harmonious and progressive development of men's innate powers.
36. *Plato* (427-347 B.C.)—Developing the body and the soul of all the perfections which they are capable of.
37. *Quintilian* (38-86 A.D.)—Character as the end of education,
38. *Rousseau, Jean Jacques* (1712-1778)—Development from within.
39. *Ruskin, John* (1819-1900)—Developing physical health, manual and moral training
40. *Russell, Bertrand* (1872-1970)—Developing four qualities in child-courage, intelligence, sensitiveness and vitality.
41. *Santayana* (1863-1952)—Providing liberal education to a minority and teaching of three R's for the masses.
42. *Schiller, Friedrich* (1759-1805)—Education as a process of emotional development.

43. *Socrates* (469-399 B.C.)—Dispelling error and discovering truth.
44. *Spencer, Herbart* (1820-1903)—Preparing for complete living.
45. *Tolstoy, Count Leo Nikolayevich* (1828-1910)—An advocate of freedom in learning
46. *Whitehead, Alfred North* (1861-1947)—Learning to be an active assimilation of general ideas which could be applied to life.

Classification and Evaluation of Definition of Education

It is clear that there are as many concepts of education as there are thinkers.

To simplify matters, we may make a two-fold classification as under:

1. Definitions which lay stress on inner potentialities.
2. Definitions which lay stress on adoption to environmental and social aspects.

Development of Inner Potentialities

Thinkers like Aurobindo, Gandhi, Sankaracharya, Tagore and Vivekanand of India and Aristotle, Nunn, Pestalozzi and Plato of the west come under this category.

Aurobindo defines education as "helping the growing soul to draw out that in itself."

Gandhi says, "By education, I mean an all-round drawing out of the best in the child and man—body, mind and spirit."

Sankaracharya says, "Education is realisation of the self."

Tagore thinks, "Education means enabling the mind to find out that ultimate truth which emancipates us from the bondage of the dust and gives us the wealth, not of things but of inner light, not of power but of love, making the truth its own and giving expression to it."

According to Vivekanand, "Education is the manifestation of divine perfection already existing in man—Education means the exposition of man's complete individuality."

Aristotle speaks of education as "the creation of a sound mind in a sound body." Education, according to him, should develop the body i.e., the physical capacities of the child and the mind which means his intellectual, emotional, moral and spiritual capacities.

According to Nunn, "Education is the complete development of the individuality so that he can make an original contribution to human life to his best capacity." The individual is a sum total of various constituents and all these must be developed. Every individual is a unique one and as such the task of education is to cater to the individual needs. The development should take place to the maximum possible extent.

Pestalozzi defines education "as the natural, harmonious, and progressive development of man's innate powers". Man is endowed with certain inborn powers and capacities and the task of education is to bring about the development of these. Due regard should be paid in the process of education to the child's nature and needs. Undue stress should not be laid on the development of some powers of the child at the cost of others. A proper balance should be struck in the development of the various innate powers of the child.

Plato said, "Education develops in the body and in the soul (of the pupil) all the beauty and all the perfection which he is capable of."

Adaptation of the Individual to Environmental and Social Aspects

In the words of Dewey, "Education is the development of all those capacities in the individual which will enable him to control his environment and fulfil his responsibilities."

According to Redden, "Education is the deliberate and systematic influence extended by the mature person upon the immature through instruction, discipline and harmonious development of the physical, intellectual, aesthetic, social and spiritual powers of the human being according to their essential hierarchy by and for the individual and social uses and directed towards the union of the educand with the creator as the final end". The ultimate goal of life is the union of the individual with God. This union can take place only when the various capacities of the child are developed for the good of the individual as well as that of society.

Thomson says, "By education I mean the influence of the environment upon the individual to produce a permanent change in his habits of behaviour, of thought and of his attitude. Environment has various aspects—physical, social and cultural. Education should facilitate the task of adaptation of the child to his environment."

Best Definition

A review of these definitions reveals that the definition given by Gandhi is the best. Gandhi had a scientific attitude of mind. He observed facts, sorted them before accepting them and after weighing them well, he drew his conclusions. Gandhi felt that while physical and intellectual development was necessary, the training of a child's heart and spirit was more important. He remarked, "By education I mean an all-round drawing out of the best in the child and man—body, mind and spirit. Literacy is not the end of education nor even the beginning. It is one of the means whereby man and woman can be educated. Literacy in itself is no education" This aim is in conformity with the one accepted by the Board of Education in England, viz., "the aim of education should be to develop to the full potentialities of every child at school, in accord always with the general good of the community of which he is a member".

'Drawing out' and not 'Pouring in'—has been stressed by Gandhi. He wrote, "We have upto now concentrated on stuffing a child's mind with all kinds of information without even stimulating or developing them."

He fully realised that nature has endowed children and youth with tremendous vitality. They have within them the springs of youth, joy and vigour. They have the God-given curiosity to wish to know things for themselves. The task of education is to use these powers. It would be wrong to suppress them. This energy should be utilised and harnessed properly.

What do we understand by "All-round"?—Man is neither mere intellectual nor the gross animal body, nor the heart or soul alone. A proper and harmonious combination of all these is required for the making of the whole man.

"True education," says Gandhi, "is that which draws out and stimulates the spiritual, intellectual and physical faculties of the children". Any programme of education that puts exclusive emphasis on one of these aspects of the human personality is against the basic principle of education.

Meaning of the term 'best in man'—The best in man is related to three aspects: body, mind and spirit, No field should remain neglected. The best in man will include the harmonious development of all the three aspects or faculties of the child.

How can we draw out the best?—The best can be drawn out by touching the hearts of children. Gandhi states, "If I was to be their real teacher and guardian, I must help them to solve the problems that faced them, and I must take along the right channel the surging aspirations of this youth".

Gandhi further explained the concept of education in his book *Basic Education* (Page 12 and 13) as, "I hold that true education of the intellect can only come through a proper exercise and training of the bodily organs, e.g., hands, feet, eyes, ears, nose etc. In other words an intelligent use of the organs in a child provides the best and quickest way of developing his intellect. But unless the development of the mind goes hand in hand with a corresponding awakening of the soul, the former alone would prove to be a poor lop-sided affair. By spiritual training I mean education of the heart. A proper and an all round development of the mind, therefore, can take place only when it proceeds 'pari passu' with education of the physical and spiritual faculties of the child. They constitute an indivisible whole."

Functional and operational definition of education—Education is a process which draws out the best in the child with the aim of producing well balanced personalities culturally refined, emotionally stable, ethically sound mentally alert, morally upright, physically strong, socially efficient, spiritually upright vocationally self-sufficient and internationally liberal.

Etymological meaning of education—Etymologically, the word 'education' is derived from some Latin words which are explained as under:

1. Education	The act of teaching
2. Educere	To lead out or to draw out
3. Educare	To bring up, to train, to nourish
4. Educo	To lead forth, to extract out

Thus education implies:

1. Act of drawing out
2. —— of extracting out.
3. —— of leading forth.
4. —— of leading out.
5. —— of teaching.
6. —— of training.

Wider Meaning of Education

Whatever broadens our horizons, deepens our insight, refines our reactions and stimulates thought and feeling, educates us. It includes all influences—cultural, domestic, economic, geographical, political, religious, social and spiritual. Even the climate, soil and surroundings educate us. In this context, the views of R.C. Lodge as given in his book *Philosophy of Education* deserve careful consideration. "In the wider sense, all experience is said to be educative. The bite of a mosquito, the taste of watermelon, the experience of falling in love, of flying in an aeroplane, of being in a storm in a small boat—all such experiences have a direct educative effect on us. The child educates the parents, the pupil educates his teachers... Everything we say, think or do educates us no less than what is said or done to us by other beings, animate or inanimate. In the wider sense, life is education and education is life."

John Stuart Mill says, "Not only does education include whatever we do for ourselves and whatever is done for us by others, for the express purpose of bringing us somewhat nearer to the perfection of our nature, it does more, in its largest acceptance, it comprehends even the indirect effects produced on character, and on human faculties, by things of which the direct purposes are quite different, by laws, by forms of government, by the industrial arts, by the modes of social life, nay even by physical facts not dependent on human will, by climate, soil and local position. Every environment, every surrounding, every activity helps to shape the human being. A human soul is in constant interaction with his environment. The interaction results in the modification of human behaviour or education."

In the words of William H. Kilpatrick, "From the broad point of view all life thoughtfully lived is education." It is said that a pupil gets one-fourth of his education from his teacher, another fourth by his own intellectual efforts, another fourth from his fellow students and the rest in the course of time through life and experience.

The wider meaning of education includes the following:

1. The process of education is a lifelong process, from infancy to old age or from 'womb to grave'.
2. It includes experiences gained through the various formal and informal agencies of education, We learn from home, school, church, cinema, club, press, travel, friends, physical and social environments.

3. We receive education many a time when we are not conscious of the fact.
4. All experience is said to be educative.

Narrow Meaning of Education

In a narrow sense education as pointed by G.S. Mill is, 'the culture which each generation purposefully gives to those who are to be its successors, in order to qualify them for at least keeping up and if possible for raising the level of improvement which has been attained.' It thus includes special and specific influences. Education thus in a narrower sense means a conscious and deliberate process, well-planned to modify the behaviour of the educand in desirable and socially approved channels and to bring about in the educand specific knowledge and skills. This point is explained as under:

1. Such a type of education is imparted in planned institutions like schools.
2. It is a deliberate, conscious and systematic influence exerted by the mature person i.e. the teacher, on the immature person i.e., the child.
3. It is limited to the teaching of ready-made material.
4. This type of education is intentional rather than incidental.
5. Knowledge is considered as the accumulated experience of the human race.
6. Education is regarded as synonymous with instruction.

Characteristics of Education

Education—A lifelong process—Education is a continuous process of development from 'womb to the tomb'. Several thinkers hold the view that education starts even before birth. In the *Mahabharta* for instance, Abhimanyu is mentioned to have learnt the skills of breaking the 'Chakrvyah' in his mother's womb.

Education—A bipolar process—John Adams has observed, "It (education) is a bipolar process in which one personality acts upon another in order to modify the development of the other. The process is not only deliberate but a conscious one. The educator has the clearly realised intention of modifying the educand (student). James S. Ross has stated, "like a magnet, education must have two poles, it is a bi-polar process."

Education—A tripolar and multipolar process—Education is also regarded as a tripolar process involving the interaction of the personality of the educator on that of the educand in a social setting which affects the modification of the behaviour of the educand. The knowledge of the nature of the educand is at once very useful and essential. Similarly the educator also must thoroughly understand himself—his assets and limitations and act accordingly in educating the educand. The social setting has to be presented by the educator to the educand in a simplied and purified manner. It must be remembered that the unconscious influence of the environment is subtle and pervasive.

The basic system of education as propounded by Gandhi emphasised three aspects (a) the student, (b) the craft or the subject, and (c) the environment—physical and social. Introducing the third element, i.e., the social environment, Dewey has emphasised the society as the source of the curriculum or subjects to be taught. Since all these three poles—the teacher the pupil and curriculum are important, education is called a tripolar process.

Education—A deliberate process—The process of education is not only conscious but also deliberate. The educator is fully aware of the fact that his aim is to develop the personality of the child along definite lines through the modification of his behaviour.

Education—A psychological process—According to the psychological aspect of the process, the educator must understand the nature, interests, capacities and limitations of the child.

Education—A sociological process—This implies that the educator must interpret and develop the endowments (capacities) of the child in a social setting. A child is a social being and as such must be educated in such a way than he becomes a useful member of the society.

Education—A child centred process—The modern educator considers the child as a 'hero' in the drama of education and assigns the central place to him. The subject matter, the teacher and the environment are all for him and not he for them. The child centred process signifies that the educator must study each child carefully and attend to his individual needs. Since the child is the focus, the school curriculum and environment must provide for his total growth taking into account all the essential areas: the aesthetic, the creative, the ethical, the linguistic, the manual, the mathematical, the physical, the scientific, the social and the spiritual.

Education—A life long process—Education is a cradle-to-the grave process, no longer a concentration on the early years. Every year, every month, every day and every minute, step by step a person learns. In the new world no one knows what the morrow will bring. And so every individual must equip himself in every moment of his life to meet the new challenges in life, Education must at all stages become self-education, so that with the tools of education acquired at school, the adult will continue his education throughout life with all the means at his disposal—the library, the reading room, camps, tours, mass media, clubs, institutions, etc. life long education is acquired through formal, non-formal and informal means of education.

Traditional versus new education—There seems to be potentially a serious philosophical conflict between the new 'manpower' interest in education and the traditional view of education's role in a free society. In the context of manpower shortage, the educational system comes to be viewed as a 'brain-power industry' whose social function is to build human beings as instruments for building national, economic and military strength. Under the old view it was taken for granted that education contributed indirectly to the economic and general welfare of the nation, but the over-reaching purpose of education in a free society was to enable individuals to realise their full human potentialities for their own sake."

Education is not information or knowledge—As observed by A. N. Whitehead, "A merely well-informed person is the most useless bore on earth". Education is not synonymous with information and knowledge. The child's mind is not be to stuffed with all kinds of knowledge. Teachers are not information mongers and walking encyclopedias. Information and knowledge must lead to constructive thinking and wisdom.

Education is not instruction—Instruction denotes passivity on the part of the child. It denotes ordering and not motivating the child. Instruction in mainly confined to communication of knowledge skills and attitude. Practical activity falls into oblivion in instruction. In the world of F.W. Roberston, "Instruction ends in the classroom but education ends with life". A UNESCO publication 'Learning To Be (1975)' has preferred the term life-long education in place of instruction. In instruction as observed by Bertrand Russell, the "school has the opportunity of instilling certain mental habits". In education, this just forms a part of education.

Education as teaching—Education has a much wider scope than teaching. Teaching is primarily and basically concerned with the knowledge of school subjects. It is on account of this reason that the diplomas and degrees like 'Licentiate in Teaching' (L.T.) and 'Bachelor of Teaching' (B.T.) have been replaced by 'Bachelor of Education' (B. Ed.). Teaching involves at least two persons, that is, the teacher and the taught but education can be self-education.

Education and training—Traditionally there is no difference between education and training. Educational institutions preparing individuals for the job of teaching were called teachers training college. Now these are called colleges of education. It is argued that we train animals like dogs, elephants and horses etc. But we educate human beings.

Education is not indoctrination—Indoctrination is concerned with the instruction of some fundamentals or rudiments. It is usually imbued with a partisan or sectarian opinion, point of view or principle. The term has connotations of a bad epithet. It is frequently associated with bigotry, 'my country right or wrong', 'my religion is the best religion'. An incalculable harm has been done by indoctrination. It leads to false pride and hatred. The two World Wars were the outcome of indoctrination which was based on the propagation of narrow nationalism. Indoctrination also implies fanaticism.

Indoctrination within limits is very desirable as it helps in bringing about a change in the behaviour or belief of an individual. It is dangerous in its extreme forms.

Education	*Indoctrination*
1. The scope of education is very broad.	1. The scope of indoctrination is very narrow.
2. All the three types of education—formal, informal & non-formal are important	2. There is extreme formality in it.
3. Education aims at the all round development of the individual.	3. It aims at changing some beliefs and attitudes.
4. It makes use of a variety of methods.	4. Lecture method is a very important method.
5. Discipline is social.	5. Discipline is very rigid.
6. All members of the society can play the roles of teachers according to situations.	6. Professional teachers are needed.

Contd

7. The whole of life is the curriculum.	7. Curriculum is limited to a belief or a dogma-economic, political or religious.
8. Social adjustment is more important.	8. The teacher determines the achievement.
9. Education is child centred.	9. Indoctrination is thought or dogma centred.
10. Education continues throughout life.	10. Indoctrination is given in a fixed time.
11. Education is needed at every stage—childhood, youth and adulthood.	11. It is more important at the junior classes as at this stage the child receives dogmas without arguments.

Education and literacy—Literacy is concerned with the traditional 3 R's, that is, reading, writing and arithmetic. It is related to acquiring knowledge of some subjects. Education, on the other hand, is related to 7 R's, that is, reading, writing, arithmetic, rights, responsibilities and their relationships and recreation.

Literacy is mainly concerned with theoretical knowledge which can be evaluated through different types of questions—essay type, short answer type and objective type. But education cannot be evaluated through these techniques. Education provides a way of life. It develops certain values. A person may pocess high literacy and even high sounding degrees but he may be labelled uneducated if he lacks human qualities. Education is concerned with the development of character and personality.

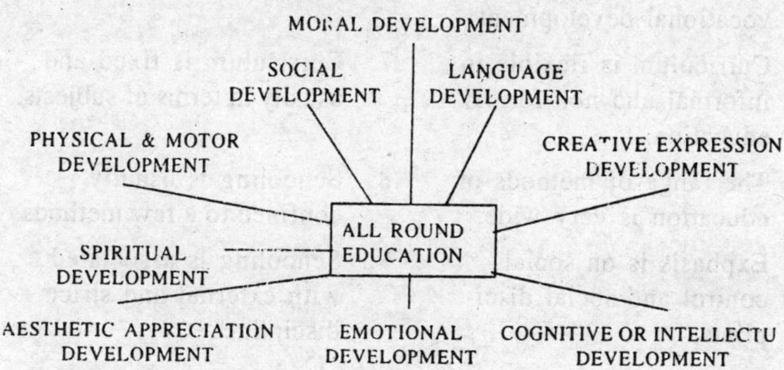

Illustration 1.1 Rounded Education

Education and Schooling

Education	*Schooling*
1. Education has three aspects formal, informal and non-formal.	1. In schooling though formal aspect assumes the most importance.
2. Field of education is very broad.	2. Schooling is a part of the field of education.
3. Education is a natural process.	3. Schooling is an artificial process.
4. Education is a continuous and life-long process.	4. Schooling starts from child's entry or admission to school and ends with his with-drawal from the educational institution.
5. Education is important at a variety of institutions home, schools and colleges, cultural religious and social institutions etc.	5. The place of schooling is limited to an educational institution.
6. Education aims at the all round development of the individual—cultural ethical, emotional, mental, physical social spiritual and professional or vocational development	6. Schooling is primarily concerned with mental development.
7. Curriculum is flexible in informal and non-formal education.	7. Curriculum is fixed and usually in terms of subjects.
8. The range of methods of education is very wide.	8. Schooling is usually confined to a few methods.
9. Exphasis is on social control and social disci-pline	9. Schooling is associated with external and strict discipline

Contd.

10. The number of teachers appointed varies according to the situation.	10. Usually number of teachers is fixed for every subject.
11. Formality and informality between the teacher-pupil go simultaneously.	11. Strict formality is observed between the teacher and the pupil.
12. Techniques of evaluation are very comprehensive. Various aspects of the development of the personality are evaluated.	12. Techniques of evaluation usually comprise essay type, short answer and objective type questions.

Why to Educate (Aims)	Whom to Educate (Child)	Who is to Educate (Teacher)	Where to Educate (School)	What to Educate (Curriculum)	How to Educate (Methods of Teaching)	When to Educate (Motivation)

Illustration 1.2 Dimensions of the Educative Process

1. *Why to educate*—This includes aims of education. The educator and the educand must be clear about the aims of education so that efforts are made in the right direction. Aims of education depend upon a host of factors: political, economic, social, geographical, religious etc. In a nutshell, education must produce socially efficient individuals.
2. *Whom to educate*—The educator must understand the educand thoroughly—his aptitudes, interests, temperaments—so that the 'best of him' is 'drawn out'.
3. *Who is to educate*—The teacher is to educate and he must thoroughly understand himself also. He must rid himself of all blemishes and remember, 'Woe to the teacher who teaches one thing with the lips and carries another in the heart.'
4. *Where to educate*—The child is to be educated in a school which must 'simplify', 'purify' and 'idealise' the enviroment.

5. *What to educate*—This leads to the contents of the curriculum which has been described as 'the environment in motion'. In a broader sense it includes all the courses, readings associations and activities that go on in the school—in the classroom, library, laboratory, workshop, playgrounds and in the numerous informal contacts between teachers and pupils.
6. *How to educate*—This involves the knowledge and technique of various methods of teaching for making the teaching-learning process dynamic, effective and inspirational.
7. *When to educate*—This is concerned with the different stages of the child so that the 'motivational' aspects may be handled and attended to psychologically.

Factors determining aims, contents and methodology of education—Education is recognised as the mirror of society and an educational institution as society in miniature. I.L. Kandel has observed, "In order to understand, appreciate and evaluate the real meaning of the educational system of a nation, it is essential to know something of its history and traditions, of the forces and attitudes governing its social organisation and the political and economic conditions that determine its development." Thus, to understand any school system it is very necessary to understand the state or the nation which shaped its schools.

The following factors have played an important role in shaping and determining the objective of education and the system of education:

1. Economic Factors
2. Geographical Factors
3. Linguistic Factors
4. Philosophical Factors
5. Political Factors
6. Religious Factors
7. Social Factors

Economic factors—Formal education is possible where production exceeds consumption. This may be the result of tremendous industrial development or favourable natural circumstances. This will depend upon the fertility of the soil, abundant mineral deposits and proper climatic conditions for work. Such conditions provide men with leisure to pursue education.

Where there is a subsistence economy, it is a far cry to afford time for formal schooling. This is the reason why poorer and undeveloped co.intries have a minimum education for their children while industrially advanced countries keep nearly all their children at school and for a longer time.

Geographical factors—The educational system in ancient Greek states presents an interesting study. Education in Sparta aimed at developing physical strength, courage and endurance and obedience because the immediate aim was to train the Spartan youth as a soldier who could protect the state from foreign aggression. Athian education, on the other hand, was richer and finer.

Linguistic factors—Language is one of the natural factors that helps and influences the growth of the educational system of a country. Nations have ties more well-knit than multilingual nations. When a multilingual nation tries to make any one language national, it results in resistance from the groups using other languages. There have been many riots in India on the linguistic issue and it still defies solution.

Philosophical factors—The philosophy of life is a great determining influence on education. All great philosophers are great educators.

Political factors—Political ideologies go a long way in determining the aims and the system of education. Different political ideologies like totalitarian or fascist, communist or socialist and democratic will call for different systems of education.

The ruled nations had a different educational system than their rulers as they were being exploited by their rulers. The system of British education was implanted in this country from purely political motives.

Religious factors—The influence of religion is very powerful as it penetrates the emotional depth of human nature. The Brahmanic system of education, the Budhist education and the early Mohammedan education were dominated by religion. Similarly, in Europe the Protestant countries were wedded to the education of the masses and the Catholic countries to the education of the classes.

Social factors—Education reflects the social pattern of society. The tremendous explosion of science and technology has shaken the old leisurely outlook on life and has created intricate problems of social adjustment. A new emphasis has been placed on literacy. A growing interest is shown in reorganising the curricula at all stages. The new forces in the social structure of the Indian society have provided a fresh incentive for educationists to pattern the educational system.

Summing Up

A.K.C. Ottaway has rightly stated "Education is an activity which goes on in a society and its aims and methods depend on the nature of the society in which if takes place."

It follows from this that the education provided within any given society will change from time to time as the society changes.

It also follows that not only will educational systems and institutions be different but each society as will have its own ideal of men or cultural heroes for the young to emulate and the development of personality will also vary from one culture to another.

Questions and Problems

A. Essay-Type Questions

1. What does the term 'education' mean? Discuss this concept by questing different thinkers.
2. Point out the significance of education. Why do we attach importance to education?
3. After giving a few definitions of education, state which of these you like the most and give reasons.
4. "By education, I mean an all round drawing out of the best in child and man - body, mind and spirit." Elucidate this statement.

B. Short-Answer Type Questions

5. What are the reasons leading to different interpretations of education?
6. Describe the chief characteristics of education.
7. Explain the educative process.
8. Write brief notes on:
   (i) Education as a tri-polar process.
   (ii) Education as a lifelong process.
   (iii) Factors determing educational aim, contents and methods.
   (iv) Education and schooling.
   (v) Education and instruction.
   (vi) Education and teaching.
   (vii) Education and training.
   (ix) Education and indoctrination.

2 Philosophy of Life and Philosophy of Education (Philosophical Basis of Education)

Philosophy of Life

Philosophy is as old as human life. Its subject matter is as wide as human experience. On account of it being an old subject with a wide gamut, it has been regarded by Francis Bacon (1561-1626) a great English philosopher as, *"the great mother of the sciences"*. Books like *science: Its Relations with Philosophy* and *Religion Physics and Philosophy by* Sir James Jean (1877-1946) and *Introduction to Mathematical Philosophy* by Bertrand Russel (1872-1970) etc. clearly show how science also looks out for philosophy. There is no aspect of life, animate or inanimate, natural or supernatural which falls outside its province or purview.

Philosophy is so deeply diffused into the wholeness of human life that Aristotle (384-322 BC) remarked, "Everyone follows a philosophy, whether he is aware of it or not". Human beings primitive or civilized, educated or uneducated, plodding or brilliant cannot escape from philosophy. Aldous Huxley (1894-1963) in his book *Ends and Means* has remarked, "Every human being has a philosophy of his own, good or bad, high or low, purely individual or common with others." He has further observed, "Men live in accordance with their philosophy of life, their concern of the world. this is true even of the most thoughtless."

Different fields of philosophy are: economic philosophy, educational philosophy, moral philosophy, physical philosophy, political philosophy and social philosophy.

Thousand of years ago Indian seers had developed a very comprehensive and well-organised system of philosophy for the guidance of an individual.

Definition and Meaning of Philosophy

Philosophy has been defined by various scholars from different angles. Some of the important definitions of philosophy are given below:

1. Aristippus (435-356 B.C.) thinks that philosophy is "the ability to feel at ease in any society".
2. In the words of Bramold, "Philosophy is a persistent effort of both ordinary and persistent people to make life as intelligible and meaningful as possible."
3. According to Cicero, Marcus Tullius (106-43 BC) "Philosophy is the mother of all arts and "the true medicine of mind."
4. Coleridge, Samuel Taylor (1772-1834) defined it as the "Science of Science".
5. Curtis, George William (1824-1892) states, "during the course of centuries, the meaning attached to philosophy has undergone many changes, and even in the present day, thinkers, are not in complete agreement about the aims and subject matter of this branch of knowledge".
6. Dumery, H. in his book the *Problem of God* (1964) defines philosophy as a "critical reflection on concrete action."
7. Henderson (1947) thinks that philosophy is a research for "a comprehensive view of nature, an attempt at a universal explanation of the nature of things".
8. Huxley, Aldous (1894-1963) observes, "Men live in accordance with their Philosophy of Life".
9. Kabir, Huyaun (1902-1969) states that philosophy "seeks to give knowledge of the whole."

10. Kant. Immanuel (1724-1804) regards philosophy as "the science and criticism of cognition."
11. According to Plato (472-347 B.C.) "He who has a taste for every sort of knowledge and who is curious to learn and is never satisfied may be justly termed as a philosopher." He has also observed, "Philosophy begins in wonder."
12. Radhakrishnan, Sarvapalli (1888-1975) considers philosophy as "a logical inquiry into the nature of reality."
13. Russell, Bertrand (1872-1970) states, "Philosophy is to be studied not for the sake of any definite answers to its question... but rather for the sake of the questions themselves, because these questions enlarge our conception of what is possible... but above all because the mind also is rendered great and becomes capable of that union with the universe which constitutes its highest goal."

Since philosophical knowledge depends on the experience and the insight of the individual philosopher, philosophy shows as wide a variety of outlook and interpretation as anyone could wish.

Indian point of view of philosophy—Prof. M. Varma in his book the *Philosophy of Indian Education (1969)* has explained it as, "(the)...Indian term *Darsana* as an equivalent to philosophy literally means seeing. The simple physiological act of seeing implies the seen and the 'seer' which is comparatively a good word for the Indian significance of the word philosopher. The 'seeing' is a vision of the entire experienced reality, it is all encompassing, for it is the vision of truth itself." According to Prof. Varma, the term philosopher requires in its derived European sense an intelligent and coherent accounting of the experience of life. It can be arrested at the intellectual level and remain a matter of logical argument. *Darsana* has an extra implication; it includes a 'realisation' an experience of the 'postulated truth' which takes it beyond mere polemics.

Etymological meaning of philosophy—The word philosophy can be traced to the Greek Word 'Philosophia' which is made up of two words—'phileo' (love) and 'sophia' (wisdom). Therefore philosophy implies 'love of wisdom'. Wisdom is not the same thing as knowledge. It is more than knowledge. Wisdom includes knowledge and goes beyond it to find relationships and to discover implications.

Different Areas of Philosophy

1. *Problems of reality*—'Metaphysics' is the branch of philosophy which deals with this problem. Questions usually discussed are - What is the nature of the universe we live in? What is reality? Such questions have been raised in the Upanishads. Mahatma Budha called the universe 'Maya'.
2. *Problem of knowledge*—This area of philosophy is known as 'Epistemology'. Questions discussed are: How do we get knowledge? How does a man know what is real? Different philosophers have provided different answers.
3. *Problem of value*—The branch of philosophy which deals with this problem is 'Axiology'. The problem of values include such questions; What are the principles of life? How do they support the view of reality? Problems of values include standards or norms of conduct.

The special branches of philosophy are called *Ethics* and *Aesthetics*. Ethics is concerned with morality and aesthetics with tastes and appreciation.

Methods of philosophy may be divided into four heads (a) speculation (b) description (c) analysis (d) prescription.

Why Do We Need a Philosophy of Life?

To take decisions and act consistently, we need a philosophy. In order to discriminate between two extremes—truth and falsehood, beauty and ugliness, right and wrong etc., one needs wisdom. Our conduct is our own and we are really free only when we rely upon inner controls and self-chosen ends. Jacques Martin (1961) states that philosophy reminds men "of the supreme utility of those things which do not deal with means but with ends. For men do not live only by bread, vitamins, and technological discoveries. They live by values and realities which are above time and are worth knowing for their own sake".

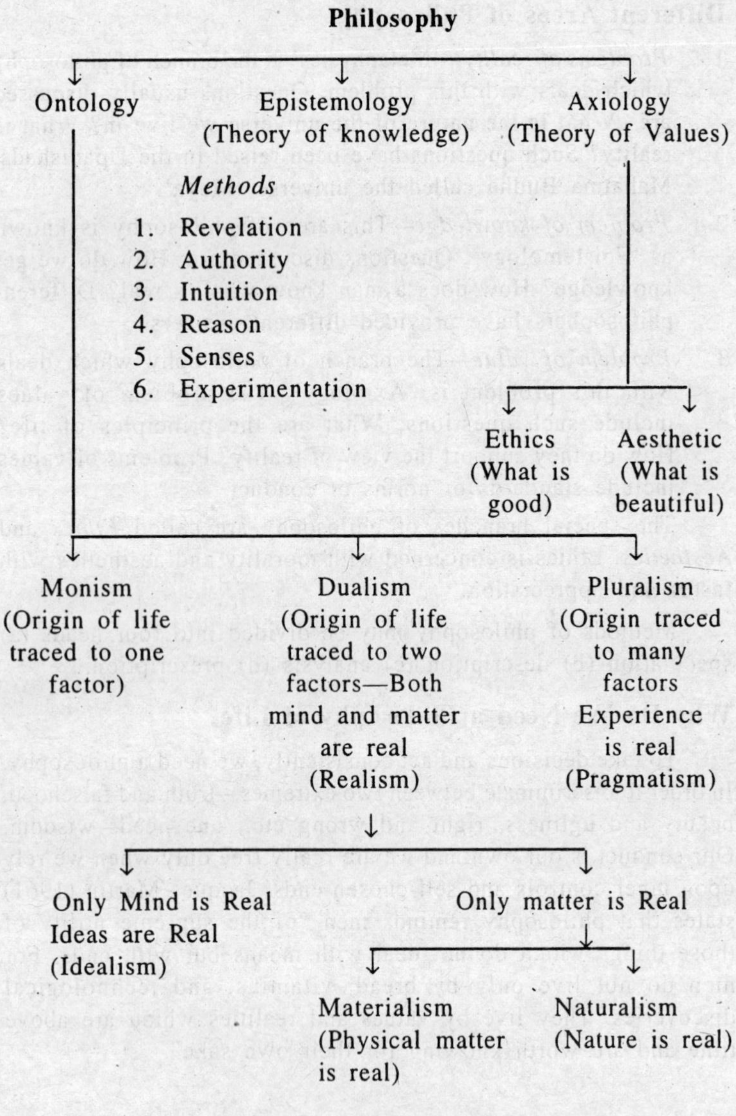

Illustration 2.1 Diagrammatic Presentation of Philosophy

Note : This is the broad diagrammatic representation of philosophy.

Hugh Stevenson (1942) in this context observes, the "capacity to believe is the most significant and fundamental human faculty, and the most important thing about a man is what he believes in the depth of his being. This is the thing that makes him what he is, the thing that organises him and feeds him, the thing that keeps him going in the fact of untoward circumstances, the thing that gives him resistance and drive. Let neutrality, confusion, indifference or skepticism enter this inner place, and the very spring of life will cease to flow. Men will quit, lose heart, yield, give up, become bitter or cynical, become sunk in bleakness or emptiness, commit suicide, turn to criminality or retreat into realism of Phantasy."

Philosophy furnishes the basis for social action as well as for personal conduct. In the words of A.C. Ewing (1964), "unless we suppose that material wealth is the only thing of value, the inability of philosophy to contribute to this would not mean that it was of no practical value. We value material wealth not for itself...but for its contribution to happiness. Now there is no doubt that one of the most important sources of happiness for those who can enjoy it at all is the search for truth and the contemplation of reality and this is the aim of philosophers".

Philosophers have been instrumental in revolutionary political and social reforms. For example, the American constitution is to a very considerable extent an application of the political ideas of the philosopher John Locke. The ideas of Rousseau played an important role in the French Revolution.

Philosophy and Science

Both philosophy and science seek knowledge. C.D. Broad has observed that philosophy "takes over the results of the various sciences to add to them the results of the religious and ethical experiences of mankind and then to reflect upon the whole. The hope is that, by this mean, we may be able to reach some general conclusion regarding the nature of the universe and as to our position and prospects in life". Again, A.C. Ewing adds, "the success of modern science would have probably never been achieved if the scientist had not taken from great original philosophers certain assumptions on which he based his whole procedure. The mechanistic view of the universe characteristic of science during the last three centuries is derived chiefly from the philosopher Descartes".

James Jean (1934) describes the inter-dependancy of philosophy and science by suggesting, "part of the value of science is intellectual. It would be a dull mind that could see the rich variety of natural phenomena without wondering how they are inter-related. Quite apart from all questions of practical utility, the modern mind feels strongly urged to synthesise the phenomena without wondering how they are inter-related. Quite apart from all questions of practical utility, the modern mind feels strongly urged to synthesise the phenomena it observes, to try to combine happenings in the internal world under general Laws."

G.T.W. Patrick describes the close relationship between philosophy and science. "They spring from the same roots the love of knowledge; and they aspire to the same end the knowledge of reality. While science describes the facts, philosophy interprets them."

Butter puts this relationship by stating, "Both are interested in knowledge But there is the difference in the kind of knowledge science seeks knowledge of facts. Philosophy seeks ultimate knowledge."

According to Dewey, "When science denotes not simply a report of the particular facts discovered about the world but a general attitude towards it as distinct from special things to do, it merges into philosophy."

Brubacher describes this relationship saying, "Science is interested in the proximate or efficient causes of facts, while philosophy is concerned with its ultimate or final causes."

Chief Characteristics of Philosophy

Philosophy as love of knowledge—As stated by Plato in his Italian *Republic,* "He who has a taste for every sort of knowledge and who is curious to learn and is never satisfied may be justly termed as a philosopher."

Philosophy as love of wisdom—The ancient Greeks believed that a person becomes wise by knowledge and understanding. The term philosophy is derived, as already mentioned, from a Greek word meaning wisdom.

Philosophy as an activity—Philosophy has been referred to a mental activity; thinking about the problems of life, its natures and purposes; the mind and its occupations, birth death and other phenomena of world; feelings, ideas, values of social life, etc. For Socrates philosophy was a daily activity. He used to invite The Athenian Citizens into arguments and discuss with them the problems of life and the world around without himself getting bored. As Russel puts it, "Philosophy proper deals with matters of interest to the general educated public and loses much of its value if only a few professionals can understand it." Henderson has also expressed himself in a similar way while defining philosophy, "Philosophy is a vigorous, disciplined, guarded analysis of some of the most difficult problems which man has ever faced"

Philosophy as a comprehensive picture of the universe—P.G. Smith has suggested three dimensions for philosophical thinking. They are comprehensiveness, penetration and flexibility. As Dewey has viewed it, "with respect to subject-matter, philosophy is an attempt to comprehend— that is gather together the varied details of the world and life into a single inclusive whole". Plato has conceived of the philosopher as a spectator of all time and all existence. It is for this reason that Brubacher has called philosophy the science of sciences.

Philosophy as a guide to a way of life—Philosophy gives a direction to life. Philosophy in India emerged as a result of reflection over the experiences and problems of life. Dr. Radhakrishnan, the great Indian philosopher has suggested this meaning to philosophy through the titles of two of his books. "The Indian View of Life" and "The Idealist View of Life". Human life is always purposeful. The purpose of life is determined by the philosophy of life. The purpose of life may be different in different cultures and societies. It depends on a host of factors. It can be materialistic or spiritualist. In ancient Sparta, the philosophy of life was to defend the country from foreign aggression and thus the aim of life was to become a soldier. The ideal Spartan was an ideal soldier. In Nazi Germany, the philosophy of life was determined by racial superiority and an individual was meant for the state. Similar was the case in communist countries. In ancient India attainment of 'Moksha' or 'Nirvana' was the guiding philosophy. In theory at least, 'simple living' and 'high thinking' is the philosophy of life in the present day India.

The Characteristics of Philosophy may be summed up as under:

1. Philosophy is a way of life.
2. — is the mother of all arts and sciences.
3. — is a dynamic and living force.
4. — is the oldest and original discipline.
5. — is a search for reality and truth.
6. — is based on the concept of enquiry.
7. — is logical.
8. — is closely related to education.
9. — is an art as well as a science.

Interdependence of Philosophy and Education

There is a close interrelationship between philosophy and education. Philosophy points out the way, and education follows it. Education thus becomes the best means for the propagation of philosophy. For the good of life, for the good of the individual and for the good of society, we need direction and this direction is provided exclusively by philosophy, which is the mother of all sciences including education. This, however, does not mean that education is enslaved by philosophy. The field of education provides a testing ground to test the truth of wisdom or direction provided by philosophy. Without the testing ground of education, philosophers would remain arm-chair theorists. A constant mutual interaction goes on between the two. It is therefore said that without philosophy education would be a blind effort and without education, philosophy would be crippled. The chief means of testing the wisdom or follies of philosophy is education which has been described as the 'dynamic side of philosophy'.

Max Black in 'A Note on Philosophy of Education', *Harward Educational Review* (spring 1956) has very aptly described the relationship in these words, "All serious discussion of educational problems, no matter how specific, soon leads to a consideration of educational aims, and becomes a conversation about the good life, the nature of man, the varieties of experience. But these are the perennial themes of philosophical investigation. It might seem a hard thing to expect educators to be philosophers, but can they be anything else?".

Fichte very rightly observed, "the art of education will never attain complete clearness without philosophy." Gentile stated, "Education without philosophy would mean a failure to understand the precise nature of education". Dewey said, "Philosophy is the theory of education in its most general phases. Education is a laboratory in which philosophical directions become concrete and are tested". If education is a set of techniques for imparting knowledge, skills and attitudes philosophy is the foundation to vitalise these. Philosophy is the foundation and education is the super-structure.

Without philosophy, education would be a 'blind effort' and without education, philosophy would be cripple."

It is stated that when we define education as the modification of behaviour the direction in which modification is to be carried out is determined by philosophy. This philosophy deals with the end and education with the means.

Education and philosophy are two sides of the same coin—life. Sir John Adams said that education is the dynamic side of philosophy. As Ross put it, "Education is the active aspect of philosophical belief, the practical means of realising ideals of life." T.P. Nunn has also said, "educational aims are correlative to ideals of life". Henderson has expressed similar views, "Educational aims cannot be determined apart from the ends and aims of life itself for educational aims grow out of life's aims. To determine what constitutes worth living has been one of the chief tasks of philosophy."

Spencer is of the view that "true education is practicable only to true philosophies".

Gentile feels that "Education with philosophy would mean a failure to understand the precise nature of education".

Bearing of Philosophy on Education

The gifts of philosophy to education are:

1. Philosophy assists education in understanding the learner, his life, his actions, ideals and problems.
2. Philosophy assists the educator in formulating beliefs, arguments, assumptions and judgements concerning learning and teaching, character and intellect, subject-matter and skill, desirable ends and appropriate means of schooling.

3. Philosophy assists education in the determined effort to find out what education should do in the face of contradictory demands of life and factors arising out of experience which bring meaning and direction to thinking.
4. Philosophy assists education in giving a unity of outlook to the diverse interests of the individual, his family community and the state.
5. Philosophy provides logical vigour, envisaging transcendence and disciplined imagination which when taken out from the person will find him a barren mass of flesh.
6. Philosophy provides reason with faith.
7. Philosophy determines what is worth-living. Education then prepares the individual for that.

All great philosophers as great educators—A close analysis of the concept of education as given by various philosophers and educators will make clear that their views on education are based on their varying concepts of reality, of knowledge, of wisdom and of values. The great philosophers of all times have also been great educators. Most of the educational movements were the expressions of their philosophical beliefs. Views of great thinkers like Socrates, Plato, Aristotle, Comenius, John Locke, Rousseau, Froebel, Dewey, H.G. Wells, Bertrand Russel, A.N.Whitehead and Aldous Huxley, offer an interesting example of the intimate connection between philosophy and education. The ancient sages in India were all educational philosophers. In recent times, this is fully illustrated in the case of Swami Dayananda, Swami Vivekananda, Sri Aurbindo, Rabindranath Tagore, Dr. Radhakrishnan, Mahatma Gandhi etc.

Philosophy and aims of education—In the words of Bode, "Unless we have some guiding philosophy in the determination of objectives we get no where at all". Robert Rusk corroborates this saying. "Philosophy formulates, what should be the end of life while education offers suggestions how this end is to be achieved". It is in this sense that philosophy becomes handy to the educator for formulating his objectives in education.

Philosophy and aims in education—"No system of education", says Acharya J.B. Kripalani, the noted Gandhian philosopher, "can be properly appraised and appreciated, unless it is studied in connection with the ideas and ideals which it represents".

The Soviet System of education can properly be understood only in the light of philosophy of Marxism and Leninism. To gain insight into the British system of education, it is necessary to have the correct perspective of the synthesis between the progressivism and the conservatism which the Butler Act tried to achieve. The Chinese, with their natural distrust of present-day education in the west, emphasise that it is the paramount purpose of the state to train the people for the purpose of the state.

In ancient Sparta, the ideal was to defend the country's honour and hence the aim of the spartan system of education was to prepare citizens to become soldiers and patriots. On the other hand, the Athenian System of education aimed at the cultural development of each individual in conformity with the Athenian philosophy of the times.

The ideals of the present philosophy in India are reflected in the Preamble, of the Constitution. These ideals of secularism, socialism and democracy are the watchwords of education.

Philosophy and curriculum—Briggs has aptly remarked, "It is just here that education seriously needs leaders—who have a sound comprehensive philosophy, of which they can convince others and who can direct its consistent application to the formulation of appropriate goals". Rusk has also emphasised, "No where is the dependence of education on philosophy more marked than in the question of curriculum".

The philosophical approach to life is the guiding factor in the determination of the curriculum. Gandhi's scheme of basic education was an expression of his philosophy. He was against the lopsidedness of the system of education as propounded by Lord Macaulay and was moved by the illiteracy and poverty of the people. His scheme of studies, therefore, emphasised crafts and the environment. He was very keen to make education self-supporting besides developing moral character. The National Policy on Education 1986 lays stress on a Core Curriculum keeping in view the needs of emotional and national integration.

To fulfil the needs of a technological society, the High Schools of the USA stressed the study of automobile repair, electronics and aeronautics in the school curriculum. Similarly, the use of calculators and computers forms an important part of the school curriculum in UK and USSR.

Philosophy and discipline—Philosophy has a great bearing on discipline in educational institutions. In a democratic set up, discipline is viewed as inner discipline as well as social discipline based on group work. In the totalitarian state, discipline is regimented and assumes the form of a military discipline, that is, unquestioned obedience and is based on fear of the educational authorities i.e. the teacher and the head. There is little concern for the individuality of the child in a totalitarian type of discipline. The idealists emphasise the impact of impression of the teacher on his students.

'Free discipline' is the slogan of the naturalist, 'Flogging the Child' was the traditional concept of discipline. Its dictum was 'spare the rod and spoil the child'. It is also believed that the child should not be given a 'long rope to hang himself'.

Philosophy and methods of teaching—Every school of philosophy has its own methods of teaching. According to the philosophy of idealism, question-answer method, lecture method and discussion method are the most suitable methods of education. Naturalism recommends learning by doing, learning by self-experience and direct experience. Pragmatic philosophy advocated project method, problem solving method and socialised techniques.

Philosophy and textbooks—Philosophy is greatly involved in the choice of textbooks. The contents of the textbooks must mirror the philosophy or way of life of the people. In a socialist society textbooks emphasise socialist philosophy. In a state dominated and ruled by religious leaders or what is known as fundamentalists, textbooks reflect tenets of scriptures. In India, since independence, there has been a great stress on emotional integration and national unity. Accordingly textbooks are being screened from time to time to ensure that they include only that matter which promotes emotional integration and national unity. Similarly, efforts are made to exclude matter that is based, on sex bias and to make sure that women are given their due place. Likewise, all references which lead to the promotion of untouchability are deleted. Textbooks are meant to spread the ideals of democracy, secularism and socialism as enshrined in the constitution.

Philosophy and the teacher—A teacher is regarded as the harbinger of the philosophy of a nation. He is the engineer of the philosophy of the students under his charge. A teacher is said to play an important role in shaping and moulding the ideals, habits, manners, tastes and ways of life and above all the character and personality of the students. It is, therefore, very essential that he must have a consistent and sound philosophy in accordance with the philosophy of the nation to which he belongs. As observed by Gentile, "The belief that men may continue to educate without concerning themselves with philosophy means a failure to understand the precise nature of education. The process of education cannot go on the right lines without the help of philosophy. Since philosophy speaks the language of analysis and reason, there is hardly any problem of education which is difficult to solve by the teacher who possesses the clear lights of philosophy".

It is felt that a basic understanding of philosophical themes on the part of all teachers regarding ancient and contemporary philosophical systems of thought will enable them to formulate their own philosophy and beliefs, help them to understand the problematic situations in the class-room discipline, under-achievement of students and many such other problems and ultimately enable them to determine the manner in which they will handle these problems.

Philosophy helps the teacher in the following ways:

1. Philosophy provides direction to the teacher.
2. — provides a way of life to the teacher.
3. — enables the teacher to think constructively and rationally.
4. — serves as a guide to the teacher to solve disciplinary problems.
5. — provides insight to the teacher to comprehend the problems of education in general.
6. — guides the teacher to undertake experiments.

Questions and Problems

A. Essay-Type Questions

1. Explain the term Philosophy. Why do we need a philosophy of life?
2. "Everyone follows a Philosophy of life whether he is aware of it or not." Elucidate this statement.
3. Illustrate the interrelationships of Psychology and Education.
4. "No where is the dependence of education on philosophy so marked than in the question of aims and curriculum of education". Explain this statement by citing examples.
5. Elucidate the statement: " All educational questions are ultimately questions of philosophy".
6. "Education is the dynamic side of philosophy." Discuss this statement.
7. "Education and Philosophy are two sides of the same coin." Elucidate.
8. Define the terms Philosophy of life and Education. How are they related? How is this knowledge useful to you as a teacher?

B. Short-Answer Type Questions

9. Briefly State the Philosophy which is the basis of the present system of education in India.
10. Write Short notes on:
    (a) All great Philosophers were great teachers
    (b) Philosophy and the teacher.
11. "The content of education is determined by the objectives of life." Explain.

3 Sociology of Education (Sociological Foundation of Education)

Origin of Sociology and its Pioneers

Although sociological concepts can be traced back to the ideas of Manu, Yagvalkya and Kautilya in India, Confucious in China and Aristotle and Plato in Greece, a formal study of sociology started only in the middle of the 19th century. The well-known French Philosopher, Auguste Conite (1798-1857) considered to be the 'Father of Sociology', used the word 'sociology' in a number of lectures to designate the application of the scientific method to the study of human nature and society.

Herbert Spencer (1820-1903) of England was the first one to write a systematic book entitled *The Principles of Sociology* (1876) in which he made an analysis of the Sociological aspects of society.

Emile Durkheim (1857-1917), a sociologist of France wrote extensively on sociological problem, As a Professor of Sociology and Education at the Sorborne University from 1902 to 1917, he wrote two books namely *Education and Society* and *Moral Education.*

The University of Chicago was the first University in the USA to start a teaching department of sociology in 1893.

Merrit and Eldrige point out that the field of the study of sociology is "human relationships."

Moore and Cole describe sociology as a "study of plural behaviour." Morris Ginsherng is of the view that, "sociology is the study of the human interaction and inter-relation, their conditions and responses."

Robbins lays stress on the fact that sociology deals with the 'whole man' in relation to all the cultural, social and biophysical backgrounds.

Meaning and Subject Matter of Sociology

From the above definitions of sociology, it is clear that the central theme in sociology is 'social interaction'. Social interaction includes interaction with cultural and other institutions, such as the family, the play and peer group, religious, economic and educational institution—in fact every form of group living. It studies the customs and traditions that grow out of these interactions, the institutions that crystallise these basic human interests and the changes that occur in these institutions. Sociology also studies the possibility of 'directing' these changes in the ultimate interest of human welfare. It helps to understand the forces that 'bring changes' and also the 'effect' of these changes on behaviour and personality development in individuals. It throws light on man as a social being. It examines social changes and social control.

Definitions of Sociology: Sixfold Classification

Almost all the definitions of sociology given by various sociologists can broadly be classified in the following six categories:

1. *Sociology as the science of society*—Sociologists like Comte, Ward, Blackmar and Gilonin, Giddings etc., define the subject as such.
2. *Sociology as the study of social relationship*—Sociologists like Mach Iver, Page and Abel stress this aspect.
3. *Sociology as the study of human behaviour in groups*—Kimball Young and his followers who have a psychological bias think of the discipline in this perspective.
4. *Sociology as the study of social structure and social phenomena*—Sociologists like Sorokin, Green, Benet and Tumain define the subject as such.
5. *Sociology as the study of the different forms of human interrelations*—Scholars like Max Weber, von Weise, Vier Kanet, Ross etc., give such definitions.

6. *Sociology as the study of social action*—Social theorists like Parsons, Merton, etc., define sociology in this way.

Some important definitions of Sociology—

Duncan states, "Sociology is the scientific study of the processes of interaction of persons and the patterns which these form in relation to biological, psychological and cultural influences."

E.T. Hiller gives this definition, "Sociology is the study of the relation between individuals, their conduct and reference to one another and the standard by which they regulate their association."

F. Le Play describes sociology as an observational science which studies actual social phenomena.

In the words of Gillian and Gillin, "Sociology in the broadest sense may be said to be the study of interaction arising from the association of living beings.

Mac Lever states, "Sociology is the study of the nature of social relationships."

Max Weber (1864-1920) a well known German sociologist considers sociology to be a "Science which attempts the interpretative understanding of social action."

Sociology of Education and Educational Sociology

There seems to be a good deal of confusion over these terms. Many authors use the terms sociology of education and educational psychology as if they are synonyms of each other. "Educational sociology or sociology of education, call it what you may, for how does any differentiation between them matter?" is the typical response of many scholars.

Prof. William Taylor of the Faculty of Education, University of Bristol points out, "It does help us to distinguish between the sociology of education, which is usually an activity and an orientation of sociologists (who may also be educators) and educational sociology which is an activity principally of educators...it (educational sociology) has tended to be hortatory rather than emperical, inspirational rather than objective and synoptic rather than analytic."

Mercer and Carr point out "The sociologist of education, it should be emphasised defines education in much broader terms than other specialists in the field of education are likely to use... Education for the former involves all aspects of the process of transmitting culture from individual to individual, The educational sociologist, on the other hand, considers his field a job-division of a developing science of education. Perhaps the education sociologist has been somewhat more "practical minded" than those scholars who have been characterised as sociologists of education. This is merely another way of saying that the sociologist of education starts his analysis from the point of view of the society as a whole, while the educational sociologist starts with the school and expands his analysis outward."

Dr. Ruhela and Dr. Vyas see the difference as "....educational sociology has always been, more or less concerned with the applied side of sociology in order to improve certain disturbing situations in an education institution whereas the sociologists of education have since their beginning been motivated by the purist traditions of sociology and as such not exceedingly concerned with its applied side."

Donald A. Hansen point out the difference as, "From one perspective, sociology can focus 'within' education, examining educational theory, practice and processes. With such a focus sociology performs such as does educational psychology and this approach is labelled (educational sociology)". From another perspective sociology can focus on education and attempt to understand educators, schools and other educational institutions in their social and cultural contexts. The "Sociology of Education" is concerned with the relationship between education and society."

Concept of Educational Sociology

Prof. W.B. Brookover points out that there were six concepts of educational sociology which flourished between 1882 and 1945.

1. Educational sociology as a means of social progress emphasised by Ward-Good, Ellwood and Kinneman.
2. Educational sociology as a *Basis for Deciding the Objectives of Education* advocated by Snednen, Peters Clements and Kinneman,

3. Educational sociology as an *Applied Sociology* stressed by Smith, Zorbugh, Kalp and Leslie Zeleny.
4. Educational sociology as an *Analyses of the Socialising Process* favoured by Ellwood, Smith and Brown.
5. Educational sociology as *Training for Educational Workers,* stressed by Zeleny and Pyne.
6. Educational sociology as an analysis of social interaction within the school and between the school and the community advocated by Walter, Lnaniecki Wilson and Cook etc.

Definition of Educational Sociology

According to Brown "educational sociology in the study of the interaction of the individual and his cultural environment including other individuals, social groups and patterns of behaviour."

In the words of Cook and Cook "educational sociology is the study of human factors in the educative process, with the aim to improve teaching and learning in all types of educational systems."

Carte's view is "educational sociology is the study of those processes of sociology that are significant for the educative process."

Ottaway observes, "educational sociology is the scientific study of the relationships between education and society."

Gene Payne, who is called the father of educational sociology explains this concept as, "By educational sociology we mean the science which describes and explains the institution, social groups and social process, that is the social relationship in which or through which the individual gains and organises his experiences These social relationships are further more regarded particularly in relation to the educational system in its evolution and changing functions."

Roucek's view is "educational sociology is sociology applied to the solution of fundamental educational problems."

From above it is concluded that educational psychology is the study of human relationships in the educative process. It is helpful in processing society. Educational sociology aims at eliminating social evils through education.

Development of Educational Psychology

It is only recently that educational sociology, a sub-division of sociology has assumed great importance as a separate subject. Among the various names associated with the growth of this subject, E. George Payne and John Dewey stand out prominently. Payne thought that a consideration of the social relationships and their place in the evolution of educational system would facilitate the understanding of education as a means of social control. Payne took three important steps to propogate the importance of educational sociology. He organised the National Society for the study of educational sociology. He edited 'the Journal of Educational Sociology' and published his famous book *The Principles of Educational Sociology* in 1928. John Dewey, the great American educational thinker popularised the subject by his publication, namely, *The School and Society* and *Democracy and Education*. He stated that the process of education has two sides—psychological and sociological. According to him, "All education proceeds by the participation of the individual in the social consciousness of the race." He regarded school as a social institution which purifies and idealises the existing social institutions.

William T. Harits, the United States Commissioner of Education, was the first educationist to emphasize that education must be based on sociology.

In 1897, Albion, W Small of the Chicago University who was the first Professor of Sociology in the USA stated. "While sociology proper is not a desirable subject for young pupils, our educational methods will be miserably inadequate to their social function until every teacher, from kindergarten onwards, is sufficiently instructed in sociology to put all his teaching in the setting which the sociological view point affords."

S.P. Dutton, Superintendent of Schools in Brookline, Massachussets expressed these views. "The school is a social institution, its aims are social and its management, discipline of methods and instructions should be dominated by this idea."

A sociologically oriented education course was started in The Normal Teacher Training Schools of Minnesota (USA) in 1895.

Colon Ascott's in "*Social Education* was perhaps the first importance book on educational sociology published in 1916.

Impact of Sociology on Education

Sociology shapes education and forms a vital force in the entire framework of education. The whole superstructure of education has depended upon social forces, needs and demands. The expectations and aspiration of a changing society are reflected through the educational system of a country or a nation. Thus, we can hardly afford to think of education in isolation today. Clarke has rightly stated, "No writer on education, however much he strive for after universal thought can wholly shake himself free from the influence of time and place."

Society is dynamic, it grows and changes and as such these social changes must not only be reflected in education but also must affect it. It is only by connecting education with the general march of events that the school can lose its isolated character. As Dewey has stated, "School must become the child's habitat to be a miniature community, an embryonic society."

Educational Sociology and the Meaning of Education

Brown has observed, "According to educational sociology education is the consciously controlled process whereby changes in behaviour are produced in the person and through the person within the group." The sociology of education focuses upon the social force through which the individual is developed, and the social relationships by which the Individual gains experience. Education is regarded not only as a conservative force but also a critical and a creative one.

Educational sociology and the aims of education—An educational sociologist always thinks in terms of the type of society that obtains at a particular time. The aims of education, therefore, according to him in an age of democracy will be those that prepare an individual for democratic living. The aim of education would be to enable the individual to live as a member of his society. Education should, "bring a change not only in the amount of knowledge gained but in the ability to do, to think, and to acquire habits, skills, interests and attitudes which characterise a person who is socially accepted, personally adjusted and socially responsible." Educational sociology aims at the socialisation of the individual. Thus the social aim of education assumes more importance than the individual aim of education.

Educational sociology also considers citizenship as an important aim of education.

Educational sociology and function of education—Payne thought that from the point of view of educational sociology there are three functions of education:

1. Assimilation of tradition,
2. Development of new social patterns, and
3. Creative and constructive role.

Dewey's ideal school is expected to perform the following functions:

1. Reflecting and epitomising the larger society outside its walls.
2. Purifying the activities of the society in its environment.
3. Simplifying the activities of the society in its environment.
4. Balancing the activities of the society in its environment.

Educational Sociology and Aims of Education

Concepts associated with social aims of education—The social aims in education finds expression in such concepts as education for social services. 'Education for citizenship, education for social efficiency, 'education for emotional integration', 'education for national unity', 'education for nationalism' and 'education for patriotism' etc.

Why social aims in education—The individual is regarded as endowed with a social nature. He is social by nature. He resides in an intricate web of social relations. Without social relations a new born baby would almost perish. An individual cannot live and develop in isolation from society. An isolated individual is a figment of imagination. A socially efficient individual is an asset to the society. He is not a drag or parasite on any individual and society . He is able to earn his livelihood. Education, therefore, should aim at the development of the individual in such a way that he becomes a useful member of the society. He should be made aware of his rights, responsibilities and relationships when living in a group.

As Dewey has observed, "Education is the process of reconstruction or reconstitution of experiences; giving it a more socialised value through the medium of social efficiency."

The Education Commission 1964-66 has also observed, "Education cannot be considered in isolation or planned in a vacuum. It has to be used as a powerful instrument of social and political change."

Limitation and Shortcomings of the Social Aim in Education

1. The social aim of education envisages the individual as a non-entity and leaves little scope for his personality and unique characteristics to flourish.
2. Aggression and violence against neighbouring countries have resulted in educational aims of this type. Militant nationalism, "my country, right or wrong," are attitudes which may develop in tender minds.
3. In recent years there has been a tendency in western countries, among the young people to rebel against the cult of 'social efficiency.' Many students prefer the development and growth of individuality and would want to give up the struggle for social efficiency.

Educational Sociology and School Curriculum

Brown, More, and Cole point out the following principles of contructing school curriculum from the viewpoint of educational sociology.

1. Curriculum should be based on the conditions, problems and needs of society.
2. It should be based on the real concerns and problems of pupils.
3. It should reflect the basic cultural values of the society it serves.
4. It should be an agent in the transmission of the highest values of the culture.
5. It should provide educational programmes and activities that give them wholesome participating roles in society. This participation is conducive to the development of responsible citizenship.
6. The curriculum must be functional in its relation to adult living and concurrently be adapted to the level of development of the child.

7. The school programme should treat with dignity all worthwhile vocations and services in community life.
8. The curriculum should develop healthy attitudes regarding human relations.
9. It should prepare the child for the world society.
10. It should prepare socially efficient individuals.
11. It should be flexible and changeable for the effective realisation of socially determined objectives.
12. It should lead to the development of genuine 'We feeling'... "a feeling that the student belongs and has a spirit of social intereaction".

Educational Sociology and Methods of Teaching

Regarding methods of teaching Moore and Cole point out "...It is through group relationships (which are encouraged in socialized methods) that an individual becomes aware of what it means to work with a purpose...purpose lies within the individual, but its source, the stimulation for its growth and nourishment, comes largely from without and for those sources to be meaningful the individual must be identified with the group—he must belong." The effectiveness of learning for social competency depends on the suitability of motives and procedures. The following are the chief characteristics of the methods:

1. The methods of teaching should enable the pupil to acquire those skills and knowledges in the classroom which are helpful to him in his adjustment to social situations.
2. The methods of teaching must seek to utilise the social forces operative in the social life with the a view of developing a capacity for social adjustment.
3. The methods should develop problem-solving and constructive thinking.
4. The socialised techniques, the project and group methods, by and large should replace the lecture and recitation method.

From education sociology point of view cooperative group patterns of learning which lay stress on group interactions, cooperative and democratic planning will always be preferable to others.

Sociology and the Teacher

It is said that the destiny of a nation is shaped in its classroom and it is the teacher who is a very important instrument in moulding that destiny. To be able to discharge such a high responsibility, it is very necessary that the teacher must become conscious of his role towards society. His behaviour should indicate his attempt to do his job properly. His personality must reflect characteristics of good citizenship. The teacher himself must be exposed to the concept of freedom egalitarianism, dignity of the individual, rights and duties etc., so that he may transmit the same to the younger generation.

Several social factors operating in a society affect systems of education. Educational sociology brings these to the notice of the teacher. This knowledge can enable the teacher to plan various educational programmes for the benefit of the economically weaker sections of society.

Educational sociology and disciples—Discipline is social through and through. It should come through participation in group activities and social service activities.

Questions and Problems

A. Essay-Type Questions

1. Describe the nature and meaning of educational sociology. How does it affect education?
2. What do you understand by sociological foundations of education? What is their impact on education?
3. How does educational sociology affect the curriculum (contents of education)? Give a few examples substantiat your answer.

B. Short-Answer Type Questions

4. Define educational sociology.
5. State the function of education according to educational psychology.
6. What are the aims of education in accordance with the sociology of education?

4 Philosophies and Their Impact on Education

4.1 Idealism

The Oldest Philosophy

Idealism is a very old philosophical thought. In India, its origin may be traced to the Vedas, the Upanishads and the Bhagawad Gita made a very comprehensive analysis of idealism. In the West its echo is found in the writings of Plato.

Chief Exponents of Idealism

1. The Vedic Rishis, and the authority of the Upanishads and the Gita.
2. Plato—A Greek Philosopher (427-347 B.C.)
3. Kant—A German Philosopher (1724—1804 A.D.)
4. Hegel—A German Philosopher (1770—1831 A.D.)
5. Froebel—A German Philosopher (1772—1852 A.D.)
6. William T. Haris—American Philosopher (1835—1909 A.D.)
7. M.K. Gandhi—An Indian Statesman (1869—1948)
8. Swami Dayananda—An Indian Philosopher (1825—1883 A.D.)

9. Rabindra Nath Tagore—An Indian Philosopher (1861—1941 A.D.)
10. Aurobindo Ghosh—An Indian Philosopher (1872—1950 A.D.)

Definition and Meaning of Idealism

Idealism maintains that the national and physical universes is subordinate to a higher degree of reality, a spiritual universe. Idealism idealises the mind and self. "Exalt the human personality" is the central theme of idealism. It considers the human personality as of 'supreme value'. It contends that the human personality constitutes the 'noblest work of God.' Man's spiritual nature is considered to be the very essence of his being.

Upanishads' Idealism

Asato ma sad gamaya,
Tamaso ma jyotir gamaya,
Mrtyor ma amritam gamaya.
Lead me from unreal to the real,
Lead me from darkness to light,
Lead me from death to immortality

—*Brihadarnayak Upanishad*

Yastu Vijnanaun Bhauati
Tasyendriyani Vasyani
Sadasviya Saratheh

He who is possessed of supreme knowledge by concentration of mind must have his senses under control, like spirited steeds controlled by a charioteer.

—*Kathopanishad*

Kant's Views on Idealism

Kant, an eighteenth century German philosopher emphasised the following attributes of idealism:

1. There are certain universal moral laws in the universe.
2. Man has an obligation to obey these moral laws.
3. The soul is immortal.
4. There is an Almighty God.

Tagore's idealism

Tagore's Prayer is as under:

"This is my prayer to thee, my lord, strike,

Strike at the root of penury in my heart,

Give me the strength lightly to bear my joys and sorrows,

Give me the strength to make my love fruitful in service.

Give me the strength never to disown the poor or bend my knees before insolent might.

Give me the strength to raise my mind high above daily trifles.

And give me the strength to surrender my strength to thy will with love"

Modern Definition of Idealism

According to Brubacher, "The idealists point out that it is the mind that is central in understanding the world. To them nothing gives a greater sense of reality than the activity of the mind engaged in trying to comprehend its world. For anything to give a greater sense of reality would be a contradiction in terms because to know anything more real than the mind would itself be a conception of the mind."

The Oxford Dictionary gives these meanings, "Idealism means representation of things in an ideal form, imaginative treatment, system of thought in which the objective of external perception is held to consist of ideas."

Rusk observes," Idealism contends that the material and physical universe known to science is an incomplete expression of reality, that it exists but to subserve, it requires to complement it a higher type of reality, a spiritual universe."

Basic Tenets of Idealism

1. Ultimate reality is mental and spiritual. The real world of the mind—the realism of ideas and of external qualities.
2. Ideas are more important than objects.
3. Man is a spiritual organism.
4. Higher knowledge is the product of interactive thinking and reasoning—a product of the mind.

5. There is an essential unity in the scheme of things.
6. Man is a part of this universe and it is the essence of his nature to work towards a rational unity in himself.
7. Man has an innate capacity to apprehend the moral value of principles.
8. The test of a good moral principle is its universal validity.

Contribution of Idealism to Education

Philosophical Principles of Idealism in Education:

1. Stress on spiritual environment.
2. Emphasis on self-realisation as the aim of education.
3. Relatively unimportant place for the child in the educative process.
4. Development of the child in accordance with adult standards.
5. Stress on disciplining the child.
6. Emphasis on book-knowledge.
7. Positive education.
8. Education as the dynamic side of philosophy.

Aims of Education

It is usually accepted that idealism has more to contribute to the aims and objectives of education than to its methods. The following are the important aims:

1. Spiritual development.
2. Self-realisation or self-actualisation.
3. Cultivation of ethical, moral and spiritual values.
4. Transmission and promotion of cultural heritage.
5. Character development.
6. Duties to self and others—industriousness, sincerity, respect for the opinion of others, modesty, cooperativeness etc.

Froebel defined the aim of education as, "In all things there reigns an external law. This all-pervading law is necessarily based on an all-pervading, energetic, self-conscious and hence external unit. This unity is God—the divine effluence that lives in each thing is the essence of each thing. The object of education is the realisation of a faithful, pure, inviolable, and hence holy life...education should lead and guide man to clearness concerning himself and in himself, to face with nature and to unity with God."

Gandhi said, "The end of all education must be building up character. What is education without character and what is character without elementary personal purity."

Dr. Radhakrishnan states, "It is the function of a university to build human beings, strive to rid them of their vanities and egotism and emancipate their minds from petty prejudices and narrow loyalties, *Sa Vidya Ya Vimuktaya*. Such enfranchised souls who fear nothing more than cowardice, who despise nothing more than insincerity are needed today for the building of our country. Whatever line you take up, disciplined dedication is necessary. Without it we cannot survive in this competitive world."

Idealism and Discipline

According to idealism, a pupil cannot realise his spiritual possibilities without submitting himself to a process of balanced external constraint which ultimately should lead to self-restraint. An idealist does not believe in 'free discipline' as it is likely to lead the child astray. An idealist attaches importance to the guidance of the teacher. Froebel, however, does not favour the imposition of the arbitrary will of the teacher. He stresses that "control over the child is to be exercised through a knowledge of the interests and expressions of love and sympathy. In general, idealists recommend direct moral instruction as an instrument of maintaining discipline".

The important features are: (a) Idealism believes in inner disciple; (b) Idealism advocates the cultivation of higher values of life through moral and religious instruction; (c) Idealism accepts restraint on freedom; and (d) It requires the teacher to present good examples because the child considers the teacher to be an ideal person to be emulated by his pupils.

Idealism and the Teacher

Idealism idealises the teacher who assumes an important role in the educative process in idealism. He is the key figure in it. He is the most important element. Education according to the idealist pattern is by and large teacher-centred, and not pupil-centred or subject-centred. His personality is the most vital influence on the pupils learning, manner, behaviour and above all his character and personality.

Froebel's metaphor of the Kindergarten, perhaps, explains best the function of the educator. The school is regarded as a garden and the teacher as the gardener whose function is to tend the little human plants in his charge carefully and to help them to grow to beauty and perfection. The human plant can grow unaided according to the laws of its own nature, yet the gardener is to see that the plant attains its finest form, it produces or gives the finest results, Ross has beautifully summed up the place of the teacher in the idealistic school when he says, "The naturalist may be content with briars but the idealist wants fine roses. So the educator by his efforts must assist the educand who is developing according to the laws of his nature, to attain levels that would otherwise be denied to him".

Idealism and Curriculum

To the idealist, any subject that provides sufficient opportunities for the development of the creative self is suitable for study.

Plato believed that the highest ideas of life was the attainment of the highest good or God and for this he suggested that the curriculum should include those subjects which lead to the inculcation of the three spiritual values—truth, beauty and goodness.

As W.C. Bagley (1913) has said, "The main aim of education is to instill ideas that will function as judgements...the subject matter of instruction (curriculum) must be totally subservient to this aim. It is the subjective attitude of the pupil that is more important". Thus the problem of curriculum should be approached from the stand point of ideas and ideals.

According to T.P. Nunn, curriculum should give place to those human activities that are of the greatest and most permanent significance in the wider world, the greatest expressions of the human spirit".

Ross summarises from Ruk a curriculum scheme for a complete ideal education.

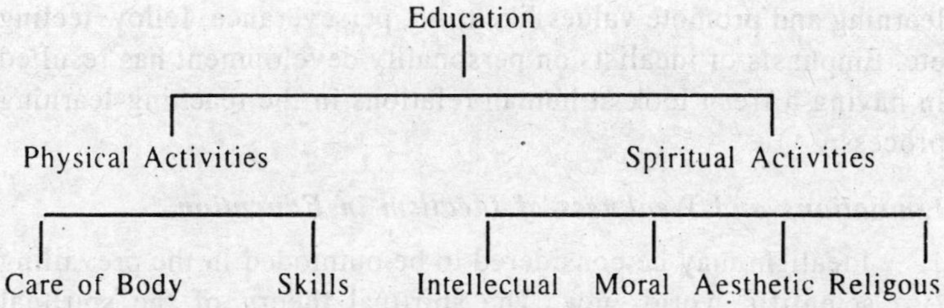

Illustration 4.1 Complete Ideal Education

Teacher-Pupil Relations in Idealims

Idealism considers the teacher a friend, philosopher and guide to the pupils. It accepts the teacher as an ideal person. Idealism makes the spirit all important. It asks the teacher to realise the divinity in the child and let the child unfold himself to make that divinity patent which at present is latent. The teacher's job in idealism is to take care of the child so that the young mind should be saturated with the idea that it has been born in a human world which is in harmony with the world around it. He guides his students so that they not only possess their heritage but also improve it steadily and proceed towards their goal steadily—each individual attains what is called 'self-realisation.'

Main Functions of the Teacher in Idealism

1. The teacher must understand his pupils thoroughly.
2. The teacher must be a personal friend and guide to his pupils.
3. The teacher should present high standards of behaviour and conduct before his pupils.
4. The teacher should have a deep knowledge of his subject.
5. The teacher should strive hard to provide a social environment in the classroom that is conducive to imitation by students.
6. The teacher should aim at inculcating in the pupils a desire to work hard.
7. The teacher should employ thought provoking techniques and thereby encourage his pupils to think for themselves.

To sum up in a world threatened by materialism, the philosophy of idealism provides light to man to restore his proper place. It stresses that educational institutions should become places for learning and promote values like truth, perseverance, fellow feeling etc. Emphasis of idealists on personality development has resulted in having a fresh look at human relations in the teaching-learning process.

Limitations and Weakness of Idealism in Education

1. Idealism may be considered to be outmoded in the prevailing scientific world-view. The spiritual theory of the spiritual universe is not considered to be in consonance with the scientific research today.
2. Idealistic concepts like 'spirit', 'mind', 'soul', 'the cosmos' have little relevance in classroom teaching.
3. The idealistic education stresses imitation of models but the younger generation prefers invention and originality rather than limitation.
4. Too much emphasis on good manners, and modesty may be mistaken for diffidence.
5. Emphasis on gaining knowledge is likely to turn education institutions into information-mongers' workshops. Schools curricula becomes overloaded with obsolete knowledge sometimes.
6. Idealistic scheme of education, by and large, pays less attention to physical, industrial, social and electronic environment of today.

4.2 Pragmatism

Pragmatism: 'Down to earth philosophy', 'Cash Value Philosophy', 'Utilitarian Philosophy', 'Worldly wise philosophy' and *'Practical philosophy'*—The essence of pragmatism is on human experience which decides the nature of things. Usually USA is known as the birth place of this philosophical thought. This philosophy developed on the basis of the needs of the people who emigrated from England and other European countries for the sake of religious freedom. They wanted to lead a new life on the basis of their new pattern of living. They were not very much interested in cultural values. They believed that only that knowledge was helpful which was helpful in changing the environment. Pragmatism holds that whatever fulfils one's purposes and develops one's life is true. All ideals are relative to situation. Pragmatism emphasises 'functional knowledge'.

Chief Exponents of Pragmatism

1. C.B. Pierce (1839-1914 A.D.)
2. William James (1842-1910 A.D.)
3. John Dewey (1859-1952 A.D.)

Meaning of Pragmatism

Historically the pragmatic approach can be traced to Protagorias, a Sophist philosopher of ancient Greece who said, "Man is the Measure of All Things." In recent times the name first appeared in 1878 in "How to Make our Ideas Clear," an article written by C.S. Pierce. He preferred to use the term "Pragmaticism." He attacked idealism and redefined truth and knowledge in terms of experience and their practical consequences. William James developed this outlook out of the American cultural milieu and became the founder and father of this, what Archit. J. Bahm calls, `down to earth' cash-value philosophy. John Dewey (1859-1952) became its leading and most influential exponent. He practised it in his laboratory school set up in Chicago in 1896. His purpose was to train pupils in co-operation and mutually useful living. Pragmatism stands between idealism and materialism—a sort of compromise. Idea or mind is the primary thing in idealism: Matter is at the centre of the universe so far as materialism is concerned. They are in fact the two "antithetical trends" in philosophy. For pragmatism "Experience" is at the centre of the Universe.

Pragmatism believes that 'reality' (world) is in constant flux. It is in a state of continuous change. It is a process. It is just like the ever changing waters of an on-going stream. There is nothing in this world which is static, permanent or eternal. If idealism speaks for ideas and ideals, pragmatism is concerned with facts based on experience only. Other equivalent names of pragmatism are 'instrumentalism' and 'experimentalism'.

William James explains the essence of pragmatism in these words, "A pragmatist turns away from abstractions and insufficiency, from verbal solutions, from fixed principles, from closed systems and pretended absolutes and origins. He turns towards concreteness' and adequacy', towards `facts', towards action' and towards power'.

Papini, an Italian pragmatist has given a very beautiful description of pragmatism. "It (Pragmatism) lies in the midst of our theories like a corridor in a hotel; innumerable chambers open out of it. In one you may find a man writing an atheistic volume; in the next someone on his knees praying for faith and strength; in the next a system of idealist metaphysics is excogitated (conntemplated upon); in the next the impossibility of metaphysics is being shown. But they all own the corridor and all must pass through it if they want a practical way of getting into or out of their respective rooms."

William James sees no difference between pragmatism and practicalism.

Dewey states, "Philosophy in order to be philosophy, should have meaning and utility in influencing the conduct of life and not a passive enquiry or contemplation." About truth he says "Truth is made just as health, wealth and strength are made in the course of experience"

In the words of Ross, "Pragmatism is essentially a humanistic philosophy, maintaining that man creates his own values in the course of activity, that reality is still in the making and awaits its part of completion from the future, that to an unascertainable extent our truths are man-made products."

James B. Prett observes, "Pragmatism offers us a theory of meaning, a theory of truth and knowledge, and a theory of reality."

A pragmatist believes in the 'non-mystical and non-spiritual' character of existence.

Forms of Pragmatism

Pragmatism has the following three forms:

Humanism pragmatism—It conceives of the truth as that which best satisfies human nature and welfare as a whole. Whatever fulfils man's purposes, derives and develops his life, is true.

Experimental pragmatism—According to experimental pragmatism truth is that which can be experimentally verified or whatever works.

Biological pragmatism—Biological pragmatism lays stress on the human ability of adaptation to the environment and that of adapting the environment to human needs.

Fundamental Principles of Pragmatism

1. Truth is that which works in practical situations. Truth changes with times.
2. Action is real, ideas are tools.
3. Man is an active being.
4. There are no absolute values of life.
5. It places its faith in man's ability to solve his problems through the logic of scientific methods and experiments.
6. It rejects all authoritarianism whether in government, religion or education.
7. Knowledge is always tentative and functional.
8. Pragmatism is a utilitarian philosophy.
9. Pragmatism has little value for the past. It takes into account the present and the future.
10. Pragmatism has little belief in the spiritual character of existence.

Characteristics of Pragmatic Education

1. Education is a social necessity. It is a means by which society renews itself.
2. Pragmatic education is progressive. It changes with the changing circumstances of life.
3. It stands for the worth and freedom of the individual.
4. Education is a continuous process.
5. It stresses the physical and social experience.
6. It regards the child as the centre of activity.
7. It makes life situations as the basis of education.
8. Experiences and experiments are the basis of parenting.
9. It considers philosophy as the outcome of educational experiments.

Aims of Education in Pragmatism

1. Social efficiency is the primary aim of education.
2. Pragmatism holds that the aims of education change with the changing times.
3. Pragmatism stresses on more and more education and continuous growth.
4. Pragmatism regards adaptation to environment as one of the major aims of education.

Curriculum

1. Pragmatism regards utility as the prime mover in the determination of curriculum.
2. — stresses upon experience curriculum.
3. — assigns a due place to the interests of the child.
4. — provides for problem-solving activities.
5. — emphasises subjects and studies like physical training, hygiene, social studies, mathematics and sciences.

Methods of Teaching

1. Curriculum provides for creative activities in the teaching-learning process.
2. It advocates purposeful activities.
3. It includes activities which lead to learning through experience.
4. Project method is considered to be an indispensable method for successful teaching-learning.
5. Principle of correlation and integration.

Role of the Teacher

1. Pragmatism regards the teacher as a helper and guide.
2. Pragmatism considers the teacher as an arranger of experience.

Discipline and Pragmatism

1. Pragmatism stresses on social discipline.
2. Pragmatism believes that discipline comes through purposive and cooperative activities.

Contribution of Pragmatism to Educational Thought and Practices

1. The pragmatic approach is based on the recognition of the needs of a technological and industrialised society. Newspapers, journals, radio and television become important media of education.
2. Pragmatism provides definite aims of education. The student is prepared to live in society and learn skills and attitudes which are required for him to live as a useful member of society.
3. Utility in the educative process is the first criterion. The school is expected to provide learning and experiences that are useful.
4. Pragmatism makes the child the centre of the educative process.
5. Teaching methods are based on 'learning by doing'. Child is put into real situations so that he may be able to grapple with them and solve the problems that arise from them.
6. Discussion, questioning, inquiring, touching and handling of situations are provided for.
7. Education is not bound by tradition. Pragmatic philosophers advise us to test everything through our own experience.
8. Pragmatism encourages a democratic way of learning through purposeful and cooperative projects and activities.
9. The teacher has to play a very challenging role in the educative process under pragmatism and he has to be very alert and watchful.

Weakness and Limitations of Pragmatism in Education

1. The pragmatic philosophy of education, by and large, ignores the place of the spirit.
2. Problems selected by the students may be unreal, having no relation with real life situations.
3. Pragmatism does not provide for regular and systematic instruction.
4. Pragmatism leaves many curricular gaps and deficiencies in the learning process.
5. It puts heavy demands on the teacher. Only a few resourceful and gifted teachers may be able to cope with the demands

of teaching in an environment set up under pragmatic conditions.

6. It does not lay adequate stress on cultural activities.
7. Pragmatism does not provide fixed goals of education.

4.3 Naturalism

The oldest Philosophy in the west, Naturalism, regards human life as a part of the scheme of nature. This is a type of philosophy to which 'nature is the whole reality'. Matter is supreme. Naturalism relegates man as a spiritual being to the background and disregards the existence of any spiritual potentialities in him. "Return to nature', 'break the chains of society' are its important slogans.

Chief Exponents of Naturalism

1. Democritus (About 400 B.C.)—A Greek Philosopher
2. Epicurus (342-270 B.C)—A Greek Philosopher
3. Bacon, Francis (1561-1626 A.D.)—An English Philosopher
4. Comenius, J.A. (1592-1670 A.D.)—A Czechoslovacian Philosopher
5. Spencer, Herbert (1820-1903)—An English Philosopher
6. Huxley, Thomas Henry (1825-1895)—An English Biologist
7. Rousseau, Jean Jacques (1712-1778)—A Swiss Philosopher

Definition and Meaning of Naturalism

In the words of Hocking, "Naturalism is a metaphysics which considers nature as the whole of reality. It excludes what is supernatural or other worldly."

George Haward Joyce states, "Naturalism is a system whose salient characteristic is the exclusion of whatever is spiritual or indeed whatever is transcendental of experience from our philosophy of nature and man."

R.B. Perry notes, "Naturalism is the philosophical generalisation of science, the application of the theories of science to the problems of philosophy". Prem Nath observes, "Naturalism is an attitude rather than a specific system of philosophy".

Rusk Writes, "Naturalism is a philosophical position adopted by those who approach philosophy from a purely scientific point of view".

James Ward, says that "Naturalism is the doctrine that separates nature from God, subordinates spirit to matter, and sets up unchangeable laws as supreme."

Main Characteristics of Naturalism

1. According to naturalism, the material world is the real world.
2. Mind is subordinate to matter.
3. Nature alone is the source of all knowledge.
4. Values are created in terms of specific needs.
5. All real values exist in nature—in living close to nature.
6. There is no possibility of any 'supernatural being,'
7. The individual is always given precedence.
8. Man creates societies only to meet some of his needs.
9. Scientific knowledge is of the highest worth.

Principles of Education According to Naturalism

1. Naturalism lays stress on physical environment.
2. Naturalism emphasises the present life of the child as the basis of education.
3. Naturalism accords an important place to the child in the educative process.
4. Naturalism advocates education in accordance with the nature of child.
5. Naturalism gives prominent place to the concept of freedom in the education of the child.
6. Naturalism has an insignificant place for knowledge from books or bookish knowledge.
7. Naturalism regards education as the dynamic side of philosophy.

Aims of Education

Herbert Spencer lays down the following objectives in his famous essay *What Knowledge is of Most Worth?*

1. Self preservation and self-expression.
2. Securing the necessities of life.
3. Raising children.
4. Citizenship training.
5. Education for leisure.

Curriculum

The chief characteristics of the curriculum are:

1. Curriculum is based on the nature of the child, his interests etc.
2. It lays stress on the subjects that are helpful in self-preservation.
3. It stresses basic sciences.
4. It gives due importance to physical and health sciences.

Man has to protect his life. Therefore, he should be given a knowledge of body and health. Training in vocational subjects is needed for self-preservation—house science for family life, social sciences for social and political life, literature and art for utilisation of leisure.

Curriculum and Methods of Teaching

Great emphasis is laid on the direct experience of things and learning by doing. Rouseau even goes to the extent of saying, "Give your scholars no Herbal lesson, he should be taught by experience alone. Teach by doing whenever you can; and only fall back on words when doing is out of question. Bookish knowledge should be as little as possible". Ross described the naturalist teaching-learning methodology as. "The naturalist educator rightly thinks less of his own exposition, much more of the learning experiences of the pupils". Important characteristics of the methods of teaching are:

1. Learning by doing.
2. Learning by experience.
3. Learning through observation.
4. Learning through heuristic method.

Naturalism and Discipline

The naturalist believes in the theory of 'Natural consequences of Discipline'. Rousseau said, "Children should never receive punishment as such—it should always come as the natural consequence of their fault". Herbert Spencer would also like the child to suffer the unavoidable consequences' or the 'inevitable reaction' of his conduct. Spencer explains this as, "when a child falls or runs its head against the table, it suffers pain, the remembrance of which tends to make it more careful and by repetition of such experiences, it is disciplined into a proper guidance of its movements."

In short, naturalism gives full freedom to the child for self-expression. It advocates 'laissez faire' (Let things go as they like). Naturalism shuns all external restraints.

Naturalism and the Teacher

Ross describes the role of a teacher in naturalism as, "The teacher is only a setter of the stage, a supplier of materials and opportunities, a provider of an ideal environment, a creator of conditions under which the natural development of the child takes place". Child is accepted as a 'hero' in the 'drama of education'.

Nature is an observer. His function is to facilitate the natural growth and learning of the child.

Contribution of Naturalism to Education

Naturalism has been a great force in bringing about a 'renaissance' in education. As a protest against the rigidity and formality of school education the naturalistic form of education presents a refreshing humanistic attitude towards learning and methods of instruction. The naturalist movement in education brought to the forefront the importance of the recognition of the child in the process of education.

Madam Montessori, in her approach to childhood, bases her method of education on naturalism.

Rabindranath Tagore's school in Shantiniketan upholds in many respects the chief principles of naturalism.

A.S. Neill's school at Summerhill illustrates the naturalistic philosophy.

Froebel's kindergarten also follows principles of naturalism.

Psychologists like Stanley Hall, Piaget and others have emphasised the child's dynamic nature which grows and develops in distinct stages; each stage having its own characteristics—infancy, childhood, adolescence and maturity. Naturalism ushered in the psychological movements, and formed the basis for child centred education, stressing freedom, initiative, spontaneity and self-expression in learning.

The main contributions of naturalism to educational theory and practice may be summed up as under:

1. Naturalism has brought to the forefront the importance and recognition of the child in the educative process.
2. Naturalism advocates that education should be a pleasurable activity for children. The child's interest in and readiness to learn a topic has been assigned due importance.
3. Naturalism stresses that education should engage the spontaneous self-activity of the child.
4. According to naturalism, methods of instruction must be inductive to make teaching effective, inspirational and attractive.
5. The concept of discipline in naturalism is very desirable. Punishment is based on the consequences of wrong deeds. Children share freedom as well as responsibility.
6. Naturalism in education draws our attention to the aesthetic aspect of surroundings. This also implies that schools should be located in natural surroundings. Education can be imparted in the open.
7. New schools and new movements came into being as a result of naturalism. Forebel's kindergarten, the Montessori method, Tagore's Shantiniketan, A.S. Neill's Summerhill are representatives of this movement.

Weakness of Naturalism in Education

1. Naturalism in its extreme form neglects books and other media. It is very difficult to assume that we can neglect the vast quantities of printed materials.
2. Physical nature alone is not sufficient for providing education.
3. Absolute freedom to child is a myth. It cannot exist. 'Child cannot be allowed the freedom to hang himself.'
4. Naturalism ignores the higher ends in the education process.
5. It is very difficult to find naturalistic surroundings for locating educational institutions.
6. Naturalism assigns very little importance to the teacher in the educative process.
7. Naturalism ignores the spiritual and moral side of man's nature.
8. Naturalism, by and large, ignores the ultimate ideals.

Summing up

The gift of naturalism to the education of the child may be aptly described in the following lines of Wordsworth from his famous 'Ode to Immortality.'

"Training clouds of glory do we come...

Heaven lies about us in our infancy...

Shades of the prison-house begin to close

Upon the growing boy."

4.4 Existentialism

The Youngest Philosophy: Conflicting Meaning

Existentialism is a modern and the youngest philosophy. It is very difficult to find its roots in any of the ancient philosophical thoughts. Existentialists are against any kind of rationalisation universalities and generalities in philosophy. They have advanced extreme subjectivism in philosophising. On account of this subjectivism, it has became difficult to talk of existentialism as a school of philosophy. In fact to write about this philosophy is neither easy nor simple but a challenging and complex one because of the inherent paradoxes and ambiguities in the philosophy itself. It is very difficult to be fully intelligible and coherent when one writes about existentialism. Contradictions and inconsistencies are fundamental to the views of existentialists. A very significant source of confusion is of the differing personal convictions of existential philosophers. For example, Soren Kierkegaard Gabriel Marcel and Gaspers are theists, where as on Jean Paul Sartre and Martin Heidegger are agnostics. Jaspers is a protestant whereas Marcel is a staunch Roman Catholic. Others remotely associated with the philosophy of existentialism are scholars like Schelling and Nietsche etc. who have influenced existential thought but they cannot be rigidly classified as existentialists.

Basic Concepts of Existentialism

Soren Kierkegaard, a Danish philosopher asserted that 'Existence Preceeds Essence!' An existentialist affirms that existence is prior to essence, that man is fundamentally free to create his essences but thinks that this is the tragedy about man. The French philosopher Sartre's monumental work, *Being and Nothingness* is basically a formulation of the theory of man. Man is nothing other than what he makes himself. If man, as the existentialists see him is indefinable, it is because at first he is nothing. Only afterwards will he be something and he himself will have made what he will be. It means that first of all man exists, turns up appears on the scene and only afterwards defines himself.

'Contingency of human life' is another significant concept of existentialism. This concept is often characterised by experience of dread, horror, uncertainty and finally limited by death. Existentialism advises us to live with these categories of contingency.

The third significant concept of existentialism is its view on freedom. In the age-long philosophical controversy of Free Will V/S Determinism, the existentialists prefer to view man as an infinitely free, responsible being. Sartre identified freedom with existence. This infinite freedom entails upon him a heavy sense of responsibility and this situation of being burdened with a heavy responsibility is the cause of dread, anguish and anxiety.

The chief characteristics of existentialism may be summarised as under:

1. Man's 'existence' is recognised.
2. Man is 'not complete' and he is in the process of 'becoming'.
3. 'Self-knowledge' is important.
4. Man has the 'freedom' and 'responsibility' in 'becoming'.
5. Man cannot accept the ready made concepts of existence. He is free to shape his life and choose his destiny.

Educational Implication of Existentialism

According to J.D. Butler, the philosophy of existentialism has not displayed any particular interest in education. Kneller has observed, "Aside from casual references such as those of Kierkegaard and Marcell to their own schooling, existentialists, we repeat, do not carry their doctrine into practical theory or policy for school behaviour". The author further observes, "The only safe conclusion to be drawn is that the last developments in this philosophic school are yet to be made and that all the avenues pursued by these men will be explored further and to some extent perhaps reconciled".

Existentialism and Meaning of Education

According to extistentialism, education should throw open to children the means to understand human suffering, misery and the dreadful responsibilities of adult life. Since man is free by nature, education must make the pupil aware of the infinite possibilities of his freedom. G.F. Kneller has put it, "An uncompromising affirmation of authentic freedom and individual uniqueness is the message of existentialism for the philosophy of education".

Existentialism and the objective of education—This philosophy regards every individual to be unique. Education, therefore, should aim at enabling every individual to develop his unique qualities to harness his potentialities and cultivate his individualities.

Existentialism and curriculum—Existentialists give more importance to humanistic studies as they believe that through the study of humanities children come to terms with human suffering, anguish, anxiety and death.

Methods of teaching—As Kneller puts it, "The existentialist favours the Socratic method, not so much because it involves 'induction' of the collection and analysis of all available evidence, nor because of its complimentary process of 'definition' whereby general values are reached from particular instances; but chiefly because it is a method that tests the inner life as a stethoscope sounds the heart".

Role of the teacher—Kneller states the role of the teacher in existentialism as, "If there is anything that the existentialist teacher can do for his students, it is to bring them to a more critical analysis and understanding of the meaning and purpose of existence, so that with time he may became more then a mere affective creature perpetuating the habits of his ancestors".

Limitations in Existentialism

1. The educational methods in existentialism appear to be impractical and inapplicable in an industrial society.
2. It requires a good deal of time and effort on the part of the teacher to develop individual relationships with the students for having a closer understanding of their personalities.
3. The terminology used in existentialism is not very clear. Concepts like 'Being', 'Meaning', 'Person', 'Existence' are ambiguous.

4.5 Humanism

Meaning of humanism—Humanism aims at gaining for man a proper recognition. In terms of the humanistic philosophy, man is an end and not a means. Man is a free agent. Humanism does not believe in supernaturalism and argues that man does not survive after death. Humanism regards that human thinking is the result of the interaction between the complex living organism and the environment. Humanism has full faith in the competency of man to solve all his problems. Humanism states that man's happiness lies in this world. Humanism believes in the freedom of man.

Main Principles of Humanism

1. Values held by the people affect history.
2. Values are relative but absolute
3. Human problems are problems of value.
4. Humanism emphasises the study of literature.

Educational Implications of Humanism

1. *Respect for ancient cultures*—Educational programmes should foster an administration and love for ancient cultures which are important sources of the growth of human civilisation.
2. *Respect for intellectuals and literary scholarship*—The younger generation must learn to respect the wisdom of the scholars as it relates to the more important field of human values. Intellectuals through their vast knowledge and intellectual ability are in a favourable position to set goals for the society.
3. *Respect for language*—The correct form of language should be taught to the student. Education must stress the use of correct and appropriate vocabulary and sentence and sentence structure through grammar and composition.

4.6 Realism

Realism is based on the belief that the physical world alone is 'objective.' Quite contrary to idealism, realism regards the worldly realities of everyday life as true.

Main Exponents of Realism

1. Aristotle (384-322 B.C) a Greek philosopher is generally recognised as the father of realism.
2. St. Thomas Aquinas (1225-1274 AD), Professor at the University of Paris tried to bring about a synthesis of Greek philosophy which stressed reason with the Christian doctrine based on faith.
3. John Locke (1632-1704), an English philosopher, gave new impetus to realism.

The rapid spread of scientific knowledge in the twentieth century led to its increased growth and its acceptance as a distinct philosophy.

Basic Concepts of Realism

The following are the five basic concepts:

1. Realism and nature of reality.
   - (i) Realism is a philosophy away from the world of ideas and is concerned with the study of the world we live in.
   - (ii) Realism believes that all knowledge is derived from experience.
   - (iii) The realist believes that the real world is the world of nature.
   - (iv) The realist believes that everything that exists in the universe is matter or energy or matter in motion.
2. *Laws of nature and realism*—The realist believes that the physical universe is operated by natural laws.
3. *Realism and science*—The realist tries to discover truth with the help of scientific methods. Such a discovery of truth helps to control the environment.
4. *Realism and religion*—There is no absolute antagonism between realism and religion, though many realists hold the view that religion is merely man-made and there is no God.
5. *Realism and value*—Most of the realists share the belief that a thing has an aesthetic value to the extent it harmonises with the beauty of nature. Many realists think that behaviour is what is socially and rationally acceptable.

Realism and Objectives of Education

Broadly speaking, there are two objectives of education according to realism:

1. Equipping students with knowledge and skill needed to understand and master their physical environment.
2. Enabling students to adjust themselves to the realities of the physical world and to adjust with adult approved behaviour.

Realism in educational practice—The realist is concerned with the systematic organisation of teaching and learning. Scientific evaluation is the most important contribution made by realism in the field of education. Realism lays stress on the use of standardised tests.

Realism and the role of the teacher—Realism does not attach much importance to the personality of the teacher. The realist also does not give any importance to the opinion of the teacher.

Realism and curriculum—The realist gives a high priority to subjects like physical sciences and mathematics.

4.7 The Electic Tendency in Education

Meaning of the Electic Tendency in Education

Electic tendency in education attempts to synthesise or to select from and to draw together aspects, ideas and values from different philosophies.

Need of an Electic Tendency

The following factors are responsible for the emergence of this tendency:

1. None of the philosophies of education provide all the answers.
2. In a multiracial and multilingual society like India, there is a great need for a philosophy which aims at synthesising diverse elements.

Educational Implications of the Electic Tendency

1. Emphasis on the individual child.
2. The powers of the mind and intellect are important.
3. The child should become a useful member of the society.
4. The curriculum should be a balanced one.

5. The interests and aptitudes of the child should be properly taken care of.
6. Teachers play an important role in the educative process.

4.8 Progressivism or Progressive Education

Meaning of Progressivism—Progressivism is the direct outcome of the influence of pragmatism on education. Progressivism advocates that the human development progresses through direct evolutionary states and every stage must be properly attended to. There is nothing absolute or rigid. Progress takes place through experimentation. Kilpatrick has been one of its most influential advocates. He has helped greatly in the spread of this movement.

The term 'Progressive Education' was first used in 1918 when the Progressive Education Association was founded in the USA under the leadership of Stanwood Cobb.

The progressive movement came as a protest against the formalism of the day in the educational field. As a matter of fact progressive education reflects the child centred view of education as advocated by great philosophers and educators like Rousseau, Froebel, Montessori, Francis W. Parker and Dewey etc.

Seven Pillars of Progressive Education

1. Freedom to the child to develop naturally.
2. Interest of the child as the motive to work.
3. Scientific study of child development.
4. Greater attention to all factors that influence a child's physical development.
5. Teacher to play the role of a guide and not that of a task master.
6. The progressive school to play the role of a leader in educational reforms movement.
7. Close cooperation between the school and the home to meet the needs of the child.

Aim of education—The advocates of progressive education stand for the education of the 'Whole personality' of the child—emotional, intellectual, physical and social.

Curriculum—It should be made of the experiences of actual daily living in various situations. It is to be made up of the sum total of the child's experiences.

Methods of teaching—The progressive education believes in group activities in which each child participates and grows personally and socially. The methods of teaching are socialised.

Agencies of education—Progressive educators are of the view that social agencies working in the field must cooperate with the efforts of the school in educating children.

In India, Progressive Movement in education was started at Bombay in 1937 by some leading educators.

It must be remembered that progressivism is not a distinct philosophy of education. It is an approach and it pervades all modern philosophies of education.

4.9 Sarvodaya

The word 'Sarvodaya' is a Sanskrit word which implies 'good of all'. Since it is aimed at the good of all, it presents a synthesis of all the good points of different Indian and western philosophies of all. According to some thinkers, Sarvodaya philosophy is ahead of all philosophies. It is very unfortunate that this philosophy has not received due attention. It believes that an individual can attain salvation only in the social cosmos. Acharya Vinoba Bhave and Kaka Kalelkar are its chief exponents.

Educational aim—A Sarvodayist thinks that the aim of education is liberation from bondage.

The educative process and the Sarvodaya philosophy—Sarvodaya education is an education for life through life. According to the Sarvodaya philosophy, knowledge should flow out of life situations. Life activities should be the core of school studies. These activities may be classified as under:

1. Productive activities.
2. Activities relating to cooperative living.
3. Activities relating to a clean, healthy and natural life.
4. Activities relating to aesthetic and cultural life.
5. Activities relating to spiritual life.

The method of instruction and Sarvodaya philosophy—"Correlation of Studies" is the main principle of the Sarvodaya method. Correlation in Sarvodaya philosophy of education is to develop an integrated personality in which the cognitive, affective and conative powers of the child are harmoniously developed. Every activity, whether manual or social or intellectual must develop all the three, the hand, the head and the heart in unison.

The problem of discipline and Sarvodaya—Sarvodaya envisages a society of free people, who will be self-disciplined rather than be disciplined through an external authority. The Sarvodaya ethics provides a good basis for freedom and discipline for the individual child. One man's freedom should not restrict the freedom of the other.

Eleven vows are being put as the motto of a disciplined life: 1. Discipline of Truth. 2. Discipline of Non-violence. 3. Discipline of Non-thieving. 4. Discipline of Brahmacharya. 5. Discipline of Non-possession. 6. Discipline of Bread-labour. 7. Discipline of the Control of the Palate. 8. Discipline of Fearlessness. 9. Discipline of Secularism. 10. Discipline of Swadeshi. 11. Discipline of Untouchability.

The teacher and the Sarvodaya philosophy—Sarvodaya envisages the teacher to be an ideal person with sound character. The pupils consciously and unconsciously limit his ways. The influence of the teacher over his pupils is very great. A teacher's conduct will always reflect the conduct of his pupils. Therefore, the teacher's character should be ideal in order to keep the pupils disciplined.

Sarvodaya and control of education—Sarvodaya neither advocates state control of education nor does it leave education in the hands of a few individuals. Sarvodaya advocated that the community should take charge of the pupils. Education should be a local affair and it should be in the hands of a local community. Each local unit should have the freedom to develop its educational unit according to its needs.

Questions and Problems

A. Essay-Type Questions

1. What is pragmatism? Which aspects of the present Indian education may be ascribed to the influence of Pragmatism?
2. Naturalism is paedo-centric (child centred). Explain this concept with reference to the role of the teacher.
3. Estimate the contribution of Pragmatism to educational thought and practice. How far are they practicable in our schools?
4. The contribution of Pragmatism is more in the areas of teaching methods rather than in the formulation of specific aims of education". Explain.
5. Enumerate and explain any three significant characteristics of the idealistic philosophy of education.
6. Illustrate how idealism has influenced educational thought and practice.
7. How would a teacher be influenced by the philosophy of idealism? Bring out the significance of idealism with reference to teacher-pupil relationship.
8. "Idealism shifts the emphasis from the natural and scientific facts of life to the spiritual aspects of human experience." Explain this statement.
9. Compare and contrast Pragmatism and Naturalism as philosophies of education.

B. Short-Answer Type Questions

10. How does Naturalism conceive the role of a teacher?
11. Point out the limitations of Naturalism in education.
12. Write notes on the educational implications of the following
    - (i) Progressivism
    - (ii) Existentialism
    - (iii) Humanism
    - (iv) Realism
    - (v) Sarvodaya

5 Indian Philosophical Traditions and Their Educational Implications

5.1 Comprehensiveness of Indian Philosophical Tradition—Bernard

Theos, in his book Hindu Philosophy (Italy) (1958) has observed, "It (philosophy) must be realistic as well as idealistic; it must not be a brutal materialism, worshipping facts and figures and ignoring values idealising science and denying spirituality. Nor must it be predominantly a philosophy of values which evades and ignores all connections with facts. It must be comprehensive enough to account for every new discovery of science; it must embrace all the concepts of religion and other philosophical systems... It is not enough merely to interpret reality as perceived by the senses; it must explain both sides of reality, the change and the unchangeable, being and becoming, permanent and impermanent, animate and inanimate. All these conditions have been satisfied by the philosophical systems of India."

Close link between Indian philosophy and religion— Prof. M. Varma in *The Philosophy of Indian Education* (1969) has emphasised that unlike Western philosophy, Indian philosophy never stood alone. It was invariably closely bound up with religion and with an ethics that had the force at once of a moral principle and a religious duty. While they are closely related like the head and the heart, their distinguishing features are as under:

Philosophy is:	Religion is:
Matter of thought	Matter of experience
Intellectual assent	Intuitive faith
View of life	Way of life
Logical justification	Experiential justification

5.2 The Vedanta Philosophy

Despite differences in detail and the exception of a purely materialist school, the Charvaka, the general spirit of Indian philosophy is a Vedantist View of life.

Sources of Traditional Indian Philosophy

The following are the chief sources from which Indian philosophy is derived.

1. Four Vedas
2. Six Vedangas
3. Four Upvedas
4. Four Brahmanas
5. One hundred and eight Upanishads (11 are most important)
6. Six systems of philosophy.
7. The Bhagvat Gita
8. Three Smritis.

Four Vedas—The four Vedas are the original and main sources of Vedic philosophy. Subsequent philosophies are based on the analysis and interpretation of the vedas.

The Vedas deal with every branch of knowledge and provide the basic knowledge of humanities, social sciences and natural and physical sciences. They deal with every aspect of human life—birth, childhood, youth, old age, death and rebirth. They point out the duties of a learned man, a student, a soldier, a householder, a warrior and an administrator etc. The Vedas have a message for all people of all nations and of all times. They embody the ways of leading a peaceful life.

The Vedas delve deep into the self as well as into the mysteries of God and nature to make life worth living. They are believed to be of divine origin.

The Vedas contain 20,358 verses: Rig Veda (10,522); Atharva Veda (5,977); Yajur Veda (1,984) and Sama Veda (1875).

Although varying dates are ascribed to the Vedas it is generally believed by scholars that the Rig Veda, the oldest of the Vedas, dates back to 4000 B.C.

The contents of the Vedic philosophy may be categorised under the following three heads:

1. The 'Gyan' or knowledge or wisdom
2. The 'Karma' or action or code of conduct
3. The 'Upasana' or dedication and devotion to God.

Central Concepts of Vedic Philosophy

Main Characteristics of the Philosophy of the Vedas

1. God is one and only one . He is all pervading, Omniscient, Omnipotent and ever present. He is the Supreme Spirit.
2. There are three entities in this universe—God, Soul and Matter.
3. The universe is real. It is not an illusion or dream.
4. This, universe is created by God.
5. The soul is immortal.
6. The ultimate aim of life is to obtain salvation (moksha) and union with god.
7. Actions are followed by results—the 'Law of Karma'. The law of Karma is nothing else but the cause and its effect.
8. The theory of 'rebirth' is a necessary corollary of the Law of Karma and immortality of the soul.
9. Knowledge of truth should be acquired and dissipated.
10. Justice should be done to all creatures.
11. All human beings should live in peace and harmony.

Philosophy to the Vedic seers was a practical aid that showed the right way of living. It determined the ideals and ways of life. For a proper understanding of the central teaching of the Vedic philosophy, it is very necessary to refer to a few concepts like 'Purushartha', 'Dharma', 'Moksha', etc.

Purusharth—Each individual has in him several desires—desire for children, desire for wealth, desire for power, common good, desire for communion with the unseen or God. Purushartha is a value which an individual seeks for the realisation of a desire or an end. The four 'Purusharthas' in a graded order are '*artha*' (wealth), '*kama*' (pleasure), '*dharma*' (righteousness) and '*moksha*' (spiritual freedom). Each value consistutes a preparatory stage for the realisation of the succeeding stage.

Artha (Wealth or material things)—This is only helpful as a means of satisfying one or the other desire of human life.

Kama—Includes physical as well as the psychological satisfaction of the natural urges of a person. Wealth or money is valuable only to the extent it serves, as a means to acquire goods. 'Artha' thus is an instrument value and it is a means to the realisation of '*Kama*'.

'*Artha*' and '*Kama*' are sought not only by man but also by all living beings.

Dharma (Righteousness)—This is confined to man. It is a spiritual value. '*Dharma*' is not only a central concept of Indian philosophy but also a unique one. It determines what we ought to do in different situations. In fact it regulates one's life. The word '*dharma*' comes from the Sanskrit root 'dhr' meaning thereby 'to hold' or to 'sustain'. '*Dharma*' denotes right action or right conduct. It has ethical and social values. It includes virtues of control of senses, charity, honesty, love, non-injury, self-restraint etc., '*Dharma*' puts a check on selfishness. '*Adharma*' is vice.

According to the social concept of Hindu '*Dharma*', the ideal life consists of four '*Ashramas*' (stages): 'Brahmacharya', the period of education, '*Garhsthya*', the life of the householder, '*Vanaprasthya*', retreat from worldly bonds and finally '*Sanyasa*', the life of a hermit.

Moksha (Liberation or salvation)—This concept sums up the aim of life in Indian philosophy. It is the realisation of the self. It is spiritual bliss. It is freedom from the cycle of births and deaths. It is becoming 'one' with God. It is the highest attainment man can have. It is the loftiest end. Philosophers and seers have prescribed different ways for the realisation of '*moksha*'. Two of these are most important. One prescribes the practice of '*niskam karma*' (selfless action), leading a pure life. The second prescribes '*dhyana*' (mediation).

According to some thinkers 'moksha' can be realised after death while others think that it can be realised in this very life. In any case the emphasis is on purity and noble deeds.

Indian Philosophy is Not Individualistic

Some critics regard Indian philosophy as individualistic, indifferent to social morality, negative and pessimistic. They sum up Indian philosophy by believing that "how to become a *sanyasi*', and `dharma' means individual perfection only."

It must be stressed that the idealist in India, while talking of the infinite goal does not neglect the immediate objectives of life. Self-realisation or salvation is to be realised in the society. The Indian philosophers very clearly, prescribed four stages of life. Each stage involved certain duties. They believed the performance of these duties would lead to liberation. Accordingly these duties and values were reflected in the curriculum. Education was considered a means of attaining salvation. Knowledge and wisdom were not gained for their sake but to make man moral and thereby assist him realise the ultimate objective of life.

Swami Vivekananda, one of the greatest exponents of Indian philosophy observed, "So long as millions live in hunger and ignorance, I hold every man a traitor who, having been educated at their expense, pays not the least heed to them.... I call him a `mahatma' who feels for the poor. Let these people be your God-think of them, work for them."

The Indian way of life or Indian philosophy propounds two paths for self-realisation: '*Pravrtimarga*' (the path of active life) and '*niviritimarga*' (the path of renuncion). The main concern of Indian philosophy is '*sarvajana sukhino bhavantu*' (happiness for all mankind). What is recommended is not 'renunciation of the world but 'self-renuciation'. Unselfishness or 'selfless' is the central point of Indian philosophy.

Educational Implication of the Vedic Philosophy

Objectives of education—It is stated. knowledge or learning makes one humble, free of ego. (A.V. VI.41). Education must give due regard to the application of learning. (Y.V. XX.12) O Lord! Illuminate the learner for a higher and happier life (A.V. VII.6.1)

Education for all—Vedas are for all (Yajur Veda-1.79.1). In other words knowlege and education should be for all

Proper environement—According to the Vedic view, through education one creates an environment conducive to attaining accomplishment of mind, intellect of thought, of purpose, of intelligence, of sense and vision. Education as Swami Dayananda means it, begins in the mother's womb. Preparation has to be made to make the womb a fit receptacle for a worthy promising soul. The mind of the pregnant mother and the environment she is in have a shaping influence on the child who is yet to be born. The parents, therefore, must have a selective environment.

Education of women—The Vedas give a very honourable and respectable status to women. They were eligible for higher education also. It is of interest to note that as many as 15 women scholars and seers contributed to several verses in the Vedas. Their names are: Angirasi Shashwati, Apala, Indrani, Lopamudra, Guhu, Romsha, Sarama, Shraddha, Surya, Urvashi, Vagambhrani, Vasukra Patni, Visvasara and Yami. It is stated, "O Learned Lady! All life is dependant on you, because you impart education to all." (R.V. II 97.17)

The Vedas accord a high position to the status of women and accordingly their education must receive priority.

Education for world peace and international understanding—The Vedas speak of one world and peace all round. Ideals and values of international understanding find their inspirations from the Vedas.

5.3 Upanishads

The word Upanishad means sitting devotedly. It brings to the mind the picture of an earnest disciple or learner learning from his spiritual guru or teacher. Apart from Indian scholars and seers, Europeans also have sung the glory of the Upanishads. In the words of Arthur Schopen hauer (1788-1860) a German philosopher, there is no study so benificial and elevating as that of the Upanishads. It has been the solace of my life. It will be the solace of my death."

The Upanishads deal with knowledge (Vidya) which nulifies or destroys ignorance (Avidya) and takes the seeker to salvation (Moksha) and to Brahma (God) and help him to understand Him in the true sense and thus liberates him from the bondage of the world. (Freedom from the cycle of births and deaths)

According to the Upanishads, self realisation comes through austerity, proper knowledge and truth. Inside the body, the self is full of light and purity and it is perceived by those who exercise self-control.

The Upanishads are the works of saints and seers. They deal with matter, soul and God and their interpretations.

Message of the Upanishads to the modern man—The modern man is crying for truth, for light and for the essence of life. The sentiments of the ancient Vedic prayers are echoed in the heart of the modern man.

"From the unreal lead me to the Real:
From the Darkness lead me to Light:
From Death lead me to immortality:"

(Brithadaranyaka Upanishad. 1.3.28)

The Isha Upanishad embodies in its very opening verse the central theme of all the Upanishads, namely, the spiritual unity and solidarity of all existence.

The second verse of the Isha Upanishad states that life is action. "In this world, one should desire to live one hundred years but only by performing actions."

Important Upnishads—Eleven Upanishads which constitute the primary object of attention are: (a) Isha Upanishad (b) Kenya Upanishad (c) Katha Upanishad (d) Prashna Upanishad (e) Mundaka Upanishad (f) Mundakya Upanishad (g) Chandogya Upanishad (h) Brithadaranyaka Upanishad (i) Attareya Upanishad (j) Taitirya Upanishad (k) Shevetashavatara Upanishad.

The period of Upanishads—It is very difficult to give the exact date of the various Upanishads. However, it is believed that the Upanishads came into being during the period 600 B.C. to 300 B.C.

Educational Implications of the Philosophy of Upanishads

Aims of Education

The principle aims of education are:

1. Acquisition of supreme knowledge.
2. Physical development.
3. Character development.

4. Spiritual development.
5. Development of social virtues.
6. Cultural development.

Curriculum—There were two types of courses—courses relating to 'Paravidya' (higher knowledge or supreme knowledge) and 'Aparavidya' (power knowledge).

The teacher and the taught (The guru and the student)—The teacher possessed virtues of affection, humility and truthfulness etc. Plain living, high thinking, disciplined routine, abstinence from pleasures, mental control and above all sincerity were the chief characteristics of an ideal teacher. The Brahmachari or the student was under the direct observation of his teacher all twenty-four hours and was also expected to lead a pious and disciplined life.

Methods of study—Listening, practice or recitation, immediate apprehension of the meaning, discourses and disputation were the methods generally followed.

The modern system of education needs to learn much from the philosophy of the Upanishads, especially in the area of aims of education and the system of organisation.

5.4 Six Systems of Philosophy

The six systems of philosophy deal with the causation of the genesis of the world and they describe six causes of this creation.

1. Naya system of philosophy (Logic) by Maharishi Gautam. It deals with matter.
2. Sankhya system of Philosophy by Maharishi Kapil. It is related to 25 elements (Tatvas). True knowledge comes by comprehending these elements like prakriti, (matter), mind (man), prithvi (earth) etc.
3. Yoga system of philosophy by Maharishi Patanjali. Patanjali, Yoga is the control of the aspiration and ambition of the mind. There are eight aspects of Yoga (a) 'Yama'—Absence of violence, untruth etc. (b) 'Nigam'—Five rules of (purity), 'Santosh' (contentment) (c) 'Tapa' (penance), 'Shauch', 'Swadhaya' (self study of scriptures) and Ishwar Pranidhan' (concentration of God), Asan (posture) (d) Pranayan (control of breath while inhaling) (e) Pratyahar (control of the mind

and sense) (f) 'Dharna' (applying the mind to some internal subject) (g) 'Dhyan' (concentrating attention on a particular subject of the mind) and (h) 'Samadhi (making attention the objective).

4. Vaishekshika system of philosophy (Metaphysics) by Maharishi Kanada. It relates to time.
5. Mimansa system of philosophy (Through Determination of a point) by Maharishi Gamini. It expounds action.
6. Vedanta system of philosophy (Theology) by Maharashi Vatsyana. It elucidates the concept of the Supreme Being.

Educational Implication

There is a great need to emphasise the eight aspects of Yoga in our educational institutions. It may be noted that yoga practices are not only for physical fitness but also for general upliftment of the individual. Yoga practised in right earnest and accepted as a way of life can be solve mental and physical problems.

5.5 The Bhagvad Gita

Ascribed to the seer Veda Vyasa, it is considered an epitome and essence of Vedic philosophy. Due the depth and vastness of the subject matter in the Gita, it has more than 300 commentaries in Indian and foreign languages.

Various dates are ascribed to composition of the Gita. B.G. Tilak, a great scholar puts 14th century B.C. as its date.

In size, the Gita is a little book of seven hundred verses, divided into 18 chapters.

Background—The Gita is in the form of a dialogue between Arjuna, a noted commander and Shri Krishna, an earthly manifestation of God—'Avatara'. The setting of the dialogue is highly dramatic. Arjuna is facing the huge army of his cousins with their supporters, many of whom are his elders including his 'guru' Dronacharya. Arjuna is to strike them for the enforcement of their claim (five Pandavas) to the part of the ancestral kingdom which is not accepted by Duryodhana, leader of the Kaurvas. The sight of his dear ones dissolves his determination to fight and he lays down his arms and thinks of renouncing the world. Shri Krishna, who is acting as his charioteer urges him to fight for his right. Krishna succeeds in persuading Arjuna who ultimately wins the struggle.

The exposition of Arjuna's duty and Krishna's exhoration to fulfill it consitutes the theme of Gita.

Principal Teachings of Gita

1. *Doing duty as dharma*—The essence of the philosophy as contained in the Gita is with inner convictions. We should discharge our duties diligently and honestly irrespective of the consequences and leave the rest to the Almighty. We must fight for justice and the right cause.
2. *Death is certain*—Death is inevitable to one who is born. One who dies, is bound to take birth. It does not, therefore, behove one to grieve over an inevitable event.
3. *Soul is immortal*—The soul is immortal and the body is perishable. The cycle of creation is a hard fact from which there is no escape.
4. *Incarnations (avatars)*—The ordered progress of the world at large is so important that God takes on special forms of prophets of incarnations from time to time to ensure its progress by appropriate guidance.
5. *Social welfare*—To be content with personal perfection is a narrow ideal. The proper ideal is to give to the world the best and the utmost that one can and to take from it the least. The wise man acts as a source of guidance and inspiration to the ignorant masses.
6. *Karma yoga*—The whole theme of the third chapter is the philosophy of action. This is also known as 'Karma-Yoga'-communication with God through action.
7. *Two ways of liberation*—According to Gita, there are two ways of liberation—those of action and knowledge. However, the order of activity is more important. It combines personal good with social good.
8. *Renunciation an attitude of mind*—The wonderful dialogue closes on the note of dedicated activity promising glory, success and prosperity to the individual who combines physical valour, with divine wisdom and is entitled Moksha or communication with God through liberating dedication.

Renunciation or 'sanayasa' is an attitude of the mind. It is not the cessation of obligatory activities but the dedication of those to God.

Educational Implications of Gita

1. *True meaning of education*—According to the philosophy of Gita, true education is that which helps one to see the existence of God.
2. *Objectives of education*—These are: (a) Developing virtuous knowledge (b) Sublimation of personality (c) Developing inner consciousness (d) Developing intellectual and logical ability (e) Developing the importance of duty in life (f) Coordinating and integrating individual and social aims.
3. *Pupil-teacher relationships*—The greatest lesson for the learner is that he must have complete faith in his teacher who should also be devoted to his work. True knowledge, learning and wisdom are acquired through ceaseless action coupled with devotion. Concentration on studies leads to enlightment and self control. The main characteristics of the learner or a devotee are:- He is a lover of knowledge and mankind. He is curious to know and has an abiding faith in his teacher. He very politely but with a subtle resolution puts questions to his teacher to solve his problems. The teacher also makes all possible efforts to enlighten his student and guide him in such a way that he attains the ideals of a self realised soul.

5.6 Gurukula (Residential or Boarding Educational Institution)

The gurukula system was one of the most important characteristics of the system of education in ancient India. It meant the stay of the student in the house of his teacher. The student was under the supervision of the teacher for twenty-four hours of the day and night. The close association of the student with his colleagues, his senior students and other scholars had an important bearing on the character and personality of the students.

The daily routine of a student was well-disciplined and marked by simplicity, endurance, a rigid adherence to the rules of hygiene and 'bramcharya' in natural surroundings, free from all unhealthy influences.

The gurukul system was best fitted to contribute to the formation of character, the building of the personality, the preservation of ancient culture and the training of the rising generation in the performance of religious and social duties.

'Far from the madding crowd', the Indian culture was born in the lap of serene and divine Nature. Surrounded by the vast natural life and multi-coloured deep forests, man began to discover harmony between his spirit and the spirit of the universe. The forests and flowers, woods and pastures, brooks and springs, deep valleys and lofty mountains gave him a spiritual message. To realise this proximity with nature, the gurukula system came into being.

5.7 The Philosophy of Smritis

The Smritis lay down the rules for the conduct of human life. The seer Manu was the first law giver to the world. The other two Smritis are: Yajnavalkya smriti by seer Yajnavalkya and Parashara smriti by seer Parashara. Here we shall refer to Manusmriti only as it is the most widely quoted one.

Manusmriti forms to a considerable extent the foundation of the Hindu way of life. Though finally compiled between 200 B.C. and 200 A.D., it is based on the Vedas. It consists of about 2,700 verses.

Besides covering subjects like administration, diplomacy, education and laws, Manusmriti deals with creation, religion and God realisation.

Manusmriti has also to say a lot on the status of women. In conformity with the Vedas, Manu has praised womanhood.

Women deserve to be worshipped; most fortunate as they are; they are the light of the house; they are the bestower of welfare and participants in all acts and rituals of dharma. Where women are worshipped, there the Gods live and where they are dishonoured, everything falls (Manusmriti 3.28 and 56). She (sister) is treated as the perfect equal of her brothers (Manusmriti 9. 130).

Brothers are urged to each give from his share of wealth to her, in case the property has been divided among them (9. 118). In the joint parental home she is as much a sharer as the brothers (9.89).

Manu, while according such a high place to women also gives words of advise to them.

Friedrich Wilhelm Nietzsche, (1844-1900) a noted German philosopher has paid rich tribute to Manusmriti "I know of no rich book in which so many tender and kind remarks are addressed to women as in the law-book of Manu; these old greybeards and saints have a way of being polite to women which has perhaps never been surpassed!"

Undoubtedly women's education needs to be promoted on the same footing as that of men.

5.8 Buddhism and its Philosophy

Sources of Information : Lord Buddha (563 to 483 B.C.) the founder of Buddhism did not write any book himself. His followers made the collections of his preachings 100 years after his death. The collection is known as '*Tripitikas* (Pitak means a box or chest) which are of three forms :

1. *Vinay Pitak*—Consisting of rules of behaviour.
2. *Sakta Pitak*—A collection of religious sermons and examples.
3. *Abhidhamma Pitak*—Descriptions of the main preachings of Lord Lord Buddha and his philosophical thought.

Origin of Buddhism—Buddhism came into being as an offshoot of the later Vedic thought. It came into prominence when during the course of time, several ills had crept into Hinduism. Buddha, the founder of this philosophy is said to be the ninth incarnation of the cosmic deity Vishnu. Buddha renounced the pleasures of princely life and practised severe penance for several years in pursuit of truth. At present about one third of the human race is Buddhist.

Principal Teaching of Buddha

Buddha's teachings are very simple and can be understood very easily. He laid great stress on human conduct and avoided reference to metaphysics which he considered to be rather superfluous. Buddha gives little attention matters like God, soul and transmigration of soul. He does not accept the divinity of the Vedas.

Buddha saw four truths:

1. The world is full of miseries.
2. Miseries are caused by desires.
3. Wordly desires can be removed.
4. These desires can be removed by following the eight-fold path.

The eight-fold path consists of:

(a) Right insight (b) Right resolve (c) Right speech (d) Right action (e) Right conduct (f) Right effort (g) Right contemplation (h) Right concentration.

By following the eight-fold path, Nirvana (salvation) can be attained.

Educational Implications

Moral education—The entire techniques of Buddhism provides directions to develop good conduct, which is also the essence of a sound system of education. To be at moral being, one must follow the noble path. The eight-fold path as preached by Buddha provides guidance for moral education and peace. Observance of purity is more important than the observance of rituals.

Curriculum—The curriculum was primarily religious and philosophical. The Vedas were not the basis of Buddhist education. Buddhist literature replaced them as the source of wisdom and morality.

Medium of instruction—In general, Pali the language of the masses was the medium of instruction. Sanskrit was also taught and used as a medium of instruction.

Educational institutions—Buddhist vihars (monasteries) i.e. residential places of the monks served as educational institutions. Most of the students were boarders. According to the Chinese traveller and scholar Hieun Tsang, there were nearly 5,000 monasteries during the 7th century A.D. Some of the vihars had large compounds. Most of the Vihars were open to all castes, and were mostly built by kings.

Universities—Buddhism contributed greatly towards the spread of education. Hieun Tsang, the great Chinese philosopher and scholar who visited India in the 7th century A.D. has paid a high tribute to the Indian system of education and learning. A large number of universities or institutes of learning sprang up where students from foreign lands came in large numbers to quench their thirst for knowledge. There were seven well-established universities: Nalanda, Vallabhai, Vikramsila, Jaagdala, Mithila, Odantapuri and Nadia. Of all these Nalanda was the greatest and most famous.

These universities were automonous. Each university had an endowment to meet its expenses. Each university had two councils to look after academic and administrative matters.

5.9 Jainism

The word Jain is derived from the term 'Jin' denoting one who has acquired perfect control over everything, that is, worldly pleasures of life. The preachings of such 'conquerors' over their senses constitute Jain philosophy. Lord Rishabhadeva was the first 'Tirthankar' (path finder) and Mahavira (599B.C.-527 B.C.) the last prophet (24th Tirthankar). It is believed that Jainism was revealed to these Tirthankars periodically. Mahavira renounced the palace, property and the family and practised severe penance for twelve years.

Two sets of Jainism came into existence. Digambara (sky clad, meaning naked) whose members go nude (now not observed strictly except in the case of very orthodox or holy) and swetambara (white clothed)

Main Principles of Jain Philosophy

1. Jainism believes in Ahimsa—Non violence or non-injury to beings.
2. It accepts the existence of immortal souls which are numerous.
3. According to Jainism, Nirvana or liberation is obtained through three jewels: Right philosophy, Right knowledge and Right conduct. (Tri-ratna)
4. Right conduct implies 5 abstinences : not to lie, not to steal, not to strive for luxury and not to strive for possessions, not to be unchaste and not to injure (ahimsa). Ahimsa is the vital principle of Jainism. All Jains are expected to be strictly vegetarian.

5. Jainism repudiates dogmatism. It rejects the idea of a creator of the world. It believes reality to be many-sided.
6. Jainism emphasises 'Syat-Vada' or 'Ane-kant-Vada' which lays the mind open to truth coming from any quarter. No proposition about the truths of life can be absolute. This generates tolerance and regard for all.

Educational Implications

1. Anekantvada of Jain philosophy implies liberalism in our thinking. Students should be trained to appreciate various approaches and accommodate difference of opinion.
2. There is an urgent need to develop the philosophy of non-violence in our educational institutions so that students acquire proper behaviour.
3. Penance or hard work is necessary for the students to acquire knowledge and wisdom.
4. Education is regarded as an instrument of salvation through non-violence, observation of continence etc.

Questions and Problems

A. Essay-Type Questions

1. Explain the philosophical thinking as contained in the Vedas. State their educational implications.
2. Illustrate the meaning of Indian tradition of philosophical thinking. What are the sources of this tradition? State their educational implications.
3. What is the Upanishad? How does the philosophy embodied in the Upanishads help in education?
4. Explain the philosophical thought contained in the Bhagvad Gita. State its impact on education.
5. Explain briefly the main principles of the philosophies of Buddhism and Jainism and their relevance to education.
6. "It is wrong to conclude that the ancient Indian philosophy is pessimistic and not meant for wordly people." Explain this statement and its educational implications.

B. Short-Answer Type Questions

7. What is the impact of the Vedic thought on the educaton of women?
8. What is the essence of the philosophy of Gita? How does it help in bringing about reforms in the present system of education.
9. State briefly the state of higher education under Buddhist influence.

6 Great Indian Educational Thinkers

6.1 Swami Dayanand (1825-1883)

A brief life sketch—Swami Dayanand's original name was Dayaram Mulshankar. He was born in a Brahman family of Gujarat. From his early life, he sought answers to many riddles of life, death, salvation, reality and truth. At the age of fifteen he left home in search of truth. He spent his life spreading the message of the Vedas. His interpretation of the Vedas has brought a new vista of knowledge and wisdom in the sphere of social reforms and educational reconstruction.

Swami Dayanand, the founder of Arya Samaj was not only a great religious and social reformer but also a great educator. The Dayanand Anglo-Vedic schools and colleges derive their inspiration from Swami Dayanand's educational principles and philosophy and are a great tribute to his personality. The educational philosophy of Swami Dayanand is contained in the second chapter of 'Satyarth Prakash'—Light of Truth.

Dayanand philosophy—According to Swamiji, there is only one God. He is all pervading and should alone be worshipped. The Vedas are the source of all true knowledge. Truth should be followed and .falsehood shunned. He founded the Arya Samaj— an organisation that works for the social, moral, religious and educational upliftment of the people.

Swami Dayanand stressed that we should treat every human being with dignity and respect regardless of his social position, caste, wealth or poverty.

Aims of education—The aims of education may be described as under:

1. Formation of character by observing rules of celibacy.
2. Acquisition of knowledge and wisdom.
3. Inculcation of love for truth.
4. Promotion of moral and spiritual values.
5. Physical development.
6. The development of the spirit of service for humanity.

Mother, father, teacher—Three Great Tutors. Only that man can become a great scholar who has had the advantage of three good tutors—Father, mother and teacher. Blessed is the family and most fortunate is the child whose parents are godly and learned. The mother's influence on the education of children surpasses that of everyone else. He alone is said to have a mother whose mother is devout and learned. Blessed is the mother who never ceases to impart a religious tone to the mind of her child from the time of conception till his knowledge is perfected.

The education of the child starts even before birth—'Sanskars'. It behoves both parents before, during and after conception to avoid the use of such foods and drinks as are intoxicating, decomposed (foul smelling), non-nutritious (dry) and prejudicial to the growth of intellect; and to use those articles that are productive of mental tranquility, health, strength, intellect, energy, and good temper—qualities that go to make a man refined. Such foods are milk butter, sugar, cereals etc.—foods and drinks that help to make the reproductive element (both male and female) of the highest quality, free from all faults and imperfections.

Concept of discipline—Those children alone become well-behaved refined and scholarly whose parents do not indulge them: but on the other hand reprimand them when necessary. Those parents and tutors who are not slow to reprimand their children and pupils (when needed) are giving them a drink of immorality; but those who indulge them are in fact, giving poison, and are thus the cause of their ruin because indulgence spoils children, whilst reprehension develops good qualities in them. Children should also feel pleased when reprimanded and feel uneasy when fondled. But parents and teachers should never reprimand them out of malice or spite, outwardly they should keep them in awe; whilst inwardly they should be tender-hearted and kind to them. Likewise, they should advise them to abstain from stealing, committing adultery, contracting habits of indolence, arrogance, drunkenness, untruthfulness, malevolence, wickedness, malice, jealously, blind-passion; and to cultivate good qualities such as truthfulness, virtue.

Noble examples to be set—A broken pledge injures a man's character more than anything else. Therefore, once you make a promise, keep it; for example, if you say to a man: "I will meet you at such a place and time", or "I will give you such a thing, at such and such time." Then, always keep your promise; otherwise, no one will ever trust you. All should therefore, speak the truth and keep their word. One should never be vain. Deceitfulness, hypocrisy, and ingratitude are painful even to the soul that harbours them. It is hypocrisy to believe one thing and say another, and thus mislead people in order to gain selfish ends. Ingratitude is that condition of mind in which you do not feel thankful to one who has been good to you.

Teacher's role—Swami Dayanand gives great importance to the role of the teacher. The Guru becomes the second parent to the child. The teacher should be good charactered and set good examples before his students.

Education for all—Swami Dayanand believed in free and compulsory education for both boys and girls.

Women's education—Swami Dayanand advocated equal opportunities for women.

Contribution of Swami Dayanand to Education

Swami Dayanand's views on the importance of education for character development, free and compulsory education, role of parents in the education of the child, teachers role and education of women and his concept of discipline are all very relevant today. It is of interest to note that there would be hardly a great educator in whose memory a chain of educational institutions exist as in the case of Swami Dayanand. This is his great contribution to education.

6.2 Swami Vivekanand (1863-1902)

A brief life sketch—Swami Vivekanand (originally Narendranath Datta) a disciple of Sri Ramakrishna made a mark of his wisdom at the Parliament of Religions held at Chicago (USA) in 1893. In his address he made a clarian call to the world: 'Help and not Fight', "Assimilation and not Destruction', 'Harmony and Peace and not Dissension.' Swami Vivekanand saw the 'divine' in the form of the poor. His call to the nation was: "O Indian! Forget not that the lower classes, the ignorant poor; the illiterate, the cobbler, the sweeper are the flesh and blood."

Swami Vivekanand spent the last fifteen years of his strenuous life in communicating his universal message of unity and tolerance. After the death of his guru Shri Ramakrishna in 1886, Swami Vivekanand organised the Ramakrishna Mission.

Principal Tenents of Vivekanand's Philosophy

1. Vedanta represents the highest spiritual and ethical values of mankind. It teaches the unity of life, divinity of man, selfless devotion and fearlessness.
2. Religion means self-realisaion.
3. Ethics and morality should be the real basis of life.
4. Love and renunciation should permeate the universe.
5. Man is the incarnation of God.
6. The best image for worshipping God is man. God resides in every human heart.
7. Service to mankind is the highest good of religion.
8. The teachings of the Upanishads have strength enough to provide solution to our social problems.
9. 'Karmayoga' is needed for the attainment of self-control and self-realisation.

Educational philosophy of Vivekananda--His educational philosophy may be encompassed within ten words, "Education is the manifestation of the perfection already in man." Like fire in a piece of flint, knowledge exists in the mind, suggestion is the friction which brings it out. Swami Vivekananda explains this by stating, "Knowledge is inherent in man, no knowledge comes from outside, it is all inside. What a man 'learns' is in reality what he 'discovers' or 'unveils', by taking the cover off his own soul, which is a mine of infinite knowledge. We say Newton discovered gravitation. Was it sitting anywhere in a corner waiting for him? It was in his own mind; the time came and he found it. All knowledge that the world has ever received came from the mind; the infinite library of the universe is in your own mind. The external world is only the suggestion, the occasion, which sets you to study your own mind. The falling of an apple gave the suggestion to Newton, and then he studied his own mind. He rearranged all the previous links of thought in his mind and discovered a new link among them, which we call the law of gravitation. It was not in the apple nor in anything in the centre of the earth."

Character building as the most important aim of education—"We want that education by which character is formed, strength of mind is increased, the intellect is expanded and by which one stands on one's own feet."

How to judge a man of character—Swami Vivekananda says, "If you really want to judge the character of man, look not at his great performances, Watch a man do his most common actions. Those are indeed the things which will tell you the real character of the great man. Great occasions rouse even the lowest of human beings to some kind of greatness, but he alone is really great whose character is great always—the same what ever be." According to him 'intellectuality' is not the highest good. 'Morality' and 'spirituality' are the things for which we strive. He remarks, "Our women are not so learned, but they are more pure." He does not consider a man as educated if he can only pass some examination and deliver good lectures. The basis of all systems, social or political, rests upon the goodness of man. No nation is great or good because its Parliament enacts this or that, but because its men are great and good.

Self-teaching—"No one was ever really taught by another. Each of us has to teach himself a child educates itself."

Living examples of teacher—"Words even thoughts, contribute only one-third of the influence in making an impression—the man two-thirds."

Discipline through positive suggestions—"We should give positive ideas. Negative ideas only weaken men. If you speak kind words to them and encourage them, they are bound to improve in time."

Concentration as the only method of education—The power of concentration is the only key to the treasure-house of knowledge."

Qualities of the learner—"The conditions necessary for the taught are purity, a real thirst after knowledge and perseverance."

Education a physical strength—"Be strong, my young friends...you will be nearer to Heaven through foot-ball than through the study of Gita."

Education to be based on western science coupled with Vedanta—"Living with the Guru and a similar system of imparting education are needed. What we want is western science coupled with Vedanta—'Brahmacharya' as the guiding motto and also 'Shraddha' (faith) in one's own self."

Education of the masses—Vivekananda gave prime importance to the education of the masses. He asserted, "The chief cause of India's ruin has been the monopolising of the whole education of the land, by dint of pride and royal authority, among a handful of men." He further observed, "If we are to rise again, we shall have to do it in the same way, that is, by spreading education among the masses." He considers that "the great national sin is the neglect of the masses, and that is one of the causes of our downfall. No amount of politics would be of any avail until the masses in India are once more well-educated, well-fed, and cared for. They pay for our education, they build our temples, but in return they get kicks. They are practically our slaves. if we want to regenerate India, we must work for them."

Women's education—Vivekananda was an ardent champion of the education of women. He remarked, "Women have many and grave problems but none that cannot be solved by that magic word: education!" What does our Manu enjoin? His view was that "our Indian women are as capable as any in the world. It is only in the homes of educated and pious mothers that great men are born. By raising the women their children will by their noble actions glorify the name of the country. Then culture, knowledge, power and devotion will awaken in the country"

Contribution of Swami Vivekananda to education—Swami Vivekanand's views on education are reflected to a great extent in the National policy on education. A special mention may be made of his views on the role of education in the making of a man, in character building, on free and compulsory mass education, women's education and his concern for the education of the down trodden and weaker sections of the society. He advocated a practical type of moral education—education through our noble acts. He very rightly stressed the importance of western science and technology along with eastern thoughts.

Swami Vivekanand made an important contribution to the educational and social reforms by founding the Ramakrishna Mission in 1899. The Mission has been running several educational institutions in different parts of the country.

6.3 Rabindranath Tagore (1861-1941)

Brief life sketch—Tagore popularly known as Gurudev was a poet and patriot, and educationist and artist, a social reformer and a religious reformer. Tagore burst into international fame when his book 'Gitanjali' won the Noble Prize for literature in 1913. He utilised the entire amount of this award of £ 8,000 for the up-keep of his famous school 'Shantiniketan' which he had founded at Bolepur in 1901. The school was opened on the model of ancient ashrams. In 1921 this school grew into a world university, called 'Visva Bharati'.

Tagore's experiences of his early education at various schools were not happy ones. The suffering and misery of a child under a heartless educational system has been forcefully brought out in his educational writings, namely, (a) 'Shiksar Herpher' (our education and its incongruities), (b) The Parrot's Training, and (c) 'Shiksa Samasya' (The problem of education).

Tagore's Philosophy: Main Principals

1. *Philosophy of humanism*—Tagore observed, "The best and noblest gifts of humanity cannot be the monopoly of a particular race or country".
2. *Synthesis of culture*—Tagore said, "Before we are in a position to stand in comparison with the other cultures of the world or try to cooperate with them, we must base our own culture on a synthesis of all the different cultures we have".
3. *True culture*—Culture brings fulfillment from the depths of the self to the faculties and aptitudes of a man as a whole.

Under its influence man spontaneously attains an all-round fulfillment, and the pursuit of knowledge for its own sake and the enthusiasm for unselfish actions become natural. True culture sets greater store by natural courtesy than mechanical observance of custom and convention. It does not encourage artificial politeness calculated to serve practical ends in human dealings. A cultured man will rather injure than humiliate himself. He is ashamed of purposely parading himself or selfishly forcing himself to the forefront. Whatever is mean or false pains him. He takes delight in respecting excellence in all spheres, because of his intimate acquaintance with all that is best in art, literature and history. He can judge and forgive and can appreciate the good point in others in spite of divergence of views. To be envious of others success is to humiliate himself.

4. *Tagore—a universalist—A messenger of freedom of mind and peace*—Tagore has expressed his feelings in the following verses.

"Where the mind is without fear and the head is held high,
Where knowledge is free,
Where the world has not been broken into fragments by narrow domestic walls,
Where words come out from the depths of truth,
Where tireless striving stretches its arms towards perfection,
Where the clear stream of reason has not lost its way into the dreary desert-sand of dead habit,
Where the mind is led forward by Thee into ever widening thought and action,
Into that heaven of Freedom, my Father, let my country awake".

Tagore's Views on Different Aspects of Education

Meaning of education—It is nothing short of the highest purpose of man—the fullest growth and freedom of soul.

Natural education—Our true education is possible only in the forest through intimate contact with nature.

Freedom of mind—The objective of education is the freedom of mind which can only be achieved through the path of education.

Children as children—It is a mistake to judge children by the standards of grown-ups. Adults ignore the natural gifts of children and insist that children must learn through the same process as themselves. This is man's most cruel and most wasteful mistake.

Subconscious mind—Children's have their subconscious mind is more active than their conscious intelligence.

Discipline and freedom—Living ideals cannot be set into clock-work arrangement. Tagore wrote, "I never said to them; Don't do this, or don't do that...I never punished them".

An ideal school—An ideal school is an Ashram were men have gathered for the highest end of life. Tagore observed. "To give spiritual culture to our boys was my principal object in starting my school at Bolepur."

Living contact between the teacher and the taught—In teaching, the guiding spirit should be personal love based on human relations. In education the teacher is more important than the method.

Teacher always a learner—Tagore pointed out, "A teacher can never truly teach unless he is learning himself. A lamp can never light another lamp unless it continues to burn its own flame."

Founding of Visva Bharati (World University)—Tagore himself describes the aims and objectives of Visva Bharati at Santiniketan as by saying, being strongly impressed with the need and the responsibility which every individual today must realise according to his power, I have formed the nucleus of an international University, as one of the best means of promoting mutual understanding; between the east and the west.

Before Asia is in a position to co-operate with the culture of Europe she must base her own structure on a synthesis of all different cultures which she has.

In this belief, it is my desire to extend by degree the scope of this University on simple lines, until it comprehends the whole range of eastern cultures—the Aryan, Semitic, Mongolian and others. Its object will be to reveal the eastern mind to the world".

The following are the various institutions developed there which form an integral past of the university.

1. Shishu Bhawan (Nursery school)
2. Path Bhawan (School Section—matriculation examination)
3. Siksha Bhawan (Higher Secondary)
4. Vidya Bhawan (College of under-graduate and post-graduate studies and research)
5. Vinaya Bhavan (Teachers' college)
6. Kala Bhavan (College of fine arts and crafts)
7. Sangit Bhavan (College of music and dance)
8. Sriniketan (Department of rural reconstruction)
9. Siksa Satra (Rural high school)
10. Silpa Sadana (College of industrial training)
11. Cheena Bhavan (School of languages e.g., Chinese, Tibetan etc.)

Tagore's Contribution to Education

Tagore combined in him the philosophy of humanism, idealism, naturalism, pragmatism and realism.

Tagore was a pragmatist and a realist. He conducted several experiments at several institutions. He also deserves credit for having attempted the revival of the ancient Indian ideals of education in the modern times and combining what is best in western arts and sciences with the manners, customs and arts of India. His stature stands out at the cross-roads of two ages—traditional and modern, of two worlds—the east and the west.

Like the ancient seers of India, Tagore sought to build up an outlook based on truth, beauty and goodness.

Tagore was a humanist. He himself said, "I have great faith in humanity." He established Visva Bharati for the entire world.

As a naturalist philosopher, Tagore surpasses Rousseau, Pestalozzi and Froebel. Fester Watson observes in the *Encyclopedia and Dictionary of Education*, "Tagore substantially adopts Rousseau's ideal of return to nature, but he included human nature, as well as external nature, basing both upon a primal sympathy." In place of the 'Negative Education' of Rousseau, Tagore wanted a richer environment of experience and idea.

While Rousseau's ideology remained theoretical, Tagore on the other hand, gave a practical shape to his ideology.

'A Poet's School' is an important writing showing the place of Nature in life and education. Children have the gift of freshness senses. They can become natural with nature and human with the human society. But the misery is that a child is offered crowded solitude in a city where man is everywhere, with never a gap for the immense non-human—nature. The inexpensive power to be happy that the children bring to this world is "constantly worn away by friction with the brick-and-mortar arrangement of life". This is why Tagore tried his best to develop in the children of his school "the freshness of their feeling for nature, a sensitiveness of soul in their relationship with their human surrounding".

He pointed out the great significance of the school atmosphere in the life of children whose mind, like the tree, has the power to gather food and nourishment from its surroundings. The cultural atmosphere keeps the mind sensitive to rich racial inheritance, glorious traditions and concentrated wisdom of ages. The school atmosphere must also develop sensitiveness of soul and allow freedom to the mind from bondage of ignorance and apathy.

Tagore was a great practitioner. He worked out his ideas and ideals in a very constructive way. The fulfillments of all his theories and concepts found expression in various directions. He 'struggled to implement his social ideal and strove to build up a social structure through education'. He created Shantiniketan to realise his educational ideals.

6.4 M.K. Gandhi (1869-1948)

One of the greatest teacher seers statesman and educated thinkers—M.K. Gandhi—Mohandas Karam Chand Gandhi came to be known as Mahatma (great soul or great seer) on account of his noble and saintly life. He is considered to be one of the greatest teachers of mankind, His contribution to the domain of education is as important as his contribution to the political thinking, the freedom of India and its social reforms.

Gandhi's educational philosophy took shape through his educational experiences at the Tolstoy Farm at Transwal in South Africa where he had gone in connection with his profession of a lawyer on behalf of a firm. His stay in South Africa for about

20 years from 1893 to 1913 was the formative period of his political as well as his educational philosophy. On the Tolstoy Farm he undertook the responsibility of educating his own sons and other children. The children had to devote 8 hours a day for vocational training and only 2 hours to book learning. Children aged 6 to 16 were very happy in 'learning by doing' and 'learning by cooperation'. After returning to India in 1914, Gandhi continued his educational experiments for a short while at Santiniketan and at Sabarmati and Sewagram, where he established his own ashrams. Sewagram Ashram is located 11 miles from Wardha. It was here that Gandhi not only conceived the idea of a new philosophy and system of education but also fought his battle for freedom.

Gandhi's publications on education are (a) Basic education (b) Medium of instruction (c) Tasks before India (d) Tasks before Indian students (e) To the students (f) Towards new education (g) True education Gandhi wrote extensively on education in 'Harijan'.

Principle Features of Gandhi's Philosophy of Life

God is the ultimate reality—According to Gandhi "God is an indefinable, mysterious power that pervades everything. God is life, truth and light. He is love. He is supreme."

Truth and non-violence—Gandhi said, "God is truth because truth or 'satya' is that which cannot be destroyed. The ultimate aim of one's life, therefore, should be the realisation of truth or God, and all that man does should be guided by this truth. Truth can be identified, at a personal level, with the 'Voice within'—the voice of conscience."

Further Gandhi says "Ahimsa (non-violence) and truth are so intertwined that it is practically impossible to disentangle and separate them. They are like the two sides of a coin...nevertheless Ahimsa is the means; truth is the end,"

Service of humanity—Gandhi observed, "The immediate service of all human beings becomes a necessary part of the endeavour simply because the only way to find God is to see Him in His creation and be one with it—I am a part and parcel of the whole and I cannot find Him apart from the rest of humanity".

Self-discipline and self-purification—Gandhi tried to personify in himself the high ideals of purity, sacrifice and service.

Righteousness and truth as the highest religion—Gandhi was of the firm view that "true religion and true morality are inseparably bound up with each other."

Ram Rajya as the concept of a society—He wanted to establish Ram Rajya which he identified with justice, peace, happiness and welfare of all.

M.K. Gandhi's Views on Education

Meaning of education and purpose—Gandhi summed up his ideas on education:

"By education I mean an all-round drawing out of the best in child and man—body, mind and spirit." 'All-round implies a harmonious development.' 'Drawing out of the best' recognizes a great potential coiled up in the child which can be realised and developed to its perfection through education. 'Body, mind and spirit' is a vision of the whole man. The first emphasis is on the body and the culmination point is the spirit. It is through practical work that one attains intellectual development. But intellectual attainment is neither the beginning nor the end of education. It is a mid-point. The individual has yet to blossom out to perfection to bring forth all that is best in him. All development, all personal advancement is in the search of truth, the realisation of the spiritual essence that is in man. Thus education cannot be confined to childhood and youth—it has to take into account the whole life of a man; and that is the significance of the phrase 'best in child and man'. So education will not be complete till one realises the Self, the perfection. Education is through life and for life. Education must take care of the whole child, the human personality, in all its aspects—physical intellectual and spiritual.

Objective of education—The ultimate objective of the new education is not only a balanced and harmonious individual but also a balanced and harmonious society—a just social order in which there is no unnatural dividing line between the haves and have-nots and everybody is assured of a living wage and the right to freedom."

Education through craft—"The uniqueness of this scheme is that education is to be given 'through' village crafts. The end in view is not to be accomplished by merely adding a village craft to the current syllabus."

Self-supporting aspect—"Self-sufficiency is not a 'prior condition', but to me it is the acid test. This does not mean that basic education will be self-supporting from the very start. But taking the entire period of seven years, income and expenditure must balance each other. Otherwise it would mean that even at the end of this training of basic education the student will not be fit for life. This is the negation of basic education. '*Nai Talim*' without the self-support basic would be like a lifeless body."

Dignity of labour—"It is a crime to make education merely literary, and to make boys and girls unfit for manual work in later life. Indeed I hold that as the large part of our time is devoted to labour for earning our bread our children must from their infancy be taught the dignity of such labour. Our children should not be so taught as to desist labour."

Methods of teaching—"Children take in much more and with less labour through ears than through their eyes."

Religious education—"To me religion means Truth and Ahimsa or rather truth alone, because truth includes Ahimsa, Ahimsa being the necessary and indispensable means for its discovery. Therefore anything that promotes the practice of these virtues is a means for imparting religious education and the best way to do this, in my opinion is for the teachers to practise these virtues rigorously in their own lives. Their very association with the boys, whether on the playground or in the class room, will then give the pupils a fine training in these fundamental virtues."

Spiritual training—"I made the children memorize and recite hymns, and read to them from books on moral training. But that was far from satisfying. As I came into closer contact with them I saw that it was through books that one could impart training of the spirit. Just as physical training was to be imparted through physical exercise, and intellectual training through intellectual exercise, even so the training of the spirit was possible only through the exercise of the spirit. And the exercise of the spirit entirely depended on the life and character of the teacher. The teacher had always to be mindful of his ps and qs whether he was in the midst of his boys or not".

Education and character—"The end of all knowledge must be the building up of character. What is education without character and what is character without elementary personal purity."

The teacher—"Woe to the teacher who teachers one thing with the lips and carries another in the heart."

Medium of instruction—"Our language is the reflection of ourselves and if you tell me that our languages are too poor to express the best thought, then I say that the sooner we are wiped out of existence the better for us."

The foreign medium—"The foreign medium has caused a brain fag, put an undue strain upon the nerves of our children, made them crammers and imitators, unfitted them for original work and thought and disabled them for filtrating their training to their family or the masses. The foreign medium has made our children practically foreigners in their own land."

Curriculum and spinning—"In any curriculum of the future, spinning must be a compulsory subject. Just as we cannot live without eating, so it is impossible for us to attain economic independence and banish pauperism from the ancient land without reviving home spinning."

Freedom but under discipline—"The pupils must have initiative. They must cease to be mere imitators. They must learn to think and act for themselves and yet be thoroughly obedient and disciplined. The highest form of freedom carries with it the greatest measure of discipline and humility. Freedom that comes from discipline and humility cannot be denied, unbridled licence is a sign of vulgarity injurious alike to self and one's neighbours."

Co-education—"Before launching on such experiments, a teacher has to be both father and mother to his pupils and be prepared for all eventualities, and only the hardest penance can fit him to conduct them."

Text books—"I have therefore, come to the conclusion that books are required more for the teachers than for the taught. And every teacher, if he is to do full justice to his pupils, will have to prepare the daily lesson from the material available to him. This too, he will have to suit to the special requirement of his class."

Women's education—"As for women's education, I am not sure whether it should be different from men's and when it should begin. But I am strongly of the opinion that women should have the same facilities as men and even special facilities where necessary."

Handwriting—"Handwriting is an art. Every letter must be correctly drawn, as an artist would draw his figures. This can only be done if the boys and girls are first taught elementary drawing."

Gandhi as an idealist—The idealism of Gandhi is reflected in the following words: "Long before I undertook the education of the youngsters at the Tolstoy Farm I had realised that the training of the spirit was a thing by itself. To develop the spirit is to build character and to enable one to work toward a knowledge of God and self-realisation and I held that this was an essential part of the training of the young, and that all training without culture of the spirit was of no use and might be even harmful.

Gandhi as a naturalist—To quote M.S. Patel, "Gandhi has a strong claim to be ranked among the leading naturalistic educators of the of the world. He cannot however be called an extreme naturalist. Like Rousseau, he believes that natural and rural environments are important educative agencies but he does not hold with him that the child should be segregated from the baneful influence of man and society. His attempt at rescuing education from the four walls of the school room cannot be passed over in silence."

Gandhi as a pragmatist—According to M.S. Patel, Gandhi's contribution to the pragmatic philosophy of education is unique. The introduction of a basic craft as the centre of education, the co-ordination and correlation of the content of the close relationship of education with actual life, the method of learning by doing, the individual initiative, the sense of total responsibility and emphasis on experiment as the means of discovering truth are some of the outstanding features of Gandhi's pragmatic philosophy of education.

Basic system of education origin and development—To materialize this vision of society Gandhi evolved a scheme of education after many trials and experiments over a period of 40 years. His ideas revolutionised the current thinking about education.

In 1937 the All India National Education conference was held in Wardha which unanimously approved of his idea and appointed a committee of leading educationalists with Dr. Zakir Husain as its Chairman to give shape to Gandhi's plan. The report of the committee embodies what is known as the Wardha Scheme of Basic National Education.

Main characteristics and features—Basic Education or Nai Talim or Wardha Education has the following main characteristics:

1. Free and compulsory education for seven years.
2. Craft as the basis of education.
3. Self-supporting education - earning while learning.
4. Three centres of correlation of all contents of the curriculum.
   (i) Craft work.
   (ii) Physical environment.
   (iii) Social environment.
5. Education related to life activities.
6. Education for citizenship.
7. Mother tongue as the medium of instruction.
8. Adequate freedom for the teacher and the taught.

Criticism of Basic Education

1. The basic system of education is based on unsound psychological foundations.
2. Craft cannot be the sole basis of education.
3. The basic system is not suitable in the age of industrialisation.
4. It neglects the personality of the child.
5. It is very expensive.
6. It does not develop the all round personality of the child.
7. It gives secondary importance to literacy.
8. In craft work also, students do not develop adequate skills.
9. The finished products of the students do not get a proper price.

Contribution and Relevance of Gandhi's Views on Education in the Modern Context

The most important point in Gandhi's scheme of education is its emphasis on relating school education to the needs of the society. He wanted to achieve this objective through a system of

'Learning while earning'. He gave an important place to the learning of craft. It will be seen from the curriculum of the present day schools that work experience and socially useful productive work find an important place. His views on early childhood education are quite relevant to-day. Parent education is stressed for the proper development of the early stages of the child. His emphasis on education through the mother tongue is the accepted principle throughout the period.

A few words of comparisons with other educators. Those who had reached similar conclusions are Rousseau, Pestalozzi, Froebel, Dewey and Karl Marx. Rousseau had advocated manual work just to eliminate prejudice against it. Pestalozzi recommended it for sense training and tried to show that industrial and intellectual training could go side by side. But Gandhi was bold enough to make craft the nucleus of the whole instruction and not an extra or additional subject. There is close resemblance between the theories of Gandhi and Froebel in so far as both lay particular emphasis on activity and constructive work in school life. Gandhi gave the constructive work of Froebel a concrete shape and a local habitation, though quite independently of him. Gandhi differs from Dewey in that he does not mean to supplement literary training with manual training, but makes manual training the means of literacy and intellectual training. Karl Marx maintained that education should be related with the productive process. But Gandhi does not attach a school to a factory or workshop. To him the school itself is the workshop where work is an essential instrument of learning.

6.5 Sri Aurobindo (1872-1950)

A patriot-revolutionary turned into a great educator, seer and thinker—Besides English, he mastered Latin and Greek and also learnt French, German, Italian and Spanish during his stay in England for 14 years from the age of 7 to the age of 21.

After his return to India, in 1893, he devoted himself to the study of Sanskrit, Marathi, Gujarati and Bengali and drank in the culture and philosophy of India. He began yoga by himself in 1904.

Aurobindo was a very brilliant student and passed the open competition for I.C.S. but did not try to qualify in the riding test.

Aurobindo's ideas on education are contained in his two books namely *A system of National Education* and *Sri Aurobindo and Mother On Education.*

Aurobindo's Philosophy of Life

Sri Aurobindo's philosophy emerged out of his own experiences, thoughts and life education. His life is based on spiritual discipline and the one end ardently sought after everything else is done is the attainment of the 'Life Divine' while living in the world. Sri Aurobindo considers yoga as the means through which one can come in contact with the true self and unite the separate parts of oneself and can also see the same divine in others. In his yoga, work is as important as meditation. His yoga is not that of a 'Sanyasi' who turns away from life in order to turn towards God. On the other hand his yoga is of the ordinary man, who has put God on the shelf, while he carries on his worldly pursuits. The seeker must experience the 'Ananda,' love, consciousness and energy of the 'Supreme.' Truth must be lived. Work done in full concentration and in the spirit of surrender which takes one's consciousness nearer to the Divine. Knowledge, work, devotion and meditation are all integrated in his yoga. The most important thing is to have an inner urge for the Divine. As Sri Aurobindo says, " one who chooses the Divine is chosen by the Divine. As the call for the Divine grows more intense, so does His help come more readily."

Aurobindo says that we must aim not only at an inner realisation but an outer realisation also—the establishment of the kingdom of God not only within the heart but also in the world of human affairs—in economics and politics. And he assures us that this is possible.

Yoga can be practised in ordinary life. If a merchant wishes to follow this yoga, his business itself is regarded as work divine and he cannot practise corruption or indulge in black marketeering. In the same way a student would look for higher values by practising yoga (self-control) and he will save himself from many useless and harmful activities.

Sri Aurobindo's Views on Different Aspects of Education

Integral education—According to Sri Aurobindo, education must emphasise the following aspects in addition to the physical psychic and mental aspects as denoted by the matter and spirit respectively. The cultivation of these aspects (a) beauty (b) power (c) knowledge and (d) love is what he called an Integral Education. Beauty is tne realisation through physical culture. Power is to be related to the control of sensations. Knowledge helps in developing the mental make up of an alert mind. Love is the formation of desirable feelings and emotions, which should be directed towards others and the commission with the Divine.

"If education is to bring out to full advantage all that is in the individual child we should first guarantee a safe custody of all that is individual. Nothing is to be lost or damaged, twisted or crushed. 'Everyone has in him something divine, something his own, a chance of perfection and strength in however small a sphere which God offers him to take or refuse.' That Divinity in man is not to be insulted, that chance of perfection is not to be lost, that spark of strength is not to be extinguished. The task of a teacher is to help the child to feel that touch of Divinity, to find that 'something', to develop it, and use it. Education should help the growing soul to draw out the best that is within and make it perfect for a noble cause."

Principles of teaching—Sri Aurobindo enumerated three principles of teaching. The first principle of true teaching is that nothing can be taught. The teacher is not an instructor or task master, he is a helper and guide.

The teacher's work is to suggest and not to impose on the mind of the students. He does not actually train the mind of his student but helps him to perfect his mind, the instrument of knowledge and encourages him every way in this process. Thus he does not impart knowledge, but shows the way how knowledge can be acquired. Knowledge is within the pupil and the pupil has to help himself to bring it out, but he needs help. Somebody must tell him where it is and how it can be 'habituated to rise to the surface'. The teacher alone can do this work.

The second principle is that the mind has to be consulted in its growth. "The idea of hammering the child into the shape desired by the parent or teacher is a barbarous and ignorant superstition."

The third principle of teaching is to work from the near to the far, from the known to the unknown. Man's nature is moulded by his soul's past his heredity and his environment. The past is the foundation, the present is the material and future is the aim—and each must find its due and natural place in any national system of education.

Teacher—a guide and helper and moraliser through personal example—The teacher is not an instructor or task-master; he is a helper and guide. His business is to suggest and not to impose. He does not actually train the pupil's mind, he only shows him how to perfect his instruments of knowledge and helps and encourages him in the process. He does not impart knowledge to him; he shows him how to acquire knowledge for himself. He does not call forth the knowledge for himself. He does not call forth the knowledge that is within. He only shows him where it lies and how it can be habituated to rise to the surface.

The Ashram school—The school was originally started in 1943 for the children of Sri Aurobindo's disciples. It expanded gradually from a Primary School to a full-fledged High School. There are resident as well as day-students.

The International Centre of Education—The objectives underlying the Centre are:-

1. To evolve a system of education for making it dynamic, ideal for society.
2. To organise an environment which may provide inspiration and facilities for the exercise and development of the five aspects of the personality—the physical, the vital, the mental, the psychic and the spiritual.
3. To emphasise the unity of all knowledge.
4. To develop the sense of oneness of mankind.
5. To discover and prepare for the role India has to play in the formation of the new international harmony.

The curriculum—It includes:

1. Psychic and spiritual studies.
2. Academic subjects.
3. Physical and health education.
4. Cultural activities like art, music, drama.
5. Vocational training
6. Education for international understanding.

Auroville—Auroville, 'the city of dawn' near Pondicherry was inaugurated by the Mother on 28 February 1968, with representatives from 121 nations pouring soil from their respective lands into a lotus shaped urn symbolising the unity of the human race. It was intended to give practical expression to Sri Aurobindo's vision of a modern, self-supporting community, whose members would take full advantage of scientific developments while laying greater emphasis on spiritual awareness.

According to its own charter, Auroville belongs to nobody in particular. It belongs to humanity as a whole. Conceived as "the city of human unity," its objective was that there should be somewhere upon the earth a place that no nation could claim as its sole property, a place where all could live freely as the citizens of the world.

Contribution of Sri Aurobindo to education—The most notable contribution of Sri Aurobindo to education is the international flavour in the development of Auroville—a city of universal culture. It is also a world university centre, a university in which continuing education from infancy to old age is envisaged to be offered. The Auroville project has the support of the Indian Government and of UNESCO.

Questions and Problems

A. Essay-Type Questions

1. "Gandhi's philosophy of education was naturalist in its setting, idealist in its aim, and pragmatic in its method and programme of work." Explain and illustrate.
2. Elucidate the significant aspects of Tagore's educational thought and assess their values.
3. What according to Swami Vivekanand ought to be the national pattern for modern India?
4. State the views of Swami Dayanand on various aspects of education and their relevance to modern India.
5. By education Gandhi means "an all round drawing out of the best in child and man, body, mind and spirit." Explain.
6. Briefly describe Gandhi philosophy of education and bring out clearly his views on the meaning, aims and methods of teaching.
7. Show how Tagore's philosophy of education is intimately connected with his philosophy of life.

B. Short-Answer Type Questions

8. State the merits and demerits of the System of Basic Education.
9. What according to Swami Vivekanand is the major aim of education?
10. Briefly describe the naturalism of Tagore.
11. Write a brief note on Shantiniketan.
12. How far does the present system of education reflect the views of Gandhi?
13. Write short notes on (a) Shri Aurobindo's Integral Education (b) Auroville.

7 Great Educational Thinkers of the West

7.1 Jean Jacques Rousseau (1712-1778)

An interesting personality—It is a of great interest to go through these lines written about Rousseau by Charles W Coulter and Richard S. Rimanoczy, in *A Layman's Guide to Education Theory* (1955),

"It is singular that this (Rousseau) depraved, neurotic, immoral Frenchman should, have exercised the influence in politics and education that he did. Opportunistic, unreliable, unscrupulous though he was in his private life, his writings had such an influence on the temper of his time that they must be considered as a turning point in education. At times, a gigolo, kept by a woman of rank, other times a liar, a thief, and the unacknowledged father of several illegitimate children by his non-confessions, he had the flesh of genius that seemed to attract friends and followers despite his personal shortcomings."

Rousseau's Publications

1. The Progress of the Act and Sciences (1750).
2. The Origin of Inequality Among Men (1753).
3. The New Heloise (1759).
4. Social Contract (1762).
5. Emile or Concerning Education (1762).

Rousseau's Philosophy of Naturalism

The key-note of his philosophy is to have a 'State of Nature', 'Natural Man' and 'Natural Civilization'. "Reason," he said "should be the guiding principle in producing both the natural civilisation and Natural Man. Rousseau said, "Everything is good as it comes from the hands of the Author of Nature, but everything degenerates in the hands of Man." Again he observes, "Civilised man is born, lives and dies in a state of slavery. At his birth he is stitched in swaddling clothes, at his death he is nailed in his coffin and as long he preserves the human form he is fettered by our institutions, Leave him alone," The ideal of the 'State of Nature' was "a simple farming community or State without evil."

Rousseau's Natural and Negative Education

When Rousseau talks of negative education, he believes that the child should be subject to a natural order and free from a social order. Negative education has the following characteristics.

1. *No place for book learning*—Rousseau does not believe in imparting education with the help of books. He holds that reading is a curse and books have no place in the education of the child. He advocates that the child should think for himself and learn with his own efforts.
2. *No formal lessons*—Rousseau is also against any formal teaching in the class. He believes that verbal lessons are a useless burden on the memory of the child and a sheer waste from the educational stand-point. The child is not able to interpret and assimilate on the basis of cause and effect theory, hence it is easily forgotten.
3. *No habit formation*—Rousseau also does not believe in any habit formation at this stage." "The only habit a child is to form is not to form any habit at all." He believes that everybody is a slave to his habits and the same may be true about the child. He was against all social habits. He however, favours natural habits and holds that the child should be left to have natural habits.
4. *Non-moral education*—The child is the purest thing in nature and therefore there is no place for any moral teaching. Morality is something which is beyond the understanding power of children. The reason behind this assumption is

that morality and reasoning do not go together. The child, therefore, should be left to learn from the lessons of nature. If he commits a mistake he will suffer and learn in a natural way. We say a burnt child dreads the fire.

5. *Back to nature*—The state of nature in which man lived long ago was a blissful state. Modern civilisation is the main cause of the misery of mankind. The alternative before mankind is to go back to nature. The customary procedures of the civilised society should be done away with and the natural state may be accepted again.

Three sources of education—According to Rousseau, the following were the three sources:

1. *Education of nature*—"The constitutional exertion of our organs and faculties is the education of nature."
2. *Education given by men*—"The uses we are taught to make of that exertion, constitute the education given to us by men."
3. *Education from circumstances*—"And in the acquisitions made by our own experience, on the objects that surround us, consists our education from circumstances."

Aims of education—Rousseau suggested the following aims of education:

1. Preparation for the struggle for existence.
2. Self-expression.
3. Autonomous development of individuality.
4. Imprisonment of racial gain.

Child centred education—In his 'Emile' Rousseau has observed, "I wish some discreet person would give us a treatise on the art of observing children, an art which would be of immense value to us, but of which fathers and schoolmasters have not as yet learnt the very first rudiment."

Rousseau believed that the nature of the child is fundamental, and it should be given its due attention. The entire concept of negative education centres upon the child.

'Emile' : A Valuable Treatise on Education

'Emile' is treatise on education cast in the form of a novel in which there are three characters; Emile, who may be regarded as 'Rousseau' while a boy, and his tutor, who is obviously Rousseau, as a man, Sophie, who is destined to be the mate of Emile.

'Emile' consists of five books or parts on training and education.

Book I deals with the infant; Book II with childhood; Book III with the preadolescent between the ages of twelve and fifteen; Book IV with adolescence; and Book V with the education of girls.

The book received a mixed reaction. On the one hand, the Parliament of Paris criticised 'Emile' very strongly and ordered it to be burnt publicly. On the other hand, in various European countries it was immediately translated into several languages as it aroused a deep interest in the problem of childhood and youth. There was general agreement that no form of education could be regarded as satisfactory which did not account for the nature of the child."

'Emile' and the curriculum—'Emile' recommends a curriculum in accordance with the nature and stage of the child.

Curriculum at the first stage from one to five years should be such that it develops strength. The child should be allowed to wander freely in the country side. His play things should be very simple such as branches with fruits and flowers.

Curriculum at the second stage between 5 to 12 should lead to the development of the senses. There will be no verbal lessons and moral instruction. He will not be instructed in language, history and geography. All learning should come by activity and experiences. Curriculum at the third stage between 12 to 15 would consist of studies that reveal nature, astronomy, science and the arts and crafts. Rousseau emphasises the learning of manual and industrial arts to make Emile independent and partly to overcome the prejudice held against manual labour.

In the fourth stage of the adolescence period between 15 to 20 years of age, the study of society, politics, economics, history and religion are the appropriate studies for the youth to understand complex social relationships.

Education of Sophie or Women's Education

Rousseau maintained that the duty of a woman towards man is "to train him in childhood, to tend him when he is a man and to counsel him throughout his life." Rousseau further stated, "Woman is made specially to please man." Hence a woman, according to Rousseau does not require knowledge but taste and prosperity of manners. He remarked "A woman of literacy education (culture) is the plague of her husband; her children, her family her servants—everybody." Sophie, therefore is to learn embroidery, lace making, the art of house decorating and house keeping, sewing etc.

Rousseau believes in the goodness of a woman. He states, " But the woman who is both virtuous, wise and charming. She, who in a word combines love and esteem, can send them (men) at her bidding to the end of the world, to war, to glory and to death at her behest. This a fine kingdom and worth the winning." For developing such qualities. Rousseau advocates that a woman must be trained carefully and strictly. Her education should be given in such a way that she remains 'chaste' and 'good' till her dying day. Instead of long sermons about piety, the parents should preach by their examples, which would be engraved on her heart.

Methods of teaching—Rousseau stressed the following:

1. Teach by doing whatever you can, and fall back upon words when doing is out of question.
2. Never substitute the symbol for the thing unless it is impossible to show the thing itself.
3. Do not teach books. "I hate books. They only teach us to talk about things that we know nothing about. To conceal their deficiencies teachers choose the dead languages—words, words, words."
4. Provide opportunities to children from their own experience and not from books.

   "Let him (the child) not be taught science, let him discover it."
5. Provide sense training.
6. Discipline—"Leave him (child) alone" "Nothing can be more foolish than to substitute our ways for them". Rousseau advocated discipline by natural consequences. He said, "If

children commit mistakes and violate the principles of nature, they naturally invite the retribution of nature."

Role of the Teacher

Rousseau wrote, "The highest function of the teacher consists not so much in imparting knowledge as on stimulating the pupil in its love and pursuit." Further he advises, "To know how to suggest is the art of teaching." Rousseau placed stress on developing the reasoning power of the child. He observed, "If ever you (teacher) substitute authority in the place of argument, he (child) will reason no longer, he will be ever afterwards be handed like a shuttle cock between the opinion of others."

Contribution of Rousseau

It is sometimes observed that Rousseau, "a vagabond without family bonds or social status with no literary training has influenced the philosophy of education, its meaning, aims, method, curriculum and organisation more than Montague with all his wisdom or Comenius with all his philanthropy, or Locke with all his reason and truth." His chief contribution may be summarised as:-

1. His emphasis on the 'discovery' and 'recognition' of childhood traits has brought about a revolutionary change in the thinking of educators.
2. His stress on the 'concrete' led to 'Learning by Doing.'
3. Rousseau anticipated the modern Heuristic Method when he declared the child as a 'discoverer.'
4. Showed the way to the teacher that he must study the child thoroughly.
5. Rousseau propounded the new gospel of faith in nature in place of the old laws.
6. Rousseau showed the value of motivation and of creating problems and of utilising the senses and activities of the child.
7. Present day emphasis on vocational education finds its root in Rousseau.
8. His conceptions of freedom, growth, interest and activity are noteworthy in educational theory and practice.
9. It is due to Rousseau that the need for sense training and physical activities in the earlier development of the child has been recognised in the modern system of education.

Limitation and Weaknesses of Rousseau's Naturialism in Education

1. *Neglect of books and other media*—Rousseau's naturalism in its extreme form neglects books and other media. It is very difficult to assume that we can neglect the vast quantities of printed materials.
2. *Limited scope for learning from nature*—Physical nature alone is not sufficient for providing education. Moreover in the present day urbanisation, it is very hard to find natural surroundings for education.
3. *Faulty conception of discipline*—His doctrine of discipline by natural consequences is also doubtful. The child at his tender age without foresight, without reason and without developing his correct understanding cannot correct his behaviour. He requires the mature and wise guidance of the parents and the teacher. If the child is left to his own judgement and wisdom, he might receive a blow, which may blow is entire personality.
4. *Outdated views about woman's education*—Rousseau does not give a fair treatment to women's education. This seems to be a very unsatisfactory side of his educational philosophy.

7.2 Johann Heinrich Pestalozzi (1746-1827)

A practical educator—Pestalozzi, a Swiss educator, began his experiments in education by teaching his own child Jacobi. He started his own school to carry out his experiments on education. The school was later on shifted to Yverdon which became a famous centre of experiments in education.

Pestalozzi's main publications are Leonard and Gertude. *How Gestude Teachers Her Children* and *Evening Hours of a Hermit.*

Important Educational Principles and Methods of Pestalozzi

1. *Aims of education*—According to Pestalozzi, "Education is the natural, progressive and harmonious development of all the powers and capacities of human beings.
2. *Child centred education*—Pestalozzi said. "I wish to psychologize education." He advocated that a child should be studied thoroughly and thereafter appropriate methods of instruction should be used.

3. *'Anschaung'* (Sense perception or observation)—He said, "Knowledge must be founded on sense perception."
4. *Use of object lesson*—Pestalozzi writes, "Teach him (child) nothing by words that you can teach him by things themselves."
5. *Nature as an educator*—Pestalozzi states, "Nature teaches better than men."
6. *Curriculum*—Pestalozzi said that the curriculum should be based on practical activities. Curriculum should include language, geometry, history, moral training, nature study, oral speech, and religious training. Agricultural and manual activities are also included.
7. *Discipline*—Pestalozzi is in favour of guiding the children to control themselves. He pleads for giving love and affection to them.
8. *Role of the home*—According to Pestalozzi, a good house is the ideal education institution for its is the centre of love and active cooperation for the common welfare.
9. *Place of school*—Schools are necessary since home cannot provide all instruction.
10. *Time table*—In Pestalozzi's school, a time table was made for the periods, each one hour long, from 6 A.M. to 8 P.M.
11. *Methods of instruction*—In Geography and Nature Study, object lessons were stressed for training in observation. The language lesson was analysed into syllables. The teaching of arithmetic was based on counting and oral work. There were graded exercises for organisation. Crafts like book binding and making geometrical models, gardening and manual work received considerable importance. Free time was provided to the children in the evening for doing whatever pleased them.

7.3 Friderich August Froebel (1782-1852)

The great aim and purpose of his life is summed up in his famous saying :

"Come, let us live for children!"

Founder of the kindergarten—It is an irony of circumstances that the founder of the kindergarten system—a system which has been accepted all over the world as a sound of system of early education, was forbidden from establishing any school by the German Government that viewed his method of education with suspicion on the ground that it encouraged socialism. This was a great shock for the great teacher and he could not long survive it. Froebel died in agony, misery and poverty in 1852.

Froebel's publications—His publications include: *The Education of Man, Pedagogies of kindergarten, Education by Development, Mother Play and Nursery Songs.*

Early life and experiences—Froebel was deprived of parental affection and the memories of his early suffering made him in later life more eager to promote the happiness of children. He lost his mother when he was only nine months. His father who got remarried was not very affectionate towards him. For a number of years, more or less, he wandered from place to place, picking up professions of one after the other different natures and failing miserably in them.

The year 1816 was a great turning point in his life when he established a small school. Thereafter he vigorously engaged himself in carrying out experiments in early education.

Main Educational Principles of Froebel's Philosophy

1. *The law of unity*—In 1826, Froebel published his famous book *The Education of Man.* In this book, he says, "The true method of education consists in considering the mind of the child as a living whole in which all the parts work together to produce harmonious unity."
2. *Creativeness of childhood*—Froebel proposed a new concept of childhood. He stressed that childhood is not merely a preparation for adulthood. Childhood is a value in itself and possesses its own creation. An adult has no right to feel superior and to interfere with the nature of children, Rather the adult must first understand the child and then guide him accordingly.
3. *Inner relatedness of all education*—This means that the educator ought to lead the child through such situations as will help to relate his experiences organically one with another. Only thus can the child realise his own personal unity and the unity inherent in the diversity of life.

4. *Totality of educational endeavour*—In order to realise the driving character of the universe and his part in it, man needs his senses and emotions as well as reasons. They all are windows of the soul. Hence Froebel emphasised the totality of educational endeavour.

5. *Concept of play and activity*—According to Froebel, "Play is the purest, most important activity of man at this stage...It gives, therefore, joy, freedom, contentment, inner rest and peace with the world. It holds the source of all that is good." Froebel recognised that play needs to be organised, and controlled on definite materials so that it may not degenerate into aimless play "instead of preparing for those tasks of life for which it is destined." There should be rational conscious guidance. Consequently, Froebel has given gifts to children to play with.

Froebel has suggested the following kinds of play at the kindergarten stage:

1. Play leading to recreation.
2. Play leading to constructive activities.
3. Play for imaginative and intellectual activities.
4. For developing cooperation.
5. Play songs.

In fact the entire programme of the kindergarten revolves around activities, play, songs and occupations that are full of action.

Function of Education

The functions of education, according to Froebel, may be summed up as, "Education should lead and guide man to clearness. It should lift him to knowledge of himself, to mankind, to a knowledge of God and of nature, and to the pure and holy life."

Froebel maintains that the aim of education is not to make the mind of the child a jumble of words. He writes, "The essential business of schoo is not so much to communicate a variety and multiplicity of facts as to give prominence to the ever living unity that is in all things." Again he writes, "Human education requires the knowledge and appreciation of religion, nature and language in their intimate living reciprocity and mutual interaction.

Without the knowledge and appreciation of the intimate unity of the three, the school and we ourselves are lost in the fallacies of bottomless, self-provoking diversity." So the aim of education is to enable the child to realise the unity in diversity.

Meaning of Kindergarten and its Objectives

Kindergarten is a German word which implies a children's garden. Froebel conceived the school as a garden, the teacher as the gardener and the students as tender plants. The teacher like the gardener is to look after the little human plants and water them to grow to beauty and perfection. Froebel discovered much similarity between a child and a plant. He believed that the process of growth and development of the plant and the child is the same. The plant grows from within according to the seed that is within, in the same way the child grows from within. He unfolds his tendencies and impulses from within.

In the words of Froebel the object of a kindergarten is "to give the children employment in agreement with their whole nature, to strengthen their bodies, to exercise their senses, to engage their awakening mind and through their senses to make them acquainted with nature and their fellow creatures. It is specially to guide aright the heart and the affections, and to lead them to the original ground of all life, to unity with themselves."

Chief Features of Kindergarten

1. *Self-activity*—Froebel said that 'free self activity' is a process by which the child realises his own nature and builds up his own word and then unites and harmonises the two. Self-activity of the mind is the basic law of a kindergarten.
2. *Play songs*—Froebel has given fifty play songs in his book 'Mother and Nursery songs'. The idea of the introduction of songs is to enable the child to use his senses, limbs and muscles and also to familiarise him with the surroundings. The child begins to use language through these songs. Each song is accompanied by a game such as 'Hide and Seek'. The selection of the song is determined by the teacher in accordance with the development of the child. There are three parts in a song.

(i) A motto for the guidance of mother or teacher.

(ii) A verse accompanied by music.

(iii) A picture illustrating the song.

3. *Gifts and occupations*—To provide activities, Froebel devised suitable materials known as gifts. The gifts suggest some form of activity and the occupations are the activities suggested by the gifts. These have been carefully graded. They possess all the novelty of play things. The order of the gift is devised in such a way that it leads the child from the activities and thoughts of one stage to another.

4. *The place of the teacher*—The teacher is not to remain passive. The teacher has to suggest the idea of occupation when gifts are offered to children. He is also required to demonstrate certain activities to them. He also sings a song with a view to helping the child form appropriate ideas.

5. *Discipline through love*—According to Froebel. "Control over the child is to be exercised through a knowledge of his interests and by the expression of love and sympathy." A teacher has important responsibilities to perform. He has to inculcate sympathetically values like love, sympathy, humility, co-operation and obedience to elders. He has to avoid external restraint and bodily punishment. The child should be made to realise that punishment depends upon his love for order, goodwill and mutual understanding. Froebel stressed that women should be trained for training children at this stage.

Froebel's Contribution to Modern Education

Froebel was the first modern educator who stressed the role of proper training and education of the pre-school child. He invited us to live for our children and love them. Froebel drew the attention of the parents teachers and other sections of the society to the fact that until the education of nursery years was reformed, nothing solid and worthy could be achieved. His emphasis on the study of the child, respect for his individuality, playway in education and engaging women teachers at the necessary stage are great landmarks in education.

7.4 Maria Montessori (1870-1952)

Brief life sketch—The first Italian lady to get the Degree of Doctor of Medicine, Maria Montessori became one of the prominent educationalists of the world. The doors of the medical colleges were closed for women in those days. How to get admission was the problem before her? She tried a trick and was successful in getting admission. She signed herself as 'M. Montessori' when she applied for admission. The authorities could never think that a lady would apply in such a manner. So they admitted her thinking she was a man. This speaks of her ingenuity! While working as a professor at the University of Rome, She got an opportunity to work in the world of mentally deficient children. She took a keen interest in their development and discovered the following points:

1. Mental deficiency results from the dullness of the senses.
2. Sense training was the best method to achieve marvellous results in their education.
3. If the method of sense training is employed to educate normal children, far better results could be achieved.

From 1907 to 1952 she spent her life in working with small children, organising Montessori schools and training teachers for the new system.

Important publications—These include: *Discovery of the Child, Education for a New World, The Secret of Childhood, The Child, Peace and Education, Child Training* and *The Montessori Method.*

M. Montessori spent a number of years in India in propagating her new method and training teachers.

Principal Features of Montessori Educational Philosophy

Principle of development from within and child centred Education—Montessori wrote, "Child is a body which grows and a soul which develops these two forms physical and psychic, have one eternal front, life it self" She believed that education of a child is from within, pointed out emphatically, "If any educational act in to be efficacious, it will be only that which tends to help towards the complete unfolding of the child's individuality." She is of the opinion that for the unfolding of the child's individuality, a suitable environment should be provided. Montessori's Children's House, a name given to a school by her, aims at providing such an environment.

All the following principles are the outcome of this child-centred philosophy.

Principle of individual development—This principle is the outcome of the principle of individual development. She believes that every child is peculiar to himself and he progresses at his own speed and rate and collective methods of teaching crush his individuality. She treats each child as a separate individual and recommends that he should be helped and guided in a manner that helps him in his proper growth and development. In the words of John Adams, Dr. Montessori "has rung the knell of class teaching."

Principle of self-education or auto education—Montessorie has shifted the emphasis from teaching to learning. She believes that self-education or auto-education is the only true education. She advocates that the child should remain undisturbed by adult interference. She has devised the didactic apparatus which attracts the attention of the children, keeps them busy spontaneously, leads them to learn the powers of movements, reading, writing and arithmetic, etc.

Principle of freedom or liberty—Her belief is that freedom is the birth right of every individual and she advocates the spontaneous development of the child through full liberty. She does not believe in putting restraints as she thinks that these may 'mar or stifle the innate powers of the child'. She says, "The school must permit the free, natural manifestations of the child if he is to be studied in a scientific manner."

Principle of no material rewards and punishments—According to her, they are incentives unnatural or forced effort and the development that comes with their help will also be unnatural.

Principle of sense training—Montessori asserts that our senses are the gate ways of knowledge and therefore on their training and development depends the acquisition of knowledge throughout life. She pointed out that the senses are very active between the ages of 3 and 7 and that a lot of learning takes place during this period. She advocates that sensory training is the key to intellectual development.

Principle of motor efficiency or muscular training—She has also attached importance to muscular training as a part of the early education of children. She believed that muscular training facilitates over other activities like writing, drawing, speaking, etc. She takes muscular activity as purely physiological in character. She stresses that running, walking, etc., all depend on muscular training.

Principle of no fairy tales—She would like to banish fairy stories from the curriculum of young children since these tend to confuse children and to hinder them in the process of adjusting themselves to the real world.

Functions and Role of the Teacher

Teacher as gardener—She thinks that a teacher should care for the child like a gardener who cares for the plant so that the natural growth of the child is properly guided and aided in the process of unfolding itself.

Knowledge of each child—The teacher should have an intimate knowledge of the mind and character of each individual. He should keep the physiological records of each child's development: his weight, height and other measurements.

The directress and not the teacher—Dr. Montessori has replaced the world 'teacher' by the word 'directress' and she thinks that the primary duty of the person in authority is to direct and not to teach. She insists that the directress should have an extensive knowledge of psychology and laboratory technique.

Doctor-cum-scientist-cum-missionary—In the words of Montessori, the directress should be partly doctor, partly scientist and completely religious, the directress should avoid scolding or suppressing the patient in order to avoid worst situations. Like a scientist she should wait patiently for the results and should conduct experiments with her material. Like a religious lady she should be there to serve the child.

Faith in the personality of the child—She should allow the child to grow according to his own inner law. Her business is to provide for suitable environments. She should provide children with suitable opportunities to think for themselves.

Moral qualities—"Virtues and not words are the main qualifications of the directress." She must banish anger which is a great sin and which prevents from understanding the child. The soul of the child, which is pure and very sensitive, requires her most delicate care. Her motto should be "I must diminish to let you grow."

Children's House: An Activity House

Montessori, with a view to giving a practical shape to her educational principle, organised. The 'Children House', a name given to school. The 'House' provides all the requirements of a 'Family House'. In fact, it has all the essentials of a good school, a workshop and a home. The main room of the building is a study room. All the rooms are well equipped according to the needs of the children and the spirit of the Montessori Method.

There are three types of exercises provided in the Children's House.

1. Exercise in practical life *i.e.*, sweeping the room, dressing, laying tables *etc*.
2. Exercise for sense training
3. Didactic apparatus for teaching language and arithmetic.

Contribution of Maria Montessori to Educational Thought and Principles

Madam Montessori's profound love and affection, keen sensitiveness, artistic imagination and exceptional sympathy for children have given a new touch to the theory and principles of education. In fact, she has ushered in a new era in child education, especially of small children at the nursery stage.

To Madam Montessori "the child was God." Her school was the temple and the duty of the temple was the essence of childhood. She further writes, "To-day there stands forth one urgent need-the reform of methods in education and instruction, and he who struggles towards this end is struggling for the regeneration of man."

By originating the Montessori Method, Maria Montessori revolutioned the concept of child education. Her impact on educational thought and practices is universal. She has also made an important contribution to the training of teachers for the pre-primary stage. Montessori ranks among the fore front educationers who advocate an environment of freedom to children.

Limitations of the Principles and Methods of Education

There is more emphasis on biological aspects and less on psychological. The method neglects the training of imagination. A lot of space and expensive apparatus are needed. The apparatus needs to be adapted to local conditions.

A Comparative Study of Montessori and Froebel

Points of Similarity

1. Both recognise the importance of early childhood education.
2. Both consider education as development from within.
3. Both stress the importance of a congenial environment for the growth and development of the child.
4. Both give due regard to the personality of the child.
5. Both believe in play-way.
6. Both stress sense training.

Points of Contrast

Froebel's Kindergarten	*Montessori Method*
1. *Philosophy*	
Froebel was basically a philosopher and kindergarten is based on philosophical principles	Montessori was basically a scientist and the method is the outcome of her scientific principles
2. *Methods*	
(i) Sense training through gifts the didactic apparatus	(i) Sense training through
(ii) Stress on play-way	(ii) Self corrective apparatus is provided
(iii) Emphasis on manual activities	(iii) Stress or daily life activities
(iv) Scope for development of imagination	(iv) No scope for fairy tales
3. *Role of the Teacher*	
The teacher is like a gardener	Teacher as directress

7.5 John Dewey (1859-1952)

A great teacher and an Encyclopedia Reader—Charles W. Coulter and S. Richard, in there publication *A Layman's Guide to Education Theory (1955)* describe the contribution of Dewey—as: "John Dewey, a great teacher, an encyclopedia reader, thoroughly familiar with the American as well as the European background of pedagogy, dedicated himself to sparking a revolution in the theory and practice of education, not only in America but throughout the world."

Brief life sketch—John Dewey, the eminent American philosopher and educator, was born in October 1859 at Burlington and graduate from the University of Vermont in 1874. He started his career as a school teacher and had the actual experience of teaching in a class room. His philosophy, therefore, is not simply speculative but based on the actual experiences in the school.

After leaving his job as a school teacher, Dewey joined Johns Hopkins University and obtained the degree of Ph.D in philosophy. Thereafter he worked as a professor of philosophy at the universities of Minnesota, Michigan and Chicago. Before he died in 1952, he was a professor of education and philosophy at the University of Columbia, New York

It was at Chicago in 1896 that Dewey founded the ideal University Laboratory School. This school served him as a scientific laboratory in obtaining knowledge of facts and laws unknown to the educationists of the universe. It was here that he tested, modified and clarified his theories after practical experience of school situations.

Important Publications of John Dewey—*My Pedagogic Creed* (1897), *Psychology and Philosophic Method* (1899), *The School and Society* (1900), *How We Think* (1910), *Democracy and Education* (1916), *Creative Intelligence* (1917), *Reconstruction in Philosophy* (1920), *Human Nature and Conduct* (1922), *Experience and Nature, Philosophy and Civilisation, Art as Experience* (1934), *Experience and Education* (1938), *Schools of Tomorrow* (1942), *Education Today* (1949).

Dewey's philosophy of education—Dewey's philosophy and programme in education has variously been termed as 'Experimentalism', 'Functionalism', 'International', 'Operationalism',

'Practicalism', and above all 'PRAGMATISM'. All these terms indicate his stress on the dynamic and ever changing character of life and education. Dewey's philosophy of life and of practices of education grew out of his experiments in the University Laboratory School, founded at Chicago in 1896.

Principle Features of Dewey's Educational Philosophy

Education is adaptation, growth and construction and reconstruction of experience and life itself—Dewey is a protagonist of the conception of education as growth and direction. Life is growing and education is the process of this ever-increasing growth. What is of enormous significance for Dewey is the present life and its possibilities. He criticised the conception of education as a 'preparation' for the realisation of some remote future goal. It is essential that the immediate situation should be interpreted in such a meaningful way that it may provide the maximum stimulus for the responsive cooperation of pupils and the utilisation of their emergies.

Dewey further explains his philosophy of education in these word, "The new philosophy of education is an experimental philosophy. All experiences cannot be educative...The traditional education gave pupils experiences but not of the right type...The business of the educator is to set a kind of experience which while being agreeable promotes having desirable future experiences. The central problem of an educator based upon experience is to select the kind of present experiences that live fruitfully and creatively in subsequent experiences. The continuity of experience is the philosophy of Educative Experience. It is held that education is a development within, by and for Experience...Education by, of, and for Experience...Thus a full integrated personality exists only when successive experiences are integrated. What is a thing for? What's its use? Action must precede knowledge. Whatever knowledge we posses has resulted from our activities, our efforts to survive. Only that which has been organised into our dispositions so as to enable us to adapt our environment to our needs and to adapt our aims and desires to the situations in which we exist is really knowledge."

Accordingly Dewey's concept of school and its curriculum are an 'eptiome' of the life experiences.

Education as a psychological and social process—"In sum, I believe that the individual who is to be educated is a social individual and that society is an organic union of individuals. If we eliminate the social factor from the child, we are left only with an absrtraction: if we eliminate the individual factor from society, we are left only with an inert and lifeless mass. Education, therefore, must begin with a psychological insight into the child's capacities, interests, and habits. It must be controlled at every point by reference to these same considerations. These powers, interests, and habits must be continually interpreted—we must know what they mean. They must be translated in terms of their social equivalents—in terms of what they are capable of in the way of social service."

Participation of the individual in the social process—Dewey said, "I believe that all education proceeds by the participation of the individual in the social consciousness of the race. This process begins unconsciously almost at birth, and is continually shaping the individual's powers, saturating his consciousness, forming his habits, training his ideas, and arousing his feelings and emotions. Through this unconscious education the individual gradually comes to share in the intellectual and moral resources which humanity has succeeded in getting together. He becomes an inheritor of the funded capital of civilization. The most formal and technical education in the world cannot safely depart from this general process. It can only organise it or differentiate it in some particular direction.

I believe that the only true education comes through the stimulation of the child's powers by the demands of the social situations in which he finds himself."

Education as a Process of Living

Education is a process of living and not preparation for future living. Education must be conceived as a continuing reconstruction of experience; the process and the goal of education are one and the same thing.

Social efficiency as the aim of education—According to Dewey, education aims at the "development of all those capacities in the individual which will enable him to control his environment and fulfil his possibilities." Dewey further said, "What nutritions and reproduction are to physiological life, education is to social."

Education in the art of living together—Social efficiency also implies cultivation of the power to join freely in the common activities.

School as a social institution—In his book *My Pedagogic Creed*, Dewey states, "I believe that the school is primarily a social institution. Education being a social process, the school is simply that form of community life in which all those agencies are concentrated that will be most effective in bringing the child to share in the inherited resources of the race, and to use his own powers for social ends." "I believe that the school must represent present life—life as real and vital to the child as that which he carries on in the home, in the neighbourhood, or on the playground."

Dewey outlines the following three functions of the school:

1. To provide a simplified social environment.
2. To provide a simplified but desirable environment by weeding out what is undesirable.
3. To provide a balanced environment of various elements in the social environment.

School curriculum and development of social insight and interest—The task of educating so many children at so many different educational levels with such a variety of abilities, needs and goods requires a completely different approach. With this increase in a diversified school population, Dewey advocates that broader curricula programmes are needed and emphasis should be placed on the total development of the person as being equally important as the intellectual and the academic. Such a curriculum acknowledges that the social responsibilities of education must present situations where problems are relevant to the problems of living together, and were observation and information are calculated to develop social insight and interest.

According to Dewey social life cannot be cut into pieces of knowledge. Departmentalisation of the curriculum and the systematic succession of studies have to be replaced by an elastic programme of activities.

The subject-matter of geography, arithmetic, grammar should come out of school situations in answer to social needs.

Methods of teaching—Professor Dewey has expounded the '*problem method*' of teaching in his books entitled *How We Think* and *Interest and Effort in Education.* It is a method with those intellectual processes that are an antecedent to induction and education. Dewey calls this as "the processes by which the mind of the individual comes into relation with the objective world. Interest and self-activity are its chief characteristic features."

Kilpatrick, one of the most famous followers of Dewey developed Dewey's techniques into the Project Method. In the Project Method, the child's interests and purposes are the most important elements and various subjects are integrated and correlated.

Discipline—Dewey explains his concept of discipline in these words, "Out of doing things that are to produce results, and out of doing on a social and cooperative way, there is born a discipline of its own kind and type. Discipline is inherent in the relations of members of the school society in pursuit of common ends."

Teacher—a guide and director—"The teacher is a guide and director; he steers the boat, but the energy that propels it must come from those who are learning. The more a teacher is aware of the past experiences of students, of their hopes, desires, chief interests, the better will he understand the forces at work that need to be directed and utilised for the formation of reflective habits."

The teacher is the prophet of the true God—"The teacher is engaged, not simply in the training of individuals, but in the formation of the proper social life."

Every teacher should realise the dignity of his calling; that he is a social servant set apart for the maintenance of proper social order and the securing of the right social growth.

In this way the teacher always is the prophet of the true God and the usherer in of the true kingdom of God.

Democracy and education—Dewey asks, "What does democracy mean save that the individual is to have a share in determining the condition and aims of his own work." Democracy means "emancipation of the mind of an individual organism to do its own work."

Contribution of Dewey to educational thought and practice—Professor Ulich in *History of Educational Thought* describes Dewey's contribution—"Dewey is one of the most astute, if not the most astute, among the modern philosophers who try to explain the quality and purpose of human life from an immanent and sociological point of view. His work offers one of the most helpful means of understanding the functioning of the human mind within a society of men who want to communicate with one another and to preserve themselves. Dewey's work encourages an experimental and scientific attitude; it prevents us from fixing our minds on things and ideas only because we happen to find them in the storehouse of tradition; it shows what men can achieve if they rely on their reason and courage instead of clinging to their prejudices; It teaches tolerance and respect for man without unduly edifying him—in short, it is a great corrective of false ideologies as well as a guide toward active, manly virtue."

"The quest for the three goals—scientific method, humanistic ethics and democratic theory—represent the great contribution of Dewey to educational theory." Observes Professor V.P. Verma, Dewey's concept of problem-solving led to the development of the project method.

Rush thinks—"In education we cannot but be grateful to Dewey for his great, services in challenging the old 'static cold storage ideal of knowledge' and in bringing education more into accord with the actualities of present-day life. The general principle underlying the developments in his philosophy and his applications of these in education appears to be that both philosophy and education should reflect the main currents of contemporary thought and incorporate the techniques that have so significantly contributed to modern industrial and social progress."

Questions and Problems

A. Essay-Type Questions

1. How does Froebel make use of the principle of self-activity in child education?
2. "Experience is the watchword of Dewey's philosophy." Illustrate.
3. Evaluate Dewey's contribution to education with reference to its aims, discipline, curriculum and method of teaching.
4. Discuss the salient features of Froebel's Kindergarten.
5. What does Rousseau mean by education according to nature: Estimate the contribution of Rouseau to child-centred education.
6. Critically examine the contribution of Pestalozzi to the development of child-centred education.
7. State briefly three main principles of Froebel in educational philosophy and describe the pattern of education which emerges out of these principles.
8. How far do you agree that John Dewey probably influenced education more than any other educator.
9. Explain Rousseau's negative education.

B. Short-Answer Type Questions

10. Give an outline of Maria Montessori's contribution to child-centred education.
11. What are the methods of teaching in the kindergarten as adopted by Froebel?
12. What are the limitations of the Montessori method of teaching?
13. Explain the significance of Froebel's gifts and occupations.
14. What according to Dewey should be the relation between the school and the society?

8

A Traditional, Developing (Emerging) and Modern Society

Concept of Society

Man is a social being. He lives in a society which is a composite of individuals and small or large groups. Society has its impact on the individuals and the individuals also influence society. History records that great individuals like Gautam Buddha, Guru Nanak Dev, Gandhi and Nehru changed the outlook of a vast section of society in accordance with their philosophy of life.

The word 'society' has several connotations and has been defined differently. For our purpose, we shall refer to only two definitions.

According to MacIver, "Society is the web of social relationships and it is always changing."

In the words of Lappise, "A society is a kind of community whose members have become socially conscious of their mode of life and are united by common sets of aims and values."

From the above it is clear that every home or family is a mini society. It consists of a web of relationships. It is always changing. In the earlier days, there were large families and now the trend is towards nuclear families. The members of a family have their own modes of life and are united by common aims and values. Likewise there may be a school cooperative society or club.

Indian society is composed of several groups and inter relations. These groups may have different aims and values but at the broader plane, they are no different from an English society or a German society.

Still a broader concept of society divides the world into two societies only—the eastern and the western.

According to Vedic thought the concept of a society is expressed in 'Vasudhev Katumbakam' (the world is a family or one society).

Dimensions of a society—Broadly speaking a society may be seen in terms of dimensions: cultural, economic, educational, political, philosophical and social, though there are large variations from region to region, there are certain common characteristics.

Cultural Heritage

Meaning of culture—Culture has been viewed differently by different scholars. Our objective here is not to discuss the views of scholars but to provide a broader view of culture. Professor S.P. Ruhela in an article 'Social and Cultural Traditions of India', published in *The Teacher and Education in Emerging Society* (NCERT, 1983) provides the following meaning of culture. Modern sociologists like Talcott Parsons and Robert Morten define culture as a system of values, i.e. preferred way or alternatives adopted by the members of a given community in almost all matters concerning their way of living—e.g. what to eat, how to dress, how to treat different categories of people like elders, children, guests, superiors, rulers etc., what interests, attitudes and goals to pursue in life, and the like. In other words, culture is concerned with preferences in beliefs, ideas, practices and ideals. It is the sum total of the "Man and his Work" as cultural anthropologist M.J. Herskovits emphasised long back. "Values occupy the most dominant place in it."

The world conference on cultural policies, held under UNESCO'S auspices, in Mexico city in 1982 gave the following definition of culture, "Culture comprises the whole complex of distinctive spiritual, material, intellectual and emotional features' that characterise a society or social group. It includes not only the arts and letters, but also modes of life, the fundamental rights of human beings value systems, traditions and beliefs."

Dr. Radhakrishnan sums up the cultural traditions of India in these words, "The ideal man of India is not the magnanimous man of Greece or the brave knight of medieval Europe but the free man of spirit who has attained insight into the universal source by rigid discipline and practice of disinterested virtues, who has freed himself from the prejudices of his time and place. It is India's pride that she clung fast to this ideal."

Assimilation, Humanism, Secularism, Toleration and Universality are the essential characteristics of Indian culture. The following prayers enshrine the traditional values of Indian culture. 'Satyam, Shivam, Sundaram'—truth, beauty and goodness

'Vasudhev Kutumbakam'—the whole world is a family.

'Sa Vidhya ya Vimuktayaya'—knowledge is that which liberates.

'Sakal Bhumi Gopal Ki'—all the land belongs to the Lord.

'Shanti Shanti'—peace, peace.

Composite Nature of Indian Culture

A composite culture is made up of various parts or elements. It means a harmonious blend of various ideas, customs, manners and values. It is the product of assimilating, borrowing and sharing of interaction between two or more streams of thought.

Indian culture is like a colour composite of a collage of patterns through which runs a thread of unity.

The composite culture of India bears the impact of the Vedas, the Upanishads, the Bhagvad Gita, Buddhism, Jainism, Bhakti Marg, and Sufism (Muslim saints), It is also influenced by the spirit of brotherhood of Islam and western culture. In essence it is based on the traditional values of assimilation, humanism, secularism, toleration and universality.

From ancient to modern age, India has produced great philosophers, saints and mahatmas, who have contributed towards the overall development of man. India has also assimilated the best from all philosophers and religions in the world. It has also assimilated many things from the various races that came to India from foreign countries and settled here.

The five most illustrious representatives of the composite culture of India during the four centuries of the medieval age and three of the modern, are Amir Khusrau (13th, 14th century) Sant Kabir and Guru Nanak (15-16th century) Prince Dara Shikuh (17th century), Raja Rammohan Roy (19th century) Jawaharlal Nehru and Mahatma Gandhi (20th century).

We have places of worship which attract in equal measures people from all faiths.

At the political level also, there have been kings like Ashoka and Akbar who worked for the promotion of a composite culture.

The geographical features may vary but a common thread of unity runs through the apparent variations. More than 900 million people in India are like a college of varying customs, dances, dresses, food and music. Dussehra attracts crowds in Kullu in Himachal Pradesh in the north. It is equally popular in Mysore in the south. Id celebration or the Christmas spirit is the same in Kashmir or Kerala. The Hindi speaking pilgrim from the north finds himself spiritually at ease in Kanyakumari. Likewise a Tamil speaking tourist finds himself spiritually at ease in Varanasi or Haridwar. The sari is in demand by women all over India whichever part they might belong to. Dosa as an item of food is relished all over the country. Dance styles, Bharat Natayam, Manipuri or Kathak are appreciated in all parts of India.

It may be recalled that the freedom struggle was inspired by a sense of unity. People belonging to this composite culture made great sacrifices.

In this variety lies the greatness of India and this reflects the composite culture of Indian society.

Educational Heritage of India

A rich educational heritage—In the words of Lord Meston, "At no period of its history has India been an altogether unenlightened country. Inscriptions, on stone and copper, the palm-leaf records of the temples, and in later days, the wide-spread manufacture of paper, all alike indicate not only the great knowledge, but also the common use of the art of writing. From the earliest times the caste of Brahmans has preserved by oral traditional as well as in manuscript; a literature unrivaled alike in its quantity and in the intellectual subtlety of its contents."

In ancient India education was wide spread. The standard of education was so high that foreign students and scholars came to India to receive education and enlightenment. To use modern phraseology, foreigners used to call themselves 'India Returned' as some of us take pride what in calling ourselves 'Foreign Returned', 'USA or UK Returned' etc. It is, therefore, no wonder that Dr. F.W. Tomas,[1] one of the most distinguished scholars has observed, "Education is no exotic in India. There is no country where the love of learning has so early an origin or has exercised so lasting and powerful an influence."

According to the *Encyclopedia Britannica,* Vol. 7, "the period...was a most creative period and metaphysics as well as mathematics and early science made noteworthy progress. It was the age of the *Upnishadas* and *Sutras.* When new branches of learning enriched the content of education."

According to a French scholar, Maspero, the Chinese Emperor Ming-ti (A.D. 58-75) sent 18 scholars to India. The names of Fa-Hien Tsang, Hieun Tsang and I-T-sing readily come to mind.[2]

The present educational scenario has to be viewed in the light of the British system of education as devised by Lord Macaulay in 1835.

Economic Dimensions of the Colonial Society

Going back, India that is Bharat was the richest and the most prosperous country in the world. It was then known as the 'Golden Sparrow'. Literally speaking 'Rivers of milk' flowed. Indian handicrafts and industrial products were known for their excellence in design and quality all over the world. From the richeness of this land and from the labour and wisdom of its people had sprung enormous wealth, great ideas, refined skills and art. Naturally, therefore, foreigners were tempted to come to India to learn as well as to loot and plunder.

The present economic scene has to be seen in the background of the British rule in India. The British rule promoted the interests of British society, its economy and industries. They deliberately

1. F.W. Thomas, *History and Prospects of British Education in India,* Cambridge, George Bell & Sons, 1891, p. 1.
2. See Chapter 5, "Indian Philosophical Traditions and Their Implications."

adopted many measures which adversely affected the indigenous industries. They wanted to make India a vast market for the sale of British goods. In fact their policy, as an eminent economist has said, was to make Indians "hewers of wood and drawers of water." The destruction of cottage industries had far-reaching effects. The pressure of population increased on land. Food crops were neglected. The economic condition of the peasants became very bad. The farmers were forced to sell their produce at a very low price to middle men. They borrowed money on heavy interest from the money lenders. The money lenders became very powerful and they established their hold on the peasants.

The British rulers manipulated the rules of customs and imports and exports in such a way that they dumped cheap machine-made British goods in India. They exported raw materials at low rates from India and imported finished goods at high rates,

Here and there, a few attempts were made to promote industries in India.

The fact, however, remains that there was a continued neglect of industrialising India. Independent India, inherited a crippled economy.

Political Dimensions of Indian Society

At the time of independence, there were more than 500 princely states in India. The British rulers left them free to join India or Pakistan. However, within a very short period after independence, these states became an integral part of India. Sardar Patel, the then Home minister of India, played a leading role in persuading and in some cases, compelling the rulers of these princely states to join India. If they had chosen to remain independent, the unity and strength of India would have been threatened. The wisdom and foresight of Sardar patel brought about an emotional and political integration of India, On account of his firmness, Sardar Patel came to be known as the 'Iron Man of India'.

Philosophical Dimensions of Society

This aspect has been discussed in Chapter 5 of this book.

Social Dimensions of a Traditional Society

Caste system—It has been one of the most important banes of the Indian social system. In the ancient time the society was divided into four Vanas on the basin of division of labour. This system, essentially had an economic dimension but with the passage of time it developeu into a caste system. The caste system led to the degradation of the worth of an individual. It led to untouchability and weakened the cohesiveness of Indian Society.

The brahmans were the first to have the privilege of getting and imparting education. For a long time they had the monopoly of "correct religious practices and of education and learning." Then came the Kshatriyas and the Vaishas. At the bottom of the social ladder were the Shudras. Buddha was the first to challenge the caste system in the sixth century BC. The next major challenge came to this from teachers and religious thinkers of medieval India. In the nineteenth century Ram Mohan Roy, Swami Dayanand and Swami Vivekanand advocated massive educational programmes for the uplift of the lower sections of the society and that of women. Early in the twentieth century, Tagore demonstrated in his school Shantiniketan, the value of education to the vitalisation of Indian society. Mahatma Gandhi, by his teaching and example stressed the need for the education of the masses.

Joint family system—The joint family system is another characteristic of the traditional Indian society. It was a necessity when the wants of the people were very few as compared modern society. Agriculture was the main occupation. Besides it was done with traditional simple implements. It was not mechanised. With the introduction of modern techniques of farming and other occupations, there has come about a great change in the concept of the joint family system. Many new occupations have affected the traditional joint family system. The joint family system has both merits as well as demerits.

Social stratification and mobility—The Indian society may be broadly divided into three social classes. These are the upper class, middle class and lower class. The middle class may be further divided into three sub-classes—upper middle class, middle class, and lower middle class. The lower class people constitute about 70 per cent of the total population. They are mostly agricultural and industrial labourers, low paid employees and daily wage earners.

Class stratification and casteism are rigidly observed in the rural areas. However, mobility from one occupation to another has been gradually becoming common.

Chief Characteristics of a Developing (Emerging) and a Developed (Industrialised) Society

The chief characteristics of a developed and a developing society are broadly as under:

Developed Society	Developing Society
1. Very high gross national net product (GNP) per capita	1. Low GNP per capita.
2. Very low infant mortality rate (number of deaths of infants)	2. High infant mortality rate.
3. High adult literacy	3 Low adult literacy
4. High life expectancy	4 Low life expectancy
5. High percentage of schooling (completing primary and secondary state)	5. Low percentage of schooling
6. Very low drop-out rates	6. High drop-out rates
7. Industry dominated economy	7. Agriculture dominated economy
8. High percentage of urban population	8. High percentage of rural population
9. Population growth rate is low	9. Population growth rate is high
10. Most of the population can afford items of comfort	10. Most of the people cannot afford such items
11. Distribution of income is fairly even	11. Most people are poor. Some are very rich
12. People are engaged in gainful employment	12. Relatively there is more unemployment and under employment
13. Production in the farms and factories is done by the latest modern techniques	13. The techniques of agricultural and production are primitive in general
14. People in general are not superstitious	15. People in general are ignorant and superstitious.

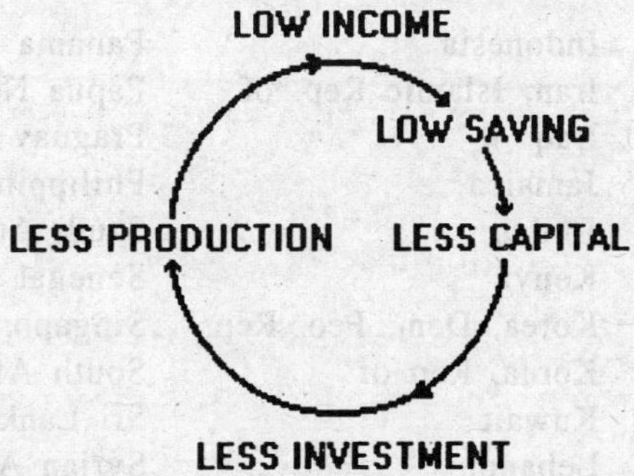

Illustration 8.1 Economic situation in an under developed country (society)

The United Nations Children Fund (UNICEF), an agency of United Nations Organization (UNO) has done the following classification of developed, developing and least developed countries.

Developed Countries

Albania	Germany	Poland
Australia	Greece	Portugal
Austria	Hungary	Romania
Belgium	Ireland	Slovakia
Bulgaria	Israel	Spain
Canada	Italy	Sweden
Czech Republic	Japan	Switzerland
Denmark	Netherlands	United Kingdom
Finland	New Zealand	U.S.A.
France	Norway	Yugoslavia (former)

Developing Countries

Algeria
Angola
Argentina
Bolivia
Brazil
Cameroon
Chile
China
Colombia
Congo
Cote d'Ivoire
Cuba
Dominican
Ecuador
Egypt
El Salvador
Eritrea
Ghana
Gautemala
Honduras
Hong Kong
India
Indonesia
Iran, Islamic Rep. of
Iraq
Jamaica
Jordan
Kenya
Korea, Dem. Peo. Rep.
Korea, Rep of
Kuwait
Lebanon
Libyan Arab Jamahiriya
Malaysia
Mauritius
Mexico
Mongolia
Morocco
Mozambique
Namibia
Nicaragua
Nigeria
Oman
Pakistan
Panama
Papua New Guinea
Praguay
Philippines
Saudi Arabia
Senegal
Singapore
South Africa
Sri Lanka
Syrian Arab Rep.
Thailand
Trinidad and Tobago
Tunisia
Turkey
United Arab Emirates
Uruguay
Venezuela
Viet Nam
Zaire
Zimbabwe

Least Developed Countries

Afghanistan
Bangladesh
Benin
Bhutan
Botswana
Burkina Faso
Burundi
Cambodia
Central
African Rep.
Chad
Ethiopia
Guinea
Guinea-Bissau
Haiti
Lao Peo.Dem.Rep.
Lesotho
Liberia
Madagascar
Malawi
Mali
Mauritania
Mozambique
Myanmar
Nepal
Niger
Rwanda
Sierra Leone
Somalia
Sudan
Tanzania, U. Rep. of
Togo
Uganda
Yeman
Zaire
Zambia

India comes in the category of a developing country/society. A comparative study of India vis-a-vis some developing countries is given towards the end of this book.

Questions and Problems

A. Essay-Type Questions

1. Describe in brief the various dimensions of a society. State whether they are interrelated or not. Give reasons in support of your answer.
2. Explain the characteristics of the composite culture of Indian society.
3. State the cultural and social factors which create hindrances in the development of Indian society.
4. Compare a developing society with a developed society by citing examples.
5. "Indian society is a developing society." Elucidate this statement.

B. Short-Answer Type Questions

6. "Culture is not merely different arts." Explain briefly.
7. List the factors that have influenced Indian culture.
8. Why do we call Indian culture a composite culture?
9. Write short notes on:
   (a) Educational heritage of India.
   (b) Colonial Indian economy.
   (c) Caste system.
   (d) Social stratification and mobility.

9 Education, Social Transformation and Socialisation

9.1 Education and Social Change

Interdependent role of education and social change—Educational and social changes are mutually reinforcing and complementary. An educational change leads over time, to a corresponding social change and social change in turn, intensifies the need for and strengthens the educational change. It may be in the reverse order, that is, social change leading to educational change and educational change intensifying the need for and strengthening social change. For instance it was the spread of education among the scheduled castes that tended to reduce the vigours of untouchability and as the practice of untouchability was loosened and weakened among them, it become possible to spread education more quickly among the scheduled castes. The spread of education among them helped to improve their socio-economic conditions and as their socio-economic conditions improved, they began to avail themselves more fully of the opportunities provided in the formal as well non-formal system of education.

The spread of education in the rural areas made the rural people politically important and their increasing political importance in turn enabled them to improve their educational status.

The spread of education among women led to changes in their social status, just as the improvement in the social status of women made it possible to spread education among them to a considerable extent.

Several other illustrations can be easily cited to show the interdependence between educational and social changes. It may also be added that the rate of social change is directly proportional to that of educational change and that both have been extremely rapid in the science and technology-based societies in the modern world.

The significance of the role of education in social change has been very aptly described by the Education Commission 1964-66: "The destiny of India is now being shaped in her classrooms...In a world based on science and technology it is education that determines the level of prosperity, welfare and security of the people. On the quality and number of persons coming out of our schools and colleges will depend our success in the great enterprise of national reconstruction the principal of which is to raise the standard of living of our people."

The International Commission on the Development of Education (1972) expressed its views, "Education must recognise itself for what it is: it may be the product of history and society, but it not their passive play thing. It is an essential factor in shaping the future, particularly at the present moment, since in the last resort education has to prepare mankind to adapt the change, the predominant characteristic of our time...It has to prepare for changes, show people how to accept them and benefit from them, create a dynamic, non-conformist, non-conservative frame of mind.

Social change towards progress—When we take for granted the phenomena for change, one question arises. Does this change that takes place in the society stand for progress? Is it in the right direction? A change may not always be towards progress. Therefore, can education allow society to drift? The answer is 'no.' Education must be used as an instrument of social progress. This means the problem of education is three fold in relation to social change.

1. To conserve as far as possible all the good points of cultural and social heritage.
2. To adjust to changing situations.

3. To create a new system of education for social progress.

Education is a constructive instrument for improving society. Brown has stated, "Education brings changes in behaviour, and if its main functions are to remain mere transmission or enrichment of culture, it will fall short of its role in a dynamic society. Education must also provide situations at all age levels but within the maturity and ability of the individual to stimulate a creativeness of mind, which can explore new horizons and bring the vision of the future into a living reality."

The child is to be led towards a better and happier future. The needs of the society are ever changing. Every successive generation aims at making improvements in the existing pattern. Education helps in reconstructing and reorganising the experience of the needs of the society and thus eliminates the unworthy features of the society and builds up a happier and better world.

Broad Areas of Social Transformation Through Education

1. Education is considered to be of immense help in realising the ideals of democracy, secularism, national integration and industrialisation.
2. Education is expected to change the values and attitudes of the people and to create in them an urge for the necessary motivation for social change.
3. It is generally believed that education will provide necessary training in skills and occupations and thus produce the needed competent personnel for manning the different specialised jobs in industrial, business, educational, agricultural and research establishments etc.
4. Education is considered to be an important means of assisting people in making them aware of their weaknesses and enabling them to gain necessary knowledge in order to achieve progress in various areas of their life in a systematic and consistent manner.

Agencies, and types of education and social change—Education starts from the cradle and continues throughout life. It is a continuous process. It takes place in and outside the educational institution. It can be imparted through formal as well as non-formal agencies of education.

In a totalitarian state education becomes a tool in the hands of the rulers to promote a totalitarian way of life. A uniform and rigid system of education is established. Everything is determined from the top.

In a democratic society social changes take place gradually through education.

The family is the first unit of social life. Social experience in the family in early childhood proves a basis for the development of personality and culture. The family, thus, can play a crucial role in assisting or subverting the larger social process though effective or ineffective social control. Therefore, parental education is of vital importance.

The educative forces of the school exert an active influence towards social change and transformation.

Organisations like youth welfare associations, child welfare organisations, Bharat Scouts and Guides, N.C.C., Red Cross, and Nehru Yuvak Kendras etc. also contribute to social change.

Mass media of communications, like press, radio and television are the other agencies of educating people regarding social change.

Educational Implications of Education as a Social Function

Simplifying and ordering the environment—A complex civilisation is too complex to be assimilated in toto. It has to be broken up into portions, as it were, and assimilated piecemeal in a gradual and a graded way. Therefore the first duty of the school is to provide a simplified environment. It selects the features which are fairly fundamental and capable of being responded to by the young. In this way it establishes a progressive order, using the factors first acquired as a means of gaining insight into what is more complicated.

Purifying and idealising environment—We cannot import into school life all that exists outside. We shall have to eliminate evil features of the existing environment. By selecting the best for its exclusive uses it strives to reinforce the power of this best.

Wider and better balanced environment—In the school there are children of diverse races, communities, religions etc. They come from different home backgrounds. So we should try to eliminate the tendency to justify one's language, speech, community or race but should train children in tolerance towards other communities, races and religions. The caste, creed and colour should not be a bar to healthy conjoint living in the school.

Teacher as an Agent of Social Change

There is a paragraph in the McNair Report on the Training of Teachers which says, "It is a truism to say that every teacher, in however humble a capacity he or she may be serving, is directly and vocationally involved in moulding the shape of things to come." "If that truism be true", observes Prof. W.O. Lester Smith of the London University, "the unsettled times in which our young citizens are going to live their lives make it necessary that those who aspire to the teach should have thought and should continue to think about the problems of society with all the intelligence at their work."

Prof. Ottaway thinks that teachers in the schools can have the most powerful influence in the community if they choose, Teachers' professional organisations and unions are among the orthodox pressure groups and they can bring their views before the public opinion and government.

An American educationist, Edmund W. Gordon, has pointed out, "It is the task of the teacher to educate—to educate for change—to educate through change—to educate for orderly planned revolution. If necessary to educate through more disruptive revolutionary action."

A teacher can convey, disseminate and develop knowledge, attitude, skills and values to the students through the following ways.

1. Direct teaching.
2. Providing opportunities to the students to practice the values of democracy, secularism and socialism.
3. The teacher himself becoming a model embodying the desired values.

A Teacher Can Also Educate Parents

Limitations of the teacher in social change—Shri S.P. Ruhela and K.C. Vyas pose this question in the context of the Indian situation, "How can they (teachers) be so (effective) when the occupation of school teachers has so far not been able to emerge as a profession in the strict sense of the term due to their effective unenlightened and key and strategic decision-making positions contraposed to another class of the elite equipped with education in vernaculars, occupying a subordinate position in the hierarchy of offices. This latter stratum is increasingly deprived of the opportunity of serving national positions demanding advanced knowledge of English."

9.2 Education and Socialisation

Significance and meaning of socialisation—Man becomes a human being only as a member of society. By nature he cannot live alone or in isolation. He is compelled by his biological and social necessities to live in a group or a society. Each of us is largely a social product. Socialisation is the process through which we learn to live in a society and learn the values of the society and the ways of thinking, doing and living that are deemed to be desirable.

The following definitions throw light on the several aspects of socialisation. Bogardus defines socialisation as, "The process whereby persons learn to behave dependently together for human welfare and in doing so experience social control, social responsibility and balanced personalities."

Cook thinks that socialisation is a process as a result of which children take on themselves the various social roles, social learning and developmental tasks.

Drever is of the view that "socialisation is a process by which the individual is adapted to his social environment (by attaining social conformity) and becomes a recognised, cooperating and efficient member of it."

Gandhi states, "I value individual freedom but you must not forget that man is essentially a social being and socialisation is the process of making a social being."

Guskin and Guskin define socialisation as "the process by which an individual learns the behaviour, the values and the expectations of others that enable him to take on particular roles in society."

Havighurst and Newgarton are of the view that "socialisation is the process by which children learn the ways of their society and make those ways part of their personality."

MacIver writes, "Socialisation and individualisation are the two sides of a single process".

Ross observes, "Socialisation is the development of we-feeling in associates and the growth in their capacity and will to act together".

Main Characteristics of the Socialisation Process

1. Socialisation is a continuous and an unending process
2. Socialisation is a visible and non-visible process.
3. Socialisation is a deliberate as well as an unconscious process.
4. A democratic approach to socialisation is preferable to an autocratic approach.
5. Socialisation process aims at enabling the individual to become a worthy member of society.
6. Socialisation improves the individual as well as the society.
7. There are several agencies and groups of socialisation—the family, the peer group, the club, the media and the school.

Role of Education in Socialisation

A noted French Sociologist, Emile Durkheim explains, the role of education in socialisation in these words, "Education is the influence exercised by adult generations on those that are not yet ready for social life. Its objective is to arouse and develop in the child a certain number of physical, intellectual and moral traits that are demanded of him by both the political society as a whole and the special milieu for which he is specially destined, more briefly, education is a socialisation of the younger generation."

Brown has brought out this function of education beautifully when he states, "Education is the consciously controlled process whereby changes in behaviour are produced in the person and through the person within the group. Education in the highest sense has taken place when external controls have been accepted as conviction by the person and have thus become internal controls. It makes for more effective participation in the total process of interaction in terms of various socially desirable values."

Role of the School in the Socialisation of the Child

The function of the present day school has considerably changed in the present scenario of rapid changes. The traditional function of the school to impart the basic skills of 3 R's is no longer considered to be adequate to meet the present challenge. Now the school must develop attitudes, skills and values of 7 R's i.e. Reading, Writing, Arithmetic (representing school subjects), Rights, Responsibilities, Relationships and Recreation. It is through a variety of school programmes comprising curriculas, co-curricular and extracurricular activities that the task of socialisation can be achieved successfully.

Class in the process of socialisation—The class provides innumerable opportunities to the children to move and mix with an egalitarian group. This is the beginning of the socialisation of the child for his future life. Here children get many chances to mix without any distinction of caste, colour or creed. The children who are selfish or self-centred learn to adjust their behaviour in terms of class norms. The teachers are expected to be vigilant so that the students do not think in terms of untouchability, caste distinctions and other prejudices.

Essential Conditions and Environment in the School for Socialisation of the Child

The task of socialisation of the child is not an easy one. The educational thinkers point out very emphatically that certain conditions in the learning-teaching situation must be created and made available in the school so that it may become an effective instrument of socialisation. These conditions are: (a) a democratic social climate in the school, (b) effective interpersonal relationships; (c) motivated learning situations; (d) school-community inter-relationships; (e) student participation and involvement in the school administration; (f) a rich programme of co-curricular activities.

Role of the Teacher in the Socialisation of the Child

A teacher can play a vital role in the socialisation of the child under his charge. He exerts a great influence upon the development of the personality of the child. For the socialisation of the child, a teacher can play an effective role in the organisation of the following programmes.

1. Community activities like camps, common meals, social service etc., should be frequently organised.
2. There should be close cooperation between the teachers and parents on matters relating to the proper socialisation of the children.
3. Various aspects of socialisation, anxiety of children and juvenile delinquency may be discussed by the headmasters, inspecting officers, teacher-educators and professional organisations in seminars or small forums.
4. Adequate stress may be laid on group activities.
5. Exhibitions on "Know Our Country" may be organised from time to time.
6. Stories depicting self-sacrifice made by great men for the cause of the general good may be told to children so that they are motivated to rise above petty gains and work for the betterment of humanity.
7. The teacher should refrain from projecting their class images on students. They should not show any discrimination. They must ensure a safe and healthy social environment in which the children may imbibe desirable values of freedom, equality, integrity, honesty, patriotism etc.
8. With proper guidance and responsibilities, the students' council can build up a sense of shared responsibility among children.
9. A proper socialisation of children very much necessitates that the ideology of the common school system be allowed to function in letters and spirit in India.
10. Children may be taken from time to time to public places like museums, courts, places of historical importance etc.
11. People engaged in different economic activities or vocations may be invited to school to give a faithful description of what they do and how useful their work is to the nation. This will enable the children to be acquainted, with those around them in the society This will also develop vocational socialisation in children.
12. Work experience should be introduced in school. This will enable the children to have first hand experiences of the activities pursued in farms and factories.

13. Children should be associated with social events like the celebration of the birthdays of leaders.
14. The school or college programme should be full of numerous co-curricular and curricular activities in which children meet, cooperate.
15. Children should be told about the socially accepted institutions in their society.
16. The introduction of a common school dress, common lunch etc., in the schools and colleges will prevent children of poor and lower middle classes from suffering due to the inflated ego of the children of the well-to-do families.
17. Teachers and parents may encourage the children to mix in inter-caste rather than intra-caste and inter-regional rather than intra-regional groups.
18. The teachers and the parents should respect the personality of children.
19. The mechanism of praise and blame, reward and punishment should be carefully used to socialize the children.
20. Proper social education may be provided to parents so that they understand the significance of the socialisation of the children.

Questions and Problems

A. Essay-Type Questions

1. What is socialisation? State the role of education in the socialisation of the child.
2. Explain the role of the school in the socialisation of the child.
3. What is socialisation? Discuss the role of the teacher in the socialisation of the child.
4. "Education must change society rather than follow social changes". Critically examine this statement and state the role of education in social change.
5. "Unless a teacher enjoys a reasonable status in society, he cannot act as an effective agent of social change". Comment on this statement.
6. "Socialisation is a process by which an individual in adapted to his social environment and becomes a recognised cooperating and effective member of it." Elucidate this statement.

A. Short-Answer Type Questions

7. What are the essential conditions for socialisation of the child in the school?
8. Distinguish between social change and social progress.
9. State the aims of social progress.
10. What are the objectives of socialisation?

10 Agencies of Education and Social Groups

10.1 Formal, Informal and Non-Formal Agencies and Types of Education

T. Raymont has very rightly stated, "Teachers are not the only educators, and schools and colleges are not only educational institutions. The other institutions though for good or ill, are unquestionably educational institutions." The word 'ill' seems to have been used in view of the criticism that only other agencies, even schools and colleges have not discharged their duties satisfactorily. In fact one writer namely Everotte Reimer has gone to the extent of writing a book entitled *School is Dead*.

It is observed that according to some educators, of all the education we receive, we learn one-fourth from our teachers, one-fourth from books, one-fourth from our colleagues and one-fourth from the environment. This indicates the types of education and the several agencies imparting education directly or indirectly, formally or informally, consciously or unconsciously and actively or passively.

In view of the changing nature of society, .the role of each type of agency of education undergoes, several changes.

Education in a wider sense takes place from the womb to the tomb. It is carried on by a number of agencies, usually classified as formal, informal and non-formal. The education imparted by these agencies is termed formal, informal and non-formal respectively.

Broad Classification of Agencies of Education

Formal (Active)	Informal (Passive)	Non-Formal (Active/Passive)
1. School	1. Art Gallery	1. Adult and social education centres
2. College	2. Cinema	2. Play-ground when regular teaching in physical education is one
3. Church	3. Home/Family	3. Professional organisation when it organises seminars and workshops
4. Home in the past	4. Library	4. Radio Persons specifically on educational programmes
5. Adult school (on regular basis)	5. Museum	5. T.V. Persons specially on educational programmes
	6. Peer and Play-Group	
	7. Play-ground	
	8. Press	
	9. Reading Room	
	10. Radio	
	11. Television	
	12. Voluntary Organisations like Bharat Sewak Samaj, Girl Guides, etc.	

Note : See the explanation under *Need for a Balanced and Integrated Approach* (on the following page).

Formal education and formal agencies—This type of education is imparted in a school or college. It is consciously and deliberately planned to bring about specific and special influence in the educand. So it is synonymous with educational institutions. The school is thus a formal agency of education. Other traditional formal agencies are; the church, the art gallery & a museum.

Informal education and informal agencies—Informal education takes into its orbit all indirect influences of the home and the society. The press, the libraries, the films and other such agencies are included as agencies of informal education. Their influence is subtle and imperceptible but at the same time very important and significant.

Non-formal education and non-formal agencies—This is an arrangement wherein flexibility is the key word. The system is an open one with regard to various aspects of education i.e., admission, curricular, place of instruction, mode of instruction, and the time and duration of instruction. Open University, open learning, correspondence education and distance are the various examples of such a system. Adult education is usually considered as a form of non-formal education.

Need for a balanced and integrated approach—There is no clear cut dividing line in classifying agencies. Even a school can take the form of non-formal agency of education when it organises adult education classes and programmes. Students in a school acquire a lot of education through informal contact a lot of education through informal contact. Nevertheless its basic classification into an agency of formal education remains intact. The press, the radio and the television are normally termed informal agencies of education. However, when they take up occasional systematic programmes of education, they assume the form of formal agencies of education. Regular school broad casts and T.V lessons, based on the school curriculum may be termed as programmes of formal education and radio and television assume the form of formal agencies of education.

The entire programme of correspondence education/distance education, open education may be classified both formal as well as non-formal depending upon the type of educational activity.

An adult school following a regular programme of education comes under the category of a formal agency of education. We should try to avert the danger of education being isolated from the subject-matter of life-experience, Here one of the weightiest problems with which the philosophy of education has to cope with is the method of keeping a proper balance between the informal, the formal and non-formal. We should beware ourselves of over-specialisation so that we do not become egoistic specialists,

Hence, we should try to incorporate the merits of informal education as far as we can and also to keep away the dangers of too much formal education. In fact with the development of new educational thought and technology and science, it has become very difficult to divide educational agencies into water-tight compartments.

Comparative Study of Formal and Non-Formal Education

Formal Education	*Non-Formal Education*
1. It is limited to period of 'being taught' as against a 'period of life' and 'work' It is imparted in educational institutions.	1. It is lifelong with learning integrated with life and work. Life is upgraded and enriched by learning.
2. It has fixed points of entry and exit. Age admission and entry qualification are prescribed.	2. It has a flexible point of entry and exit, re-entry and re-exit and so on throughout the life-span of the individual.
3. It is geared to impersonal goals of knowledge acquisition, It is examination oriented.	3. It is a process of enabling the individual to understand his own needs, the environmental situation, the societal goals and mutual relationships.
4. It is employment-oriented.	4. It is motivated by individual growth, self-renewal and maximising human potential.
5. It has fixed concepts and contents in its curriculum.	5. It has a diversified content in a fixed curriculum which is responsive to learner and environmental needs.
6. It is imposed by 'give' on the 'receiver' with little interaction between the two.	6. It is a process of sharing, exploring, analysing and judging together with maximum participation of the learners.
7. It fosters an uncritical command obedience.	7. It develops an open-end, critical and self-reliant awareness.

Contd.

8. It works on the principle of weeding out 'failures'.	8. It works on the principle of universal success through universal learning satisfaction.
9. It nurtures the status quo and discourages deviation.	9. It encourages healthy points of departure towards progress.
10. It works within a fixed social frame and hence gets quickly out of step with social change.	10. It anticipates and prepares for change for the future.

A Comparison of Formal and Informal Education

Formal Education in Formal Agency	*Informal Education: Life Long Education in Informal Agency*
1. It is planned, keeping in view some definite aim.	1. It has no definite aim.
2. It is imparted through formal lessons or well planned means.	2. It is not imparted through any formal lesson or planned means.
3. There is a definite course to be covered during a definite period.	3. There is no such definite course and period.
4. Both the teacher and the taught are aware of the process through which education is imparted.	4. They are not conscious of the process.
5. It is organised by some agency, say the managing committee or the government.	5. There may not be any organising body behind the process.
6. It starts and ends at a particular age.	6. It is a life long process. It has neither any end nor beginning. It continues for the whole life.
7. It puts a mental strain both on the teacher and the taught.	7. Being natural does not strain any body.

Contd.

8. It observes several formalities	8. No formalities are observed.
9. Only qualified teachers work	9. Education can be obtained from anybody.
10. There are regular and set programmes.	10. It takes place naturally.
11. A specific time table is followed.	11. There is no specific time table.

10.2 The Home as an Agency of Education

Importance of the home/family as an agency of education—From time immemorial, home and family has been playing an important role in the training and education of a child. It is the first place or institution where we learn our first lessons of living together, working together, helping each other and learning lessons of mutual help and adjustment.

The family or the home is an important agency of education and has been exercising an everlasting and immediate influence on the behaviour, character, conduct and personality of its members. The education of the child is not the exclusive responsibility of the school. Parents can and should play an important role in shaping and building the career of their children.

According to Ballard, "Originally, the family was the all-inclusive social institution. All human activity centred in blood-bound groups, hence all human relationships were comprehended by it. It is only within comparatively recent times that the school order expanded beyond the control of the family group."

Crow and Crow observe, "In rural areas the young child may be almost entirely dependent upon his family for his early education in human relationships. As a result, the influence upon him of home conditions and family attitudes is more potent than it, is for the child whose home appears to be in an urban area."

Frank indicates the importance of the family as "it is the only institution which is an essential agency for child rearing, socialisation, and for introducing the child to the culture of the society, thereby shaping the basic character-structure of our culture and forming the child's personalty." Henderson states, "A child's education begins in his home."

Joseph Mazzine was right when he said that the child comes to have the first lesson of citizenship on mother's knee and father's kiss.

Ramont describes the educative influence of the home in these words, "The home is the soil in which spring up those virtues of which sympathy is the common characteristic. During the earliest and most impressionable years, the family is the child's entire social environment, and though the social circle widens when he goes to school and begins to form outside friendships, yet the family remains for some years the largest and most central portion of the circle."

Russell is of this view, "Home gives the child the experience of affection and of a small community in which he is important. He has also the experience of relation with people of both the sexes and different ages, and of the multifarious business of adult life."

Young and Mack are right when they say, "The family is the oldest human group and the basic one. While the particular form of family structure may and does vary from society to society, the central foci of family activities everywhere are child rearing and the initial induction of the child into the culture of a society in fact socialisation."

Swami Dayanand laid a great stress on the good 'sanskars' on the child from the very beginning.

Mahatma Gandhi was greatly influenced by his mother. It was Jija Bai who had imbued Shivaji with the virtues of value, The great scientist Jagdish Chandra Bose got an insight into his scientific ingenuity from his mother's conversation during childhood.

The importance of the family/home may be summed up in the words of E.B. Castle, "It is simply the home more than the school that determines the quality and direction of any child's life, and that the teacher's work is fulfilled or destroyed by the operation, for good or ill, of this major factor in the education of any child. In the home, the child is provided with security or denied it; here his emotional needs are satisfied or starved, his waywardness corrected or neglected; here he is cherished with the creative discipline or spoiled as a parent's plaything; here are standards learned and values slowly appreciated. The teacher soon knows what has happened in the home; the attitudes of the parents are as quickly divulged by the child as the politics of his father's breakfast table. And do what he may, the teacher will seldom win the battle between bad home influence and good living unless as by divine providence often happens, the innate goodness of the child eventually overcomes shortcomings of its home."

Educational Functions of the Family

The family is expected to perform the following roles;

1. *Proper physical development*—For proper physical development of the child, the home should provide for good, healthy surroundings and rest. The home should be airy and well-ventilated.
2. *Proper moral environment*—Since morality cannot be taught, it can only be learnt. It is, therefore, essential that the older members of the family set good examples before the younger ones.
3. *Opportunities for participation in household responsibilities*—Children should be associated with the management of the household affairs. By participating in such activities children learn to subordinate their interest for the sake of the family.
4. *Development of intellectual, aesthetic and practical interest of the child*—It is very important that the parents should try to find out the interests of the children and take necessary steps for their development.
5. *Understanding of the child's nature*—The intelligent parent would seize of every opportunity to gain knowledge of child psychology. He would consider a child to be an adult in miniature. He would show neither leniency nor strictness in dealing with children.
6. *Understanding the importance of play in the education of the child*—It is a wrong notion on the part of the parents to think that play is a waste of time and, therefore, not allowing them to play. They should provide ample opportunities for play.
7. *Opportunities for self-expression*—Parents should encourage their children to participate in various recreational and constructive activities. They should provide them with newspapers, magazines and books of short stories.

8. *Special responsibility for religious-education*—Right type of religious education should be provided by the home.
9. *Realisation of the limitations of the school*—The parents should realise the importance of the work of the school, its limitations and cooperate with the school authorities in furthering the progress of their children.

Industrialisation and urbanization have greatly effected the role of the home in these areas (a) providing moral education (b) providing religions education (c) providing social contact and (d) providing vocational guidance.

Summing up

In short, homes where children are regarded as a sacred trust by the guardians, where there is the proper climate for the child to develop good ideals, habits, modes of thinking and behaviour, where the relationships between members are smooth and harmonious, make the task of the school easy and ensure good education for children. An educationist has observed, "A wise father is more than a hundred school masters. The mother's face is the child's first lesson-book. Home makes the man."

10.3 School as an Agency of Education

Significance of a School

A school is a social institution set up by the society to serve its ends. It is one of the most important formal agencies of education. It plays a major role in moulding the ideas, habits and attitudes of the children with a view to producing well balanced personalities; physically strong, mentally alert, emotionally stable, culturally sound and socially efficient. Informal agencies of education such as the Church and the home fail to satisfy the increasing educational requirements of a complex society and thus are losing their hold on the people. In the modern times the school has assumed a very great importance.

H.G. Wells has observed, "A world whose schools are unreformed is an unreformed world." S. Bala Krishna Joshi writes, "The progress of a nation is decided and determined not in the legislatures where passions and prejudices warp judgement and vitiate the laws that may be framed, not in courts where punishments more often harden, than reforms offenders, not in factories where men become mechanised and think of their individual interests instead of the common, no, but in school where the minds of the future citizens are moulded, where the habits, attitudes and outlook of those that are to shape and preside over the destinies of the nation are formed."

According to Nunn, "A nation's schools...are an organ of its life, whose special function is to consolidate its spiritual strength, to maintain its historic continuity, to secure its past achievements, to secure its past achievements, to guarantee its future. Through its schools a nation should become conscious of the abiding sources from which the best movements in its life have always drawn their inspiration, should come to share the dreams of its nobler sons, should constantly submit itself to self criticism, should purge its ideals, should reinform and redirect impulses."

John Dewey thinks, "the school is primarily a social institution. Education being a social process, the school is simply that form of community life in which all those agencies are concentrated that will be most effective in bringing the child to share in the inherited resources of the race to use powers for social ends."

In the opinion of the Secondary Education Commission of 1952-53, the secondary school of the future must be transformed into an activity school—we do not visualise this school as merely a place of formal training whose main concern is to communicate a certain prescribed quantum of knowledge but rather as a living and organised community which is primarily interested in training its pupils in what we call the gracious "art of living."

In the words of Kandel, "The school exists to accelerate the impact of the essential aspects of culture which prevails in the society." Harold Rugg thinks of the school as an "enterprises which prevails in the society."

The Kothari Commission 1964-66 observed that the destiny of India is shaped in the her classrooms.

Functions of the Present Day Schools

The functions of the present day schools may be stated as under:

1. *Manysided education*—'Teach the 3 R's was the conception of a traditional school. The slogan of a present school is Teach the 7 R's i.e., Reading, Writing, Arithmetic, Recreation, Rights, Responsibilities and Relationships.

2. *Training for democracy*—The present school must prepare students for a democratic society by providing them democratic experiences. The students should be trained in 'the art of living together' and made to realise the implications of the terms, 'rights and duties' of a responsible member of a democratic society. The secondary education has greatly stressed the importance of equipping its students adequately with civic responsibilities.
3. *Conservation of culture*—The school is an important institution which conserves the morals, customs and ways of social life and passes it on to the students. We cannot be cut off from our social and natural environment. Education is the transmission of technical skills and cultural traditions from one generation to another and a school discharges this function very effectively.
4. *School as an agency of social reform*—Mere conservation of the culture is not enough. Ryburn feels, "The progressive school can never be content that the present generation should simply remain where their fathers were."
5. *Development of a scientific attitude*—The school should develop a spirit of scientific enquiry in the students. Their ability to use information should be developed. They may be given training to apply information, to judge, to be able to see the consequences of a course of action, to bring an active forward looking intelligence to bear on a solution, and to think creatively.
6. *School life closely connected with life outside*—The school life should be closely related to the real life of the community so that the students may be trained to grapple with the problems which they will meet in later life. K.G. Saiyidain writes, "No school in the country-side can capture the loyalty or the imagination of the villagers, if it is divorced from the realities of their life and their main interests and preoccupations."
7. *Value of interdependence*—We cannot escape from social relationships in real life. A school must provide situations in which the students may be gradually led to understand the relationships in community, country, and in the world at large. The school should set up situations which provide constant practice in social and co-operative living. It must encourage activities through which the child can make a personal contribution in group enterprise, co-operative instead of competitive individualism.

8. *Opportunities for the full development of the child*—In place of being subject-centred, the present school is child-centred. Our approach is to be psychological and not logical. The school must aim at producing the highest type of personality possible. The personality of the child is an invisible whole and the child is to be taught in body, mind and spirit. A progressive school will aim at providing opportunities to pupils to develop all the three in co-ordination with one another and so to develop the whole personality.
9. *Recognition of individual differences*: Individual differences of children must be appreciated and opportunities provided to them for the growth of their talents in accordance with their capacities. It must be remembered that no two children are alike in native endowment. A school should endeavour to provide for each individual pupil suitable opportunities to use and develop his natural aptitude, and inclination in the special course of studies chosen by him.
10. *Passion for social justice*—India is a land of many castes, creeds, religions and dogmas. The present day school must kindle in the hearts and the minds of the students a passion for social justice based on a sensitiveness to the social evils and exploitation which corrupts the grace of life.
11. *Responsibility for moral education*—In the past, moral education was given by the Church and family. In the modern time the school has been called upon to cater for moral education. An increasing importance is being given to character-building aspects in the schools.
12. *Responsibility for vocational education*—Apprenticeship system provided vocational education in ancient and medieval times. In ancient India vocation was on family basis, the son learnt the vocation by working with the father. In the present complicated economic society, neither of the systems is helpful. It has, therefore, become necessary for the schools to impart vocational education to students.
13. *Freedom for self development*—For the development of a creative mind, freedom for self development and freedom for activity must be given in a school. "This freedom will not be the licence it is sometimes supposed to be. It will be the controlled freedom of an individual living in a community of which he is one part, and his fellow pupils and teachers

are the other parts. It will be a freedom from an exaggerated force or undue influence on the part of the teacher, a freedom for the particular pupil to use his particular talents and capabilities and to develop his personality along his own line, under the guidance of the teacher," writes Ryburn.

14. *School as a place of productive activity*—Practical activities like socially useful productive work and work experience should form an integral part of school programme.
15. *Programme of the school visualised as unity*—The Secondary Education Commission 1952-53 stressed that the entire programme of the school should be visualised as a unity and inspired by a psychologically, congenial and stimulating approach.
16. *School as an epitome of life outside*—The school should serve as a mirror of society's activities but in a simplified, purified and balanced way.
17. *School as a centre of community service*—W.K. Mccharen writes, "A community school is one whose programme is designed for useful and effective learning on the part of the children and one which helps to improve the quality of living in the community, one which serves the total population of the community, and seeks to evolve its purposes out of the interests and needs of the people in community."

Summing up

In the words of S. Bala Krishna Joshi, "A school is not a mere brick and mortar structure housing a miscellany of pupils and teachers; a school is not a market place where knowledge is doled out to unwilling consumers of varying capacities; a school is not a railway platform where a heterogeneous crowd gathers with diverse objects; a school is not a vigorous reformatory where juvenile suspects are kept under vigilant watch; a school is a spiritual organism with a distinctive personality of its own, a school is a vibrant community centre, radiating life and energy all round, a school is a wonderful edifice, resting on the foundation of goodwill—goodwill of the public, goodwill of the parents, good will of the pupils. In a word, a well-conducted school is a happy home, a sacred shrine, a social centre, a state in miniature and bewitching Brinda Van, all beautifully blended into a synthetic structure."

10.4 Cooperation Between the School and the Family (Parents)

Why cooperation—Teachers are interested in the welfare of their students; they want them to develop emotionally ethically, mentally, physically and socially, as do the parents. Hence the obvious need for cooperative efforts on the part of the teachers and students who are the custodians of the welfare of children. George Tomilson has very rightly stated, "Let us fashion our homes and organise our schools with the well being of children always in mind. In particular, remember that any clash between parents and teachers must always be harmful to the child. Harmonious working together can bring us the results we want." In the words of S. Bala Krishna Joshi, "Close cooperation between the parent who is the first teacher and the teacher who is the second parent is the very foundation on which rests the fruit fullness of the training imparted in our institutions."

Methods of securing cooperation—In view of the mass illiteracy in our country, the initiative for the home-school cooperation rests upon the teachers. To quote S. Bala Krishna Joshi, "Parental cooperation cannot be had by learned discussion on the subject, or by periodical pamphlets posted to the parties. It cannot be created overnight. We cannot wake up one fine morning and find the parents pitchforked into cooperation. It is based on a series of silent acts of sincere service of children. It is the natural consummation of devoted deeds of dedication at the shrine of Duty." All possible avenues should be explored to establish contacts with the parents. The following are some of the main methods of securing the cooperation of the parents and making them interested in school work:

1. Dealing with parents in a friendly manner.
2. Personal contacts and mutual consultations about the progress of the child.
3. School reports, that is, casual letters to parents, and progress report cards.
4. Sufficient notice to the parents regarding the change of books or other requirements.
5. Acquainting the parents with the weaknesses of the students well in time.
6. Meeting with the parents of children with in particular class.

7. Inviting parents to witness training and skills displayed by children in various fields.
8. Organising special campaigns like literacy etc.
9. Home visits by teachers.
10. Annual prize distribution function.
11. Open day school and inviting parents to see the regular activities and programmes.
12. Celebration of parents days.
13. Organising career conferences.
14. Organsing lectures on currents educational problems and trends in educational theory and practice.
15. Associating parents in the management of the school.
16. Formation of parents-teachers association.
17. Making the school a centre of community service, adult education classes. Use of school library for parents. Cleanliness of roads and streets etc.
18. Parents participation in the improvement and the school—raising funds for the school, awarding scholarships to the needy, donating books, arranging mid-day meals, constructing rooms, donating and for the school and rendering other several types of assistance to school.

10.5 Community/Society as a Social Group in Education

A community is an organised social group with some degree of 'we feeling'. Browns defines community, "By a community I mean a small, diversified group of people—young and old, male and female, with different skills and abilities, living together as kin neighbours. It is a face to face, primary group in which many of the major functions of life are carried on cooperatively within the group itself." Cook and Cook observe, "a community is an organised way of life within a geographic area. It is in more detail a population aggregate inhabiting a delimitable area, sharing historical heritage, possessing a set of basic institutions, participating in a common life, conscious of local unity and able to act together in solving problems which involve public interest."

Educational functions of a community—A community and especially a village community is undoubtedly an important agency of education. In metropolitan towns like Delhi, minority communities like the Tamil community, Bengali Community have established their education institutions to promote the education of their children. These communities also make specific provision for the conservation and promotion of their culture in the educational institutions.

Some of the important educational functions performed by a community are:

1. Establishing and maintaining educational institutions.
2. Formulating different aims of education, of course keeping in view the national goals.
3. Making provision for universal education.
4. Providing suitable environment.
5. Providing adult education.
6. Establishing libraries and reading rooms.
7. Making provision for vocational education.
8. Setting up community centres.

10.6 Community and the School

A two-way traffic—The observations made by the Secondary Education Commission 1952-53 are worth noting, "What we would like to see is a two-way traffic." This statement implies that on the one hand the school is to organise its entire programme on the aspirations and needs of the community and on the other hand the community is to ensure that the school possesses adequate equipment and other resources for its efficient working. In fact the role of the community comes first as it initiates the opening of the school. Schools are established to serve the community.

The school as a centre of community service—A school can serve the community in the following ways:-

1. Linking curriculum with the needs of the community.
2. Organising social service clubs/leagues or squads for undertaking various programmes of community service,
3. Setting up adult education centres.
4. Celebration of national days and festivals.
5. Providing a special section of library books useful for adults.
6. Formation of parents-teachers association.
7. Organising campaigns like literacy.
8. Making school as a centre for utilsing leisure time meaningfully.

School Improvement Programmes Undertaken by the Community

The following is an illustrative list of school improvement programmes:-

1. Donating land for the school.
2. Construction of a few rooms or the entire school building.
3. White washing or repairs to school building.
4. Construction of school compound walls.
5. Provision of sheds for cooking meals.
6. Donating land for playground.
7. Donation of land for agricultural and other purposes.
8. Painting of blackboards.
9. Repair of school furniture.
10. Supply of free uniform and other articles.
11. Supply of grain, firewood etc.
12. Supply of utensils for free meals.
13. Supply of radio and T.V. sets.
14. Provision of drinking water.
15. Helping school in enrolment and retention of students.
16. Providing first aid etc.

10.7 Peer Groups and Play Groups

Peer group—Peer groups are generally formed during adolescence. In western societies peer groups of the opposite sex are common. In developing countries like India, peer groups are yet in infancy but their influence has been steadily growing. The peer groups primarily operate in the area of vocational, recreational and social activities. They also provide sex education. A peer group assists the individual teenager in the process of self-identification and individualisation. A peer group is fairly independent of external control and supervision. Its members tend to withdraw psychologically and socially from the family, the church and the school but they do not withdraw physically because of their economic dependence. A peer group serves as an important social agency of education during adolescence.

Play group—Play groups of children consisting of children from two or more families exercise a considerable influence on their personality development and consequently on their education.

The following are the educative values of the activities of the play groups.

1. Children learn to cooperate with other children.
2. They learn the qualities of followership as well as leadership.
3. Children develop social attitudes.
4. Children learn to go beyond 'ego-centric interests.
5. Play groups provide opportunities to children to mix up with children of different socio-economic strata of society.
6. Working in play-groups, children learn to respect other's rights and privileges.
7. Play groups provide all the advantages which play in general provides for a child's development in the emotional, mental and physical areas.

10.8 Continuing Correspondence, Distance and Open Education

Nomenclature of continuing and distance education—Several terms for distance education are often used simultaneously depending upon the situation of a particular country. Yet all these terms connote the same meaning. Among the various terms used inter changeably are:

1. Continuing Education, 2. Correspondence Education, 3. Correspondence Learning, 4. Correspondence Teaching, 5. Distance Education, 6. Distance Learning, 7. Distance Teaching, 8. External Degree Programme, 9. External Studies, 10. Extra-Mural System, 11. Home Study, 12. Independent Study, 13. Independent Learning, 14. Life-long Education, 15. Non-Formal Education, 16. Off Campus Study, 17. Open Education, 18. Open Learning, 19. Open School, 20. Open University, 21. Out of School Education, 22. Postal Courses, 23. Teach Yourself Programme, 24. Tele University, 25. University of the Air, 26. University Without Walls.

Distance education caters to all sections of society and especially to those who, on account of several reasons are unable to pursue full time regular courses. In service personnel, housewives, disabled persons, under privileged people, people residing in remote areas, school drop outs, etc. all can avail of the courses offered.

Characteristics, Merits and Demerits of Distance Education and Formal Education

Distance Education	*Formal Education*
1. It concentrates on the needs of the learner.	1. It puts the institution first.
2. It takes into account the convenience of the learner.	2. It is teacher centred.
3. It is flexible in the sense that a course can be completed in a number of years.	3. A course is tobe complemented within a given period.
4. It is indirect education as it is not centred on face to face communication.	4. It is direct education as it is centred on face to face communication.
5. It uses media like computer, radio and television.	5. Print word is the most prominent element.
6. It is part-time education.	6. It is full-time education.
7. It is less expensive.	7. It is relatively expensive.
8. It lacks a certain kind of vitality which only the presence of a teacher can generate.	8. It provides vitality with the presence of the teacher.
9. It is flexible with regard to qualification for entry.	9. It is rigid.
10. It may or may not be for a degree or diploma.	10. It is for a degree or diploma
11. There is separation of the learner from his peer group.	11. Learners are in close contact.
12. It is a system of mass education.	12. Education is imparted in a group.
13. It is available even in areas where there is no school or college.	13. It is not possible without an educational institution.

Contd.

14.It is available even to those with poor health or disadvantageous physical conditions or any psychological conditions that inhibit them from undergoing institutionalised education.	14.It is not available to such groups as they cannot attend educational institutions.
15.It looks for unorthodox modes and means of educating all those who are willing to be educated.	15.It depends upon conventional means of education.

Brief history of distance education in India—University of Delhi was the first university to starts correspondence courses in higher education in 1962.

Andhra Pradesh opened the first Open University in the country in 1982.

The Indira Gandhi National Open University (IGNOU), New Delhi came into being in 1985.

The open school providing school education through correspondence courses was established in 1979.

Distance education covers about 11 per cent of the total enrolment in higher education.

Objective of the open university—Broadly, the objectives of an Open University are:

1. To provide greater equality of opportunity and access to higher education;
2. To provide educational opportunities for those who missed such opportunities when they were young and joined careers;
3. To provide opportunities to those adults who would like to have access to higher education throughout their live; and
4. To help those who want to learn new subjects or renew or update their knowledge while in service.

Courses—Long-term programmes include degree courses, undergraduate as well as postgraduate courses. The short-term programmes comprise diploma and certificate courses. In addition, there will be a fairly heavy emphasis on continuing and extension education.

Features and Merits of the Open University

1. Relaxed entry regulations—it does not debar a student from studying on account of lack of formal qualifications.
2. Self-pacing—one can study according to one's own pace and convenience.
3. Freedom and flexibility in choosing any combination of courses.
4. Transfer of credit from one programme to another and from one University to another, either conventional or non-conventional.
5. Education is home-based and not classroom-based.
6. Instead of depending on the teacher only for teaching, communication technology is used to provide multi-media teaching.
7. Quality of teaching is high because it taps the best expertise available in the country for preparing its educational programmes.
8. It offers not only degree, diploma and certificate courses but also other programmes such as extension, enrichment community oriented and continuing education.

Making Continuing Distance and Open Education More Effective

1. Proper planning and announcement of the programme.
2. Proper selection of editors.
3. Preparation of adequate material in regional languages.
4. Optimum utilisation of infrastructural facilities.
5. Printing of material—without errors
6. Suitable guidelines for correspondence students.
7. Coordination with postal authorities.
8. Regular checking of assignments.
9. Cost-effectiveness of distance education.
10. Systematic utilisation of educational technology.
11. Periodical evaluation of the programme.

10.9 Mass Media as an Agency of Education

Meaning of mass media—Mass media are means of communication that reach a large number of learners or people, with a common message.

In early times, the teacher was the only medium of communication for children. He taught his students orally. During the course of time the invention of the printing press, led to the printing of books. Then came newspapers. Now for quite some time new mass media like radio and T.V. are increasingly used in education. They reach large members and also help in improving the quality of education.

Significance of mass media in education—Prof. Marshall McLuhan who has written extensively on 'understanding media' explains the relationship of the electronic media and education in these words, "In education this means that the one-way method of imparting knowledge to passive students has ended. They exist and live already in a field of information which the new media have created for them since. they were born (true of western society of USA, Canada, for example) a rich field which teaches more than the absolute school curricula....'the walls of the classroom fade away'. Education will no longer depend entirely on obtaining knowledge through the printed page. The vital approach to learning is fast changing to total sensory involvement (visual, auditory, motor and tactile) in the process of acquiring knowledge." Another media expert Carlton W.H. Erickson observes, "In recent years technology has swept through society from research laboratories into manufacturing communications, the space age and finally now education.

Educational implications of the mass media—The mass media are expected to be useful in education in the following respects:

1. Providing quality learning experiences.
2. Catering to larger number of students.
3. Offering communication advantages in terms of physical control of stimuli—magnifying pictures and films—enabling close observation.
4. Providing multi-sensory stimuli auditory and visual stimuli and multirange stimuli.
5. Serving as storage banks of information on pictures, audio and video tapes, discs,, films and slides—useful for reusing replaying and reviewing in the classroom.

10.10 The Radio as an Educational Aid

Significance of the Radio as an Educational Aid

R.G. Reynolds describes the potential of the radio as an instructional aid "Radio is the most significant medium for education in its broadest sense that has been introduced in the turn of the 20th century. As a supplement to classroom teaching its possibilities are almost unlimited. Its teaching possibilities are not confined to the five or six hours of the school day. It is available from early morning till long after midnight. By utilising the rich educational and cultural offerings of the radio, children and adults in communities, however remote, have access to the best of the world's stores of knowledge and art. Some day its use as an educational instrument will be as common place as textbooks and blackboards."

The chief merits of the radio as an instrument of educational aid may be listed as under:

1. Enriching of school programme.
2. Furnishing latest material.
3. Bringing the school into contact with the world around.
4. Developing critical thinking.
5. Developing leisure time interest and appreciation.
6. Providing opportunities for student participation.
7. Providing an alternative approach to the education of out of school children.
8. Serving as a training component for teachers.
9. Imparting vocational skills.
10. Popularising science with a view to developing scientific outlook.
11. Promoting emotional and national integration.
12. Providing information about population education, energy conservation, preservation of wild life etc.

Suggestions for Improving School Broadcasting Programmes

1. The school broadcasts should not be merely course lessons but should have a wider horizon of application in day-to-day life.

2. The school broadcasts should be planned according to the needs of the syllabus, students and concerning teachers.
3. Teachers should occasionally meet, discuss and plan the type of assistance required on mass media instructional facilities.
4. The radio programmes should be intended to give supplementary information to the various topics in the syllabus.
5. Good planning and administration is highly needed so as to make the programmes effective and worthwhile.
6. Broadcasting time should be suitable to schools.
7. Broadcasts should be made in a pleasing style.
8. Broadcasts should be made in easy and simple language.
9. Every school should have at least one member of the staff trained in the media. It will be proper if a few teachers are given training in this filed.
10. Adequate feedback should be provided.
11. There should be proper follow-up on school broadcasting programmes.
12. Adequate listening facilities should be provided in schools.

A brief history of school broadcasting—The year 1920 is termed as a great landmark in the history of school broadcasting. The British Broadcasting Corporation (B.B.C.) is a pioneer in the field. Ever since its start in 1920, school broadcasting has made rapid strides. In India, Bombay Radio Station was the first to put out items of general interest to school children in 1929. From April 20, 1929, the Corporation of Madras introduced regular school broadcasts for half an hour on all weekdays. Similar programmes were introduced by Calcutta Station in 1932.

The All India Radio (Akashvani) has daily school programmes on a variety of topics.

Questions and Problems

A. Essay-Type Questions

1. Distinguish between formal informal and non-formal education. Explain the significance of each.
2. Show how home and school are complementary to each other in educating a child.
3. Discuss the role played by the home as an agency of education. What changes are noticeable in present and traditional roles?
4. Describe the role played by an active agency of education.
5. "School is the most important agency of education." Discuss.
6. "School is a miniature society." Explain this statement and point out the role of the school in education.
7. "School is an epitome of society". Elucidate this statement and bring out the role of the school.
8. What do you mean by mass media? What is its role as an agency of education?
9. Discuss the functions of the family in the education of the child.

B. Short-Answer Type Questions

10. What is the role of the peer group in the development of a child's personality?
11. In what ways can the school and the community cooperate?
12. State the function of the community as an agency of education.
13. State briefly the significance of continuing education.
14. Point out the importance of an Open University. What are its chief characteristics?

11 Curriculum

Meaning and Definition of Curriculum

Curriculum is the sum total of the school's efforts to influence learning whether in the class-room, on the playground or out of school. In fact curriculum has been described as, "the environment in motion." It includes "the totality of experiences that a pupil receives through the manifold activities that go on in the school— in the classroom, library, laboratory, workshop, playgrounds and in the numerous informal contacts between teachers and pupils. In this case, the whole life of the school becomes the curriculum which can touch the life of the students at all points and help in the of evaluation balanced personality. Curriculum is considered as a tool in the hands of the artist (the teacher) to mould his material (the pupils) in accordance with his ideal in his studio (the school) "The curriculum is an aid in the process of adjusting the child to the environment in which he functions from day to day and in wider environment in which he will have to organise his activities later.

Definition of Curriculum

According to the American Association of School Administrators (1953) "In recent years the curriculum has been most commonly defined as all of the directed learning experiences of children and youth under the influence of the school".

Blond's Encyclopedia of Education (1969) defines "curriculum as all the experiences which a pupil has under the guidance of the school."

J Francis Brown (1984) states, "curriculum is all the learning which is planned and guided by the school."

Derek Rowntree in *Dictionary of Education* (1981) notes, "curriculum can refer to the total structure of ideas and activities developed by an educational institution to meet the learning needs of students and to achieve desired educational aims."

Education Commission 1964-66 has conceived the school curriculum "as the total of learning experience that the school provides for the pupils through all the manifold activities in the school and outside, that are carried on under its supervision. From this point of view, the distinction between curricular and extra-curricular work ceases to exist, and a school camp and games and sports are curricular or rather co-curricular activities."

Good's Dictionary of Education considers curriculum as "a body of prescribed educative experiences under school supervision, designed to provide an individual with the best possible training and experience to fit him for the society of which he is a part or to qualify him for a trade or profession."

J.P. Hills in *Dictionary of Education* (1982) writes, "A simple way of considering the curriculum in to see it in terms of four facts: content, methods, purposes, evaluation."

C.K. Nolan and W. Cook Watter in *Encyclopedia of Educational Research* (1960) regards curriculum as "all the educational experiences that a learner has under the guidance of a teacher."

Etymologically the term 'curriculum' is derived from the Latin word 'currere' which means 'run'. Thus Curriculum means 'a course' to be run for reaching a goal.

From above, the concept of curriculum may be explained as:

1. A curriculum includes all the subjects activities and experiences for the development of the child.
2. All these subjects, activities and experiences are under the guidance and supervision of teachers.
3. All these subjects, activities and experiences are offered in the school inside the classroom, in the farm, the laboratory in the workshop, in the playground etc.

4. Some portion of the curriculum is for all pupils while other portions may be in accordance with individual needs..
5. A diversified curriculum is provided in Class XI in the 10 + 2 pattern of education.

National Goals

Curriculum and modernisation of societ—The modernisation of a society is tied up with the contents of the curriculum. Broadly speaking this implies in terms of curriculum objectives:

1. The development of a scientific outlook from early childhood.
2. Loosening of bonds of dogmatism and dispelling of superstition, fatalism, dogmatism and passive resignation.
3. Promoting the capacity to think rationally to enquire and judge for himself and to contribute to the stock of human knowledge.
4. The development of productive capacity.
5. The development a synthesising attitude towards science and culture.
6. Development of values of a secular, socialist and a democratic state.
7. Development of values of emotional integration and national unity.

Philosophical, Psychological and Sociological Basis of Curriculum Construction

Neither philosophy nor sociology nor psychology can on its own justify a curriculum to be used as the sole basis for curriculum planning. Illustration 11.1 though oversimplified illustrates the complexity of the task :

Patterns of curriculum organisation—Following are some of the important patterns of curriculum organisition:

1. Subject-centred pattern of curriculum.
2. Student centred pattern of curriculum.
3. Activity centred pattern of curriculum.
4. Experience centred pattern of curriculum.
5. Work centred pattern of curriculum.
6. Correlated pattern of curriculum.
7. Integrated pattern of curriculum.
8. Core pattern of curriculum.

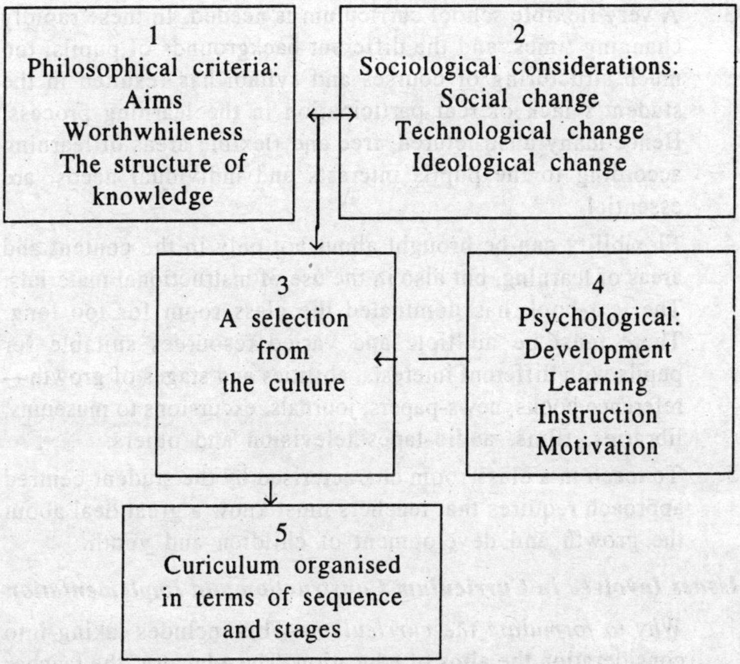

Illustration 11.1 Showing Curriculum Planning

Flexible and Student's Needs Centred Curriculum

The student-centred curriculum considers the student a 'hero' in the drama of education and places more emphasis on the student rather than the subjects. It should be in accordance with the three A's—Age, Ability and Aptitude of the student.

The following are the important characteristics of a child-centred curriculum:

1. The interests of the pupils facilitate their learning. Most of the young pupil's interests are socially derived; hence it makes the programme more life-related.
2. In terms of the highly developed Indian social organisation, co-operation is important. Therefore finding common interests and working together in terms of a unifying element bring about growth in life-related skills.

3. A very flexible school curriculum is needed. In these rapidly changing times, and the different backgrounds of pupils, too much structuring of courses and syllabi has resulted in the student's lack of real participation in the learning process. Hence many unstructured, free and flexible areas of learning according to the pupils interests and individual needs, are essential.
4. Flexibility can be brought about not only in the content and areas of learning, but also in the use of instructional materials. The text-book has dominated the class room for too long. There must be multiple and varied resources suitable for pupils with different interests, abilities and stages of growth—reference books, news-papers, journals, excursions to museums, libraries, films, audio-tapes television and others.
5. To teach in a class-room characterised by the student-centred approach requires that teachers must know a great deal about the growth and development of children and youth.

Issues Involved in Curriculum Construction and Implementation

1. *Why to formulate the curriculum*—This includes taking into consideration the aims of education. The educator, the teacher and the learner must be clear about the aims of education so that right efforts are made.
2. *For whom to formulate the curriculum*—The curriculum is to be formulated for the learner. It is, therefore very important that the curriculum shall be formulated according to the needs of the students, their individual differences, ages and stages.
3. *What to include in the curriculum*—This leads to the contents of the curriculum and the curriculum is described as the environment in motion'. In a broader sense it includes various subjects, activities and experiences.
4. *Where to use the curriculum*—The curriculum is used in and outside the school—in the classroom, library, laboratory, workshop, playgrounds and in the numerous informal contacts between teachers and pupils etc.
5. *When to use the curriculum*—This is concerned with the different stages of the child so that 'motivational aspects' may be handled satisfactorily.

6. *How to use the curriculum*—This involves the knowledge and techniques of various methods of teaching—learning for making the teaching— learning process dynamic, effective and inspirational.
7. *Who is to use the curriculum*—The teacher and the students are the main consumers. The teachers must understand themselves also.
8. *Who is to formulate the curriculum*—The formation of curriculum is a joint enterprise in which teachers should play a dominant role. The views of the learners should also be given their due importance.
9. *What type of resources to be used in the curriculum*—With the rapid advances in science and technology new learning resources are coming into use. A judicious use of the traditional and modern audio-visual aids should be made.
10. *How to evaluate the outcomes of the curriculum implementation*—This is concerned with the success of the learners as well as of the teachers. Outcomes are evaluated by a number of tests.
11. *How to bring about the required changes in the curriculum*—Curriculum must be evaluated from time to time so as to make it conform with the changing needs.

Principles of Curriculum Construction

1. Conservation of Culture.
2. Principle of future-orientation.
3. Principle of creativity.
4. Principle of activity.
5. Principle of preparation for life.
6. Principle of child-centred education.
7. Principle of maturity.
8. Principle of individual differences.
9. Principle of horizontal and vertical articulation.
10. Principle of linking with life.
11. Principle of balances of activities and subjects.
12. Principle of flexibility.
13. Principle of leisure.

14. Principle of productivity.
15. Principle of nationalism.
16. Principle of democracy.
17. Principle of socialism.
18. Principle of secularism.
19. Principle of internationalism.

Teachers Participation in Curriculum Planning

Recognition of the fact that no real progress can take place without the teacher' involvement in curriculum development came only a few decades ago even in the advanced countries of the west and that too after numerous failures in curriculum revision. Prior to that curriculum revision was done in much the sameway as it has been done in India. The decision about the overall purpose of schools and universities, the general scope and structures of their programmes was taken by public men, experts and administrators without the benefit of any real participation by teachers. Today, planning and action by teachers are promoted in these countries. Individual and cooperative efforts by teachers to decide when, how and what to teach, to revise courses, select content, plan units and produce teaching aids has become a common practice. The reliance on text-books and prescribed courses of study has diminished.

Several curriculum development studies have clearly shown that a significant improvement has taken place where the participation of teachers was both more extensive and more inclusive and where more teachers were involved in decision-making and in the production of materials. This led Krug to conclude in 1957 that "teacher participation in curriculum planning today is to be regarded not as a pleasant gesture to the teachers, but rather as an indispensable part of the process."

Theoretically speaking teachers may be called curriculum makers but seldom has the business of curriculum making in India secured the wide-spread participation of the general body of teachers. In spite of all the lip service to the teachers key role in improving instruction, their participation in curriculum planning and preparation of content and teaching materials has so far received very little practical recognition. Indian teachers have been merely, "implementing to their best of abilities and resources the curriculum and syllabi prepared by outsiders and prescribed by the State Directorate of Education. In actual practice the 'textbook' has become synonymous with the 'curriculum' in so far as the actual implementation of the curriculum is concerned."

Sometimes representatives of teachers are associated in the development of the curriculum at the national and state levels. The NCERT and State Councils of Educational Research and Training organise various courses for teachers to provide opportunities for participation in curriculum development and implementation.

Curriculum and Syllabus

A UNESCO publication entitled "Preparing Textbook Manuscripts' (1970) has differentiated between the curriculum and syllabus: "The curriculum sets out the subjects to be studied, their order and sequence and so ensures some balance between humanities and science and consistency in the study of subjects, thus facilitating inter-subject links. It follows that the curriculum determines the amount of school-times allotted to each subject, the aim of teaching each subject, the place of the motor skills which take time to acquire and, possibly, the variations between rural and urban school teaching. The curriculum in the schools of developing countries is often directly related to the requirements for developments. The syllabus determines the basic content of instructions in a given subject and the range of knowledge and skills which the pupils must acquire and establish in detail the themes and individual points to be studied in each school year... the syllabus is a refined detail of the curriculum at a particular stage of learning for a particular subject."

Questions and Problems

A. Essay-Type Questions

1. Explain the term curriculum. How is it related to national developments? What is its philosophical and sociological basis?
2. What is curriculum? Why should it be made flexible?
3. Explain the concept of the child-centred curriculum. In what ways is it different from the subject centred curriculum?
4. What do you mean by Curriculum? What are the various issues involved in its construction and implementation?

B. Short-Answer Type Questions

5. List the principles of curriculum construction.
6. Differentiate between child-centred and subject centred curriculum.
7. State the role of teachers in curriculum planning.

Part II

Education in a Developing (Emerging) Society

12

British System of Education in India

State of Education Before the British Rule in India

The indigenous system of education prevalent in India before the advent of the British rule was well developed. Prof. A.N. Basu in his book *Education in Modern India* has observed, "The elementary system was intended for the masses. It was a widespread system of education consisting of numerous primary schools scattered all over the country-side. Practically every village had its primary school." It is said that in Bengal alone, there were around the year 1835, a hundred thousand such schools. M.R. Paranjape has also observed, "At the beginning of the nineteenth century, there existed a fairly wide spread organisation for primary education in most parts of India."

The most significant feature of indigenous education in India was that schools were not meant for a particular caste or class of society. They were open to everyone who wanted to study. Higher education was also easily available.

Educational Policy of the British in India

Howell in his book entitled *Education in British India (1872)* has aptly described the educational policy of the British in India. "Education in India during the British Government, was first ignored, then violently and successively opposed, then conducted on a system now universally admitted to be enormous and finally placed in its present footing."

Macaulay as the architect of the English system of education in India—Lord Macaulay came to India as Law Member of the Council of Governor-General of India in June 1834. He was a learned scholar of English literature. He was appointed as the Chairman of the Society of Public Instruction, Bengal by Lord William Bentick, the Governor-General of the East India Company. At that time a violent controversy regarding the medium of education was in full swing. Lord Macaulay was asked to give his views.

Lord Macaulay submitted his Minutes in March 1835 which were accepted and consequently laid the foundations of the English system of education. In his Minutes Lord Macaulay made the following important observations.

1. A single shelf of a good European literature was worth the whole native literature of India and Arabia."
2. About the teaching of Sanskrit and Arabic, Macaulay wrote in his Minutes. "We are to teach false history, false astronomy, false medicine, because we find them in the company of a false religion".
3. He observed in his Minutes that it was possible through English education to bring about " a class of persons, Indian in blood and colour, but English in tastes, in opinion, in morals, and intellect."
4. About the English language he said, " It stands preeminent even among the languages of the West... It is likely to become the language of Commerce throughout the seas of the East.

In a letter to his father in 1836, Macaulay wrote, " Hindus are much influenced with education. There is no Hindu who may keep faith in his religion after studying English. I have full confidence that if your education policy succeeds, there will be no idolator left in Bengal. All this will be done naturally without my religious preaching and interference."

Bentick's resolution, 1835—William Bentick the Governor-General accepted Lord Macaulay's Minutes and passed a resolution in 1835, "the great object of the British Government ought to be the promotion of European literature and science among the natives of India: and that all the funds appropriated for the purpose of education would be best employed on English education alone."

After Bentick's proclamation, schools began to be established to teach European literature and science. Preference in Government service began to be given to those who were educated in English schools.

Significant Events in Education from 1835 to 1947

The Despatch of 1854—The Despatch of 1854 popularly known as Wood's Despatch after the name of Charles Wood, the President of the Board of Control, became a landmark in the history of education in India. It was made very clear that the object of education was the diffusion of European knowledge.

Establishment of universities 1857—The establishment of Universities in the Year 1857 was another landmark in the English system of education in India.

The Hunter Commission of 1882—The Commission anticipated a diversified instruction at the secondary stage of education.

The University Commission 1902—The main impact of this Commission was that secondary schools had to be recognised by the Universities.

Gokhale's resolution on primary education (1913-1914)—Gokhale's resolution on primary education was rejected in the Imperial Council but it focused attention on primary education.

The Sadler Commission or the Calcutta University Commission (1917)—It contained the most comprehensive study of the Indian system of education from the secondary stage to the university.

Hartog Committee Report (1929)—Its main feature was that it defined the concept of wastage and stagnation in primary education and suggested remedies.

Abbot Wood Report (1936-37)—Two experts Abbot and Wood made recommendations on technical and general education.

Wardha Report or Basic Education (1935)—Gandhi realised that the system of education introduced by the English rulers in India did not meet the needs and aspirations of India. He therefore, evolved a new system of education known as Nai Talim or Basic Education.

The Sargent report (1944)—The Central Advisory Board of Education asked John Sargent who was the Educational Adviser to prepare a report on post-war the educational development. This report contained a detailed review of the system of education and visualised a system of universal, compulsory and free education for all boys and girls between the ages of 6 and 14, the senior Basic or the middle school being the final stage in the school carrer of the majority of the future citizens.

Main Drawbacks of British System of Education in India

1. It was not related to the needs of India.
2. It was an urban system of education in a rural country.
3. English dominated the curriculum.
4. The system of education was too bookish.
5. It was examination-oriented.
6. It was very wasteful.
7. It produced clerks by and large.
8. It followed a single track.
9. It was unplanned.
10. It neglected vocational, commercial and technical training.
11. It was very expensive.
12. It created a wide gulf. Between an elite class educated in English and the masses who remained illiterate.
13. It led to contempt for manual work.
14. The rate of illiteracy become very high.

Positive effects of english education—It is believed by several thinkers that the introduction of the English language led to the opening of the doors of the West to the East. They are also of the view that even at present after about five decades of independence though the influence of tradition persists, the impact of the west on the attitudes, dress habits and manners etc. of the educated class obvious. Much of the organistation of a democratic state, the structure of its institutions and the political principles underlying them are largely European in inspiration. Similarly, it is said that the social reforms in the Hindu society and the movement for the removal of untouchability reflect western influence to a considerable extent.

Questions and Problems

A. Essay-Type Questions

1. Elucidate the merits and the demerits of the educational system introduced by the British.
2. Who was Lord Macaulay? Why did he introduce the English system of education in India? What were its efforts?

B. Short-Answer Type Questions

3. Briefly describe the main characteristics of the system of education in India.
4. Write a note on the positive effects of the system of education as introduced by the British in India.

13 Education in the Indian Constitution

Constitution as the Mirror of Educational Philosophy

The Constitution of a country reflects the aspiration, hopes, ideals and values of its people. It is therefore, natural that education should find an important place in this important document. It provides the concept of the economic and social order for which the youth of the country should be educated.

The Preamble of the constitution is described as an identity card of the constitution. It contains the 'epitome' of the objectives to which the people of a country are permanently committed.

The Preamble to the Constitution of India summarises its aim and objectives. It reads as follows:

We the People of India, having solemnly resolved to constitute India into a *Sovereign Socialist Secular Democratic Republic* and to secure to all its citizens:

Justice, social economic and political;

Liberty of thought, expression, belief, faith and worship:

Equality of status and of opportunity, and promote among them all;

Fraternity assuring the dignity of the individual and the unity and integrity of the Nation;

In Our Constituent Assembly this twenty-sixth day of November, 1949 do *Hereby Adopt, Enact and Give to Ourselves This Constitution.*

Note: Three new terms—Socialist, Secular and Integrity were added to the original text of the Preamble when in 1976 the Government passed the 42nd Amendment.

Education in the Concurrent List—Till 1976 education was a State subject but with the 42nd Amendment to the Constitution which received the President's assent on December 18, 1976, it was put on the Concurrent List.

Various Constitutional Provisions Relating to Education

Article 21A. (Inserted in 2002) Right to Education. The state shall provide free and compulsory education to all children of the age of six to fourteen years in such manner as the state, by law, determine. This article was inserted in the constitution in the year 2002 by the constitution (Eighty-sixth Amendment, Act, 2002).

27. Freedom as to payment of taxes for promotion of any particular religion—No person shall be compelled to pay any taxes, the proceeds of which are specifically appropriated in payment of expenses for the promotion or maintenance of any particular religion or religious denomination.

28. Freedom as to attendance at religious instruction or religious worship in certain educational institutions—(1) No religious instruction shall be provided in any educational institution wholly maintained out of State funds.

Article 28 (2): Nothing in clause (1) shall apply to an educational institution which is administered by the State but has been established under any endowment or trust which requires that religious instruction shall be imparted in such institutions.

Article 28 (3): No person attending any educational institutions recognised by the State or receiving aid out of State funds shall be required to take part in any religious instruction that may be imparted in such institution or to attend any religious worship what may be conducted in such institution or in any premises attached thereto unless such person or if such person is a minor, his guardian has given his consent thereto.

Article 29 Protection of minorities language and culture— (1) Any section of the citizens residing in the territory of India or any part thereof having a distinct language, script or culture of its own shall have the right to conserve the same.

(2) No citizen shall be denied admission into educational institution maintained by the State or receiving aid out of State funds on grounds only of religion, race, caste, language or any of them.

Article 30. Right of minorities to establish and administer educational institutions—(1) All minorities, whether based on religion or language shall have the right to establish and administer educational institutions of their choice.

(1) In making any law providing for the compulsory acquisition of any property of an educational institution established and administered by a minority, referred to in clause (1), the State shall ensure that the amount fixed by or determined under such law for the acquisition of such property in such as would not restrict or abrogate the right guaranteed under that clause.

(2) The State shall not, in granting aid to educational institutions discriminate against any educational institution on the ground that it is under the management of a minority, whether based on religion or language.

Article 45 Provision for early childhood and education to children below the age of six years. The state shall endeavour to provide early childhood care and education for all children until they complete the age of six years. (This was substituted for previous Article 45).

Article 46. Promotion of educational and economic interests of Scheduled Castes, Scheduled Tribes and other weaker sections— The State shall promote with special care the educational and economic interests of the weaker sections of the people, and in particular, of the Scheduled Castes and the Scheduled Tribes, and shall protect them for social injustice and all forms of exploitation.

Article 337. Special provision with respect to educational grants for the benefit of Anglo-Indian community—During the first three financial years after the commencement of this Constitution, the same grants, if any, shall be made by the Union and by each State 2 for the benefit of the Anglo-Indian community in respect of education as are made in the financial year ending on the thirty-first day of March 1948.

Article 350A. Facilities for instruction in mother tongue at primary stage—It shall be the endeavour of every State and of every local authority within the State to provide adequate facilities for instruction in the mother-tongue at the primary stage of education to children belonging to linguistic minority groups and the President may issue such direction to any state as he considers necessary or proper for securing the provision of such facilities

Article 62. The institutions known at the commencement of this Constitution as the National Library, the Indian Museum, the Imperial War Museum, the Victoria Memorial and the Indian War Memorial, any other like institution financed by the Government of India wholly or in part and declared by Parliament by law to be an institution of national importance.

Article 63. The institutions known at the commencement of this Constitution as the Banaras Hindu University, the Aligarh Muslim University and the [3][Delhi University; The University established in pursuance of article 371E] any other institution declared by Parliament by law to be an institution of national importance.

Article 64. Institutions for scientific or technical education financed by the Government of India wholly or in part and declared by Parliament by law to be institutions of national importance.

Article 65. Union agencies and institutions for—

(a) Professional, vocational or technical training, including the training of police officers; or

(b) the promotion of special studies or research; or

(c) scientific or technical assistance in the investigation or detection of crime.

Article 66. Co-ordination and determination of standards in institutions for higher education or research and scientific and technical institutions.

Article 67. Ancient and historical monuments and records, and archaeological sites and remains, 4 [declared by or under law made by Parliament] to be of national importance.

Educational and cultural relations with foreign countries— Entry 13 of the Union List—Participation of international conferences, associations and other bodies and implementing of decisions made thereat.

3. Subs. by the Constitution (Thirty-second Amendment) Act, 1973, s. 4, for "Delhi University and" (w.e.f. 1-7-1974)

4. Subs. by the Constitution (Seventh Amendment) Act, 1956, s. 27, for "declared by Parliament by law."

Responsibilities of the Central and State Governments in Education

Responsibilities of the Central Government in Education—A perusal of the constitutional provisions reveals that the Central Government is expected to play a significant role in the field of education. Though the Ministry of Human Resource Development, Department of Education, Government of India, discharges the major responsibility in the field of Education on behalf of the Government of India, yet there are other Ministries at the Centre which also perform functions in the field of education. Broadly speaking, the following are the major functions performed by the Ministry of Human Resource Development, Government of India.

1. *Planning of education*—So far eight Five-Year Plans have been formulated. Educational Planning is an integral part of the overall planning of national development.
2. *Appointment of committees and commissions for educational reforms*—Since independence over a hundred committees and commissions have been appointed to suggest educational reforms.
3. *Setting up organisations*—To carry out educational plans, the Government of India has set up organisations like the University Grants Commission (UGC), the National Council of Educational Research and Training (NCERT), National Institute of Educational Planning and Administration (NIEPA) etc.
4. *Direction and advice*—The Central Government provides direction and advice through the Central Advisory Board of Education and the conferences of Education Ministries, Secretaries and Directors of Education.
5. *Control*—Since the centre provides grants to states, it exercises a check on the proper utilisation of grants for educational purposes.
6. *Equalisation of educational opportunities*—The Centre has initiated a number of schemes in the field of education for providing adequate opportunities.

7. *Administration of education in Union Territories*—The Centre is directly responsible for education in a Union Territory.
8. *Clearing house function*—The Department of Education serves as a depository of information and ideas of education, research, training and statistics. From time to time it brings out useful information on various aspects of education.
9. *Liaison with UNESCO*—The Department of Education carries out some programmes in cooperation with UNESCO. The Indian National Commission for cooperation with UNESCO is that agency through which these programmes are organised.
10. *Promotion of cultural contact*—The Department of Education also takes suitable steps for the promotion and propagation of cultural contacts not only within the country but also outside.
11. *Opening central institutes*—The Department of Education is directly responsible for the running of a few universities, National Libraries, Museums, Art Galleries, Central Schools, and Navodaya Vidyalayas.

Central Advisory Board of Education

The Central Advisory Board of Education is the oldest and the most important advisory body of the Government of India on education. The Union Minister of Human Resource Development is its Chairman. It includes distinguished educationists from all parts of the country and representatives of the Government of India and States, the Parliament and the Universities. The functions of the Board include advising to advise the Government of India on educational development and also appointing committees for important educational matters.

Role of the State Government in Education

Education, though on the Concurrent List, the State Governments have the major responsibility in the field of education. The State Departments of Education, which are the principal agency of the State Governments, are expected to perform the following functions:-

1. Establishment and maintenance of State run educational institutions.
2. Giving grants-in-aid to private recognised educational institutions.

3. Organising inspection and supervision of schools.
4. Upgrading curricula periodically, preparing textbooks, teachers guides and other aids.
5. Giving recognition to schools.
6. Prescribing the standards to be maintained in consultation with expert bodies.
7. Recruiting teachers and determining other conditions of service.
8. Establishing and maintaining State Evaluation Units.
9. Collecting and disseminating educational statistics.
10. Carrying out education reforms as suggested by expert bodies appointed by the State or the Central Government.
11. Encouraging voluntary organisation to participate in the running and maintenance of schools.

Education in the Concurrent List

Meaning of Concurrence in Education—Concurrence in Education implies that both the Central Government and the State Governments have the right to make legislation and education. In case of any dispute on any educational matter, the Central Government would have the overriding powers.

As already mentioned subject to certain promises education was a state subject till 1976. Thereafter it came on the Concurrent List.

Arguments in Favour of Making Education a Concurrent Subject

1. Ensuring uniformity in the pattern of education all over the country.
2. Better implementation of educational policies.
3. Better utilisation of educational funds.
4. Quality leadership from the Central Government.
5. More possibility of improvement in educational standards.

Arguments Against Making Education a Concurrent Subject

1. Decentralisation of education is in accordance with democratic ideals.
2. States are in a better position to appreciate local educational needs

3. Education in the hands of the Central Government only is likely to lead to red tapism.
4. Educational interests of the minorities are likely to be more safeguarded under State Governments.
5. The backward regions have better chances of getting more attention.
6. According to the dictum 'Unity in Diversity', a State government would be in a better position to conserve and promote its own culture.

A Meaningful Partnership

The National Policy of Education 1986 revised in 1992 has described the relationship between the Central Government and State Governments as that of 'a meaningful partnership'. The 1986 policy in part 3, para 13 has observed. "The Constitutional Amendment of 1976, which includes Education in the Concurrent List, was a far-reaching step whose implications—substantive financial and administrative—require a new sharing of responsibility between the Union Government and the States in respect of this vital area of national life. While the role and responsibility of the States in regard to education will remain essentially unchanged, the Union Government would accept a larger responsibility to reinforce the national and integrative character of education to maintain quality and standards (including those of the teaching profession at all levels), to study and monitor the educational requirements of the country as a whole in regard to manpower for development to carter to the needs of research and advanced study, to look after the international aspects of education, culture and Human Resource Development and, in general, to promote excellence at all levels of the educational pyramid throughout the country. Concurrence signifies a partnership which is at once meaningful and challenging; the National Policy will be oriented towards giving effect to it in letter and spirit."

Questions and Problems

A. Essay-Type Questions

1. State the provisions that have been made in the Indian Constitution for education.
2. " We are not in favour of fragmenting education and putting one part in the Concurrent List and the other part in the State List." Examine this statement.
3. What is concurrence in education? Are you in favour of putting education in the Concurrent List. Support your answer with arguments.

B. Short-Answer Type Questions

4. Explain the meaning of 'meaningful partnership' in education.
5. List the important functions of the Central Government in education.
6. Point out the role of a State Government in education.

14

Education and the Changing Indian Society
(Education and National Development)

Emerging Concerns and Imperatives

India is on the move towards transformation from a traditional society into a new society based on the aspirations, ideals and ideas contained in the philosophy enshrined in its constitution. These are the directions and guidelines on which our entire socio-economic political system is to be based. These may be seen the light of eight explosions as indicated below:

Explosion	*Changes Needed in Society*
1. Explosion of aspirations and expectations	Society is to be based on the ideals of quality, fraternity, justice and liberty.
2. Explosion of fundamentalism	i. Promotion of secular ideals, ii. Emotional integration, iii. Appreciation of a composite culture.

Contd.

3. Explosion of information and knowledge	i. Rational approach ii. Shunning superstitions iii. International outlook.
4. Explosion of population	Small family norm and control of population.
5. Explosion of poverty	i. Raising living standards ii. Bridging the gulf between the rich and the poor.
6. Explosion of pollution	i. Protection of environment ii. Protection of health.
7. Explosion of science and technology	i. Making the optimum use of science ii. Developing harmony between science and culture.
8. Explosion of corruption	Developing ethical, moral and spiritual values.

Educational Implications of the New Concern and Imperatives of the Changing Indian Society

It is a truism to say that there is hardly any field or sector of national development which is not influenced by education in some form or other. The National Policy on Education 1986, as modified in 1992 has observed, "The country has reached a stage in its economic and technical development when a major effort must be made to derive the maximum benefits from the assets already created and to ensure that the fruits of change reach all sections. Education is the high way to that goal."

To meet the challenges of change as reflected in the new concerns and imperatives of the changing Indian society, education, through its contents and methods of teaching, etc. must include the following functions:

1. Fulfilling constitutional obligations—universalisation.
2. Producing equality of opportunity.
3. Preservation of cultural heritage.
4. Strengthening emotional and national integration.
5. Building character and inculcating values.

6. Promoting ideals of secularism and democracy.
7. Protection of environment and conservation of natural resources.
8. Observation of small family norms.
9. Inculcation of the scientific temper.
10. Interfacing between the world of work and education vocationalisation of education.
11. Utilisation of media and technology.
12. Evolving a child centered approach for the all round development of the child.
13. Facilitating creative expression.
14. Developing a global perspective.

National Development—The term national development is very comprehensive. It includes all aspects of the life an individual and the nation cultural, democratic, emotional, economic, intellectual, material, moral, physical, spiritual and social. All aspects of development are very important and interrelated also. If one aspect remains undeveloped, others are also affected. National development is not synonymous with economic development though economic development is an important facet of national development.

According to the noted economist John Vaizey, "National development is the total effect of all citizen's forces and addition to the stock of physical, human resources, knowledge and skill."

The United Nation Decade Report has defined it thus, "National Development is growth plus change. Change in turn is social and cultural as well as economic and qualitative as well as quantitative."

Broad Indicators of National Development—There was a time when Gross National Product (GNP) per capita was considered to be the only indicator of national development. Although there are no universally accepted indicators of national development, yet reliance is usually made upon the indicators given below:

1. Infant mortality rate under 5 years of age.
2. Infant morality rate under 1 year of age.
3. G.N.P. per capita.
4. Life expectancy at birth.
5. Total adult literacy rate.
6. Percentage of age completing primary school.

7. Total population.
8. Population below the poverty line.
9. Availability of fundamental rights.
10. Per capita availability of calories.

Problems of National Development

1. Increasing per capita income.
2. Raising standard of life of the people.
3. Modernising society.
4. Promoting emotional and national integration.
5. Promoting universalisation of elementary education.
6. Raising adult literacy rate.
7. Keeping population under control.
8. Developing democratic, secular and social values.
9. Bringing about a synthesis between moral and scientific values.

Education and National Development

It is not without significance that the report of the Education *Commission* 1964-66 has been titled *Education and National Development*. The Education Commission has observed. "If the pace of national development is to be accelerated, there is need for a well-defined, bold and imaginative educational policy and for determined and vigorous action to vitalize, improve and expand education."

The Commission further observed that education cannot be considered in isolation or planned in a vacuum. It has to be used as a powerful instrument of social, economic and political change and will, therefore, have to be related to the long-term national aspirations and the programmes of national development on which the country is engaged and the difficult short-term problem it is called upon to face.

The Commission has rightly observed, "In a world based on science and technology it is education that determines the level of prosperity, welfare and security of the people. On the quality and number of persons coming out of our schools and colleges will depend our success in the great enterprise of national reconstruction whose principal objective is to raise the standard of living of our people."

The National Policy on Education, 1986 has observed, "The country has reached a stage in its economic and technical development when a major effort must be made to derive the maximum benefit from the assets already created and to ensure that the fruits of change reach all sections. Education is the high way to that goal." The modified NPE 1992 also endorsed the above statement.

Problems of National Development and Education

1. Education to develop such skills as lead to increased production.
2. To include such aspects as are helpful in the modernisation of Indian society.
3. to promote values of emotional and social integration.
4. To promote democratic ideals.
5. To promote socialism.
6. To strengthen secular values.
7. To work for the inculcation of ideas of international understanding.
8. To promote the small family norm.
9. To develop environmental awareness.
10. To bring about a synthesis between cultural values and scientific values.

Questions and Problems

A. Essay-Type Questions

1. Explain the state of society as visualised in the Indian Constitution.
2. Illustrate the needs of the present day Indian society and explain how education can meet these needs.
3. What are the new challenges before the Indian society? To what extent can education meet these challenges?
4. What is national development? What are the indicators of national development. State the role of education in national development.

B. Short-Answer Type Questions

5. State the main functions of education in the changing Indian society.
6. List the main features of a developing society like India.

15 Education for Cultural Development and Modernisation

15.1 Cultural Development and Education

Essence of Indian culture—The spirit of Indian culture is truly reflected as stated by Dr. S. Radhakrishnan in his book *Our Heritage,* in the following verses of the Rig Veda,

Meet together, talk together:

May your minds comprehend alike:

Common be your action and achievement:

Common be your thoughts and intention:

Common be the wishes of your hearts:

So may there be union amongst you.

King Asoka in one of his edicts has said, "Do not quarrel about religion, concord is meritorious. Do not imagine that you have a complete hold on truth. You may not have it; no religion has a monopoly of Truth; you may try to know the God above all gods who is expressed in different ways and different individuals.

(Note : See Chapter 8 dealing with the Composite Nature of Indian Culture)

Meaning of Culture

Different interpretations of culture—There seems to be no set meaning of the word 'culture'. It has been defined differently by various thinkers. Some of the most important definitions are given below. These throw adequate light on the meaning of 'culture'.

Mathew Arnold, in his book *Culture and Anarchy* defines culture as "a study of perfection as the best that has been thought and known.".

Thomas Arnold thinks, "culture looks beyond machinery ... culture has one great passion—the passion for sweetness and light."

According to Brown, both material and non-material are dependent upon each other. But culture cannot be defined. It is better to describe it. The culture of people is the way of life of that people, the things its people value, the things they don't value, their habits of life, their works of art, their music, their words, their history, briefly what they are, what they do and what they like. By material elements is meant the whole of man's materials civilisation, tools, weapons, clothings, machines and industry. By non-material elements is meant language, art, religion, morality, law and government.

T.S. Elliot thinks that the term culture "includes all the characteristic activities and interest of people".

Dayanand (Swami) states, "culture consists of the acceptance of truth and abandonment of untruth."

Ellwood says, "culture includes all of man's material civilisation, tools, weapons, clothing, shelter, machines and even its system of industry." This appears to be a very broad concept of culture and we will be stretching this concept too far.

Emerson observes, "The foundation of culture, as of character, is at last the moral sentiment."

Gandhi remarks, "culture is the foundation, the primary thing. It should show itself in the smallest detail of your conduct and personal behaviour, how you sit, how you walk, how you dress, etc. Inner culture must be reflected in your speech, the way in which you treat visitors and guests, and behave towards one another and towards your teachers and elders."

Nehru thinks, "culture is the widening of the mind and of the spirit."

Russell points out, "Genuine culture consists in being a citizen of the universe, not only of one or two arbitrary fragments of space and time. It helps man to understand human society as a whole, to estimate wisely the ends that communities pursue, and to see the present in its relation to the past and future."

Rabindranath Tagore has expressed the concept of Indian Culture in his *Gitanjali* in the following verses.

A Hymn to India

In this land did once resound a hymn unceasing
to the one, the primal source and wonder of creation,
the music of many hearts mingling in that one harmony,
and minds, disciplined and dedicated, had poured
their diverse offerings into one sacrificial flame,
and to their chant had awakened.
A mind magnificent, all embracing, all absorbing,
Break open the door to the vision of the sacred flame,
of the spirit's unceasing endeavour—
for we must gather again with bowed heads
on the shore of this vast sea of humanity
that is India.

Behold the sacred fire with its blood-red flame of sorrow
Ours is the sorrow and in its flame we must burn within—
so has Fate decreed.
Welcome pain, welcome anguish that makes us one again,
freed of fear, freed of the load of shame!
This agony unbearable shall end
in the spirit's rebirth, vast and boundless,
the night has run its course and the Mother awakes in her spacious abode
on the shore of this vast sea of humanity
that is India

Come ye Ayran, come non-Aryan, Hindu, Muslim, come,
come ye English, come ye Christians, welcome every one,
Come Brahmin, cleanse your mind and clasp the hand of all,
come ye outcaste, come ye lowly, fling away the load of shame!

Come, one and all, the Mother's crowning,
the sacred jar is yet to fill
and all must join that the water be consecrate
on the shore of this vast sea of humanity
that is India.

(Stanzas from Bharatatirtha, first published in Gitanjali—Bengali 1910)

Taylor defines culture as, "that complex whole which includes knowledge, belief, art, morals, law, custom and any other capabilities and habits, acquired by man as a member of society."

The University Education commission 1948-49 visualises—"culture is an attitude of mind, an inclination of the spirit and those who yearn for it, wish to have a vision of greatness, sit in the presence of nobility, see the highest reach and scope of the spirit of man". According to the Commission, "Our art and literature, our law and history belong to the mainstream of our culture. Every Indian student should get to know the main outlines of the history of India, which is not a mere chronicle of dates and defeats, of follies and failures. He should know the lives of the heroes who express the spirits of our civilisation, the seers of the Vedas, the Buddha and Sankara, Asoka and Akbar. A habitual vision of greatness is the way to cultural growth."

The UNESCO sponsored World Conference on Cultural Policies held in Mexico city in 1982 declared that "culture comprises the whole complex of distinctive spiritual, material, intellectual and emotional features that characterise a society or social group. It includes not only the arts and letters, but also modes of life, the fundamental rights of the human being, value systems, traditions and beliefs."

Education and Culture: Education as an Act Agent of Cultural Development

A UNESCO publication entitled *Culture and Development* (1994) explains the interrelationship of education and culture. "Whereas culture is the key which unlocks the creative potential of a community or society, education is the tool which could shape and guide the development of that potential while at the same time, channelling it in directions which respond to the community's own aspiration. There is a constant interaction between education and culture—if it is the former that sheds light, it is the latter that provides perspective. Education is infused by culture, but since cultural models and meaning are mainly transmitted through education; the former could be considered in a sense, to be an effect of education. Education could therefore be regarded as being, possibly, the most powerful agent for cultural development or change, and not merely a neutral mechanism for cultural transmission."

Transmission of cultural heritage—To perpetuate present progress we should transmit the cultural heritage. Only physical reproduction is not sufficient; we should equip the new generation with our attainments in all fields of life. Here was should exploit the innate tendencies, needs and interests of the children for the purpose of education, Our education should also be in consonance with the mental 'make-up' of the students.

Improvement of the culture of society—Without improvement society will stagnate. Education is not only to reflect the cultural conditions but also to improve them. With the advancement of science and technology our ways of life are also undergoing tremendous change, If we would not cope with the present advancement there would be a 'cultural lag'. We must adjust ourselves with the fast changing world. So education must adapt itself to the changing conditions. But as always happens some new things are not very desirable. So we shall have to guard ourselves against the tendency of schools to import everything new in the society. If old and out-moded things are to be discarded we shall have to be vigilant against blind and slavish imitation of the new developments. It is through education that we can prepare students to evaluate the past and understand the present and to be prepared for the future. In short the students should be taught to get inspiration from the inspiring past, to live in the dynamic present and to face the challenging future.

National Policy on Education, 1986 and as Modified in 1992 on "The Role of Education in Cultural Development."

The National Policy has described the cultural perspective and its relation with education as under.

1. The existing schism between the formal system of education and the country's rich and varied cultural traditions needs to be bridged. The preoccupation with modern technologies cannot

be allowed to sever our new generations from the roots in India's history and culture. De-culturisation, de-humanisation and alienation must be avoided at all costs. Education can and must bring about the fine synthesis between change-oriented technologies and the country's continuity of the cultural tradition.

2. The curricula and process of education will be enriched by cultural content in as many manifestations as possible. Children will be enabled to develop sensitivity to beauty, harmony and refinement. Resource persons in the community, irrespective of their formal educational qualifications, will be invited to contribute to the cultural enrichment of education, employing both the literate and oral traditions of communication. To sustain and carry forward the cultural traditional models will be supported and recognised.

3. Linkages will be established between the university system and institutions of higher learning in art, archaeology, oriental studies etc. Due attention will also be paid to the specialised disciplines of Fine Arts, Museology, Folklore etc. Teaching, training and research in these disciplines will be strengthened so as to replenish specialised manpower in them.

Role of the schools in conserving cultural heritage— For the adoption of culture, one must participate in the activities of the society. An educational institution must provide a good model of culture. It should provide opportunities in the art of living together.

The curriculum of the school must reflect the cultural values of the society.

Fine Arts, i.e., music, dance, and drama should be encouraged.

Educational tours to art galleries and museums etc. should be organised.

Cultural functions should be organised in the school from time to time.

Modernisation of education and cultural renaissance—In this context we cannot do better than to quote Pandit Jawaharlal Nehru, "Can we combine the progress of science and technology with the progress of the mind and spirit also? We cannot be untrue to science because that represents the basic fact of life today. Still less can we be untrue to those essential principles for which India has stood in the past throughout the ages. Let us then pursue our path to industrial progress with all our strength and vigour and, at the same time, remember that material riches without toleration and wisdom may well turn to dust and ashes."

Education should transmit the culture to the new generation and transformation outlook of the young towards life in the light of the past, in the context of cross-cultural influences and in the light of future requirements of the individual and the society.

15.2 Modernisation of Indian Society and Education

Meaning of modernisation—The twin slogans of development and modernisation can be heard echoing all over the world. Modernisation, with different aspects and several features has not only become a comprehensive concept in coverage but also complex in its structure. Modernisation means a process of change—change in behaviour. The very concept of modernisation warrants radical changes—changes in the traditional society in different walks of life. In general modernisation is marked by industrialisation, urbanisation, socialisation, vocationalisation, technologisation of agriculture, economy, education, commerce, transport, and communications etc. It also means rationalisation of ways of thinking and behaving. Modernisation means a process of change—change of a traditional society into a society based on science and technology. Modernisation is marked by industrialisation, urbanisation, vocationalisation, use of technology in education, development of means of agriculture, communication and transport etc.

Characteristics of Modernisation

S.C. Dubey (1967) provides the following characteristics of modernisation.

1. Empathy. It implies the capacity to see ourself in the situation of others.
2. Mobility. It means equipping persons for rational situational and structural choices
3. High participation. It indicates the increasing participation of people in social activities.

4, 5 & 6 Interest articulation, interest aggregation and institutionalised political competition. These characteristics recognise the vital role that interest and power groups and power relations play.

7. Achievement orientation. This refers to 'inner concerns' that motivate and sustain economic growth.
8. Rational ends-means calculation. It is believed that people with high achievement motivation learn faster and work harder to reach high level goals.

9, 10 & 11. New attitudes to wealth, work, savings and risk taking; faith in the desirability and possibility of change; economic, political and social discipline; and capacity to put off immediate and short run satisfactions for higher satisfaction in the long run. These attributes of modernisation relate to certain attitudes, motivations and values that are very essentially interlinked with the cultural and social implications of modernisation.

M. Inklets lists the following characteristics of modernisation.

1. Acceptance of new ideas.
2. Curiorisity for acquiring latest knowledge.
3. Adoption of new techniques and methods.
4. Emphasis on the present rather than the past.
5. A practical and realistic approach to the world.
6. Faith in equal justice.

In the words of Black Bellah, "The most distinctive feature of modern society is its adoption of science and technology. On this basis, societies are increasing their productivity. Science based technology has other-significant utilisation of social and cultural life and it involves fundamental social and cultural changes which are broadly described as modernisation".

The Education Commission 1964-66, explains the concept of modernisation as, "Modernisation aims, amongst other things (adoption of a science based technology, keeping pace with the explosion of knowledge and quick almost breath taking rate at which social changes take place) at creating an economy of plenty which will offer to every individual a larger way of life and a wide variety of choices."

Main Components of Modernisation

1. *Explosions of various kinds*—Explosion of knowledge, explosion of attitudes, explosion of interests, explosion of expectations, explosion of frustration and explosion of values.
2. Decentralisation of power.

3. Industrialisation.
4. International outlook.
5. Mass education.
6. Materilistic outlook.
7. Mechanisation.
8. Pragmatic attitude.
9. Rational outlook.
10. Respect for the dignity of the individual.
11. Secular values.
12. Scientific temper.
13. Socialist ideas.
14. Vocationalisation.
15. Universal brotherhood.
16. Urbanisation.

Modernisation is not westernisation—These two terms should not be used synonymously. Modernisation does not necessarily imply the adoption of western manners, habits, modes of dress, cultural and other values. For instance, Japan is a modern country. It has adopted science and technology in different areas like agriculture, commerce and industry but it is still wedded to many of its past cultural values.

Modernisation is not discording all traditional values—According to Thomas, "It is true that new values are merging as a result of the changes in society. The emergency of new values does not mean that traditional values have been wiped out."

Modernisation and Science and Spiritual Values Society

The Education Commission 1964-66 which went into all aspects of education at all stages and its relationship with national development observed, while discussing its role in the context of modernisation, "A basic distinction between traditional and modern societies is the development and use by the latter of science-based technology which helps modernisation of agriculture and development of industries. In a traditional society, production is based largely on empirical processes and experience on trial and error, rather than on science, in a modern society it is basically rooted in science."

The commission has further stressed that "science based technology has other important implications for social and cultural life and it involves fundamental, social and cultural changes which are broadly described as modernisation."

While emphasising the role of science in the modernisation of the society, the Education Commission equally stresses the role of spiritual values. It states, "Modernisation does not mean—least of all in our national situation—a refusal to recognise the importance of or to inculcate necessary moral and spiritual values and self discipline. Modernisation, if it is to be a living force, must derive its strength from the spirit."

We should learn to harness science but must also learn not to be dominated by science.

The imbalance of Atom and Ahimsa or to put it differently, man's knowledge and mastery of 'outer space' and the 'space within his skull' must be redressed.

India has made many glorious contributions to world culture, and perhaps the grandest of them all is the concept and ideal of non-violence and compassion sought, expounded and lived by Buddha and Mahavira; Nanak and Kabir, Vivekanand, Raman Maharishi and Gandhi and which millions after them have striven to follow.

Concluding remarks—India is on the move again—with the promise of a new renaissance in the making. The most powerful tool in the process of this renaissance and modernisation is education based on moral and spiritual values on the one hand and on the other on science and technology. In this context we cannot do better than to quote Pt. Jawahar Lal Nehru, "Can we combine the progress of science and technology with the progress of mind and spirit also? We cannot be untrue to science because that represents the basic fact of life to-day. Still less can we be untrue to those essential principles for which India has stood in the past throughout the ages. Let us then pursue our path to industrial progress with our strength and vigour and at the same time remember that material riches without toleration and compassion and wisdom may well turn to dust and ashes!"

General Characteristics of a Traditional and a Modern Society

Traditional Society	*Modern Society*
1. Agriculture	
i. Old implements	i. Use of fertilisers, machines and tractors etc.
ii. Dependence on animals for various agricultural operations	ii. Big farms
iii. Dependence on rain	iii. New Multipurpose projects
2. *Economic*	
i. Old approaches to production and distribution	i. New approaches
ii. Small scale production	ii. Large scale production
3. *Education*	
i. In terms of 3 R's	i. In terms of 7 R's
ii. Low literacy	ii. High literacy
iii. Education for a few	iii. Universal Schooling
iv. Use of Slate, blackboard and the like	iv. Education of the masses
	v. Use of new media.
4. *Family*	
i. Large families	i. Small families
ii. Joint Family system	ii. Nuclear family
5. *Health*	
i. High mortality rate	i. Low mortality rate
ii. High birth rate	ii. Low birth rate
6. *Industry*	
i. Home based	i. Factory based
ii. Cottage industries	ii. Small scale, large scale industries
iii. Manual work	iii. Use of electricity
	iv. Use of machinery
7. *Political*	
i. Village or tribal authority	i. Political parties
ii. Very few voters	ii. Adult suffrage

Contd

8. *Religion*	
i. Belief in rituals	i. Rational outlook
ii. Fixed beliefs	ii. Secular beliefs.
9. *Social*	
i. Caste system.	i. Loosening of caste barriers
ii. Untouchability	ii. Removal of imtouchability
iii. Low status of women	iii. Better status of women.

Negative effects of modernisation— Modernisation has also led to some disruptive tendencies: communal disturbances, disquiet, violence and provincial, regional and national conflicts. It has also created many economic and social problems. Material values of life sometimes dominate spiritual values. In the developing countries, in the initial phases there appears a wide gulf between the rich and the poor. Modernisation is also responsible for the 'explosion of frustration' among many sections of society.

Obstacles in the modernisation of Indian society—Since independence, India has been on the path of modernisation. Considerable progress has been achieved in different areas of national life. Yet there is far more to achieve. Progress is not as rapid as it should have been. In this regard, the following constraints and obstacles may be mentioned:-

1. Gap between ideals and actuals.
2. Old cultural beliefs and traditions.
3. Closed type of society.
4. Poverty of the masses.
5. Illiteracy of the masses.
6. Population explosion.
7. Narrow religions faiths and beliefs.
8. Narrow loyalties.
9. Lack of unity.
10. Lack of political stability.

Education and Modernisation of Indian Society

Education is the most powerful tool in the process of modernisation. It must be remembered that an old fashioned and static system of education cannot meet the demands of a rapidly changing society. Therefore education is also to be modernised. Thus modernisation through education shall have to go side by side with modernisation of education.

Role of Education in the Modernisation of Indian Society

1. Education for developing skills to increase production.
2. Education and equalisation of educational opportunities.
3. For the promotion of emotional and national integration.
4. For the establishment of a socialist pattern of society.
5. For the promotion of democratic values.
6. For the promotion of secular ideas.
7. For developing a wider outlook.
8. For synthesising cultural and scientific values.

Transformation of Education for Modernisation

Aims of education and modernisation—In this context we may quote the Kothari Commission of Education (1964-66), "The very aim of education has to be viewed differently—it is no longer taken as concerned primarily with the imparting of knowledge or the preparation of finished product, but with the awakening of curiosity, the development of proper interests, attitudes and values and the building up of such essential skills as independent study and the capacity to think and judge for oneself without which it is not possible to become a responsible member of a democratic society."

Science-based education—We are at a crucial stage in the process of development and transformation and in this context the role of science (using the word in its broadest sense) is of the utmost importance. Science education must become an integral part of school education and ultimately some study of science should become a part of all courses in the humanities and social sciences at the university stage.

The quality of science teaching also has to be raised considerably so as to achieve its proper objective and purposes, namely to promote an ever-deepening understanding of basic principles to develop problem solving, analytical skills and the ability to apply them to the problems of the material environment and social living and to promote the spirit of enquiry and experimentation.

Vocationalisation of education—The need to provide some correctives to the over-academic nature of formal education has been widely recognised. In the curricula of most contemporary school systems particularly in the socialist countries of Europe, a place is found, for what is variously called, 'manual work' or 'work experience'. At present, the intelligentia consists predominantly of the white-collared professionals and students of humanities, while the proportion of scientists and technical workers in its rank is quite small. To achieve this, greater emphasis must be placed on vocational subjects, education and research.

Universalisation and mass education—The proportion of persons who have so far been able to receive education is very small. This will have to be increased. It is very essential to produce educated and skilled citizens and to train an adequate and competent intelligentia to modernise society quickly.

Education for social and national integration—Social and national integration is crucial to the creation of a strong, united country, which is an essential pre-condition for modernisation.

Development of skilled manpower—There can be no hope for mondernising the agricultural economy of the country unless the farmer is ready to adopt techniques that increase yields and to move out of his age-long conservatism. The same is true of industry. The skilled manpower needed for the relevant research and its systematic application to agriculture, industry and other sectors of life can only come from a development of scientific and technological education.

Dynamic methods of teaching—In a modern society, knowledge inevitably ceases to be something to be received passively. It is something to be actively discovered. If this is rightly understood it would involve a revolution in traditional education. Where 'to know' has come to mean 'to know by heart', where respect for all inherited knowledge is vigorously cultivated and where the assimilative faculties tend to be emphasised to the neglect of the critical and creative ones. In India, as in other countries where similar conditions prevail, this would require the introduction of a new technology in teaching as well as educational planning and management.

Harmony between science and spirituality—Vinoba Bhave has described the present age as the 'age of science and spirituality'.

The pursuit of material affluence and power should be harmonised with the higher values. The concept of the mingling of 'science and spirituality' is of special significance for Indian education.

Study of foreign languages—It is important to encourage the study of important foreign languages on a more extensive scale for a variety of academic and practical purposes. Russian, French, German, Japanese, Spanish and Chinese besides English are important world languages of communication and for acquiring knowledge and culture.

Modernisation and the teacher—The teacher through his outlook in life and through his methods of teaching can promote ideas of modernisation.

Gandhi and Modernisation of Indian Society

Gandhi's ideals in this context may be summed up by "I do not want my house to be walled in on all sides and my windows to be stuffed. I want the culture of all lands to be blown about my house as purely as possible. But I refuse to be blown off my feet by any".

Universalisation of Education and Modernisation of Indian Society

Universalisation of education implies education for all, irrespective of caste, colour, creed sex or age.

Broadly speaking universalisation of education relates to (a) the education of children covering age group 6 to 14 as stipulated in Article 21A (Previously it was Article 45) of the constitution, (b) Education of the illiterate adults between 15-35 years of age.

Universal elementary education goes a long way in the modernisation of a society. J.P. Naik an eminent Indian educator of our country has very aptly observed, "The progress of primary education is an index of the general, social and economic development of the country as a whole." Various studies have amply demonstrated that countries which have made proper provision for primary education are far ahead of those with inadequate provision.

Likewise adult education plays a crucial role in the modernisation of society.

Keeping in view the pivotal role of education in national reconstruction, the World Conference on Education for All, held at Jomtien (Thailand) in March 1990 made the World Declaration on Education for All.

Questions and Problems

A. Essay-Type Questions

1. Discuss how the concepts of conservation of culture and development of culture are used in planning educational programmes in a developing country like India.
2. What is meant by culture? What is composite culture? State ways and means for the conservation and promotion of culture through education.
3. What is meant by modernisation ? Discuss how far education helps in the modernisation of India.
4. State how far the present system of education is able to meet the demands of a modern society. Suggest suitable measures is this regard.
5. Suggest ways and means of making our schools and teachers as instruments of modernisation of society?
6. "Education and modernisation are inter-dependent Discuss."
7. Define modernisation. Discuss why is it needed? What is the role of education in it?

B. Objective-Type Questions

8. "Modernisation is not westernisation". Explain
9. "Modernisation without spiritualisation is meaningless". Elucidate.
10. List ten important characteristics of modernisation.

16 Education for Democracy, Secularism and Socialism

16.1 Education for Democracy

Meaning of democracy—Without going into the numerous definitions of democracy we may go into the spirit of democracy as reflected in them. In simple words, it is considered a way of life, meaning thereby that the individual should have the freedom to think independently and exercise his judgement freely with regard to all economic, educational ethical, political and economic issues. Democracy thus must become a part and parcel of our lives. Democracy should not be confined to local, state or parliamentary elections, and combats among parties. Political democracy cannot stand in isolation.

The economic aspect of democracy implies that the economic power should be shared by the people.

The ethical aspect of democracy rests on the faith that each individual is entitled to full respect for his dignity and worth.

The social aspect of democracy means equality irrespective of caste class, creed, sex and wealth.

The spirit of democracy may be explained by assigning ideals, or values to each letter of the word democracy. 'D' stands for division of authority and power

— for dignity of the individual

‘E’ Stands for equality

‘M’ Stands for mutual understanding
— for mass education

‘O’ Stands for open mindedness
— for objective attitude

‘C’ Stands for co-operation
— for classless society

‘R’ Stands for rational thinking
— for respecting other’s ideas
— for relationship between rights and responsibilities

‘A’ Stands for adult franchise

‘C’ Stands for concern for others
— for constructive and creative approach

‘Y’ Stands for yearning for living and working together.

Attributes of a democratic citizen—According to the Secondary Education Commission, “To be effective a democratic citizen should have the understanding and the intellectual integrity to sift truth from falsehood, facts from propaganda and to reject the dangerous appeal of fanaticism and prejudice. He must develop a scientific attitude of mind to think objectively and base his conclusions on tested data. He should also have an open mind receptive to new ideas and not confined within the prison walls of outmoded customs, traditions and beliefs.

It should neither reject the old because it is old nor accept the new because it is new, but dispassionately examine both and courageously reject whatever arrests the forces of justice and progress.”

The essence of a democratic society is not only the tolerating but the welcoming of differences which make for the enrichment of life.”

Democracy and education—Prof. Dewey in his book *Democracy and Education* has explained the relationship very clearly between education and democracy in these words “an undesirable society is one which internally and externally sets up barriers to free intercourse and communication of experience. A society which makes provisions for participation in its good of all its members on equal terms and which secures flexible readjustment of its institutions through the interaction of the different forms of associated life is so far democratic. Such a society must have a type of education which gives individuals a personal interest in social relationships and control and the habits of mind which secure social changes without introducing disorder."

Education in a democracy—A few implications:

1. The right to education becomes a fundamental right in a genuine democracy.
2. Education is essential to a citizen to function as a voter and a legislator.
3. Education is essential to enable voters to comprehend and intelligently discern the programme of parties.
4. It is necessary to enable citizens to prepare themselves for securing the means of livelihood.
5. It is essential for participating intelligently in the social and other processes, which require attitudes, oreintation, skills and emotional states.
6. It is essential for a citizen to comprehend the laws of the land.
7. The right to vote, the right to participate intelligently in shaping the policies of the state, demand not merely the right to education but the right to education in the language of the people.

Democracy and aims of education in India: The Secondary Education Commission (1952-53) has suggested the following aims of education of a democratic society.

1. Development of democratic citizenship.
2. Improvement of vocational efficiency.
3. Development of personality.
4. Development of qualities of leadership.

Development of democratic citizenship implies: (a) clear thinking (b) receptivity to new ideas (c) clearness in speech and writing (d) the art of living in a community (e) passion for social justice (f) tolerance (g) true patriotism (h) internalism.

Democracy and curriculum—Curriculum should be based on these principles: (a) principle of relating contents to the aspiration and needs of the people (b) principle of child-centred education (c) principle of diversification (d) principle of vocational education.

In short curriculum should be 'life cenetred', 'activity centred' and 'Child Centred.'

Democracy and methods of teaching—Learning by doing, 'activity methods, 'Dalton Plan', experimental method, socialised recitation and project method etc. should be adopted.

Democracy and discipline—Discipline should be self discipline and social discipline.

Democracy and the teacher—The teacher himself should possess a democratic outlook. He should show due respect to the personality of the child. Individual differences of children should be attended to.

Democracy and school administration, management and supervision—There should be a proper division of powers and responsibilities. Decentralisation and human relationships should be the watchwords of the educational administrator.

Functions of the School in a Democracy

According to Thomas H. Briggs, "The school is truly the guardian of democracy" Kilpatrik describes the concept of a school in a democractic set up: "Kilpatrik states: "The effective school in a democracy must give its pupils an intelligent understanding of the issues of democracy, make them well disposed towards democracy as a way of life, and make them skilful in the cooperative activities through which democracy must function."

The functions of the schools in the process of educating students in democratic values and principles are three fold:

1. To convey to the students the meaning of democratic values ideals and principles and their implications for conduct in the various life situations.
2. To enable the students to incorporate these values, ideas and principles in their daily conduct, in and out of school.
3. A democratic school introduces radical changes in respect of methods, discipline and administration.

Methods of Educating the Students in a Democratic Way of Life

1. *Respect of individual personality*—The school administrators should show regard to the individuality of the members of the staff and the students.
2. *Introduction of self-government in schools*—The students may be associated with the management of the school rules.
3. *Provision for manual work*—Manual work goes a long way in making the students realise the dignity of labour.
4. *Equal opportunities for admission*—In the matter of admitting students in schools, there should be made no distinction of caste, creed, colour or wealth. This is very essential for promoting the cause of social justice.
5. *Encouragement to group work*—Group activities should be encouraged to provide opportunities to the students to participate in the affairs of the group.
6. *Democratic methods of teaching*—'Learning' by 'doing' rather than by 'rote learning' should be aimed at.
7. *Promotion of self-expression*—With a view to promoting self-expression among the students, debate, declamation contest etc. may be planned.
8. *Opportunities for social service*—Social work will bring the students into direct contact with the community and enable them to understand its problems.
9. *Vocational effciency*—Craft education is very helpful in preparing our students with a practical bias.
10. *Development of hobbies*—Hobbies are very helpful in preparing the students to make the best use of their leisure.
11. *Hostel life*—Whenever possible hostel life opportunities should be provided to the students. This is an effective way of training the students in the art of living together.
12. *Student parliament*—Student's unions and parliaments may be formed in the schools and the office-bearers of these elected.
13. *Visits to legislatures*—Such visits provide the students first hand opportunities to see for themselves the working of a democracy.
14. *A democratic teacher and his role*

    (i) A teacher himself sets democratic examples.

(ii) A students are teacher-guided.

(iii) The students are guided by the teacher in the choice of many activities.

(iv) The groups suggests and proposed supplementary work — all which is reviewed and appraised by the group.

(v) The students aid in planning the academic work, make suggestions and proposals.

(vi) The pupils share with teacher in establishing standards of achievement.

(vii) The students share with the teacher the responsibility of appraising their work.

(viii) Students are encouraged by the teacher to make suggestions concerning their work.

(ix) Students are encouraged to correct their mistakes.

(x) The daily programmes is elastic and can be changed as the group decides.

(xi) The teacher adopts an exploratory attitude.

(xii) The teacher tries to understand the child.

(xiii) The teacher is sympathetic.

(xiv) The teacher tries to find reasons for misbehaviour.

(xv) The teacher takes into consideration the individual differences of the students.

(xvi) Children are encouraged to show affection.

(xvii) Every child is provided with an opportunity to contribute and to lead a group.

(xviii) Materials and books are provided for all mental levels in a grade.

(xix) Students are grouped properly.

(xx) The students express themselves freely.

(xxi) Curriculum is flexible to meet the needs of each child.

(xxii) Teachers co-operate with the counseller to study problem students.

(xxiii) Teachers encourage parents to visit the school for a closer relationship between home and school.

(xxiv) School environment is reflected by the stude t's remark, "I like School."

(xxv) Students committees assume responsibility for selecting equipment and suppliers needed.

16.2 Education for Secularism (Secularisation of Education)

Concept of Secularism

The word secularism did not occur in the Indian Constitution as enacted on 26 November, 1949. However, subsequently it was incorporated in its Preamble with the 42nd Constitutional amendment in 1976.

H.V. Kanat, a veteran Parliamentarian expounded the concept of secularism in the Constituent Assembly, "When I say that a State should not identify itself with any particular religion, I do not mean to say that a State should be anti-religious or irreligious. We have certainly declared India to be a secular state. But to my mind, a secular state is neither a godless state, nor an irreligious nor an anti-religious State. In short, by a secular State is meant that the State shall not make any discrimination whatsoever on the ground of religion or community against a person professing any particular form of religious faith. This means in essence that no particular religion in the State will receive any patronage or protection".

Dr. B.R. Ambedkar, the principal architect of our Constitution explains secularism in the following words:

"Secular State does not mean that it shall not take into consideration the religious sentiments of the people. All that Secular State means is, that this Parliament shall not be competent to impose any particular religion upon the rest of the people. This is the only limitation that the Constitution recognizes. (Parliamentary Debates, 1951), VOL— III, Part-II)

Dr. Radhakrishnan, former President of India explained secularism as follows: "When India is said to be a secular state, it does not means that we reject the reality of an unseen spirit or the relevance of religion to life or that we exalt irreligion. It does not mean that secularism itself becomes a positive religion or that the State assumes divine prerogatives. Though faith in the Supreme is the basic principle of the Indian traditions, the Indian state will not identify itself with or be controlled by any particular religion. We hold that no one religion should be given preferential status, or unique distinction, that no one religion should be accorded special privileges in national life or international relations for that would be a violation of the basic principles of democracy and contrary to the best interest of religion and Government. This view of religious impartially, or comprehension and forbearance, has a prophetic role to play within the national and the international life."

(Discovery of Faith, p. 184)

Dr. Rajendra Prasad, the first President of India has very clearly observed that becoming secular, India has not been anti-religious or irreligious. He stated, "There are some who think that because we are a secular state we do not believe in religion or spiritual values. Far from being so, it really means that in this country all are free to profess or preach the faith of their liking and that we wish well of all religions and want them to develop in their own way without any hinderance."

Jawaharlal Nehru, the first Prime Minister of India has explained the secular nature of our State. "It means while religion is completely free, the state including in its wide fold various religions and cultures, gives protection and opportunities to all and thus brings about an atmosphere of tolerance and cooperation."

Webster's New Collegiate Dictionary explains the word secular as "(a) relating to the wordly or temporal (b) not povertly or specific religious and (c) not bound by monastic vows or rules".

Asoka's secular outlook is one or the landmarks not only of Indian civilisation but also of the human civilisation itself. He made a passionate appeal not for the toleration of all religious sects but also to develop a spirit of reverence towards them. He pleaded for restraint of criticism of other religions and sects.

India as a secular State: Ours is a secular State. It means that the State shall not discriminate against the followers of a particular religion. All Indians—Hindus, Muslims, Sikhs, Christians and others have the freedom to practise their religion.

Secularism has been made one of the basic elements of the structure of the Constitution of India. According to the fundamental right to practise religion was confered on all person by Article 25 and 26, protection against levy of tax for promotion of any religion was conferred under Article 27.

The characteristics of a secular State are:

1. The State as such has no religion of its own.
2. It does not accord preferential treatment to the followers of any faith.
3. It does not discriminate against any person on account of his faith.
4. All citizens are eligible to enter government service irrespective of their faith.

Universal Values of Secularism—Most prominent values of secularism are: love, reverence, tolerance and truth.

Educational Implications of Secularism

According to Brubacher secularism has "no religious point of view while it has a theory of moral education." Brubacher has also observed, "If the secularist has any religion at all it is likely that scientific doctrine constitutes the presuppositions of that religion and that scientists are its high priests."

Many postive steps have been taken to promote secularism in the country. It is laid down in the Constitution that religious minorities are free to establish their educational institutions. The state does not debar any such educational institution from grants.

Secularism is a philosophy of moral education. Secular behaviour springs in the school from the influence of the school, through the conduct and behaviours of the teachers themselves and life in the school community as a whole.

All the activities and programmes of the schools must strive for the inculation of values of love, truth and tolerance.

Secular Outlook

A secular outlook implies the following:

1. It treats all religions on an equal footing.
2. It permits freedom of religion.
3. It permits freedom of worship.
4. It views all individuals as citizens with equal rights.
5. It implies tolerance.
6. It has faith in rational thinking.
7. It encourages moral and spiritual values.
8. It believes in co-existence.

9. It stresses free inquiry.
10. It implies freedom of our mind from dogmatic ideas.

Increasing concern is expressed every day about the general deterioration in values in contemporary social life. It is always the acts of immorality that have sown the seeds of unhappiness, hatred, jealousy and enmity in society. The same immorality is exhibited in the form of mass copying, indiscipline and turmoil in the educational institutions. There is need for appropriate educational action to meet these challenges. The National Education Policy (1986) has stated, "The growing concern over the erosion of essential values and an increasing cynicism in society has brought to focus the need for readjustments in the curriculum in order to make education a foreceful tool for the cultivation of social and moral values."

Religious and moral education in secular India—The Constitution of India has laid down the following provisions in connection with religious and moral education in educational institution.

Constitutional provisions-Article 19(1)—"Subject to public order, morality and health and to other provisions of this part, all persons are equally entitled to freedom of conscience and the right freely to profess, practice and propagate religion."

Article 21—"No person may be compelled to pay any taxes, the proceeds of which are specifically appropriated in payment of expenses for the promotion or maintenance of any particular religion or religious denomination."

Article 22(1)—. "No religious instruction shall be provided in any educational institution wholly maintained out of State funds.

Provided that nothing in this clause shall apply to an educational institution which is administered but has been established under an endownment or trust which requires that religious instructions shall be imparted in such institutions.

(2) No person attending any educational institution recognised by the State or receiving aid out of State funds shall be required to take part in any religious institution or to attend any religious worship that may be conducted in such institution or in any premises attached there to unless such person, or if such person is a minor his guardian has given his consent thereto."

Article 30 (1)— "All minorities whether based on religion or language, shall have the right to establish and administer educational institutions of their choice.

(2) The State shall not, in granting aid to educational institutions, discriminate against any educational institution on the ground that it is under the management of a minority, whether based on religion or language."

A person can be a secularist but not a religious person if religion is narrowly conceived in terms of certain rituals. Similarly a religious person believing in and performing certain rituals may not be a secularist.

16.3 Socialism and Its Educational Implications

Meaning of socialism—Socialism has its origin in Europe as a revolt against capitalism in the 19th century. Its salient ideas spread all over the world. There are different brands of socialism especially those shaped by Karl Marx and Lenin in Russia, Mao in China and Gandhi in India.

Gandhi like Marx aimed at the establishment of a classless society but on the path of non-violence, service, truth, cooperation and decentralisation of power. Gandhi called it 'sarvodaya', that is, 'good of all'. In 1947 in an editorial under the caption 'who is a socialist' Gandhi wrote, "Under socialism all the members of the society are equal—none low, none high...Even as members of the individual body are equal, so are the members of society. This is socialism. Under it, the prince and the peasant, the wealthy and the poor, the employer and the employee are all on the same level." He has further observed, "Only a truthful non-violent and pure hearted socialist will be able to establish a socialist society in India and the world."

A perusal of the course of estabilishing a socialist society in Europe would reveal the occurrence of class wars and shedding of a lot of blood.

Objectives of a socialist society—Broadly speaking the basic objectives of a socialist or socialist pattern of society is to establish a society based on equality of opportunity in economic, political and religious fields.

Chief Features of a Socialist Society or Socialism

1. Socialism aims at social justice.
2. It aims at equality.
3. It aims at establishing a classless society, free from exploitation, oppression and disparity.
4. It aims at establishing a society based on mutual cooperation and fellow feeling.
5. It pre-supposes public ownership of the means of production.
6. It aims at abolishing the capitalist system.
7. It aims at the active participation of the individual in the productive process of society.
8. It aims at developing necessary skills and favourable attitudes towards work.

Educational Implications of Socialism

Aims of education and socialism—Emphasis on (a) social development of an individual, (b) education for citizenship and (c) socialisation of the individual.

Contents or curriculum—(a) more emphasis on core curriuculum, (b) subject matter stressing equality, (c) study of socialistic movements and (d) socially useful productive work and work experience

Methods of teaching—(a) socialised recitation techniques, (b) project method, (c) problem method and (d) team teaching.

Educational measures for promoting a socialist society—Various Committees and Commissions have suggested many measures in education which conform to a Socialist pattern of society. The Kothari Commission has observed, "One of the important social objectives of education is to equalise opportunity, enabling the backward or under privileged classes and individuals to use education as a lever for the improvement of their condition. Every society that values social justice and is anxious to improve the lot of the common man and cultivate all available talent, must ensure progressive equality of opportunity to all sections of population. This is the only guarantee for the building up of an egalitarian and human society in which the exploitation of the weak will be minimised."

Teaching of socialism—It is the responsibility of the educational institutions to bring about adequate awareness regarding socialism among the teachers and students so that the young people are armed with knowledge which will enable them to chart the course of the nation towards the goal of socialism.

The following are the three main ways in which a school can convey positive attitudes and values regarding socialism to students:

1. Direct teaching of socialism.
2. Living the values and attitudes to be learned through the organisation of various activities.
3. Teachers becoming models embodying the desired values and attitudes.

Textbooks and socialism—As an impact of socialism, textbooks at the school stage, by and large, have been nationalised, The contents of textbooks are oriented and regulated according to the national policy and ethos. Efforts are being made to keep the price range of textbooks within the easy reach of the parents.

Equality of opportunity in education—The Kothari Commission has rightly observed. "On grounds of social justice as well as for the furtherance of democracy it is essential to make special efforts to equalise educational opportunities between these groups."

Ways and Means of Providing Equality of Opportunity in Education

1. Tuition free education to economically weaker sections of students.
2. Free textbooks and uniforms to the weaker sections.
3. Establishment of book banks.
4. Award of scholarship.
5. Granting of loans.
6. Day-study centres and lodging houses.
7. 'Earn and learn' facilities.
8. Special facilities for girls.
9. Special stress on the education of the backward sections of societies—tribals, slum areas, hilly areas etc.
10. Meeting the needs of slow learners and the handicapped.
11. Running and maintenance of state/government schools.

12. Equality of opportunity in admission.
13. *Common school system*—A common school system of public education should be evolved in place of the present system which divides the management of school between a large number of agencies whose functioning is inadequately co-ordinated. It should be maintained at an adequate level of quality and efficiency so that no parent would ordinarily feel any need to send his child to the institutions outside the system such as independent or unrecognized schools. Such a step will be very helpful towards eliminating the segregation that now takes place between the schools for the poor and the underprivileged classes and those for the rich and the privileged ones. The existing 'caste' system in education will largely disappear.

Questions and Problems

A. Essay-Type Questions

1. "If democracy is to be a stable form of the government of a country, education for democracy must be introduced in schools." Discuss this statement.
2. What is democracy. What are its essential features and educational implications.
3. Discuss the relationship that exists between democracy and education. State the role of a teacher in promoting democratic ideals.
4. "Education for the socialistic pattern of society is the need of the hour." Discuss.
5. "Liberty and equality are the two great principles of democracy." How can we promote them through education?
6. Discuss the concept of equalisation of educational opportunity with special reference to Indian society.
7. What are the characteristics of a secular state? What are its educational implications?

B. Short-Answer Type Questions

8. State the characteristics of a democratic citizen.
9. What are the chief characteristics of socialism?
10. Explain secularism.
11. State briefly the Gandhian concept of socialism.

17 Modernisation of Indian Society and Adult Education

Meaning of Adult Education

Adult education, basic education (not in the context of Gandhi's system of basic education), functional literacy, literacy, mass education and social education—all these connote the same meaning.

UNESCO (1974) defined the concept by stating, "The term adult education denotes the entire body of organised educational processes, whatever content, level and method whether formal or otherwise, whether they prolong or replace initial education in schools, colleges and universities as well as in apprenticeship, whereby persons regarded as adults by the society to which they belong develop their abilities, enrich their knowledge, improve their technical or professional qualifications and bring about changes in their attitude or behaviour in the two-fold perspective of full personal development and participation in balance and independent social, economic and cultural development."

Adult Education and National Development

From the definition given above, it is obvious that adult education should be resolute oriented towards national development and should be an integrated part not only of national education plans but also of plans and projects for development in all sectors of national life.

It is an important and traditional function of adult education to bring knowledge to the people especially the knowledge which concerns them deeply, for exampie, knowledge of the basic essentials of a healthy life, civic education, etc. As a large part, of the Indian population is illiterate, literacy has become one of the part most important programmes of social education and is an index of its progress.

Since India has resolved to recover her place in technology in response to the demands of modern times, it is the function of adult education to serve as a smooth and effective channel between centres of research and the homes and hamlets in which the common people live. It aims to bring down to the people the benefits of new knowledge that is being continually created in laboratories and also the knowledge that is already there, but is not available to them.

Adult education should enable everyone to study his or her role as a parent and member of a community; as a wage earner and as a responsible citizen. It must also give opportunities for vocational employment.

Adult literacy, being an essential element in the overall development, must be closely linked to economic and social priorities and to present and future manpower needs.

One of the essential functions of adult education is to awaken in the people an appreciation of the significance of the country's Five-year plans and to enthuse them for participation in it.

Men everywhere function in groups and a distinctive group is a cluster around a leader. The quality of a group is therefore largely a product of its leadership and if the Indian people have to justify their aspiration, it can be done only by improving the quality of leadership in the villages and towns of India. This is a responsibility which adult education alone can shoulder.

Adult education is helpful in national development by promoting the ideals of a composite culture, emotional integration and national unity.

The National Literacy Mission (NLM), launched in 1988 observed "The NLM will concentrate on the 15-35 age group which is crucial for the country's development. On its understanding of the significance of national and social integration of productivity and a new work ethics and of family, planning depends the course of our country's future."

Aims and Objectives of Adult/Social Education

The aims and objectives of social education are to transform the society. Social education should enable every one to study his or her role as a parent and as a member of a community, as a wage-earner and as a dutiful citizen. Social education should also offer opportunities for vocational employment. It will also develop religious and civic consciousness and social advantage so as to enable the learners to participate directly in the government after becoming literate and to co-operate actively with educated citizens. Such an education will seek to inspire them to take a keen interest in the affairs of the state, all developmental plans and allied programmes. This education will bring out the best that is in the individuals and foster habits of healthy life.

Scope of Adult Education in the Indian Context

In normal conditions programmes of adult education presume universal literacy. In the Indian context 50 per cent of the people are unable to read and write and naturally, liquidation of illiteracy becomes a matter of immediate national concern.

The scope of adult education is as wide as life itself. Its requirements are somewhat different from those of the normal school system. It depends upon the support it receives from several agencies, particularly the universities and public institutions and libraries. The effectiveness of the programmes of adult education depends upon competent administrative machinery.

Recent Programmes in Adult Education

Adult education policy statement (1978)—The Government of India resolved to wage a relentless struggle against literacy to enable the masses to play an active role in social and cultural change.

National Adult Education Programme (NAEP) 1978—NAEP was launched on 2, October 1978. It was proposed to cover the entire population in the age group 15-35 by the end of 1983-84. The programme, by and large, could not be implemented properly and results were far below expectation.

Adult Education and National Policy on Education, 1986—The NPE envisages that the whole nation must pledge itself to the eradication of illiteracy, particularly in the 15-35 age group. The National Programme of Adult Education is to be a phased time-bound programme covering 40 million by 1990 and another 60 million by 1995. Its aim will be (a) strengthening of the existing schemes, (b) launching of Mass Programmes for Functional Literacy, (c) organisation of various programmes of continuing education, (d) strengthening of technical resource system, (e) mounting of Technological Mission of Eradication of Illiteracy, (f) involvement of a dynamic management system to ensure the effective delivery of the learning inputs and, (g) the institution of an effective Management Information System and evaluation.

A vast programme of adult and continuing education has been undertaken through various ways and channel, including:

1. Establishment of centres in rural areas for continuing education;
2. Worker's education through the employers, trade unions and concerned agencies and government;
3. Post-secondary education institutions;
4. Wide promotion of books, libraries and reading rooms;
5. Use of radio, TV and films, and reading rooms;
6. Creation of learners' groups and organisation;
7. Programmes of distance learning;
8. Organising assistance in self-learning; and
9. Organising need and interest based vocational training programmes.

National Literacy Mission (NLM)—The NLM was launched in the month of May 1988 to impart Functional Literacy (a term used of Adult Education by NLM) to 80 million illiterate person in the 15-35 age group—30 million by 1990 and an additional 50 million by 1995.

The Mission has given the following components of functional literacy:

1. Achieving self-reliance in literacy and numeracy:
2. Becoming aware of the causes of their deprivation and moving towards amelioration of their condition through organisation, and participation in the process of development;

3. Acquiring skills to improve the economic status and general well-being;
4. Imbibing the values of national integration, conservation of the environment, women's quality, observance of small family norm, etc.

Salient Features of the NLM

1. Priority to weaker sections.
2. Honorarium to adult education workers.
3. Involvement of several agencies.
4. Post literacy and follow-up programmes.
5. Setting up of National and State Boards of Adult Education.
6. Setting up of National Institute of Adult Education, New Delhi.
7. Various programmes of non-formal education.
8. Utilisation of mass media for adult education.

Total literacy campaign (TLC)—Greatly encouraged by the success of the TLC in district Ernakulam (Kerala) in January 1990; it has been started in the central district of the country. Its chief features are:

1. It is a voluntary effort campaign.
2. It is implemented by Zilla Saksharta Samitis (District Literacy Committees) under the District Collector.
3. Suitable primers for the adults are developed.
4. It aims at enlisting the cooperation of all sections of the population.

Jan Shikshana Nilayam (JSN)—Under the National Literacy Mission, several thousand post literacy centres or libraries, called Jan Shikshana Nilayam have been established. A JSN caters to a cluster of 4-5 villages covering a population of almost 5,000. A JSN is introduced to perform two important functions (a) to upgrade the knowledge of the adults and (b) to serve as 'windows' for securing information on various development programmes.

Table 17.1

Adult Literacy Rate of India Vis-a-Vis Select Countries (2009)

S.No.	*Country*	*Adult Literary Rate*
1.	Afghanistan	28%
2.	Bangladesh	54%
3.	Bhutan	56%
4.	Canada	100%
5.	China	93%
6.	**India**	**64%**
7.	Greece	97%
8.	Hangary	99%
9.	Iran	71%
10.	Indonesia	70%
11.	Italy	100%
12.	Japan	10%
13.	Mexico	92%
14.	Myanmar	90%
15.	Nepal	57%
16.	Pakistan	55%
17.	Poland	99%
18.	Russian Federation	100%

Source : *The State of the Word's Children 2009.*

Evaluation of the Adult Education Programme

The progress in the field of adult education has been far from satisfactory. Several functionaries and especially the honorary workers supply fictious enrolment figures. The report of the Controller and Auditor General of India (CAG), tabled in the Lok Sabha on 19 May, 1992, makes very dismal reading. Out of 406 voluntary agencies evaluated by the audit, as many as 140 needed improvement, 77 were not capable of undertaking literacy programmes, and the performance of 86 agencies was categorised as wholly unsatisfactory for their bonafides were doubtful.

It has been gradually becoming a fashion to obtain suitable grants from the government in the name of promotion of adult education. There has been loud talk of Total Literacy Campaigns (TLSC) in almost all the districts of the country. In several cases, a 'bogus' enrolment is shown and tall claims made. Hundreds of associations and organisations on paper flourish in the name of adult education. Such gimmicks should stop.

If the past is any index, substantial progress in the field of adult education is a 'mirage'. Without a firm political will, backed by a firm realistic programme, we are likely to repeat our past mistakes and waste crores of rupees.

Questions and Problems

A. Essay-Type Questions

1. Explain the concept adult education. State its role in the modernisation of Indian.
2. Describe the recent attempts made in India for the promotion of adult education. State the promotion of adult education in India. State the reasons why these efforts have not been successful. Suggest suitable measures.

B. Short-Answer Type Questions

3. Write a short note on the National Literacy Mission.
4. State the objectives of adult education.

18 Primary/Elementary Education

18.1 Primary Education and National Development

J.P. Naik, an eminent educator of our country has very aptly described the importance of primary elementary education in these words, "The progress of primary education is one index of the general, social and economic development of the country as a whole." A well planned and properly implemented system of Education at this stage plays a very significant role in laying down the proper foundation of child's cultural, emotional, ethical, intellectual, moral, physical, social and spiritual development. Primary education also contributes a lot to foster values of emotional and national integration. Studies have clearly established that countries which have made adequate provision for primary education are far ahead of those with inadequate provision. In this context it must be remembered that in developing countries, the majority of the population can have access to primary education only. It is, therefore, extremely important to make a sufficient investment at this level of education.

18.2 Nomenclature of Primary Education

Usually the terms elementary, basic education and primary education are used interchangeably. The National Policy on Education has used elementary education for classes I to VIII. The NCERT, in its publication entitled *National Curriculum for Elementary and Secondary Education: A Framework* (1988) mentions elementary education (8 years) divided into primary stage (5 years and upper stage (3 years). The Ministry of Human Resource Development, Department of education uses elementary education and under it includes primary classes (classes I to V) and middle (classes VI to VIII). There is a good deal of class variation in the years of schools at the two stages. Generally speaking elementary education refers to the combination of two stages of education—primary stage of education covering classes I to V (age group 6 to 11) and upper primary classes covering VI to VIII (age group 11 to 14). Thus the elementary stage consists of classes I to VIII and age group 6 to 14.

The primary stage consists of classes I to V (5 years) in 20 states Union Territories. States where the primary stage consists of classes other than I to V are Assam, Gujarat, Karnataka, Kerala, Maharashtra, Meghalaya, Dadra and Nagar Haveli, Goa, Lakshadweep, Mizoram and Mahe and Yaman region of Pondicherry. Of these in Gujarat, the primary stage consists of classes I to VIII.

Middle stage consists of classes VI to VIII in as many as 20 states and UTs. Exceptions are Andhra Pradesh, Assam, Gujarat, Karnataka, Kerala, Maharashtra, Meghalaya, Dadra and Nagar Haveli, Goa, Daman & Diu, Lakshadweep, Mizoram and Mahe region of Pondicherry. These is no middle stage in Gujarat. In Meghalaya, middle stage consists of classes IV to VI, in others it consists of classes V, VI and VII.

Age of admission—Minimum age for admission to class I is generally 5 + or 6 years. In 18 states UTs, the minimum age for admission to class I is 5 + years and in 121 states UTs, it is 6 + years. In 2 states UTs, there is no age restriction.

Medium of instruction—The regional language or the mother tongue is the medium of instruction at the primary stage in most of the states and UTs. Facilities for studying in a medium other than regional languages vary considerably.

18.3 Universalisation of Elementary Education (UEE) and Constitutional Provisions

The universalisation of elementary education has been one of the most important goals of educational development in India since independence. It means making education available to all children in the age group 6 to 14 (classes I to VIII). It found expression in Article 45 of the Indian Constitution as a Directive Principle of State Policy where it reads under the caption *"Provision for Free and Compulsory Education for Children*—The State shall endeavour to provide, within a period of ten years, from the commencement of the Constitution, for the free and compulsory education for all children until they complete the age of fourteen years." In other words this task should have been completed by 1960. However this resolve could not be accomplished on account of several problems such as the rehabilitation of displaced persons after partition and lack of resources. As a result the target date had to be revised first to 1970, then to 1976 and later on to 1990. The target date, according to the National Policy on Education, 1986 was 1995. The modified National Policy on Education 1992 has further revised the target date. It reads, "It shall be ensured that free and compulsory education of a satisfactory quality is provided to all children upto 14 years of age before we enter the twenty first century. A national mission will be launched for the achievement of this goal."

Universalisation of elementary education or compulsory primary education implies three aspects, (a) universalisation of provision of schools within the walking distance of the child, (b) universalisation of enrolment of all children in the age group 6 to 14 and (c) Universalisation of retention of all students, meaning thereby that once a child joins a primary school at the age of 6, he should remain these till he complete all 8 classes.

Progress in the universalisation of elementary education— There has been a phenomenal progress in the expansion of elementary education in India since independence. Enrolment in classes I to V increased 7 times during the period 1950-51 to 2006-07.

In classes VI to VIII, enrolment during the same period, increased 17 times. Overall increase in classes I to VIII was 8 times. The following table illustrates this expansion.

Table 18.1

Enrolment in Primary and Middle Classes (2006-2007)

	Enrolment	*1950-51*	*2006-07*	*Increase*
1.	Enrolment in classes 1 to V	19.02 million	132 million	7 times
2.	Enrolment in classes VI to VIII	3.1 million	52.0 million	17 times
3.	Enrolment in classes I to VIII	22.3 million	184 million	8 times

Source : *Selected Educational Statistics* 2007-2008, Ministry of Human Resource Development.

Notwithstanding this increase, as stated earlier, we are far behind our commitment of compulsory universal elementary education. Here four aspects must be noted: (a) we are able to cover about 75.5 per cent of the population in the age group 6 to 14 the, (b) coverage of population in backward and tribal areas and also of girls is far below the national average, (c) the drop-out rates are very alarming, (d) many of the primary schools lack adequate facilities like buildings, drinking water facilities etc. on the one hand and blackboards, charts, etc. on the other hand.

Problems of Universalisation of Education

1. Low priority to primary education.
2. Inequality of educational opportunity.
3. Low enrolment of the backward sections of the society.
4. Stagnation.
5. Wastage,
6. Low enrolment of girls.
7. Apathy and poverty of the parents.
8. Defective curriculum.
9. Uninspiring methods of teaching.
10. Lack of suitable reading and writing material for children.
11. Lack of qualified teachers.

12. Frequent transfer of teachers.
13. Lack of effective inspection and academic guidance by the inspecting staff.
14. Failure to enforce compulsory attendance.
15. Lack of a suitable admission policy.
16. Conservative attitude towards co-education.
17. Inadequate and unattractive school buildings.
18. Poor nutrition of children.
19. Existence of large number of incomplete primary schools.
20. Lack of part-time facilities.
21. Group rivalries of local bodies.
22. Meagre financial outlays.
23. Population explosion.

Measures for the Promotion of Universalisation of Education

Priority to elementary/primary education—Primary education should be developed on a priority basis and the percentage of the budget under this sector should be suitably raised. There has been a decline in this sector. From 56 per cent of the total educational budget spent on primary education during the First Plan, it came down to 33 per cent in the Sixth Plan and 37 per cent in the Seventh Plan.

In the case of higher education, the percentage increased to 12 per cent from 9 per cent during the same period. It is, therefore, very essential that priority should be given to elementary education.

Wide Variation in Enrolment and Equalisation of Educational Opportunities

There are wide variations in enrolment ratio in different states. The Table 18.2 illustrates that enrolment in classes I to V was as high as 150.4% in Madhya Pradesh and as low as 94.7% in Bihar. In classes VI to VIII the ratio was 96% and 39% respectively. Table 18.2 provides the state of variation in enrolment rates.

Table 18.2

Enrolment Ratio in Some Bigger States (2006-2007)

S.No	*State*	*Classes I to V*	*Classes VI to VIII*
1.	Andhra Pradesh	96.5	74.5
2.	Bihar	94.7	39.0
3.	Gujarat	120.1	75.4
4.	Karnataka	107	88.8
5.	Madhya Pradesh	150.4	96.0
6.	Maharashtra	113.6	101.5
7.	Tamil Nadu	117.8	109.2
8.	Uttar Pradesh	113.7	53.6
9.	West Bengal	102.7	70.5

Source: *Economic Survey 2008-2009.*

The hard core of non-enrolled children at the elementary stage are in highly populated states like Bihar, Rajasthan and Uttar Pradesh as shown above. Again there is less enrolment of children belonging to backward agricultural landless labourers, high areas, rural areas and also urban slum areas etc.

The problem of inequality of educational opportunity may be considered at several levels and with reference to different sections of society, as follows:

1. Inequality that exists between one State and another.
2. In a State the prevailing inequality between one district and another.
3. In a district, unequal educational opportunity in different areas.
4. Inequality of educational opportunity between boys and girls.
5. Inequality of education opportunity that now prevails between the different sections of society; advanced castes versus scheduled castes and scheduled tribes; upper and middle classes versus lower classes; economically better off classes versus poorer section, etc.

Causes of inequality of educational opportunity—On the basis of the experience reported in the different States, the following causes which now tend to create inequality of educational opportunity may be listed:

1. Varying economic conditions. Some States are economically advanced while others are lagging behind.
2. Social and psychological reasons—apathy towards girl's education, particularly in socially backward groups of people.
3. Varying literacy levels in states, districts, and localities.
4. Existence of inaccessible and isolated small habitations particularly in hilly and forest areas.
5. Varying occupational opportunities prevailing in different areas.
6. Lack of suitable and adequate accommodation for running schools.
7. Dearth of suitably qualified teachers, particularly women teachers, and teachers for tribal areas.

Effective and Deliberate Steps to be Taken for Bringing About Equality in Educational Opportunity

The financing of elementary education where equality of opportunity is to be achieved without delay should be separated from financing of other sectors of education and treated on a special footing. Special financial assistance must be given to all States on the Principle of Equalisation in order to enable them to fulfil the directive of Article 45 of the Constitution. The extent of the States' effort and the quantum of assistance from the Centre should both be decided by the Equalisation Authority, that is, the Central Government while equalising at the State level. Similar principles should be adopted by the State quantum at the District level and by the District, when equalising at the local level.

Special Programme Towards Equalisation

1. Free distribution of mid-day meal to the poor and needy children.

2. Supply of free textbooks and clothing to the poor children.
3. Directive by the centre to backward States to concentrate on the clearance of the backlog of non-attending boys and girls.
4. Setting up of school improvement committees for undertaking an intensive drive for bringing non-attending children to schools and also to see to it that enrolled children are retained in schools. Where school management committees already exist, they may be entrusted with this task.
5. Steps may be taken to enforce attendance, at least to the extent of issuing warning notice and attendance orders to the parents of defaulting children.
6. Whenever necessary, the prescribed teacher-pupil ratio may be relaxed while sanctioning new schools and additional teacher units in backward areas.
7. Provision of part-time schooling may be arranged for those children who are unable to attend regular schools.
8. Intensifying social education programmes in backward areas and among socially backward groups of people for education the parents.
9. Special targets may be fixed for enrolment by the State Government from year to year for each district; greater attention being paid to backward districts and areas.
10. Separate targets for the enrolment of children of groups of backward classes may also be fixed at State and District levels.

Table 18.3

Share of Elementary Education in the Overall Investment in Education During the Plan Period

(Percentage)

Plan/Sector	*Elementary Education*	*Secondary Education*	*Higher Education*
First Plan (1951-56)	56	13	9
Second Plan (1956-61)	35	19	18

Contd.

Third Plan (1961-67)	34	18	15
Plan Holiday (1967-1969)	24	16	24
Fourth Plan (1969-74)	30	18	25
Fifth Plan (1974-78)	35	17	22
Sixth Plan (1980-85)	33	21	22
Seventh Plan (1985-90)	37	24	16
1990-92	37	22	12
Eighth Plan Outlay (1992-97)	47	18	8

Source: Compiled form Five Year Plans, Planning Commission, New Delhi.

Popularisation of Universal Education in the Backward Areas Including Tribal Areas

1. *Teacher training*—Maximum academic qualifications of candidates belonging to backward areas for teachers training may be relaxed the teachers working there should be acquainted with local dialects.
2. *Introduction of tribal dialects and medium of instruction*— In tribal areas, having a large population where people do not understand the regional language, tribal dialects may be introduced as the medium of instruction wherever possible in the initial stage and then they should be integrated with the general educational system and may be taught regional languages. But in the tribal areas where the children understand the regional language, it can be used as a medium of instruction. Such practice will reduce the rate of wasteage and stagnation and also create interest among the children.
3. *Suitable curriculum for the schools*—There is a need for evolving a suitable curriculum for the schools functioning in tribal areas. This curriculum may be science-oriented but

culture-based. The curriculum should be so framed that this should include the various aspects of tribal life and culture.

4. *Economic incentives to parents*—Since the tribal people are economically backward and the children have to take part in different activities of economic pursuits, the parents do not care for the education of their children because this sustains an economic loss. Thus some economic incentive may be given to students, but not to parents to prosecute their studies. The timing of the schools may be adjusted according to the local needs.
5. *Provision of hostels and extension of ashram schools*—Whenever possible, the schools functioning in tribal areas may be provided with hostels which will solve many problems. Extension of Ashram schools, use of youth dormitories may also solve some of the problems.
6. *Provision of suitable school accommodation*—All the schools functioning in tribal areas should be provided with suitable accommodation.
7. *Encouragement of participation of tribal percents*—Participation of tribal parents in the educational programmes may also be encouraged. The awareness and interest regarding the utility of education for the children should be created among the parents.
8. *Provision of audio-visual aids*—Provision of audio-visual aids for the development of education of tribal children is essential and may be made available as soon as possible.
9. *Opening of non-formal education centre*—These centres may cater to the needs of drop-outs and adult women folk of the community.

18.4 Drop-Outs, Stagnation and Wastage

The drop-out rate implies the percentage of children leaving elementary or secondary stage before completion. Stagnation means failure in class, that is, repetition of class or classes by pupils. Wastage means drop-out of pupils and its consequent wastage.

Causes of both stagnation and wastage are by and large, the some.

Table 18.4

Drop-out Rates (1990-91 and 2005-06)

Category	*Classes (I-V)*		*Classes (I-VIII)*	
	1990-91	*2006-07*	*1990-91*	*2006-07*
Total	42.60	29.0	60.90	50.82
SCs	49.40	34.2	72.09	57.3
STs	62.52	50.0	78.57	70.9

Source: *Educational Statistics*, 2006-2007.

The above figures clearly show that the drop-out rates are very high. About 40 per cent students who join class I, leave school before the competition of class V and as many as about 57 per cent leave school before class VIII.

A UNICEFF Publication entitled *The State of the World's Children* 2009 provides the following data on universalisation of education.

Table 18.5

Universalisation of Education: Comparative Data on Select Countries

Country	*Percentatge of Children reaching grade 5*	*Country*	*Percentage of Children reaching grade 5*
Bhutan	90	Finland	100
Afghanistan	50	Sweden	100
Pakistan	37	Sri Lanka	97
Bangladesh	90	Germany	99
India	**73**	Japan	100
Indonesia	88	Switzerland	100
China	95	USA	99
France	100		

Source: *The State of the World's Children, 2009.*

From the above it is concluded that strenuous efforts are needed to come upto the level of developing countries. It is also to be remembered that the years of schooling bear a close relation with productivity.

Causes of Wastage (Drop outs) and Stagnation

Some of the important causes are:

1. Illiteracy and apathy of the parents towards the education of their children in the backward areas.
2. Book centred curriculum.
3. Irregular attendance of the students.
4. Curriculum not related to life situations
5. Uncongenial environment at home
6. Poverty of the parents and children's help in their earning if they do not attend school.
7. Inefficient teaching.
8. Defective system of examination.
9. Poor health of the children.
10. Malnourishment of the children.
11. Stagnation in class I, on account of the following reasons.
    - (i) Heterogeneity of the age composition of students. Some children join late and they find it difficult to adjust psychologically with their peers who are of a lower age.
    - (ii) Making fresh admission throughout the year.
    - (iii) Over-crowding in the class.
    - (iv) Inability of the teachers to use play-way techniques which can assist in initiating the children pleasantly to school life.
    - (v) Poor teaching of beginning reading.

11. Rigid school time table.
12. Uninspiring overall school environment.

Suggestions for Tackling Drop-out Wastage and Stagnation

1. *Making school environment attractive*—The overall environment of the school should be made attractive. A primary school should have a playground attached to it. The spirit of play-way should be predominant. There should be no over crowding in classes so that a teacher could play individual attention. There should be audio visual aids to excite the curiosity of the students.

2. *Adjusting school timings and vacation*—There is need for adjusting the school vacations suitably so as to make them synchronise with the sowing and harvesting of crops. It may be mentioned in this connection that a few States have already taken this step.
3. *Providing part-time education*—Facilities for part-time education need to be greatly expanded. The cost of part-time education can be reduced by arranging classes in the regular school building in the evening and employing the same staff by giving them some extra allowance.
4. *Providing facilities to needy students*—Student whose parents are poor should be provided certain facilities such as a free supply of books and stationery, free uniforms and even stipends. Provision of subsidised mid-day meals should be made by enlisting the co-operation of the local community.
5. *Educating parents*—The parents need to be educated about the importance of education in individual and social development. A massive programme for removing adult illiteracy should be taken up. An educated parents is the best guarantee to ensure that his children also get education. A climate for education should be created by pressing the mass media such as the radio and television into service.
6. *Removing social evils*—Steps should be taken to remove social evils such as early betrothal or marriage. Social taboos against the education of girls in mixed schools even in the age group 6-11 should be removed. This can be done through persuasion and propaganda.
7. *Changing admission policy*—All the children to class I should be admitted at the beginning of the session. Normally no child should be admitted to school after two months of the beginning of the session.
8. *Establishing ungraded schools*—As suggested by the Kothari Education Commission lower primary schools should be ungraded. The idea underlying ungraded schools is to enable each child to progress at his own speed.
9. *Reforming examination system*—Evaluation should be continuous and there should be automatic promotions subject to regular attendance.

18.5 Qualitative Improvement in Elementary Education and Issues Involved

Multiple Steps for Improving Elementary Education

Side by side with the expansion of education facilities at the elementary level, efforts have also been made to improve the quality of education so as to make it more responsive to the aspirations and the needs of the people. It is to be remembered that improving the quality of education is a slow and gradual process. Another point regarding this aspect is that improvement is a constant process. Changes in science and technology necessitate changes in the teaching-learning process, contents and materials. As J.P. Naik has observed, "it includes several programmes, such as improvement of textbooks, adoption of better methods of teaching and evaluation, intensive utilisation of available facilities, maintaining contact with the community, individual guidance to students, inculcation of social and moral values etc., which do not need much investment in terms of physical or monetary terms. But their success depends essentially upon the competence of teachers, their identification with the interests of the students committed to their care."

Improvement in the quality of elementary education raises many issues which may briefly be stated here. In fact the issues of wastage, stagnation, drop-outs and improvement in education are inter linked. Some of these issues have already been discussed.

1. Curriculum renewal.
2. Textbook improvement.
3. Better teaching methods.
4. Effective teacher education or training.
5. Provision of material facilities in the schools.
6. Improving the working of one-teacher schools.
7. Progressive methods of evaluation.
8. Democratisation and humanising school administration and supervision.

18.6 Operation Blackboard

Background—The National Policy on Education expressed a great concern for the non-fulfilment of the constitutional provisions regarding universalisation of elementary education. It, therefore, resolved to complete this task by 1995. While doing this, it was felt that a comprehensive scheme for bringing about qualitative changes in the elementary education was needed urgently so that the problems of drop-outs, stagnation and wastage could also be satisfactorily handled, side by side the quantitative expansion of elementary education.

Meaning and components of the scheme of O.B.—'Operation Blackboard' aims at the substantial improvement in facilities in elementary schools all over the country. Operation Blackboard lays down the minimum level of facilities to be provided to all elementary schools which have so far been established. It also prescribes the minimum level of funding for all primary schools to be opened in future.

Use of the word 'Operation' indicates that there is an urgency in this programme its goals are clear and well-designed and the government is determined to achieve these goals with the cooperation of the people within a pre-determined time-frame.

There are three components of Operation Blackboard:

1. Provision of at least two reasonably large rooms that are usable in all weathers, with a deep veranda, along with separate toilet facilities for boys and girls.
2. Provision of at least two teachers, as far as possible, one of them a woman, in every primary school.
3. Necessary land for construction of school buildings, including land for games and sports has to be provided by the local community.

Implementation—Since it was not possible to provide all the above mentioned facilities to all schools at the same time, on account of financial constraints, the implementation was phased over a period of three years 20 per cent of community developments to be covered in 1987-88, 30 per cent in 1988-89 and the remaining 50 per cent in 1989-90.

The 'Operation Blackboard' envisaged the coverage of all primary school run by the Government, Local bodies, Panchayati Raj institutions.

Role of the Central and State Governments in the implementation of the blackboard scheme—For the effective implementation of the scheme the Government of India has undertaken a great responsibility in this scheme. Funds for the construction of buildings have to be arranged by State Governments under the schemes of National Rural Employment Programme (NREP) and Rural Landless Employment Guarantee Programme (RLEGP).

The following guidelines have been issued to the States regarding the construction of school buildings:

1. Each of the rooms to be constructed should be 30 square metres in area and the depth of the verandah should be approximately 9-10 feet. Even if there are two rooms in existence at present whose area is less than the recommended area, new rooms should be constructed.
2. Separate toilets for boys and girls must form a part of construction activity. Toilets should be so constructed that they inculcate desired toilet habits among children.
3. The design of the building should provide scope for expansion. Every effort should be made to utilise local materials to keep the cost low. The building should be adequate without being ostentatious, and should merge with the environment. It should also be ensured that there is built in space for storage of equipment. Well-plastered blackboards should also form part of the structure itself in the rooms, as well as at both ends of the verandah.

The role of the local community has been defined in the scheme as follows:

1. Necessary land for construction of school buildings, including land for games and sports has to be provided by the local community.
2. The local community preferably Village Education Committees, have to give a formal undertaking that they will accept responsibility for repair and maintenance of the building.
3. The local community has also to accept responsibility for an appropriate fencing around the school compound.

Provision of essential commodities include teaching learning equipment, textbooks, charts, toys, work experience equipment, play materials, primary science kit (NCERT), mine tool kit (NCERT), mathematics kit, Reference books, books published by the National Book Trust etc., musical instruments, chalk and duster etc.

During the period 1987-88 to 1993-94 over 95 per cent of the blocks in the country comprising over 95 per cent of the primary schools were covered.

Suggestions for the Successful Operation of the Scheme of Blackboard Operation

1. The State Government should devolve all decision-making powers concerning Operation Blackboard to the Education Complexes which would seek consultation from DIETs on the one hand, and the school concerned and the Village Education Committee, on the hand, for planning and implementing the scheme.
2. The schools and the Village Education Committees made fully responsible for UEE in their respective areas, should undertake a micro planning exercise for working out their requirements under Operation Blackboard and be accountable for its implementation.
3. Operation Blackboard must be given the status of one of the priority strategies for UEE, but, at the same time, it should be ensured that investment is made only one those items whose need has been established by the teachers and other related persons on the basis of micro-planning and classroom requirements.
4. For posting women teachers in the villages, it would be best to select them locally, wherever possible, or else make provision for their accommodation, security and other support services.

18.7 Minimum Levels of Learning (MLL)

The strategy of minimum learning aims at laying down learning outcomes expected from the students after following a course. It also lays down measures for the realisation of these standards. MLLs were laid down by a committee set up in 1990. The Department of Education Ministry of Human Resource Development has organised a number of seminars to explain the concept of MLLs and chalk out strategies for its implementation. Projects covering 2,000 primary schools, 10,000 teachers and about 3.86 lakh students have been planned in this context.

The main steps by which MLL is to be introduced in schools are (a) an assessment of the existing level of learning achievement; (b) a definition of the MLL for area and the time-frame within which it will be achieved, (c) re-orientation of teaching practices to competency based teaching, (d) an integrating of continuous, comprehensive evaluation of student learning with classroom teaching, (e) review of textbooks and revision where required, (f) the provision of necessary inputs including provision of physical facilities, teacher training, supervision and evaluation, etc., to improve learning acquisition of MLLs.

18.8 Curriculum Reforms, UNESCO, UNICEF etc.

The following are the important projects:

1. Primary Curricular Reform Project with UNICEF assistance.
2. Nutrition Health Education and Environment Sanitation (NHEES), covering about 100 primary schools in each of the 9 states in which it is in operation.
3. Primary Education Curriculum Renewal (PECR) in operation in 15 states, 30 primary schools in each state.
4. Development Activities in Community Education and Participation (DACEP) is in operation in 13 states, with 100 community education centres in each state.
5. Area Intensive Education Project for. Human Resource Development (AIEP) for the promotion of elementary education of girls.
6. Early Childhood Education (ECE) in, 11 states. Children Media Laboratory, NCERT, provides play materials.

Non-Formal Education at the Elementary Stage

Non-formal education for children also has to receive equal importance. Unlike for the adults the needs here are two-fold. The first is to help those children who desire to join the formal set-up of education for certificate oriented courses or higher studies to cover, within the shortest possible time, the courses that their counterparts have covered in the formal schools. For the other children not desirous of certificate-oriented education, programmes of functional education have to be organised on the same lines as those for the adults.

Non-Formal Education and National Policy on Education, 1986 and 1992—The Policy envisages:

1. A large and systematic programme of non-formal education will be launched for school drop-outs, for children from habitations without schools, working children and girls who cannot attend whole-day schools.
2. Modern technological aids will be used to improve the learning environment of NFE (Non-Formal Education) centres.
3. Talented and dedicated young men from the local community will be chosen to serve as instructors and particular attention will be paid to their training.
4. Steps will be taken to facilitate their entry into the formal system in deserving cases.
5. All necessary measures will be taken to ensure that the quality of non-formal education is comparable with formal education.
6. Effective steps will be taken to provide a framework for the curriculum on the lines of the national core curriculum, but based on the needs of the learners and related to the local environment.
7. Learning material of high quality will be developed and provided free of charge to all pupils.
8. NFE programmes will provide a participatory learning environment, and activities such as games and sport, cultural programmes, excursions, etc.
9. Much of the work of running the NEF centres will be done through voluntary agencies and Panchayati Raj institutions.
10. The provision of funds to these agencies will be adequate and timely. The Government will take over-all responsibility for this vital sector.

It is estimated that there are about 2 lakh non-formal education centres (80,000 for girls only) with about a 60 lakh enrolment. The programme covers 18 States and Union Territories.

Questions and Problems

A. Essay-Type Questions

1. What are the difficulties in implementing the constitutional provision for universal compulsory education? Suggest suitable measures for its early implementation,
2. To what extent have the constitutional provisions regarding compulsory provisions been fulfilled. Describe the measures taken in this regard.
3. What measures may be taken for improving the quality of primary education?
4. Briefly explain the terms 'drop-outs, 'stagnation' and 'wastage'. What steps should be taken to minimise these?
5. What are the various aspects of equality of opportunity in elementary education? Suggest measures for tackling the situation.
6. "At the elementary stage of education in India the problem is not only of enrolling children but also of retaining them." Explain this statement.
7. What is the meaning of 'Operation Blackboard'? What is its significance in the universalisation of elementary education?

B. Short-Answer Type Questions

8. Briefly describe the various schemes launched in the field of elementary education with the help of UNICEF.
9. State the role of non-formal education in the promotion of elementary education.
10. List measures for the promotion of elementary education among the backward sections and tribal areas.

19 Secondary Education

19.1 Significance and Nomenclature of Secondary Education

Significance of secondary education—Since the secondary stage of education coincides with the adolescence period, it becomes the most crucial period. It is the terminal stage of a large number of pupils who enter life. It assists them to become useful members of a complex modern society.

Secondary education provides a teacher for the primary schools. In general, the minimum qualification for admission in an elementary teacher training institute or school is the completion of the secondary schooling.

Secondary education leads to higher education. It is expected that students completing this stage should have the requisite maturity to pursue higher education.

In view of the importance of the secondary education in the Socio-Economic reconstruction of the country, the Secondary Education Commission 1952-53 outlined the four aims of secondary education (a) development of democratic citizenship, (b) improvement of vocational efficiency, (c) development of personality and (d) development of qualities of leadership.

Nomenclature of Secondary Education

Secondary Education is the second level of schooling that falls between the elementary-primary level and higher educationl college level. Before the introduction of the 10+2+3 patterns of education in India, there were several patterns of secondary education.

According to a publication entitled *Selected information on School Education in India* (1991), published by the Department of Education, Government of India, the secondary stage consists of class IX-X in 20 states/UTs. In other states/UTs, it consists of class VIII-X. Senior Secondary (10+2) intermediate stage consists of classes XI-XII in all the states/UTs. In 1992-93, there were 62,984 high schools and 18,880 higher secondary schools (New pattern). There were also 2,222 intermediate/junior colleges in Andhra Pradesh, Assam, Karnataka, Maharashtra, Manipur, Mizoram and Nagaland.

Brief History of the Pattern of Secondary Education in India

The Secondary Education Commission recommended the new educational structure for Secondary education after the 4 or 5 years of Primary or Junior Basic Education:

1. A Middle or Junior Secondary or Senior Basic stage which should cover a period of 4 years;
2. A Higher Secondary stage which should cover a period of four years.

The Education Commission 1964-66 envisaged the pattern of education as, "a pre-school stage of 1-3 years, a primary stage of 7-8 years (divided into lower primary of 4 or 5 years and higher primary of 3 years in general education, or 1-3 years in vocational education), a higher secondary stage of 2 years of general education or 1-3 years of vocational education and a higher education stage of 3 years of more for the first degree course."

The National Policy on Education (1968) stated, "The ultimate objective should be to adopt the 10 plus 2 plus 3 pattern, the higher secondary stage of two years being located in schools, colleges or both according to local conditions.

The National Policy on Education, 1986 states, "The National System of Education envisages a common educational structure. The 10+2+3 structure has now been accepted in all parts of the country. Regarding the further break-up of the first 10 years efforts will be made to move towards an elementary system comprising

5 years of primary education and 3 years of upper primary, followed by 2 years of High School."

The modified NPE, 1992 observes, "Efforts will also be made to have the +2 stage accepted as a part of school education throughout the country."

19.2 Problem of Secondary Education and the Secondary Education Commission, 1952-53

Background of the appointment of the commission—India had recently achieved its political freedom and after careful consideration it decided to transform itself into a democratic and secular republic. This required that the educational system must contribute in the development of habits, attitudes and qualities of character which should enable its citizens to bear worthily the responsibilities of democratic citizenship. This required a review of secondary education.

Accordingly the Government of India set up the Secondary Education Commission in September 1952 under the Chairmanship of Dr. A Lakshmanaswami Mudaliar, Vice-Chancellor, Madras University.

The Commission submitted its recommendations in 1953.

Main Recommendations of the Commission

The Secondary Education Commission surveyed education in India and made recommendation for its reconstruction. Among its most important recommendations, mention may be made of the following:

1. Aims of secondary education.
2. Duration of the secondary education.
3. Curriculum of the secondary education.
4. Establishment of multipurpose schools.
5. Provision of educational and vocational guidance and counselling.

Aims of Secondary Educational

The commission recommended four aims, keeping in view the needs of a democratic India as envisaged in the constitution.

Development of Democratic Citizenship

This implies the development of these qualities-(a) clear thinking, (b) receptivity to new ideas, (c) clearness in speech and writing, (d) education in the art of living in a community, (e) passion for social justice, (f) development of tolerance, (g) development of true patriotism.

Improvement of Vocational Efficiency

This includes (a) creating an attitude of dignity of work, (b) doing all work efficiently, (c) promotion of technical skills, (d) increased productivity, (e) provision of diversified courses.

Development of Personality

(a) Appreciation of cultural heritage, (b) cultivating rich interests, (c) development of hobbies.

Development of Qualities of Leadership

It was considered very essential for the successful functioning of our democracy.

Establishment of Multipurpose Schools

The Commission recommended that multipurpose schools should be established to provide for the individual differences of students to use and develop their natural aptitudes and inclinations in the special courses of studies chosen by them.

Evaluation of the report—The impact of the report on educational reforms in the country was negligible. The report did not give due attention to the financial consideration in the implementation of its recommendations. It did not suggest short term and long term strategies for carrying out the reforms. The scheme of multipurpose schools could not make headway. The commission did not state in clear terms the duration of each stage of school education. The commission also did not visualise a definite framework for vocationalisation of secondary education.

19.3 Education Commission 1964-66 on the Restructuring of Secondary Education

Appointment of the commission—Independence of the country in 1947 raised high hopes that the colonial system of education would undergo a radical change to meet the requirements of independent India. But in spite of a number of committees and commissions, each examining a particular level of education, satisfactory progress was not made. It was, therefore, felt that a comprehensive educational policy dealing with the aspects of education at all levels was needed. Accordingly the Government of India appointed the Education Commission in 1964 to advise the Government on the national policy of education. The Commission gave its recommendation sin 1966. It is popularly known as the Kothari Commission after its Chairman, D.S. Kothari.

Main Recommendations of the Commission

The Commission's recommendations covered almost each aspect of education. However, the following are generally considered to be most significant.

1. Significant role of education in national development and productivity.
2. Stress on science education.
3. Vocationalisation of secondary education.
4. 10 + 2 + 3—uniform educational structure for the entire country.
5. Introduction of work experience as an integral part of school education.
6. Ten years of schooling of general education.
7. Specialisation or streaming in classes XI and XII.
8. Increase in instructional days and minimising holidays.
9. Neighbourhood concept of schools.
10. Establishment of book banks.
11. Provisions for adequate number of scholarships.
12. Identification of gifted students and special programmes for them.
13. Adequate residential facilities in schools.
14. More attention on the education of the backward classes.
15. Development plan for education in each district
16. Two sets of curricula.
17. Prescriptions of three or four textbooks for each subject.
18. Importing of moral and religious education.

19. Guidance and counselling as an integral part of school programme.
20. Rich co-curricular programme.
21. Evaluation as a continuous process.
22. Establishment of school complexes.
23. Developing a wide range of correspondence courses.
24. Suitable pay scales for teachers.
25. Creation of an Indian Education Services like I.A..S. and other Allied Services.
26. Education Acts to be passed by all states.
27. Three language formula.

Evaluation of the report—The Education Commission report is an achievement, a mine of information and wisdom and source of guidance and inspiration. The recommendations of the Commission led to the formulation of the National Policy on Education 1968— The first policy on education in independent India. The introduction of the new pattern of education in also on account of the recommendations of the Commission. The establishment of book banks owes its origin to the report of the Commission. As recommended by the Commission work experience has been made an integral part of the curricula. The Commission's recommendation on the pay scales of teachers are regarded as the 'Magna Carta' for teachers. The scheme of vocationalisation of school education could not be implemented effectively.

Nevertheless in several areas, the recommendation of the commission remained on paper. For example, (a) creation of school complexes, (b) development of 'Neighbourhood' concept of schools, (c) creation of an All Indian Education Service, (d) equalisation of educational opportunity to the weaker sections, (e) establishment of a suitable machinery for assessing manpower needs, (f) continuous evaluation, (g) implementation of the three language formula.

19.4 Duration of Higher Secondary/Senior Secondary Education

The Secondary Education Commission 1952-53 made the following recommendations:

1 Under the new organisational structure, education should commence after a four or five year period of primary or junior basic education and should include: (a) the middle or senior basic or junior secondary stage of 3 years, and (b) higher secondary stage of 4 years.

2. During the transitional stage, the existing High Schools and the Higher Secondary Schools should function on the lines laid down.

3. The present Intermediate stage should be replaced by the Higher Secondary stage which should be of four years' duration, one-year of the present Intermediate being included in it.

4. As a consequence of the preceding recommendations the first degree course in the university should be of three years's duration.

5. For those who pass out of the High School, there should be provision for a pre-university course of one-year, during which period three scheme of studies should be planned with due regard to the needs of the degree or the professional course to be taken by the students and special emphasis should be placed on the quickening of intellectual interests, training in methods of study at college and the study of English so long as it continues to be the medium of instruction at the university.

6. Admission to professional colleges should be open to those who have completed the higher secondary course, or have taken the one-year's pre-university course.

7. In the professional colleges, a pre-professional course of one year should be provided for the students, preferably in the professional colleges themselves. As a transitory measure, these may be held in the degree colleges where facilities exist, till professional colleges are able to provide for such courses.

For about 11 years after the submission of the report, no action could be taken on the recommendation of the Commission. The situation was reviewed by the Education Commission 1964-66 which recommended the structure as under:- .

1. One to three years of pre-school education.

2. A ten-year period of general education which may be sub-divided into a primary stage of 7 to 8 years (a lower

primary stage of 4 to 5 years and a higher primary stage of 3 or 2 years), lower secondary stage 3 or 2 years of general education or one to three years of vocational education.

3. A higher secondary stage of two years of general education or one to three years of vocational education.
4. A higher education stage having a course of three years or more for the first degree, followed by courses of varying duration for the second or research degrees.

19.5 10 + 2 + 3 Pattern of Education

Origin of the New Pattern of Education

On the recommendation of the Education Commission, the Government of India issued in 1968 a National Policy Statement on Education for the country. The statement read, "It will be advantageous to have a broadly educational structure in all parts of the country. The ultimate objective should be to adopt the 10+2+3 pattern, the higher stage of 2 years being located in schools, colleges or both according to local conditions." The Government of India, Ministry of Education, appointed a National Committee in 1973 to formulate practical measures for the introduction of the new pattern of 10+2+3. The new pattern was first introduced in 1975 in secondary schools affiliated to the Central Board of Secondary Education. Now almost all the States and Union Territories have adopted the pattern.

In 1993, there were about 63,000 High School and 19,000 Higher Secondary Schools (new pattern).

Significant Characteristics of the New Pattern Duration—(a) It provides for a common 10 years of schooling, (b) the total years of schooling is 12 years in place of 11, (c) the first degree course is of three years duration, (d) the first university degree can be obtained after 15 years of study, (e) it calls for a selective approach to upgrade the existing secondary schools (schools of 10 years and eleven years of schooling).

Curriculum—(a) It includes the compulsory study of two languages, mathematics, science, social studies, work experience, physical education in classes IX and X. (b) It provides for streaming of courses in classes XI and XII. (c) It provides for two levels of courses—advanced and ordinary in some subjects.

Vocational courses and Socially Useful Productive Work (SUPW)—(a) It aims at establishing a close link between the school and the environment by modifying the present emphasis on theoretical aspects of education. (b) It provides for an appropriate opportunity to students to take up vocational courses.

Merits of the New Pattern

1. *Education and productivity* —The major thrust in the 10+2+3 pattern has been towards linking education with productivity by means of providing useful work experience and vocational courses.
2. *Strengthening national unity*—The uniformity of educational structure in all parts of the country is expected to generate a feeling of 'oneness' among the students.
3. *Specialisation at the appropriate time*—Modern Research findings in the field of education point out that streaming of pupils into specialised groups from Class IX is undesirable. The New Pattern provides reasonable opportunities at the appropriate time to the students to take decisions about the particular stream to be studied by them after a term.
4. *Inter-state adjustments*—Uniformity of structure facilitates education of the mobile population which is continuously increasing in the country. Differences in structures and standards cause considerable inconvenience to students migrating from State to State.
5. *Implementation of national programmes of schoolimprovement*—A broadly uniform pattern in all parts of the country is intended to facilitate the implementation of educational programmes, production of books and teaching material, reforms in evaluation and training of teachers.
6. *Mature students*—With a 2-year preparation, instead of one year after Class X, students will become more mature and be able to do more advanced work than is possible now.
7. *Rasing of standard of education*—The indiscriminate rush to universities may be stemmed and more places in colleges my be released for those best fitted for higher education. This would tend to raise the standard of higher education.
8. *Vocationalisation of education*—Vocationalisation is an essential and urgent reform intertwined with the new pattern

and the programme for this purpose will have to be based upon detailed man-power estimates formulated on the basis of district surveys.

9. *Education for employment*—The new pattern envisages great help in providing employment after completing secondary education.

10. *Upgrading for the first degree course*—Now, why 15 years! Besides other things, the standard of education will have to be raised if India has to, take her rightful place among nations. No advanced country in the world honours a young man with the award of a first degree in less than 15 years of preparation and hard work. In the USA, the high school is up to 12th grade which is followed by a 4-year course in a college or university leading to a bachelor's degree. In the USSR, the complete secondary education ends with grade 10 and then begin 5 years of higher education in a university. In England, after 13 years of schooling, 3 years are needed in a college or university to obtain the first degree. Thus it will take a total 16 years in USA, 15 years in USSR and 16 years in England to be awarded the first degree. This is why a graduate from India will not be considered equivalent to a graduate in U.K. and therefore a graduate needs to graduate again in U.K. before pursuing higher education for which B.A. is the minimum qualification. The 10 + 2 + 3 pattern provides the answer.

Limitations

1. *Expensive scheme*—The addition of one year to school education involves a lot of expenditure on the part of the Central and State Government and also to private organisation.
2. *Heavy financial burden on parents*—The parents have to support their children and provide education to them for 12 years instead of 11.
3. *Loss of one year*—Earlier Students could join professions or other avenues after 11 years of schooling and now they need 12 years. Likewise they graduated after 14 years of study as against 15 years now. Thus they lose one year.
4. *Heavy curriculum*—Students are overburdened with too many subjects and too much subject content.

5. *Ill equipped schools*—The Scheme of vocationalisation could not work satisfactorily as necessary facilities could not be provided.
6. *Non-recognition of vocation courses*—In several cases students who pursue vocational courses find it different to pursue higher education on the one hand and on the other are not adequately equipped to take up a vocation.
7. *Non-banking of work experience*—Work experience has been defined as participation in productive work in school, in a workshop, in a factory, on a farm etc. but in implementation, by and large, its linking with productivity is conspicuously absent.
8. *Teacher training*—Adequate provision has not been made for providing and training suitable teachers for work experience.
9. *Lowering of standard in certain subjects*—The curriculum has very little relevance to life situations. It is likely to lower the standard in various subjects. An example will make this point very clear—a student now studing in Class XI and taking up commerce, would have studied only 2 periods in Class IX and X, whereas in the old pattern he used to study for about 16 periods. In the old pattern, a student would have studied commerce for about 24 periods in Classes IX, X, XI whereas now in four years, i.e., Classes IX, X, XI, and XIII he would be studying commerce for about 18 periods only. This implies that after studying commerce for four years in the new pattern i.e., in Class IX-XIII, a student would not have gained the same knowledge as he would have gained in the old pattern by studying commerce for 3 years. This would mean that as far as the question of specialisation is concerned, the new pattern certainly puts the students at a disadvantage. Thus it may be stated that from the specialisation point of view, 10 + 2 would be less than the previous 8 + 3.
10. *Not-child centred*—The compulsory introduction of mathematics and science in classes IX and X robs the children of their freedom. Why should a child study these subjects if he has no aptitude for them. It is common experience that the compulsory study of these subjects aggravates the problem of drop-outs.

New Pattern: A Fad, A Fraud and A Fallacy

The new pattern is considered a fad by its critics because it is based on the assumption that the compulsory teaching of mathematics and science upto Class X will lead to the development of a scientific temper of mind of the students.

The critics call it a fraud because its implementation has been only 'showy' and the authorities failed to provided necessary facilities.

It is also pointed out by critics that it is a fallacy to assume that the addition of one year in schooling will lead to making students more mature and knowledgeable.

Suggestions for the Effective Implementation of 10+2+3 Pattern

1. Rational use of funds.
2. Training and reorientation of teachers.
3. Vocational Courses to be linked with the environment.
4. Survey of vocational opportunities and provision of vocational courses accordingly.
5. Proper selection of schools for opening class XI and XII and also of vocational courses.

19.6 Diversification or Streaming of Courses

Meaning of diversification—Diversification of courses implies providing varied courses to students. Before the introduction of the 10+2 pattern of education, diversification was done in class IX and thereafter it began to take place in class XI.

Why Diversification at the Higher Secondary Stage

1. *Individual difference and education according to three as*—The fundamental principle of education is that it should be according to the age, ability and aptitude of the students and especially at the adolescent stage so that they derive the most benefit. It is observed that at the higher secondary stage of education there emerge masked individual differences which must be catered to.
2. *Varied needs of the country*—The country needs craftsmen, engineers, doctors, managers etc., for different fields and industries. The resources of the country are to be utilised to the maximum. The same set of people, trained in the same

occupations or trained for the same services can hardly meet the growing demands of trade, industry, commerce and agriculture etc.

3. *Age of specialisation*—The modern age is the age of specialisation: plus 2 stage seems to be the most suitable occasion for the diversification of courses as the interests and abilities of students are adequately developed and they are in a better position to take decisions about their future career. At the age of 13, under the old pattern, students were required to take decisions regarding their future career at an early date. The recent world trends in secondary education is providing for diversification and specialisation at the age of about 15 years or senior stage of secondary stage.

19.7 Ishwarbhai Patel Review Committee and Socially Useful Productive Work

Main Recommendations of the Ishwarbhai Committee, 1977-78

The Review Committee was appointed in 1977 under the Chairmanship of Dr. Ishwarbhai ex Vice-Chancellor, Gujarat University to review the syllabuses and textbooks prepared by the NCERT for the 10+2 pattern of education.

The Committee made the following recommendations:-

1. Introduction of socially useful productive work in place of work experience.
2. Broad syllabus frames in stead of a detailed syllabus.
3. Exclusion of subjects like economic, commerce and psychology in class IX and X/
4. Deletion of some portions in some subjects.
5. Freedom to various agencies to develop textbooks.
6. No rigid time-table in classes I-IV/V.
7. Only two books, that is, one for Mathematics and the other for environmental studies, apart from the textbook in one language at the primary stage.
8. No homework in classes I-IV/V.
9. No rigid academic year.
10. Stress on self-study.

Socially Useful Productive Work (SUPW)

One of the most important recommendations of the Ishwarbhai Patel Committee report was to introduce socially useful productive work as an integral part of the school curriculum for classes I to X. It suggested that about one-fifth of the total school time-table should be devoted to this aspect of the curricula.

According to the Committee, SUPW is 'purposive, meaningful, manual work resulting into either goods or services which are useful to the community'.

Objectives of Socially Useful Productive Work—It aims at:

1. Acquainting children with the world of work and services of the community and developing in them a sense of respect for manual workers.
2. Developing a desire to be useful members of the society and contributing their best to the common good.
3. Inculcating a positive attitude of team work and socially desirable values like self-reliance, dignity of labour, tolerance, co-operation, sympathy and helpfulness.
4. Helping in understanding the principles involved in the various forms of work.
5. Leading children to participate increasingly in productive work, as they go from one stage of education to another, and there by enabling them to earn while they learn.
6. Providing opportunities for creative self-expression and for the development of problem solving abilities.

Flexible contents—The contents of socially useful productive work should be need-based and depending upon the problems of child, the school and the community. Therefore, it will be very flexible in nature and no fixed programme can be prescribed in all the schools at a time. Even the details of the programme may vary from year to year in the same school according to the changing needs.

Three phases of SUPW—From the point of view of the learning and skill development process, experience in every productive work or service has to be provided in three phases, (a) exploration of the world of work with the help of observation discussion and very simple manipulation, (b) experimentation with materials, tools and techniques, (c) work practice in the form of work projects or crafts/trades and services. This aspect should be reflected in the plan of the contents.

Difference Between Socially Useful Productive Work and Other Similar Activities

1. The programme of Socially Useful Work is different from crafts in this respect that whereas the work experience aims at developing manipulative skills only, the former aims at harmonious development of the whole man, that is, his body, mind, heart and spirit.
2. The programmes of work-experience lack the components of social usefulness and in practice are not even casually correlated to other subjects. The remunerative aspect of this programme is also given high priority at the cost of creativity and scientific planning and intelligence performance.
3. Originating from the Gandhian concept of education, Socially Useful Productive Work is a tool for inculcating Gandhian values—truth, non-violence, self-reliance, dignity of labour, co-operation, classless society etc.

Implementation of a Programme of Socially Useful Productive Work

1. Adequate overall planning.
2. Setting up of necessary infrastructure.
3. Proper selection of the contents of SUPW.
4. Preparation of suitable instructional material.
5. Training and orientation of a teacher to take up SUPW.
6. Creation of necessary climate for the introduction of SUPW.
7. Liaison with different organisations.
8. Periodical supervision of the work.
9. Evaluation of the programme.

19.8 Navodaya Vidyalayas: Peace Setting Schools

Concept of Navodaya Vidyalayas—Para 5.14 of the National Policy on Education observed that it is universally accepted that children with special talent or aptitude should be provided opportunities to proceed at a faster pace, by making good quality education available to them irrespective of their capacity to pay for it. Accordingly the NPE envisaged the setting up of the Scheme of Navodaya Vidyalayas. Para 5.15 of the revised NPE 1992 illustrated the scheme as "Pace-setting residential schools, Navodaya Vidyalayas, intended to serve this purpose have been set up in most parts of the country on a given pattern, but with full scope for innovation and experimentation. Their broad aim will continue to be to serve the objective of excellence complied with equity and social justice (with reservation for the rural areas, SCs, and STs.) to promote national integration by providing opportunities to talented children from different parts of the country to live and learn together to develop their full potential, and most importantly, to become catalysts of a nation wide programme of school education."

Chief Characteristics of Navodaya Vidayalayas

1. They cater to the needs of the talented students.
2. Primarily, they are rural based. Seventy-five per cent seats are reserved for rural areas.
3. They are residential.
4. Education is provided free of charge.
5. They have reserved seats for SCs and STs as per their actual population in the district subject to a minimum of nationally prescribed figure of 15 per cent and 7.5 per cent for SCs and STs respectively.
6. A certain portion of students come from other states.
7. They are expected to foster national integration by providing opportunities of learning and living together.
8. It is expected that in these schools, the three-language formula would be implemented in its true spirit.
9. Selection of admission is based on different types of scholastic aptitude texts which aim at eliminating the element of subjectivity.
10. These schools are expected to encourage experimentation and innovations.
12. It is envisaged that these schools would become catalysts of a nation-wide programme of school improvement.

Organisation of Navodaya Vidyalayas—A Navodaya Vidyalaya Samiti, an autonomous organisation in the Ministry of Human

Resource Development has been set up. These schools are affiliated to the Central Board of Secondary Education, Delhi.

The Central Government bears 100 per cent expenditure for running these institutions and it is the responsibility of the State Governments to provide a plot of land, about 30 acres in area, free of cost.

Eventually the Central Government plans to open one such school in every district. This target is likely to be achieved by the end of the Eighth Five-Year Plan. Upto 1994, there were 339 sanctioned Vidyalayas in the country.

Adverse Comments on the Scheme by the Ramamurti Report (1990)

1. The Scheme itself is very costly—with high capital expenditure and high per student expenditure; government support for this high cost education for a selected few, while lakhs of children are denied their legitimate claims for provision of moderately good education is discriminatory and inconsistent with the principles for which a democratic republic committed to equity and social justice stands.
2. The scheme caters only to a microscopic minority of the total school population.
3. It is an exclusive system inconsistent with the long-cherished common school system of public education.
4. A matter of investigation is whether a majority of those who have received admission in the Navodaya Vidyalayas do really come from families of agricultural workers, share-croppers, rural artisans, the poor, marginal farmers, etc.
5. Teaching of science through English and social science through Hindi is pedagogically unsound.
6. The operational design of Navodaya Vidyalayas fails to fulfil the original policy mandate of NPE in the light of the points made below:
   (i) It is true that 'children with special talent or aptitude should be provided opportunities to proceed at a faster pace, by making quality education available to them. However, in operational terms, it does not necessarily mean that such children need be separated from the rest in special residential schools in order to be nurtured.

(ii) There can be varying perceptions of what constitutes 'special talent or aptitude.'

7. Navodaya Vidyalayas were started in great haste, without the necessary infrastructure or operational facilities which reveals a lack of proper planning.
8. Experienced staff could not be made available in the beginning on account of unattractive terms of deputation.

19.9 Vocationalisation of Education

Meaning of Vocationalisation of Education

The National Review Committee (1977-78) under the chairmanship of Dr. Malcolm S. Adiseshiah, appointed to review the curriculum of the +2 stage of school education with special reference to vocationalisation of education explained the concept of vocationalisation at the higher secondary stage in these words, "The vocationalised spectrum of the Higher Secondary schools is learning of skills or a range of skills through the study of technologies, related sciences, and farm or other practical work. This vocationalised training must be distinguished from technical/ vocational education imparted in the I.T.I.s technical high schools, agricultural or industrial polytechnics, where a certain level of skill as craftsman or technician or extension agent is aimed at and attained. The Vocationalised spectrum that is referred to embraces in the UNESCO language "those aspects of the educational process involving, in addition to general education, the study of technologies and related sciences and the acquisition of practical skills, aptitudes, understanding and knowledge relating to occupations in the various sectors of economic and social life. Such an education would be an integral part of general education and a means of preparing for an occupational field and an aspect of continuing education."

Why Vocationalisation of Education

The Education Commission 1964-66 pointed out, "another programme which can bring education into closer relationship with productivity in to give a strong vocational bias to secondary education and to increase the emphasis on agricultural and technological education at the university stage. This is of special significance in the Indian situation where, the educational system has been training young persons so far mostly for government services and the so called white collared profession."

Para 5.16 of the National Policy on Education 1992 states, "The introduction of systematic, well planned and rigorously implemented programmes of vocatonal education is crucial in the proposed educational reorganisation. These elements are meant to develop a healthy attitude amongst students towards work and life, to enhance invidual employability", to reduce the mismatch between the demand and supply of milled manpower and to provide an alternative for those intending to pursue higher education without interest or purpose. Efforts will be made to provide children at the higher secondary level with generic vocational courses which cut across several occupational fields and which are not occupation-specific".

The merits of the vocationalisation of education may be listed, as under:

1. Vocationalisation education is related to productivity.
2. It enhances employability.
3. It prepares for self-employment.
4. It inculcates dignity of labour.
5. It reduces the mismatch between the demand and supply of skilled manpower.
6. It provides an alternative for those pursuing higher education without particular interest or purpose.
7. It is helpful in the maximum utilisation of the human and national resources of the country.

The Vocational Course

The Adiseshiah National Review Committee in its report *Learning To Do - Towards a Learning and Working Society* (1987-88) recommended that special attention has to be given to the self-employment factor. Vocational education at this level should, as far as possible, not duplicate what the ITI's or Technical High Schools are at present offering. The main thrust of the proposed vocationalisation will be on rural, agricultural and related vocations. The duration of a vocational course should normally be two years in so far as the instruction in the schools in the formal system is concerned. The courses requiring lesser duration than two years may be pursued through non-formal systems such as part-time and evening courses, correspondence courses, etc., and the institutions should be free to offer such courses through non-formal channels.

Courses and Allocation of Time—The Committee has recommended the following course and allocation of time for the vocationalised spectrum:

Course	*Time Allocation*
1. Language(s)	15%
2. General Foundation Course	15%
3. Elective Subjects (60% for practical work)	70%

Vocational electives—Any one vocational course to be offered out of 64 courses divided into 8 categories:

1. Agricultural and related vocations
2. Business and office management
3. Para-medical
4. Educational service
5. Local body and other services
6. Journalism
7. Home Science related vocations
8. Other general services.

National Policy on Education 1992—Suggested the following courses:

1. Vocational education will also be a distinct stream, intended to prepare students for identified occupation spanning several areas of activity.
2. Health planning and health services management should optimally interlock with the education and training of appropriate categories of health manpower through health-related vocational courses.
3. Efforts will be made to devise suitable vocational courses based on agriculture, marketing, social services etc.
4. An emphasis in vocational courses will also be on the development of attitudes, knowledge and skills for entrepreneurship and self-employment.

Vocational targets and slow progress—The NPE 1986 proposed that vocational courses cover 10 per cent of higher secondary students by 1990 and 25 per cent by 1995. But taking into consideration the slow progress in their area, NPE 1992 proposed that vocational courses cover 10 per cent of higher secondary students by 1995 and 25 per cent by 2000. The progress, however, cannot be said to be satisfactory. According to the *Annual Report 2000-2001*, of the Ministry of Human Resource Development, Vocational Stream was provided in 6800 Senior Secondary Schools with 10 lakh students. Considering the total enrolment of about 282 lakh students, the situation in vocational courses does not seem to be encouraging.

The following are some of the important reasons of the slow progress of vocationalisation of education.

1. Traditional disregard for manual work.
2. Indifference of the community involvement in providing facilities.
3. Failure to control the expansion of general secondary education.
4. Failure to check the rush for higher general education.
5. Unfavourable wage prices for middle-level skilled workers as against white collar job operators.
6. Failure to delink degrees from jobs.
7. Unfavourable prevailing social attitudes and inability to reconcile ourself to the idea of going into the vocational stream.
8. Lack of adequate infrastructure for making suitable provisions for vocational courses.

Measures for Popularising Vocational Courses

The Adiseshiah Report made the following recommendation which, by and large, are still relevant even to-day.

1. *Work-based learning*—Learning must be based on work either through what the Ishwar Bhai Patel Committee calls socially useful productive wok or through vocationalised courses.
2. *Agriculture-oriented vocational courses*—Vocational courses should be in agricultural and related rural occupational areas

and in managerial, commercial, health and para-medial vocations and not through opening vocational courses at this level in the manufacturing, industrial and engineering occupations.

3. *Curriculum*—The curriculum should be so structured that the courses lend themselves to imparting instruction in terms of well connected modules to enable the students to choose and combine them according to their needs.

4. *Suitable text-books*—In order to impart instruction in vocational courses, in agricultural and related subject, books be written on a priority basis to suit local conditions and made available to the schools. In some general education and commercial subjects where textbooks produced in other countries are suitable, these books may be adapted and translated into Indian languages.

5. *Teachers of vocational courses*—At the start there should not be insistence on post-graduate qualification in respect of teachers of vocational courses. What is needed is the means of developing the required skills and competencies in particular vocations and for this, services of persons who have had actual on-the-job experience may be fruitfully utilised to teach vocational courses. Part-time teachers may also be appointed wherever necessary.

6. *Pre-service and in-service training of teachers*—Both pre-service and in-service teacher education should be so organised as to bring about the proposed changes at this stage of education. The Universities, the Teachers Training Colleges, State Councils of Educational Research and Training (SCERTs), State Institutes of Education, State Institutes of Science Education, NCERT, Boards of Secondary Education, Agricultural Universities, institutions like ICAR and all others who are engaged in the preparation of orientation of teachers should be actively involved in this task.

7. *Vocational survey*—With regard to offering of vocation alised courses in rural or urban schools, a vocational survey of the area—metropolitan, block, taluk, district or State—be undertaken, such surveys being done even in cases where the vocational courses have started.

8. *Location of schools in the rural sector*—In the selection of schools, it is recommended that the location of schools in the rural sector be given priority. Since little or no vocationalised education facilities are readily available for rural students, it is recommended that all the new school should be constructed in rural areas and should be adequately equipped..
9. *Use of available facilities*—To economise on the financial investment on infrastructural facilities, it is recommended that the spare capacity in all these schools be used and the enrolment be increased through running double shifts wherever it is feasible and wherever further education demands for technical skills and competencies arises in neighbour heads.
10. *Recruitment Policy*—Vocationally qualified persons should be preferred to graduates and be entitled to the pay scales available to the graduates so long as the jobs performed are the same or similar.
11. *Organisation of vocational education*—A suitable organisation of National Council and State councils of vocational education should be set up.
12. *Apprenticeship facilities*—Suitable apprenticeship facilities should be extended to all the students who complete vocational courses.
13. *Delinking jobs from degrees*—This is very essential to check undue rush to colleges. Moreover appropriate training will prepare for various jobs.
14. *Financial Resources*—Any expenditure on vocationalisation of education should be considered as a national investment and an investment for the future.
15. *Tertiary level courses*—Tertiary level courses will have to be organised for those who pass the Higher Secondary courses of the academic stream and want to pursue vocational courses.
16. *Selection of vocational courses*—The provision of vocational courses in the backward areas may be given priority.
17. *Vocational survey*—With regard to the offering of vocationalised courses in rural or urban schools, a vocational survey of the area— metropolitan, block, taluk, district or state—be undertaken; such surveys being done, even in cases where the vocational courses have been introduced.

18. *Role of different agencies in vocationalisation*—The establishment of vocational courses or institutions will be the responsibility of the Government as well as employers in the public and private sectors; the Government will, however, take special steps to cater to the needs of women, rural and tribal students and the deprived sections of society. Appropriate programmes should also be started for the handicapped.
19. *Opportunities for professional growth*—Graduates of vocational courses should be given opportunities, under predetermined conditions, for professional growth, career improvement and lateral entry into courses of general, technical and professional education through appropriate bridge courses.
20. *Non-formal vocational courses*—Non-formal, flexible and need based vocational programmes should also be made available to neoliterate youth who have completed primary education, school drop-outs, persons engaged in work and unemployed or partially employed persons. Special attention in this regard should be given to women.

19.10 Overall State of Secondary/Senior Secondary Education in India

Secondary education as the weakest link—It is generally observed that as compared with the elementary education and higher education, we have given a very low priority to secondary education. A perusal of the various provisions regarding education in the constitution would reveal that while there is Article 45 concerning elementary education, entries 62, 63, 64, 65 and 66 of List I include higher education, there is no such mention of secondary education. It is therefore, obvious that secondary education has been rather neglected and it has remained the weakest link.

In spite of the recommendations of several national committees and commissions on education and the formulation of the National Policy on Education, 1986 and the revised Policy Formulation 1992 and also Programmes of Action 1986 and 1992, secondary education in general continues to suffer for the reasons stated below:

1. It is bookish in nature.
2. It is examination dominated.
3. It is not suited to the needs of the country.
4. It is geared to university education.

5. It prepares for clerical jobs, by and large.
6. It is not self-employment oriented.
7. It does not develop dignity of labour.
8. It does not develop the necessary manpower for various industries.
9. It is restrictive in scope.
10 It is English-dominated.
11. Methods of teaching are usually dull and mechanical.
12. It fails to develop good work habits.

The National Policy on Education 1986 and 1992 on functions of Secondary Education, states:

1. Secondary education should expose students to the differentiated roles of science, the humanities and social sciences.
2. It should provide children with a sense of history and national perspective.
3. It should give children opportunities to understand their constitutional duties and rights as citizens.
4. It should develop a healthy work ethos.
5. It should develop the values of a humane and composite culture.
6. There should be a core curriculum.
7. It should provide manpower for economic growth.
8. Main emphasis should be on consolidation.
9. Children with special talent or aptitude should be provided opportunities to proceed at a faster pace.

Suggested Reforms in Secondary Education

1. Emphasis should be laid on consolidation of secondary education and not its expansion.
2. A systematic, well planned and vigorously implemented scheme of vocationalisation of education is the need of the hour.
3. Schools of general education, by and large, have failed to provide effective vocational education to students. It is, therefore, necessary that we give a second look to this aspect.
4. It is better if instead of opening ill-equipped Navodaya Schools (Pace Setting Schools), some existing schools in the rural areas are converted into model schools.

5. All the existing schools must be provided with necessary staff and equipment.
6. Provision for scholarship may be made on a large scale.
7. The present system of examination and evaluation should be made more realistic and objective.
8. New schools with adequate infrastructure should be opened in the areas inhabited by the economically weaker sections.
9. The concept of common school and neighbourhood schools should be given a fair trial.
10. Administration and supervision of schools should be made more functional.

19.11 Curriculum Reconstruction in India

A brief history of curriculum reconstruction in India—Since the introduction of the colonial system of education in the country on the recommendations of Lord Macaulay in 1835, it had been felt strongly by the leaders as well as by the masses in general that the curriculum was bookish and did not meet the requirement of the country. After independence the people of India got the opportunity to realise this aspiration. In the following lines, an overview of this direction is presented.

1. The first major attempt was made by Gandhi when he formulated the Basic System of Education in 1937. This was confined to elementary education.
2. The secondary Education Commission 1952-53 suggested a diversified curriculum at the secondary stage.
3. The Education Commission 1964-66 suggested a common curriculum for classes I to X and streaming of courses in class XI.
4. The curriculum as suggested by the Education Commission began to be implemented in a phased manner in 1975 when 10 + 2 + 3, commonly known as new pattern was introduced.
5. In 1977 some modifications were made in the curriculum on the recommendations of the Ishwarbhai Patel Committee.
6. In 1978, The adiseshiah Committee gave its recommendations on the vocationalisation of education.
7. After the formulation of the National Policy on Education 1986, the NCERT prepared a model curriculum known as the National Curriculum for classes I to X. It was based on the thrusts as contained in the National Policy on Education.

It is being revised from time to time.

The Central Board of Secondary Education, Delhi and State Boards of Education modified the curriculum at various stages keeping in view the National Policy on Education.

Secondary Education and Curriculum Reconstruction

The first major attempt to reconstruct the curriculum at the secondary stage of education was made after the recommendations of the Secondary Education Commission 1952-53. The Commission felt that the prevailing curriculum was not in conformity with the rapid changes that had taken place in the country after independence. It found the following defects in the curriculum.

Curriculum Suggested by the Secondary Education Commission 1952-53 (IX to XI)

Keeping in view the changed political, economic, social and cultural set-up of the country, the Secondary Education Commission, 1952-52 envisaged the following curriculum of a Higher Secondary School.

1. (i) Mother tongue or Regional language or a Composite course of the mother tongue and a classical language.
   (ii) One other language to be chosen from among the following:
   (a) Hindi (for those who have not studied it in the middle stage).
   (c) Advanced English (for those who had studied English in the earlier stage).
   (d) A modern Indian language (other than Hindi).
   (e) A modern foreign language (other than English)
   (f) A classical language.
2. (i) Social Studies—general course (for the first two years only).
   (ii) General Science including Mathematics—general course (for the first two years only).
3. One craft to be chosen from the following list (which may be added to according to needs).

   (a) spinning and weaving, (b) wood work, (c) metal work, (d) gardening, (e) tailoring, (f) typography, (g) workshop practice, (h) sewing, needle work and embroidery, and (i) modelling.

4. Three subjects from one of the following groups:

   Group I (Humanities)—(a) A classical language or a third language not already taken, (b) History, (c) Geography, (d) Elements of Economics and Civics, (e) Elements of Psychology and Logic, (f) Mathematics, (g) Music, and (h) Domestic Science.

   Group 2 (Science)—(a) Physics, (b) Chemistry, (c) Biology, (d) Geography, (e) Elements of Physiology and Hygiene not to be taken with Biology, and (f) Mathematics.

   Group 3 (Technical)—(a) Applied Mathematics and Geometrical Drawing, (b) Applied Science, (c) Elements of Mechanical Engineering, and (d) Elements of Electrical Engineering.

   Group 4 (Commercial)—(a) Commercial Practice, (b) Book-keeping, (c) Commercial Geography or Elements of Economics and Civics, and (d) Shorthand and Type-writing.

   Group 5 (Agriculture)—(a) General Agriculture, (b) Animal Husbandry, (c) Horticulture and Gardening, and (d) Agriculture, Chemistry and Botany.

   Group 6 (Fine Arts)—(a) History of Arts, (b) Drawing and Designing, (c) Painting, (d) Modelling, (e) Music, and (f) Dancing.

   Group 7 (Home Science)—(a) Home Economics, (b) Nutrition and Cookery, (c) Mother Craft and Child Care, and (d) Household Management and Home Nursing.

5. Besides the above, a student may opt for one additional subject from any of the above groups irrespective of whether or not he has chosen his other options from that particular group.

Summary—A review of the above shows that a student of Higher Secondary class was expected to take up the following subjects:

1. Two languages of which one should be his mother tongue.
2. A general course in social studies and general science, if he has not taken up these or allied subjects among his optionals.
3. Special subject chosen from any one group.
4. One craft.
5. One additional subject (optional).

School Curriculum and the Education Commission, 1964-66

Need for a radical reform of school curriculum—The commission stated, "The explosion of knowledge in recent years and the reformulation of many concepts in the sciences have highlighted the inadequacy of the existing school programmes and brought about mounting pressure for a radical reform of school curriculum. A unified approach should be taken to the framing of the entire school curriculum a new definition of the content of general education and a new approach to the place of specialisation."

The following chief characteristics of the curriculum were proposed by the Education Commission.

1. Common curriculum for the ten years as against for eight years as suggested by the Secondary Education Commission.
2. Diversification of courses in class XI and not class IX as recommended by the Secondary Education Commission.
3. Provision for ordinary and advanced courses beginning with class IX. There was no such provision in the recommendations of the Secondary Education Commission.
4. Introduction of work experience for developing the dignity of labour.
5. School curriculum to be upgraded through research.
6. Teachers be oriented to the revised curriculum through in-service education.
7. Adequate freedom to be given to schools to devise the curriculum suiting their needs.
8. The standard of attainment to be clearly defined at the end of each sub-stage.
9. Wider choice of subjects in class XI as there were no grouping of subjects. eg. Humanities, Science etc.
10. Implementation of the modified three language formula to be taken up.
11. No differentiation to be made in the curriculum of boys and girls.
12. Home Science to be made an optional subject for girls and not as a compulsory subject.

Subject areas in the higher secondary classes (XI and XII) were as follows:

1. Any two languages, including any modern Indian language and any classical languages.
2. Any three subjects from the following:
   (a) Any additional language (b) History (c) Geography (d) Economics (e) Logic (f) Psychology (g) Sociology (h) Art (i) Physics (j) Chemistry (k) Mathematics (l) Biology (m) Geology (n) Home Science.
3. Work Experience and Social Service.
4. Physical Education.
5. Art or Craft.
6. Education in Moral and Spiritual Values.

After the publication of the report, there were several deliberations which resulted in the Education Policy Resolution 1968. Later on in 1975, the New Pattern of Education 10+2+3, came to be implemented in a phased programme. The New Pattern incorporated the recommendations of the Education Commission with slight modifications.

National Policy on Education and the Curriculum

The National Policy on Education 1986, laid down the guiding principles of curriculum reconstruction, keeping in view the national reconstruction and the role of education in it. Broad features of the guide lines as contained in parts III, V and VIII of the NPE are summarised below:

1. *Common core curriculum*—The National System of Education will be based on a national curricular framework which contains a common core along with other components that are flexible. The common core will include the history of India's freedom movement, the constitutional obligations and other content essential to nurture national identity. These elements will cut across subject areas and will be designed to promote values such as India's common cultural heritage, egalitarianism, democracy and secularism equality of the sexes, protection of the environment, removal of social barriers, observance of the small family norm and inculcation of the scientific temper. All educational programmes will be carried on in strict conformity with secular values.

2. *Curriculum at the secondary stage*—Secondary education begins to expose students to the different roles of science, the humanities and social sciences. This is also an appropriate stage to provide children with a sense of history and national perspective and give them opportunities to understand their constitutional duties and work ethos and of the values of a humane and composite culture. This will be brought about through appropriately formulated curricula. Vocationalisation through specialised institutions or through the refashioning of secondary education can, at this stage, provide valuable manpower for economic growth.
3. *Value education curriculum*—This will be adjusted to make education a forceful tool for the cultivation of social and moral values.
4. *Three language formula*—This will be implemented more energetically and purposefully.
5. *Media and educational technology*—Efforts will be made to provide computer literacy to as many secondary level institutions as possible so that the children are equipped with necessary computer skills to be effective in the emerging technological world.
6. *Environment education*—Mathematics education, science education, work experience, sports and physical education and Education for international understanding—the NPE made a special mention of strengthening these subjects in the curriculum.

National Curriculum for Elementary and Secondary Education (1988)

With a view to carrying out the directives in the NPE, the National Council of Educational Research and Training (NCERT), New Delhi prepared a model National Curriculum for Elementary and Secondary Education. The same was adopted by State Boards of Education and other agencies after making some modifications. The curriculum was based on the following basis and national concerns.

1. Equality of educational opportunity.
2. Preservation of cultural heritage.
3. Constitutional obligations.
4. Strengthening of national identity and unity.

5. Character building and inculcation of values.
6. A global perspective.
7. Protection of the environment and conservation of natural resources.
8. Observation of small family norms.
9. Future-oriented education.
10. Education for all-round development.
11. Evolving a child-centred approach to education.
12. Facilitating creative expression.
13. Inculcation of the scientific temper.
14. Interface between education and the world of work.
15. Continuous and comprehensive education.
16. Utilisation of media and education technology.
17. Minimum levels of learning.
18. Core-curriculum.

Scheme of Studies (Classes I to X)

		Subject and Stages	*Percentage of Time*
1.	**Elementary Education** (8 years)		
	1.	*Primary Stage* (5 years)	
	(i)	One language-the mother-tongue/ the regional language	30%
	(ii)	Mathematics	15%
	(iii)	Environmental Studies 1 and II	15%
	(iv)	Work Experience	20%
	(v)	Art Education	10%
	(vi)	Health and Physical Education	10%
		Total	100%
	2.	*Upper Primary Stage* (3) years	
	(i)	Three languages	32%
	(ii)	Mathematics	12%
	(iii)	Science	12%
	(iv)	Social Science	12%
	(v)	Work Experience	12%

(vi)	Art Education	10%
(vii)	Health and Physical Education	10%
	Total	100%

2. Secondary Stage (2 years)

(i)	Three languages	30%
(ii)	Mathematics	13%
(iii)	Science	13%
(iv)	Social Science	13%
(v)	Work Experience	13%
(vi)	Art Education	9%
(vii)	Heath and Physical Education	9%
	Total	100%

Curriculum for Higher Secondary Classes (XI and XII) (Central Board of Secondary Education, Delhi)

Academic stream—It includes

1. I and II languages (Core/Elective) out of about 30 languages:- Classical, Modern Indian languages and European languages.
2. III to V, three electives out of the following :- Economics, Political Science, Geography, History, Sociology, Psychology, Philosophy, Mathematics, Physics, Chemistry, Biology, Engineering, Drawing, Business Studies, Accountancy, Home Science, Fine Arts (one out of Painting, Graphics, Sculpture, Applied Arts and Commercial Art), Music, Dance, Agriculture, Physical Education, Insurance and Computer Science.
3. VI, General Studies.
4. VII, Work Experience.
5. VIII, Physical and Health Education.

Vocational Stream

I and II Languages as in the case of academic streams

III Vocational course (equivalent to three electives).

IV General Studies/General Foundation.

V Physical Education and Health Education.

Role of Teachers in Curriculum Planning

Several curriculum development studies have clearly shown that significant improvement has taken place where participation of teachers was both more extensive and more inclusive and where more teachers were involved in decision-making and in the production of materials. This led Krug to conclude in 1957 that "teacher participation in curriculum planning today is to be regarded not as a pleasant gesture to the teachers, but rather as an indispensable part of the process."

Theoretically speaking teachers may be called curriculum makers but seldom has the business of curriculum making in India secured wide spread participation of the general body of teachers. In spite of all lip service to the teachers' key role in improving instruction, their participation in curriculum planning and preparation of content and teaching materials has so far received very little practical recognition. Indian teachers have been merely 'implementing' to the best of their abilities and resources, the curriculum and syllabi prepared by outsiders and prescribed by the State Directorate of Education. In actual practice the 'textbook' has become synonymous with the 'curriculum' in so far as the actual implementation of the curriculum is concerned.

Sometimes representatives of teachers are associated in development of the curriculum at the national and state levels. The NCERT and State Councils of Educational Research and Training organise various courses for teachers to provide opportunities for participation in curriculum development and implementation.

General Characteristics of the Organisation and Procedures for Curriculum Development

The following considerations should be kept in view in organising the curriculum:

1. Organisation of curriculum is a cooperative affair and as such all the agencies concerned should work in close cooperation.
2. More importance should be given to the teachers in the formulation of the curriculum.
3. Views of the learners should be given their due importance in planning-learning experiences.

4. Curriculum should be continuously revised through action research.

19.12 Language Problems

Complex problem—Of the many problems which the country has faced since independence, the language question has remained one of the most complex and intractable and it still continues to be so. At the same time there is no doubt that the development of a proper language policy can also assist materially in social and national integration.

In our pluralistic society, use and development of languages in the education context is riddled with complexities. The Ramamurti Report (1990) pointed out that there are 1,652 mother tongues in India. There are over 100 languages spoken by about 700 million people.

Official language—Article 343 (I) states, "The official language of the Union, shall be Hindi in Devanagari script."

2. Notwithstanding, in clause (1), for the period of fifteen years from the commencement of the constitution, the English language shall continue to be used for all the official purposes of the union for which it was being used immediately before such commencement. This period of 15 years has been extended from time to time.

Article 350 A: (Inserted in 1956)-*Facilities for Instruction in mother tongue at primary stage*—It shall be the endeavour of every state and of every local authority within the state to provide adequate facilities for instruction in the mother-tongue at the primary stage of education to children belonging to linguistic minority groups; and the President may issue such directions to any state as he consider necessary or proper for securing the provision of such facilities.

Languages in the eighth schedule of the constitution—The fifteen languages are (1) Assamese (2) Bengali (3) Gujarati (4) Hindi (5) Kannada (6) Kashmiri (7) Malayalam (8) Marathi (9) Nepali (10) Oriya (11) Pubjabi (12) Sindhi (13) Tamil (14) Telugu (15) Urdu.

The Three Language Formula

The Central Advisory Board of Education (CABE) in 1956 examined at length the complex problem of the teaching of the languages in relation to the needs of the country and the requirements of the constitution. It devised a formula known as the Three-Language Formula which was somewhat modified and approved by the conference of Chief Ministers held in 1961. It was further modified by the Education Commission 1964-66.

Lower primary stage—(Classes I to IV or V) The study of only one language should be compulsory—the mother tongue or the regional language at the option of the pupil.

Higher primary stage—(Classes V or VI to VII) Only two languages should be studied on a compulsory basis: (a) the mother tongue or the regional language and (b) the official or the associate official language of the union.

Lower secondary level—(Class VIII to X) A study of three languages should be obligatory; and a student should be under an obligation to study either the official language of the Union or the associate official language which he had not elected at the higher primary stage.

Higher secondary classes—Only two languages need to be made compulsory and the students should have the option to select any two of the three languages studied earlier or a combination of any two languages taken from the following groups: (a) Modern Indian Languages (b) Modern Foreign Languages

Implication of the Three Language Formula

1. At the lower primary stage, in the vast majority of the pupils, the language of study is likely to be the regional language which will also be their mother tongue. Some children belonging to the linguistic minorities may also opt for instruction in the regional language because of its advantages, but this cannot be forced on them. Such children have the right under the constitution to have facilities provided for their education through their mother tongue. It is also desirable that facilities for such children should, therefore, be provided on an 'optional' basis from class III onwards. The Commission does not recommend the teaching of English as a second language at this stage.

2. At the upper primary stage, for almost all the pupils in the Hindi areas, English will probably be the second language but a large proportion of the pupils in non-Hindi areas may also opt for Hindi. Facilities should also be provided for the study of a third language on an optional basis, so that the children in Hindi areas whose mother-tongue is not Hindi and the children in non-Hindi areas who have taken English as the second language may study the official language of the Union, if they so desire.

The three language formula and the national policy on education—The 1968 Policy on Education observed, "At the secondary stage, the state governments should adopt, and vigorously implement the three language formula which includes the study of a modern Indian language, preferably one of the southern languages apart from Hindi and English in the Hindi-speaking states, and of Hindi along with the regional language and English in the non-Hindi speaking states."

The National Policy on Education 1986 reiterated that the Education Policy of 1968 had examined the question of the development of languages in great detail, its essential provisions can hardly be improved open and are as relevant to-day as before. The 1986 policy however, noted that the implementation of part of the 1968 policy has been uneven. It therefore emphasised that this policy needs to be "implemented more energetically and purposefully."

Difficulties in the Implementation of the Three Language Formula

1. Political compulsions, vested interests and lack of political will.
2. Heavy burden of the study of three languages on the children:
3. Heavy financial burden on the institutions for engaging teachers of different language.
4. Less time available for having adequate knowledge of a language.
5. Lack of motivation on the part of the students to learn three languages.
6. Compulsory study of three languages is not in conformity with the spirit of 'child centred' education.

7. Neglect of classical languages like Sanskrit and Persian.
8. Little motivation among the children of the northern states to learn a southern language and resistance against the learning of Hindi in the non-Hindi speaking areas.

Questions and Problems

A. Essay-Type Questions

1. What are the problems of secondary education in India? Suggest measures to improve its quality.
2. In the new pattern of 10+2+3 education, what are the purposes and objectives of Higher Secondary schools? To what extent have these been realised ?
3. Why was the new pattern of education introduced in India State its salient features.
4. "It is generally said that the curriculum at the secondary and higher secondary stage is over burdened." Explain this statement and support your answer with arguments.
7. Prepare a case for the vocationalisation of Secondary, Higher Secondary education in India.
8. Describe the state of vocational education in the country and highlight the problems faced therein.
9. Discuss the need, value and problems associated with the issue of channelising and diversifying students to different streams.
10. Describe the pattern of Secondary and Higher Secondary education as recommended by the Secondary Education Commission and the Kothari Commission.
11. Differentiate Work Experience from Socially Useful Productive Work.
12. Why was the scheme of Navadaya Vidyalayas introduced? State its merits and limitations.
13. Write an essay on the language problem in India.
14. Explain the main features of the three language formula. How can it be implemented more effectively?

B. Short-Answer Type Questions

15. State briefly the objectives of secondary education in India.
16. Write short notes on the main recommendations of the Secondary Education Commission and the Kothari Commission.
17. State the guidelines suggested in the NPE for the reconstruction of the curriculum.
18. "Secondary education is the weakest link in the educational structure." Comment upon it briefly.
19. "In the new pattern of education, school education has been extended by one year." Comment upon this statement.

20 Higher Education

20.1 Higher Education in Ancient India

The world's first universities were founded in India thousands of years ago. Detailed descriptions of nine ancient universities are still available. These are: Kanchi, Kannauj, Kashi (7th century BC), Mithila (Videha), Nadia, Nalanda, Taxila, Valabhi and Vikramshila. Almost all of them had three important characteristics: (a) free education (b) autonomous nature and free of state control (c) students coming to these universities were from foreign countries like Burma, Ceylon, China, Korea and Tibet.

We read in the Ramayana that 'Vyavahare' (Law) was a specialised subject at Taxila (Taksasila). The Mahabharata also refers to Taxila. Chanakya, the Prime Minister of Chandragupta Maurya is said to have had his education at Taxila.

Nomenclature of higher education in India—The preamble of the Act of 1857 by which the first three universities of Calcutta, Bombay and Madras were established stated, "for the better encouragement of her majesty's subjects of all classes and denominations within the Presidency of Fort William in Bengal and other parts of India in the pursuit, of a regular and liberal course of education it has been determined to establish a University at Calcutta for the purpose of ascertaining by examination the persons who have acquired proficiency in different branches of Literature, Science and Art and of rewarding by academic degrees as evidence of their respective attainments and marks of honours proportioned there unto."

The Indian University Education Commission 1902, recommended, "We think it desirable that there should be uniformity in the nomenclature of the examinations and degrees in Arts and Sciences at the different universities. We therefore suggest that the three examinations should be called the Matriculation Examination the Intermediate Examination and the Examination for the Degree of B.A. or B.Sc. respectively."

Indian Universities Act, 1904 gave the universities the right of teaching along with right of conducting examinations.

The University Education Commission 1948-49 observed, "the standard of admission to the University courses should correspond to that of the intermediate examination etc. after the completion of 12 years of study at a school and an intermediate college."

The Three year Degree Estimates Committee of the UGC, 1956 recommended that the three year degree course should be introduced in as many universities as possible.

On the recommendations of the Education Commission 1964-66, the Natural Policy on Education called upon to have a uniform pattern of education 10+2+3 (3 year degree course).

India has now a uniform pattern of education called 10+2+3 which implies 10 years of schooling at the secondary level, 2 years at the higher/senior secondary school or intermediate/ junior college level and 3 years at the first degree level of non-professional education. The duration of the degree courses at the first degree courses in professional subjects varies according to the requirement of each profession and so is the entry qualification. For example, the duration of the first degree course in engineering and technology is 4 years, that of architecture is 5 years and that of medical course is 4 ½ years after the senior secondary stage (class XII)

Constitutional provisions—Under the constitution (original) education was a state subject to Articles 63, 64, 65 and 66. With the constitutional Amendment of 1976, all education was brought under the Concurrent List.

Higher educational institutions include colleges, universities, 'Institutions Deemed to be Universities', 'Institutions of National Importance' etc. There are government colleges as well as aided colleges.

Universities are of various kinds; with a simple faculty or many faculties, teaching or affiliating or teaching cum affiliating, one campus or multicampus, language universities, technological universities, agricultural universities, special institutes of medicine, science, engineering, technology, social sciences, culture etc.

20.2 Types of Universities

Affiliating universities—The universities recognize external colleges offering instruction in its courses of studies. They are diffused over a large area and keep within their fold scattered colleges.

The unitary universities—A 'Unitary' university has been defined as, "One usually localised in a single centre, in which the whole of the teaching is conducted by teachers appointed by or under the control of the university". It has full control over its administration, teachers and teachings.

The federal universities—The main characteristics of a university of this type are: (a) the university and its constituent colleges are situated in close proximity of each other. (b) each constituent college is actively engaged in a work of a university standard. (c) each constituent college is prepared to forgo some measure of its autonomy in order to share in and contribute to the type and government of the university as a whole. (d) the actual teaching , as far as possible, be provided by the constituent colleges under the guidance of the university.

20.3 University Grants Commission (U.G.C.)

The University Grants Commission was set up by the Government of India under an Act (3 of 1956) of parliament in 1956. The functions of the Commission in Section 12 of the Act are: It shall be the general duty of the Commission to take, in consultation with the universities or other bodies concerned, all such steps as it may think fit for the promotion and coordination of university education and for the determination and maintenance of standards of teaching, examination and research in universities, and for the purpose of performing its functions under the Act, the Commission may:

1. Inquire into the financial needs of the universities;
2. Allocate and disburse the funds of the Commission, grants to the universities;
3. Recommend to any university the measures necessary for the improvement of university education and advise the university upon the action to be taken for the purpose of implementing such recommendations;
4. Advise any authority on the establishment of a new university or on proposals connected with the expansion of the activities of the university.
5. Collect information on all matters, relating to university education in India and other countries as it thinks fit and make the same available to any university.

20.4 Growth of Universities in India

In 1957, Calcutta, Bombay and Madras Universities came into existence with the faculties of arts, law, medicine and engineering. Subsequently, several Acts relating to the University education were passed. In 1882, the Punjab University was established at Lahore and in 1887, the Allahabad University came into being. All the five universities were mere affiliating and examining bodies. They did not do direct teaching work.

The number of Universities increased from 27 in 1950-51 to 408 (Universities Deemed Universities and Institutions of National Importance) in 2008-2009. The number of colleges rose from 700 to 22,000 during the some period. Enrolment increased from 2.6 lakhs to 123.7 lakhs. Enrolment of women students was 50 lakhs. Enrolment in the faculty of Arts, Science and Commerce was 51 per cent, 21 per cent and 17 respectively.

The number of teachers was nearly 6 lakhs.

Table 20.1

Expansion of Higher Education in India Since Independence *(Lakhs)*

Item	*1950-51*	*2008-2009*
1. No. of pupils at the university stage studying in arts, science and commerce	6 lakhs	123.7
2. Percentage to total population in the age group 17-23	0.8%	About 11
3. No. of arts, science and commerce (including research) colleges	542	22,000
4. No. of universities, institutes, deemed as universities and institutes of national importance	27	408
5. Autonomous college	nil	281

Source: *UGC Annual Report, 2008-2009.*

Table 20.2

Percentage of Age Group Receiving Tertiary Education (Higher Education) in a Few-Developed and Developing Countries (Estimated 2007)

Developed countries	*Percentage of age group receiving Higher Education*	*Developing countries*	*Percentage of age group receiving Higher Education*
1. USA	70	1. Philippines	45
2. France	35	2. Panama	40
3. Germany	40	3. Venezuela	30
4. Japan	45	4. Egypt	25
5. UK	30	5. Thailand	25
6. USSR	35	6. Mexico	20
		7. Brazil	15
		8. Turkey	15
		9. India	11

Table 20.3

Expenditure on Higher Education in India

Plan		*Percentage of total Expenditure*
First Plan	(1951-56)	9 (140)
Second Plan	(1956-61)	18 (480)
Third Plan	(1961-66)	15 (870)
Plan Holiday	(1966-69)	24 (770)
Fourth Plan	(1969-74)	25 (1,950)
Fifth Plan	(1974-79)	22 (2,050)
Sixth Plan	(1980-85)	22 (5,590)
Seventh Plan	(1985-90)	16 (12,010)
	1990-92	12 (5,880)
Eighth Plan Outlay	(1992-97)	8 (15,160)

Note : Figures in parentheses are in million of rupees

Source : *Compiled from from Five Year Plans, Planning Commission.*

20.5 University Education Commission, 1948-49

Appointment of the commission—The first major step taken in the field of education immediately after independence was the appointment of the University Education Commission under the Chairmanship of Dr. S Radhakrishnan, a distinguished scholar and former Vice-Chancellor of Banaras Hindu University, who rose to the position of the second President of India. The Commission went into all aspects of university education in India and made detailed recommendations for its reform. The report of the Commission is a document of great importance as it has guided the development of University Education in India after independence.

Major Recommendations of the Commission

Aims of Education—

1. To teach that life has a meaning.
2. To awaken the innate ability to live the life of soul by developing wisdom.
3. To acquaint with the social philosophy which should govern all our institutions—educational as well as economic and political.

4. To train for democracy.
5. To train for self-development.
6. To develop certain values like fearlessness of mind, strength of conscience and integrity of purpose.
7. To be acquainted with cultural heritage for its regeneration.
8. To enable us to know that education is a life-long process.
9. To develop an understanding of the present as well as of the past.
10. To impart vocational and professional training.

Objectives of universities—In broad terms, the functions of the universities in the modern world may be said to be the following:

1. To seek and cultivate new knowledge, to engage vigorously and fearlessly in the pursuit of truth, and to interpret old knowledge and benefits in the light of new needs and discoveries.
2. To provide the right kind of leadership in all walks of life, to identify gifted youth and help them develop their potential to the maximum.

Teaching staff—There would be four classes of teachers—professors, readers, lecturers and instructors. Promotion from one category to another to be solely on grounds of merit.

Standard of teaching—The standard of admission to the university course should correspond to that of the Intermediate examination i.e., after the completion of 12 years of study at a school and in the Intermediate College.

To avoid overcrowding at universities and colleges, the maximum number in the arts and science faculties of a teaching university be fixed at 3,000 and in affiliated colleges at 1,500.

The number of working days be substantially increased to ensure a minimum of 180 in the year, exclusive of examination days.

Religious education—All educational institutions should start work with a few minutes for silent meditation.

In the first year lives of the great religious leaders like Gautama the Buddha, Confucius, Zoroaster, Socrates, Jesus, Sankara, Ramanuja, Madhava, Mohammad, Kabir, Nanak, Gandhi be taught.

In the second year some selections of a universal character from the scriptures of the world be studied.

In the third year, the central problems of the philosophy of religion be considered.

Medium of instruction—The federal language be developed through the assimilation of words from various sources and the retention of words which have already entered into Indian languages from different sources.

International technical and scientific terminology be adopted, the borrowed words be properly assimilated.

For the medium of instruction for higher education, English be replaced as early as practicable by an Indian language which can not be Sanskrit on account of vital difficulties.

Pupils at the Higher Secondary and University stages be made conversant with three languages—the regional language, the federal language and English (the last one in order to acquire the ability to read books in English); and

For the federal language one script, Devanagri, be employed and some of its defects be removed.

English be studied in High School and in the Universities in order that we may keep in touch with the living stream of every growing knowledge

Major Recommendations of the Education Commission 1964-66 on University Education

Duration—The duration of the first degree course should not be less than three years. The duration of the second degree course may be 2 to 3 years. Admission to the first degree course should be after 12 years of schooling:

Utilisation of facilities—(a) Emphasis should be laid on programmes of intensive utilisation of existing facilities (b) the number of instructional days should be increased to about 36 weeks (216 days) in a year (excluding 27 days for examinations). (c) vacations should be utilised fully through participation in studies, social service camps, production experience, literacy drives etc.

Raising standards—Efforts should be made to raise the standard of the university degree by adding one year of content. Universities and colleges should assist secondary schools in improving their efficiency.

Part-time education—Part time and own time education should be developed.

Pay scales of teachers as decided earlier should be implemented immediately. These are: Lecturer—Rs 500-950; Reader—Rs 700-1250 and Professor 1000-1600.

20.6 National Policy on Education and Higher Education, 1986 and 1992

Important directions and observations contained in the policy are as under :-

Aims and functions of higher education—Higher education provides people with an opportunity to reflect on the critical social, economic, cultural, moral and spiritual issues facing humanity. It contributes to national development through dissemination of specialised knowledge and skills. It is therefore a critical factor for survival. Being the apex of the educational pyramid, it also has a key role in producing teachers for the educational system.

Emphasis on consolidation—In the near future, the main emphasis will be on consolidation of and expansion of facilities in existing institutions.

Autonomy—Autonomous Colleges will be helped to develop in large members.

Admissions—Admission will be regulated according to capacity.

Courses—Courses and programmes will be redesigned.

Research—Research in Universities will be provided enhanced support.

Correspondence courses and open education—Open learning system will be strengthened.

20.7 Problems of University Education

University Autonomy

Meaning of autonomy—Autonomy implies assuming full responsibility and accountability. The proper scope of university autonomy lies principally in three fields:

1. The selection of students;
2. The appointment and promotion of teachers;
3. The determination of courses of study, methods of teaching and the selection of areas and problems of research.

Autonomy for universities is not claimed merely as a matter of right or privilege. The case for it rests on the obvious ground that, without it, universities cannot discharge effectively their principal functions of teaching, research and service to the community and that only an autonomous institution, free from regimentation of ideas and pressure of party power politics can pursue truth fearlessly and build up, in its teachers and students habits of independent thinking and a spirit of enquiry unfettered by the limitations and prejudices.

In considering the question of university autonomy, we must recognise three (somewhat over-lapping) levels, as it were, at which it functions.

1. Autonomy within a university, e.g., autonomy of the departments, college, teachers and students in relation to the university as a whole;
2. Autonomy of a university in relation to the system, e.g., the autonomy of the university in relation to another or in relation to the UGC and the Association of India Universities; and
3. Autonomy of the university system as a whole, including the UGC and the Association of Indian Universities in relation to agencies and influences emanating outside that system, the most important of which are the Central and State Government.

University finances—University autonomy cannot become real and effective unless adequate provision is made to meet the financial requirements of universities and colleges. While the UGC has been established as an autonomous body to provide the necessary financial resources to the universities without government control or interference, state universities have to depend, for their maintenance grants and matching share, on the funds provided directly by the State Governments. This is an important source through which they can and sometimes do seek to curb the freedom of the universities. This is obviously undesirable.

State Governments should deal with the universities with understanding and imagination and place adequate financial resources at their disposal to enable them to carry out their obligations in an efficient way. It would also be desirable if they seek the advice of the UGC in the matter.

Universities must be free from Government Control—Addressing the 44th Annual Convention of Delhi University, Dr. L. Mudaliar criticised those "who feel that it is their duty to direct, control and otherwise supervise the working of a university" and said, "if today it is considered that a university should be treated in the same manner as a department of government or a local body and if a university is to be controlled by the transient personages in authority that rise and fall in a democracy, the future not only of the university but of the country is at stake."

Temple of learning and university autonomy—Dr Mudaliar further said, "a university was a temple of learning which the "iconoclast" could not be allowed to desecrate by introducing methods of control which may find a place in the market-square or the hustings. And yet, the tendency to play this role among those who believe that they have the democratic authority is great indeed."

Dr. Mudaliar went on to say, "To fix terms of office for the Vice-Chancellor of a University, to determine how he should be selected by a democratic government, to even prescribe conditions for his dismissal, to issue directions, controls and various other orders through many a subordinate official of a hierarchy is certainly not the way to allow a university, a temple of learning, to function.

"I do not want to be misunderstood", he added, "there have unfortunately been lapses on the part of some of those who have been incharge of Universities and who should have known better. Lapses there are in every form of administration and if anyone were to say there have been no lapses in the political, the economic and the social structures of society, he would be under delusion."

Dr. Mudaliar asserted, "the fundamental fact has to be realized that as a temple of learning, as far as possible, no hands should desecrate this sacred shrine: no laws should be passed which will make it appear that a university is but a handmaid of the political government of the day."

"In a political democracy, men may come and men may go; fashions may change; slogans may alter and the very objectives of a democratic government, the very principles that may be laid down by such democracy may vary with the changing moods of democracy; these, however, cannot and should not alter the structure of a temple of learning and if they do, the future of the country is very much at stake."

Autonomy of Colleges

Autonomy of a college implies that a college and its teachers assume full responsibility and accountability for the programmes they provide. This includes content and quality of their teaching, and the admission and assessment of their students. Unless this basic condition is first met it will not be possible to tackle the problem of relevance satisfactorily or to diversify and relate curriculum to local needs and conditions and what is more important to give greater individual attention to the students on the basis of their needs and aptitudes. This alone will make it possible for institutions of higher learning to become communities of teachers and students engaged in an agreed and mutually satisfactory joint pursuit of truth and excellence.

Conditions of the Success of Autonomous Colleges

It would be necessary to ensure that the terms and conditions of service for teachers prescribed by the government and the University Grants Commission continue to subserve the needs of national integration and development.

The concept of an autonomous college requires continuous appraisal and reviews in order to justify its recognition as an autonomous college.

One or two colleges in a district may be chosen for giving the status of an autonomous college. These colleges should be assisted to realise their potential and given autonomy to develop new courses in relation to the needs of the local region and its development.

Students and teachers should be given freedom to express their reviews freely.

Evaluation yardsticks for performance should be formulated carefully and accordingly performance measured.

Access to Higher Education and Admission Policy—since independence, enrolment in higher education has increased over 13 times. However, the facilities have not increased proportionately. It is also a fact that only about 7 per cent of the population gets higher education. There is also the problem of the unemployed educated youth.

On the one hand, we cannot ignore the increasing demand for higher education from all sections of the people and especially the weaker sections who consider it an almost exclusive channel of vertical mobility. On the other hand, we cannot also ignore or under-emphasise some aspects of the situation such as the inability of the economy to absorb its products, the growing spectre of educated unemployment, lack of resources in men, materials and money which often makes expansion lead to dilution of standards, and the unacademic considerations that drive thousands of young persons to the universities.

Selective admissions—Three main elements needed for operating a programme of selective admissions in higher education are:

1. The determination of the number of places in an institution in relation to teachers and facilities available to ensure that standards are maintained at an adequate level;
2. Prescription of eligibility criteria by the universities; and
3. Selection by the institution concerned of the best students from amongst those who are eligible and seek admission.

Part-time and Own-time Education—The opportunities for part-time education through programmes like evening colleges, and for own-time education through correspondence courses should be extended as widely as possible.

Improvement of standards—The standards of education need to be defined in the wider sense of the all-sided development of the personality of the individual and his commitment to social objectives and these would have to be substantially improved and continually raised to suit the changing needs of the country. The system of double standards in educational institutions—one for the rich and the well-to-do and the other for the large majority of the people—should be done away with. All children, both rich and poor, should rub shoulders with each other in a system of common schools at the elementary stage; and in all post-elementary education. Access to the pace-setting institutions should be available to all talented children, irrespective of their social or economic status. Methods of identifying talents by test which do not discriminate against children from disadvantaged background should be devised and a preference should be given to those from disadvantaged backgrounds even if their talent-rating is lower. For such children, special remedial coaching and training will have to be provided, and the appropriate methodology evolved with care. It is true that the maintenance and improvement of standards would need physical inputs, such as good teachers and better learning tools and facilities. But they depend more basically on discovery and cultivation of talent and the creation of a climate of dedicated hard work in all educational institutions. It is these programmes that need to be developed on the basis of a high priority.

Admission to a college should be in accordance with its capacity.

Tutorials should be organised effectively. Teachers should be motivated to attend classes.

Evaluation should be continuous.

Main Problems of University Education

1. Wastage in university education which is as high as 50 per cent.
2. Falling standards of education.
3. Imbalance in the ratio of students studying humanities, social sciences and other sciences.
4. Foreign medium of instruction.
5. Irrelevance of higher education.
6. Lack of basic facilities.
7. Lack of proper guidance.
8. Undue stress on examination.
9. Absenteeism in classes both of students and teachers.
10. Political rivalries.
11. Student and staff activism.
12. Unemployment of the educated youth.

Major Reforms to be Undertaken

The problem of higher education in India is a problem of quality, equality, relevance and of matching the preparation with the needs of the economy.

The system of higher education is now in a state of crisis, due to uncontrolled and unplanned expansion, inadequate inputs in terms of money, materials and talent, falling standards in a large proportion of institutions, weakening of student motivation, increase of educated unemployment, weakening of discipline and dys-functionalities created by the adverse effect of socio-economic problems, a lack of relevance, and significance, and because of undue political interference by subjecting universities to political and partisan pressures and lack of a national consensus in dealing with such a situation. It is obvious that universities cannot function smoothly without adequate support from the Government. This crisis continues to deepen with the passage of time and spreads not only to the entire educational systems but back again into the society itself. If this crisis is to be resolved quickly and successfully, three basic conditions will have to be fulfilled:

(1) The Government should take hard decisions on delinking most of the jobs from degrees, provide large additional investment needed to discover and develop talent, and provide satisfactory conditions of work, revision of recruitment policies, etc. It should also support the universities in taking hard decisions on selective admission, regulate of opening any new colleges, provide satisfactory conditions of work and protec university autonomy.

(2) The teachers and students should carry out their part of the responsibility through intensive efforts to improve standards and the whole academic community should strive to serve society, through sustained, dedicated work, and commitment to the pursuit of knowledge, excellence, and national development.

(3) A nation-wide effort should be organised to achieve a simultaneous breakthrough on the social as well as educational fronts.

The tasks of educational reconstruction thus require an intensive, coordinated and collaborative effort on the part of all the agencies involved—the centre, states, public, teachers, students and administrators. Instead of trying to blame each other (and each one of these has its own share of achievements as well as failures) all these agencies should work together to bring about an educational and social transformation on a scale commensurate with the size and complexity of our problems. If this can be done, there is no doubt that we shall soon be able to create a new educational system and a new society.

Student Indiscipline/Unrest

Student unrest: a global phenomenon—Although student indiscipline is a global phenomenon, yet we can hardly ignore it in India. It is to be taken up seriously and effective measures adopted to save the country from plunging into chaos.

Causes of students' unrest—These may broadly be classified as under :-

1. The loss of leadership by teachers.
2. Growth of economic difficulties.
3. General loss of idealism.
4. Defective educational system.
5. Political interests.
6. General unrest in the country.
7. Inefficient administrative machinery.
8. Generation Gap.

Remedial Measures for solving the Problem of Unrest

Constructive approach and development of social consciousness—The Kothari Commission left, "the key to the successful handling of young people is not found now-a-days in a multitude of restraints and reprimands or in the infliction of continuous penalties. These devices may have to be resorted to in extreme cases but wholesome student attitude and life cannot be created by negative and repressive measures. The true sanction of discipline lies in the development of the social conscience of the under-graduate body as a whole rather than in punitive measures of precautionary vigilance. As is society so in the university laws are observed because they are approved by reason rather than because they are imposed by force. Indiscipline should be terminated by the good sense of the students".

Curriculum reforms—The curriculum should not remain bookish. It should be made practical and functional. Four important measures are needed.

1 Restructuring examination system.

2 Delinking degrees from jobs
3 Democratisation of educational system.
4 Changing methods of class-room teaching.

Involvement of students—The students should be given the opportunity to develop self-respect and self-reliance through an attitude of trust rather than live in an atmosphere of suspicion and fear. Good student government integrates the college community, imparts a wholesome social atmosphere, fosters common ideals and loyal pride in an institution but most important, provides training for good citizenship and social responsibility. It gives scope for the right type of student political activity, which helps to develop the capacity to play the role of citizens in a republican form of government and a democratic society. It replaces the undesirable tendencies towards undermining respect for constituted authority and leaving youth a prey to propaganda of conflicting ideologies.

Promoting a sense of values—The teachers and the educational administrators must set up high standards of values and ideals before the students. It should always be remembered that example is better than precept. Students should also be encouraged to associate themselves with various types of projects for the upliftment of the community.

Welfare measures for promotion of good discipline—The National Cadet Corps is a very useful form of developing discipline and orderly habits among students. Opportunities for recreation, sports, amenities of social life, especially for students residing outside hostels (who are often neglected) all play their part in good discipline.

Restoring the leadership of teachers—Leadership can only be restored to them by their sincerity, faith and enthusiasm in the work. Efforts must also be made to improve their service, conditions and status.

Universities should be divorced from party politics—Students should not be encouraged to engage in party politics though we think it desirable that they take a wholesome and proper interests in elections and a good government. The situation calls for firm but judicious action on the part of college authorities. Further deterioration in morals should be prevented.

Co-operative and integrated efforts—Students discipline is a co-operative venture in which the teachers, the students, the parents, the political leaders, the public, the press and the educational administrator must join hands and make concerted efforts to create a suitable climate conductive to student growth and welfare. The fate of society depends upon the calibre of the product of our educational institutions.

Questions and Problems

A. Essay-Type Questions

1. Explain the broad objectives of higher education in India. State to what extent they are being fulfilled.
2. Elucidate the main problems of higher education in India. Suggest suitable solutions.
3. "There is a general feeling in the country that the standard of higher education in India has been gradually declining." Explain this statement.
4. What is the meaning of autonomy in higher education? What are its chief aspects? State the necessary conditions for its efficient working.
5. "Autonomy and accountability are interrelated." Explain this in the context of higher education.
6. What are the courses of student indiscipline/student unrest in India? Suggest suitable measures.

B. Short-Answer Type Questions

7. Write short notes on the recommendations of the University Education Commission, 1948-49.
8. Write brief notes on the following:
   (a) Kothari Commission, 1964-66 on higher education in India.
   (b) Medium of Instruction at the higher education stage.
   (b) U.G.C

21 Girls and Women Education

Significance of Girls and Women Education

The National Policy on Education (NPE) 1986 and the modified policy in 1992 and Programme of Action 1992, commit the entire educational system to work for women's equality and empowerment, and accord a high priority to the education of women. Education of women plays an important role in the socio-economic development of a country.

The ancient people of India gave an honourable place to women in society. According to the Vedas, women should have the opportunity to attain knowledge of the Vedas from the four corners of the word (Rig Veda 14.9.64). More than 400 verses in the Vedas are ascribed to 24 women seers. In the Vedas, a woman has been called 'Updeshtril (Knowledge giver) and this indicates women working as teachers.

The Rig Veda (2.47.17) proclaims, "O Learned Lady! All life is dependent on you, because you impart education to all."

In the Manusmriti (2.145) it is stated, "From the point of view of reverence due, a teacher is ten-fold superior to a mere lecturer, a father a hundred fold to teacher, mother a thousand fold to a father."

Again it is written in Manusmriti, "Where women are honoured, there the gods delight, and where they are not there all work and effort comes to naught."

Swami Dayanand Saraswati (1825-1883)) in his book *Satyarth Prakasha* has observed, "If the husband be well-educated and the wife ignorant or vice versa, there will be constant state of warfare in the house. Besides, if women were not to study, where will the teachers for girls' schools come from? Nor could ever the affairs of the State, the administration of justice and the duties of married life, that are required of both husband and wife (such as keeping each other happy, the wife having the supreme control over all household matters) be carried on properly without thorough education of men and women."

Swami Vivekanand (1863-1902) points out, "If you do not raise the women who are the living embodiment of the Divine Mother, don't think that you have any other way to rise. All nations have attained greatness by paying proper respects to their women. That country and that nation which does not respect women has never become great, nor will ever be in future. You will find in the Vedic and Upanishadic age Maitreyi, Gargi and other ladies of revered memory have taken the place of Rishis. In an assembly of a thousand Brahmanas who were all erudite in the Vedas, Gargi boldly challenged Yajnavalkya in a discussion about Brahman."

Gandhi (1869-1948) has observed," I am strongly of the opinion that women should have the same facilities as men and women should be given special facilities where necessary."

Jawaharlal Nehru (1889-1964) wrote, "I have always been strongly of the opinion that while it may be possible to neglect men's education, it is not possible to neglect women's educations."

Dr. Radhakrishnan has very emphatically stated, "women are human beings and have as much right to full development as men have. The position of women in any society is a true index of its cultural and spiritual level."

The University Education Commission 1948-49 observed, "There cannot be educated people without educated women. If general education had to be limited to men or to women, that opportunity should be given to women for then it would most surely be passed on to the next generation." The Education Commission 1964-66 wrote, "in the modern world the role of the women goes much beyond the home and the bringing up of children.

She is now adopting a career of her own and sharing equally with man, the responsibility for the development of society in all its aspects. This is the direction in which we shall have to move. In the struggle for freedom, Indian women fought side by side with men. This equal opportunity will have to continue in the fight against hunger, poverty, ignorance and ill health. The Resolution on the National Policy on Education (1968) stressed the importance of women education in these words, "the education of girls should receive emphasis not only on grounds of social justice but also because it accelerates social transformation."

The United Nations Declaration on the Elimination of Discrimination against Women (1967) took note of the great contribution made by women to social, political, economic and cultural life and the part they play in the family and particularly in the rearing of children and recommended the following in Article 9 of the Declaration, "all appropriate measures shall be taken to ensure to girls and women, married or unmarried, equal rights with men in education at all levels."

Phenomenal progress since independence—The importance of education of women has been recognised since the achievement the of independence. Accordingly strenuous efforts have been made in this area. The following figures reveal that literacy among women has increased proportionately as compared with men. Yet much more is needed to bring it at par with men.

Table 21.1

Sexwise Literacy Rate (1951-1991)

Year	*Persons*	*Make*	*Females*
1951	18.33	27.16	8.86
1961	28.31	40.40	15.34
1971	34.45	45.95	21.97
1981	43.56	56.37	29.75
	(41.42)	(53.45)	(28.26)
1991	52.11	63.86	39.42
2001	65.38	75.85	54.16

Source : *1991 Census. 2001 Census,* Registrar-General and Census Commission, New Delhi, 1991 and 2001.

Note:

1. Literacy rate for 1951, 1961 and 1971 related to population aged five years and above. The rates for the 1981 and 1991 relate to the population aged seven years and above. The literacy rates for the population aged five years and above in 1981 have been shown in brackets.
2. The 1981 rates exclude Assam where the 1981 Census could note be conducted. The 1991 Census rates exclude Jammu and Kashmir where the 1991 Census could not be conducted.

Progress of girl education at elementary. There has been a rapid progress in girls education since independence. Table 21.2 illustrates that enrolment of girls in classes I to V increased 11 times as against 4 times of boys during the period 1950-51 to 2005-06. At the middle stage (classes VI to VIII), enrolment of girls increased 37 times as against 12 times of boys. Table 21.3 shows that there is still a wide gap in the enrolment ratio of girls and boys.

Table 21.2

Enrolment of Girls' Education vis-a-vis Boy's Education at the Elementary Stage.

Stage/Class/Age group	*1950-51*	*2005-06*	*App. Increase*
1. Enrolment at Primary Stages I-V (6 to 11 Years)			
(a) Girls	5.4 million	60.9 million	11 times
(b) Boys	13.8 million	69.7 million	5 times
Total	19.2 million	130.6 million	7 times
2. Enrolment at the Middle/Upper Primary Stage Classes VI-VIII (Age group 11-14)			
(a) Girls	0.5 million	18.5 million	37 times
(b) Boys	2.6 million	28.5 million	12 times
Total	3.1 million	47.01 million	5 times

Source: *Annual Report, 2006-07. MHRD, Government of India.*

Table 21.3

Enrolment Ratio of Girls and Boys (2005-2006)

Classes	*Girls*	*Boys*	*Total*
Classes I to V	104.7	110.7	107.8
Classes VI to VIII	65.1	74.3	69.9

Source : *'Economic Survey 2002-2003'.*

Table 21.4

Number of Women vs Men in Higher Education (1950-51 and 2007-2008)

Year	*No. of Women Per 100 Men*
1950-1951	14
2007-2008	68

Source: *UGC Annual Report 2004-2005.*

The number of women enrolled in institutions of higher education increased from 40,000 in 1950-51 to about 51 lakh in 2007-2008, recording an increase of more than 140 times. The enrolment of women as a percentage of total enrolment increases, from 10% in 1950-51 to 40.6% in 2007-2008.

Table 21.5

Number of Teachers at the School Stage (1950-51 to 2006-07) *(In thousand)*

Year	*Primary*			*Upper Primary*		
	Female	*Male*	*Total*	*Female*	*Male*	*Total*
1950-51	82	456	538	13	73	86
1960-61	127	615	742	83	262	345
1970-71	225	835	1,060	175	463	638
1980-81	342	1,021	1,363	253	598	851
1990-91	473	1,143	1,616	356	717	1,073
2006-07	850	1400	2250	670	1650	2320

Table 21.6

Number of Teachers at the High/Secondary and Higher Secondary Stage (1950-51 to 2005-2006)

Year	*Female*	*Male*	*Total*
1950-51	20	107	127
1960-61	62	234	296
1970-71	155	474	629
1980-81	254	658	912
1990-91	420	920	1340
2000-01	577	1184	1761
2004-05	800	1300	2100

Problems of women education and measures of popularisation— From time to time the following Committees and Commissions have expressed concern regarding the slow progress of girl's and women's education in India:

1. The University Education Commission, 1948-49.
2. Smt. Durgabai Deshmukh Committee, 1959.
3. Smt. HasnaAMehta Committee, 1962.
4. M. Bhaktavatsalam Committee to look into the causes of public support particularly in rural areas for girls education and to enlist public cooperation.
5. Education Commission, 1964-66.
6. Resolution on the National Policy on Education, 1968.
7. Resolution of the Committee on the Status of Women in India, 1974.
8. Challenge of Education, 1986.
9. National Policy on Education, 1986.
10. Programme of Action, 1986.
11. Ramamurti Report, 1990.
12. Janardhana Committee Report, 1992.
13. Modified National Policy on Education, 1992.
14. Programme of Action, 1992.

Causes of Slow Progress

1. Economic backwardness of the rural community.
2. Lack of proper social attitudes in the rural areas for the education of girls.
3. Lack of educational facilities in rural areas.
4. Lack of women teachers.
5. Lack of proper supervision and guidance due to inadequate women personnel in the Inspectorate.
6. Lack of proper incentives to parents and children.
7. Lack of adequate incentives.
8. Lack of suitable curriculum.
9. Co-educational aspects.

Suggested Measures for Removing Economic Backwardness of the Rural Community

1. Free uniforms and free books to the needy and deserving females should be provided.
2. Attendance scholarships which serve as a compensation to the parents should be given. This will also ensure reduction of wastage and stagnation.
3. Mid-day meals should be made available free of charge.

Developing a Proper Social Attitude in Favour of Girls' Education in Rural Areas.

1. To study the problems relating to women's education and to get detailed scientific data, a thorough research should be taken up by the Institutes of Education in different states and co-ordinated at the national level.
2. Separate schools for girls at the middle and high school stages should be established where needed.
3. School mothers in co-education primary schools should be appointed.
4. Creches and nursery classes wherever possible should be opened.
5. Public opinion in favour of girls' education should be created.

Provision of Adequate Educational Facilities in the Backward and Rural Areas

The target in the Eighth Plan should be to have at least one primary school within a radius of one kilometre from every home which is within the walking distance of a child.

1. Hostel for girls at the middle and high school stages.
2. Maintenance stipends to girls residing in hostels for meeting their board and lodging expenses, at least in part.
3. Subsidised transport facilities, wherever necessary and possible.
4. All priority to be given to the construction of suitable buildings for girls' schools.
5. Free education for girls up to the School Leaving Certificate Examination.

Suggestive Measures for Meeting the Shortage of Women Teachers

1. A large number of training institutions have to be provided for women, especially in the backward states. These institutions should generally be located in rural areas and they should generally recruit their trainees from that area.
2. Condensed course centres should be started in these backward areas to open up avenues to adult unqualified women for employment as teachers. Wherever possible such centres should be attached to the training institutions.
3. A large number of quarters for women teachers should be provided, particularly in rural areas. Our target in the Seventh Plan should be to provide at least 50 per cent of the women teachers with quarters in primary schools.
4. All women teachers employed in rural areas should be given an adequate rural allowance.
5. Special stipends should be given to girls in high and higher secondary schools with an aptitude for teaching.
6. Whenever possible husbands and wives should be posted in the same place even if they work in different departments of the government.
7. Free training should be imparted with stipends to all candidates of training institutions.

8. In-service education training should be given to untrained women teachers who have put in at least two years of service. The period of training in education should be treated as on duty.

Proper Supervision and Personnel Guidance

1. Increase in the number of women inspecting officers, particularly in the backward states, at different levels including State level and Directorate level.
2. Provision of adequate transport for all district women inspecting officers.
3. Adequate office staff and equipment.
4. Residential facilities to all women officers at all levels.
5. Adequate funds at the disposal of the State Council for closer contact with rural areas.

Social Education for Adult Women

The problem of girls, education is related to the education of adult women. This problem can be tackled in the following ways:

1. By teaching simple skills like sewing, knitting, handicrafts, etc., and knowledge of basic principles of health and food habits.
2. New attitudes towards community living, family planning, supersitution, caste, etc.

Adequate Incentives to the Students

1. The number of attendance scholarships should be doubled in the Eighth Plan.
2. The allowance of the school mothers should be enhanced so that qualified women may be attracted to take up the work.
3. The number of maintenance stipends should be doubled in the Eighth Plan and the rate of such stipends should be adequately increased in view of the rising prices all over the country.
4. The number of sanitary blocks in co-education primary schools be adequately increased during the Eighth Plan.
5. Larger allocation of funds should be made in the budget for construction of hostels for girls during the Eighth Plan.

Curriculum Reforms

The Curriculum, by and large, has not met the requirements of women. The following suggestions made by the Smt. Hasna Mehta Committee (1962) deserve careful consideration:

1. No differentiation should be made in the curricula for boys and girls at the primary and middle stages of education.
2. Steps should be taken to improve the instruction of home economics.
3. Steps should be taken to improve the teaching of music and fine arts and liberal financial assistance should also be made available to girls' schools for the introduction of these courses.
4. Universities should review periodically the provision they have made for the courses designed to meet the special needs of girls and take necessary action to remove the deficiencies discovered.

Co-Education

Meaning of co-education—Co-education implies the education of the boys and girls together in the same classes of a school, admission to the school being secured by pupils of both sexes on equal terms and opportunities and freedom being provided for the association of both the sexes in intra and extra-school activities. Co-education does not mean just the admission of girls into boys' educational institutions for the purpose of receiving instructions.

Co-education is not a modern concept. Thousands of years ago, in the Vedic Bharat, boys and girls acquired their knowledge and wisdom in the Tapovans (Forest Temples of Learning). Sisters and brothers, as they were known, being pupils of the same guru, developed a sweet relation far from any elements of sex passion.

Various Committees and Commissions on Education

The University Education Commission (1948-49) favoured separate schools between the ages of 13 to 18.

The Secondary Education Commission's (1952-53) view was that where it is possible separate schools for girls should be established.

The National Committee on Women's Education (1959) recommended co-education as a general policy at the primary, middle and secondary stage but separate secondary schools for girls in rural areas. It also stressed that adequate attention should be paid to the special needs of girls in co-educational institutions.

Smt. Hansa Mehta Committee (1962) recommended the adoption of co-education as the general pattern at the elementary stage with a vigorous propaganda to overcome resistance to co-education. As a transitional measure, it observed, that separate primary or middle schools might have to be provided in case of a large demand.

The Education Commission 1964-66 laid stress on establishing separate schools for girls at the secondary stage.

The National Committee on the Status of Women (1974) favoured co-education as a long term policy.

Merits Claimed for Co-education

In the opinion of Gandhi, "Co-education must be allowed and boys and girls must cultivate a healthy and harmonious relationship, based upon a strong moral code."

Economic factors—Co-education enables us to meet the increasing demand of education for girls and women. Wc can hardly afford to open separate educational institutions. There is a lack of funds, adequate buildings and equipments for providing separate education for girls.

Psychological consideration—Hayward wrote, "Future mothers should not have to confess with tears, that they do not understand boys". Boys and girls should not be brought up as strangers. Greater contact between boys and girls results in a sense of comradeship and they would be able in courses of time to approach each other without giving that undue emphasis to the sexual side that is but natural in the present circumstances."

Humanising effect—Co-education has a humanising influence on boys and girls in that tendencies to extremes of masculinity and femininity are checked. It makes the girls less shy and makes the boys more refined. The mixing of boys and girls is natural as the feminine mind gains from association with boys and vice versa.

Disciplinary problems are solved—Discipline becomes easier to maintain because boys wish to stand well in the eyes of the girls and vice versa; the punishment of a fault is feared more than it would be in separate institutions.

Modification in personality traits—It is generally believed because of co-education, boys learn perseverance, conscientiousness and industriousness from girls and the latter learn independence, self-reliance and resource from boys.

Increase in purity—It is felt that boys become more modest by co-education, the girls less ignorant and sentimental and consequently less liable to make a grave matrimonial mistake in life. There is less underground excitement and more excitement of a natural and obvious kind.

Intellectual benefits—There is no doubt that attendance in the classes becomes almost cent per cent. Besides women can teach some subject better than men and thus we can make out a good case for co-education. Addison once said, "Female friendship is necessary for intellectual development."

Homely atmosphere—Co-education enables us to have a polished home.

Better domestic life—It would be developed through co-education.

Reduction in mental diseases—Dr. Freud believed that co-education alone could keep young people free from diseases of the mind.

Demerits and Limitations of Co-education

Free mixing up creates troubles—Dr. Stanley Hall writes: "During the early years of adolescence when the baby is rapidly changing and a sense of an awkwardness and reticence is felt, the two sexes should not intrude upon each other." Since in our tropical country sex consciousness develops at an early age, free mixing is fraught with danger.

Less attention to girls—Girls suffer. It is generally seen that in co-educational institutions adequate facilities are not provided for girls.

No thorough cleansing of the mental make-up—Co-education is a farce in many cases as we have not taken to this business in the right spirit. There must be a sane attitude and a proper and healthy outlook.

Unhealthy effects on intellectual pursuits—Sometimes it is said, "Men cannot study when women are around and that if women are let into a college, they are likely to get round some of the professors and marry them and then 'good-bye' research and higher thought".

Separate needs of men and women—Dr. Joad has remarked, "Girls tend to be more interested in their immediate surroundings, in what is pretty and ornamental, boys in what is more remote from them, in what is useful, in what is general and what is abstract. Boys seek expression in investigating, exploring, constructing, girls through artistic and emotional channels". Rousseau has also talked in the same tune, "A man seeks to serve, woman seeks to please, the one needs knowledge, the other taste. To be pleasing in his sight, to win his respect and love, to train him in childhood, to tend him in manhood and to console, to make his life pleasant and happy, these are the duties of women for all time." The same type of education for boys and girls is hardly suitable.

Physiological factors—Co-education may not prove useful as a uniform programme of physical and mental activities for both the sexes would affect the health of adolescent girls.

Undue emphasis on make-up—There is a feeling that co-education results in girls using gorgeously bordered saris which are gazed at by the boys. The boys come immaculately dressed. There is every possibility that shy glances, stealthy eying and admiring gazes will lead to various unhealthy practices.

Separate code of discipline—The discipline that is suitable for a boy is not as a rule equally suitable for a girl.

Distraction of attention—Mixing of person of both sexes at the adolescent stage, when the sex urge is at its highest pitch, is not advisable. It distracts the attention of both boys and girls and hampers their progress in studies.

Danger to morals—The strongest objection is from the moral point of view. Emotional disturbances are likely to take place. Pupils are exposed to sex appeal and morals are at risk with co-education.

Questions and Problems

A. Essay-Type Questions

1. Prepare a case for the education of women.
2. What are the cuses for the slow progress of women education in India? Suggest suitable measures in this regard.
3. Write an essay on co-education.

B. Short-Answer Type Questions

4. List any six committees and commissions that have made recommendations on women's education.
5. Compare the progress of women education in 1950-51 and in 1992-93.

22 Physical Education and Health Education

22.1 Physical Education

Significance of physical education and sports—In view of the great importance of physical education and sports the NPE 1992 considers these as an integral part of the learning process and includes it in the evaluation of performance. It further observes, "a nation wide infrastructure for physical education, sports and games will be built into the educational edifice." It has been rightly observed, "a ton of knowledge bought at the expense of an ounce of health which is the most ancient and precious form of wealth and worth, costs more than its value." Swami Vivekanand has stressed the importance of well-built bodies in these words, "what India needs to-day is not the Bhagwad Gita but the football." The message of this statement is very clear. A weak person cannot follow the teachings of the Gita. Only a strong man can follow it.

Meaning and concept of physical education—It has been stated by C.L. Brown," Physical education is concerned with strength and endurance".

In the words of Jay B. Nash, "Physical education is that field of education which deals with big-muscle activities and their related responses."

C.C. Cowell states, "Physical education is the social process of change in the behaviour of the human organism originating primarily from the stimulus of social big-muscle-play and related activities."

In the words of secondary Education commission, "It includes all forms of physical activities" and games which promote the development of the body and mind!

Aims of Physical Education

Montaigne rightly observes,. "Physical education does neither train up the soul nor body but the whole man." Froebel aptly stated, "early education must deal directly with the physical development and influence the spiritual development through the exercise of the senses." The Education Commission stresses that physical education should contribute not only to physical fitness but also to physical efficiency, mental alertness and the development of certain qualities like perseverance, team spirit, leadership, obedience to rules, moderation in victory and balance in defeat.

Among the important aims of physical education, the following deserve special mention :-

1. Conservation of health.
2. Development of well-built bodies.
3. Development of qualities like endurance, self-control, courage, etc.
4. Development of social behaviour and qualities relating to society, e.g., obedience, cooperation, leadership and followership, etc.
5. Development of regular habits of exercise and play.
6. Development of regular health habits.
7. Development of neuromuscular skills.
8. Development of a healthy attitude towards leisure and the ability to use leisure in wholesome ways.

Physical education and education—Physical education and education are inseparably united together. They go hand in hand. It has been said, "education without physical education is a bottomless vase and physical education without education is a trunkated cone."

Physical education and physical training—Physical training is a part of physical education. The scope of physical training is limited and it refers to the training aspect of the body. It is traditionally regimental in its scope and enables an individual to gain physical fitness through certain conditioning. It contributes to mental and moral development. It leads to team work.

Programme for Physical Education

Development activities—

1. Exercise tables, 'dands', 'baithaks' and yogic exercises.
2. Fundamental movements, such as, walking, running throwing, jumping, climbing and balancing.
3. Mimetics and story plays.
4. Stunts, pyramids, weight training and conditioning exercises.

Rhythmics—

Rhythm fundamentals, rhythm games, folk dances, social dances, singing games, community singing, Indian rhythmics, 'garba', 'phugdi', 'himma', 'tipri', etc.

Games, Sports, and Athletics—

Games—

1. Major games, such as kabaddi', 'kho-kho', volleyball, basketball, hockey, cricket etc.
2. Dual games such as tennis, table tennis, badminton, ring tennis, etc.
3. Recreative games, minor games, relays, social games, group games, lead-up games, etc.

Sports—Cycling, canoeing, shooting, riding, skating etc

Athletics—Running, jumping, throwing, walking and relays.

Formal Activities—Drill and marching, light apparatus, callisthenics, mass P.T. exercises.

Apparatus—Parallel bars, vaulting, beam, roman rings, ropes, pommel horse, single bar, 'malkhamb', etc.

Combatives—Wrestling, boxing, judo, 'lathi' fight, dagger fight, farigadga, sword fight, simple contests and mass combatives based on 'attack and defence.'

Aquatics—Swimming, diving and life saving.

Self-testing Activities—All types of tests.

Camping and Outdoor Activities—Hiking, cross country, camping and mountaineering, picnics, excursions etc.

Special Activities—Demonstrations, ceremonial parades, singing the National Anthem, flag salutations, practical projects, citizenship training etc.

Physical education is not merely to be confined to the playground but should pervade the class-room. Physical education in the class-room may take the following forms:

1. Direct instruction emphasising the necessity of having a good physique.
2. Suggestions regarding the maintenance of good health.
3. Emphasis on right postures.
4. Provision of good seating and lighting arrangements in the class-room, thereby impressing upon them the importance of studying under healthy surroundings.
5. Providing ample opportunities to the children for physical activity.

Physical drill—It consists of the following types of exercises:

1. Preparing or warming up, running in a circle, marching etc.
2. Corrective exercises.
3. Educative exercises
4. Psychological exercises
5. Recreative exercises

Physical drill should be organised regularly and properly graded. 'Simple to complex' and 'easy to difficult' should form the basis of physical drill. The duration of the period of exercise should depend upon the age and strength of the students. A good system of physical exercises would give strength to all parts of the body.

Gymnastics and athletics—Gymnastics and athletics are two important forms of physical education. The effect of gymnastic exercises is internal and primary. They are based on sound principles. Each exercise has its own value for a specific purpose. Gymnastic exercises are very helpful in teaching correct postures. Gymnastic exercises with apparatus (Bars, Horse, Ladder etc.) are greatly liked by the boys as these involve a great degree of skill and difficulties. Gymnastic exercises like marching, easy exercises in jumping and skipping, aesthetic dancing and folk dancing appeal to the girls.

Athletic activities include running, jumping, disc throwing, hammer throwing and weight throwing, etc.

In carrying out gymnastics, the following points should be taken into consideration:

1. Lessons and exercises should be purposive and not at random.
2. A shirt and shorts are sufficient.
3. Postures should be good.
4. The boys should not be held in a straight position for a long time.
5. The gymnastic exercises should be correlated with material and play.
6. All material should be kept in order.

Yoga—"Yoga as a system which promotes an integrated development of the body and mind" receives special attention in the NPE 1992. Efforts are being made to introduce yoga in all schools. To this end, it is being introduced in teacher training courses.

Play-ground as the 'Uncovered School'

On account of the important values of games and sports, it is said that "The Battle of Waterloo was won on the playgrounds of Eton." It may be recalled that Eton is one of the prestigious public schools in England and it has produced several distinguished politicians, generals and statesmen of England. "The play-ground is said to be the cradle of democracy". Various games and sports organised on the play-ground contribute a lot towards the development of qualities needed to be an ideal citizen of a democracy. The play ground helps in the inculcation of the following values.

1. Teaches cooperation and team work.
2. Provides opportunities for leadership.
3. Imparts training in becoming good followers.
4. Promotes physique and health.
5. Develops qualities like courage, patience, perseverance and steadfastness etc.—qualities needed in life situations.

6. The playground teaches the important lesson that the important thing in life is to struggle whole heartedly.
7. Satisfies the biological and psychological needs of children.
8. Develops 'esprit de corps' or the 'we feeling' or feeling of true loyalty.
9. Enables children to make profitable use of leisure time.

We may sum up the importance of games and sports with a quotation from Aldous Huxley, "like every other instrument that man has invented sport can be used either for a good or for evil purpose. Used well, it can teach endurance and courage, a sense of fair play and a respect for rules, co-ordinated effort and the subordination of personal interest to those of the group. Used badly, it can encourage personal vanity and group vanity, greedy desire for victory and hatred for rivals, an intolerant 'esprit de corps' and contempt for people who are beyond a certain arbitrarily selected pole. In either case sport inculcates responsible cooperation."

Principles of Organising Physical Education

1. Greater facilities should be provided in educational institutions in the form of equipment, playgrounds and funds.
2. Incentives in the form of credit for achievements in sports should be provided.
3. Health, power of endurance, physical well-being of young people should be developed by improvement in nutrition.
4. Planned coaching at all stages is essential. There is a vast talent potential in the country which should be exploited by intensive and planned coaching.
5. Sports and games should be organised in rural areas through vyayamshalas, vyayam mandals, akharas, etc., and in co-operation with community projects. Sports festivals should be organised and sports events encouraged on the occasion of fairs. Indigenous sports like Kabaddi and indigenous style of wrestling should be encouraged.
6. Where separate playgrounds cannot be made available for each educational institution, a common pool for a group of institutions should be created.
7. Standard equipment should be manufactured in the country so as to be available at cheap rates to all and facilities for its manufacture should be provided.

8. For the development of sports and games in the country it is essential that umpiring and refereeing should be of a high order.
9. All teachers below the age of 40 should actively participate in many of the physical activities of students and thus make them a lively part of the school programme.
10. Full records of physical activities of the student must be maintained.
11. The training in physical education should be comprehensive enough to include all aspects of health education.
12. The teachers of physical education should be associated with the teaching of subjects like Physiology and Hygiene and given the same status as other teachers of similar qualifications.
13. Play-grounds should be provided with the minimum area as given below:

Category	*Boys Schools*	*Girls Schools*
(a) Secondary / Senior Secondary School	5 acres	4 acres
(b) Middle School	3 acres	2 acres
(c) Primary School	½ to 1 acre	½ to 1 acre

14. Schools having an adequate playground may be required to permit its use by the neighbouring schools.
15. In cities and towns where open space is not available for every school, sports complexes may be formed.
16. Physical education should become an integral part of school education.

Competitions and Tournaments

Objectives of competitions and tournaments—The Greeks were perhaps the first to realise the importance of competitions and started the Olympics in order to keep their youth healthy, brave and strong enough to fight battles against their enemies. From the Greeks, the idea of competitions in games spread to Europe and other countries of the world. The great philosopher Bertrand Russell rightly observed, "I do not think ordinary human beings can be happy without competition for competition has been, ever since the origin of man, the spur to most serious activities". There is no doubt that competition is the hard fact of life. The progress of nations depends upon competition. The following are the main objectives as well as outcomes of competitions and tournaments.

1. They serve as great motivators to students.
2. They provide training in facing life situations.
3. They inculcate sportsmanship among students.
4. They give training to students to strive for excellence.

Harmful effects of competitions—There is no rose without a thorn. If we are not cautious enough when picking a rose its thorn is sure to prick us. In the same way competitions are not an unmixed blessing. In general the following are the limitations and the general objections raised.

1. They benefit a few students only.
2. They are expensive in time and money.
3. They sometimes cause physical injuries.
4. They may cause emotional injuries.
5. They tend to foster over specialisation.
6. They may encourage professionalism and commercialism.
7. They sometimes give rise to unsocial feelings.

Principles of organising competitions—To be effective the programme will be:

1. Closely coordinated with the general instructional programme, and properly articulated with the other departments of the school;
2. Such that the number of students accommodated and the educational aims achieved justify the use of funds for its support;
3. Planned in such a way as to result in opportunity for many individuals to explore a wide variety of sports and to set reasonable limits for each listed sport;
4. Controlled in such a way as to avoid the element of professionalism and commercialism which tend to grow up in connection with widely publicised 'Sports' contests.
5. Kept free from the type of contest which involves a gathering of so-called 'all stars' from different schools to participate in contests which may be used as a gathering place for representatives of certain educational institutions or professional

organisations who are interested in soliciting athletic talent for their teams;

6. Include educative exercises to reach all non-participating students and community followers of the school teams in order to ensure a proper understanding and appreciation of the sports skills and of the need for adherence to principles of gamesethics;
7. Engender respect for the rules and policies under which the school conducts its programme.
8. Ensure that all schools use reasonable care in avoiding any participation in a contest sport between participants of normal high school age and participants who are appreciably above or below normal high school age.
9. Permit competition between teams of comparable maturity.

22.2 Health Education

Significance of health education—It has been rightly said, "If wealth is lost, nothing is lost. If health is lost, something great is lost." Locke's famous saying a "sound mind in a sound body" is true for all ages. Ben Johnson has stated, "O Health! Health! The blessing of the rich! The riches of the poor! Who can buy thee at too dear a rate since there is no enjoying this world without thee." Similarly Herbert Spencer writes, "the preservation of health is a duty and few seem conscious that there is a thing called physical morality."

Meaning of school health programme—The school health programme consists of procedures that contribute to the maintenance and improvement of the health of pupils and school personnel including health services, healthful living and health education.

General Objectives of Health Education in School

1. Making the student realise the necessity of having good health.
2. Giving information regarding health rules.
3. Developing health habits among children.
4. Developing certain skills concerning health e.g., training in first aid, etc.
5. Enabling them to understand the educative value of sanitation, cleanliness and healthful living.

6. Developing a will to listen to rules relating to health.
7. Developing better human relationship in matters concerning health.
8. Acquainting them with the causes and remedies of general diseases.
9. Influencing parents and other adults to better habits and attitudes through the health programme of the school and to make the school an effective agency for the promotion of the social aspects of health education in the family and community as well as the school itself.

Scope of health education—It includes all such instruction that enlightens a student about activities and functions contributing to preservation, promotion and restoration of health. By means of a health education programme the spread of disease in the school-going children can be checked. A thorough knowledge of health rules underlines the needs of the study of anatomy and also the symptoms of common diseases of children. A practical knowledge of causes and diagnosis is equally essential. School health education also includes knowledge about the environment, equipments and routine of the school as well.

Scope of School Health Programme

Healthful School living or Health Protection	Health Instruction	Health Services
• Hygiene and sanitation of the school plant. • Good ventilation. • Appropriate furniture. • General cleanliness. • Proper mid-day meals.	• Imparting instruction regarding the development of adequate health and safety knowledge, attitudes and skills.	• Medical inspection. • First aid. • School Clinic. • Correcting medical defects among students and school personnel. • Special classes for exceptional children. • Control of communicable diseases.

Illustration 22.1 School Health Programme

Six Phases of the School Health Programme

1. Health appraisal or medical inspection.
2. Health counselling and follow-up.
3. Emergency care in schools.
4. Communicable disease control.
5. Identification and education of the handicapped children.
6. Health of school personnel.

Medical Inspection of Students

A systematic medical inspection of students is one the most important means of taking care of the physical well-being of the students. Although this system has been in existence for many years, yet it has failed to achieve the desired results. The Secondary Education Commission has observed the following defects in the prevailing system:

1. It is done in a very superficial manner.
2. The remedial measures suggested are often not carried out.
3. Follow-up work is practically absent.
4. Effective cooperation has not been established between the parents and the school authorities.

Suggestions for Making Medical Inspection Effective

1. It should be thorough and comprehensive. It should not merely concern itself with the height, weight and chest measurements but should also concern itself with ears, teeth, eyes, nose, heart and lungs etc. In fact no part of the body should be left unexamined as far as possible.
2. Students with serious defects should be examined more frequently.
3. Remedial measures should be taken to remove defects.
4. Three copies of the report should be prepared. One should be sent to the parents, another should be kept by the teacher-in-charge and the third one should be kept by the medical officer.

Follow-up work—It has been rightly stated that medical inspection is of little or no use unless proper 'follow up' work is undertaken. The parents and the teachers should cooperate. Immediate action should be taken after the medical inspection is over..

Methods for Imparting Health Education

Personal cleanliness—The daily morning inspection of the cleanliness of the students by the teacher is very helpful in enforcing personal cleanliness.

Development of habits regarding air—Stress should be paid on the need of fresh air at all times and especially while sleeping. The students should be asked not to cover their mouths at night. They should be taught to breathe through their noses.

Training in first-aid habits—First-aid training should be provided and students should be instructed to give immediate attention to cuts and bruises.

Vaccination and inoculation—At times of epidemics, precautionary measures should be suggested to them and they should be vaccinated and inoculated.

Development of hygienic food habits—The students should be taught to take the right type of food in a suitable quantity. They should be warned of the danger of over-eating. They should be asked not to take sour food. The students should be made to understand the importance of drinking plenty of water.

Selection of suitable physical exercises—A variety of physical activity programmes should exist in a school.

Formation of good classroom habits—A wise teacher would always pay due attention to the postures of the students. The students may be instructed to keep pens and pencils out of the mouth and to use a handkerchief while coughing.

Development of better human relations in matters concerning health—Every student should be asked to make it a point to do his best for the betterment of the health of his friends, relatives and neighbours and the entire community.

Medical inspection and follow-up work—A thorough medical examination of each student should be conducted once a year at least and appropriate follow-up action taken.

Practical activities to be organised for the promotion of health—(a) arranging lectures. (b) demonstrations (c) story telling (d) group discussions (e) health posters (f) health projects (g) health weeks. (h & i) health books or diaries (j) films and film strips (k) visits to dispensaries and hospitals (l) health clubs (m) health lessons through radio (n) T.V. lessons and health information (o) sanitary and health boards in each school (p) essay competitions (q) health squads (r) school cleanliness projects (s) community cleanliness projects (t) doing practical work like (u) keeping water safe (v) disinfecting wells (w) constructing composite pits (x) keeping refuse in basket (y) regular cleaning of latrines and urinals. (z) trimming nails and cleaning teeth etc.

Sanitation

Sanitation is the science of keeping the class rooms and their surroundings clean and conducive to health. The following are the important problems and methods of protecting sanitation in a school.

1. Protection of the water supply in the school.
2. Keeping the school lavatories clean;
3. Keeping the laboratories in a perfectly clean condition.
4. Filling up holes.
5. Removing shrubs and heaps of wastage.
6. Ensuring cleanliness in the school canteen.
7. Keeping checks on vendors and ensuring that they supply fresh food articles to students during recess and at other times.
8. Keeping the play-field fit for play

Developing Appropriate Sanitation Sense

1. Talks on sanitation
2. Exhibitions on sanitation.
3. Organising sanitary weeks.
4. Practical activities relating to sanitation as mentioned above.

Safety Education

With the use of new technology in our daily life and in school, the need for safety education has assumed special importance.

Safety Education in the Classroom

The following points should be kept in view:

1. The stair cases should not to be too high or two steep. They must be so broad as to accommodate an onrush at times. They should have side support to a reasonable height.
2. The cement flooring should not be too polished.

3. Projection of nails and wooden pieces should be removed.
4. There should be no broken pieces of glasses hanging anywhere.
5. There should be proper ventilation in the classroom.
6. Drinking water places should not be marshy, muddy or slippery as children under such conditions are likely to slip and fall down.
7. All bottles in the laboratories with poisonous chemicals should be labelled in bold letters.
8. Fire extinguishers should be fixed on the walls.
9. Electric wires, switches, etc. should not be kept uncovered.

Safety Education in the Playground

1. The playground should be fenced properly.
2. All pitfalls, rat holes, etc. should be removed through periodic inspection.
3. Playing materials and equipment should be checked every now and then to ensure safety.
4. Placards giving instructions should be displayed at proper places.

Safety Education in the Home

1. Students should be told that they should be careful while going near the well and the kitchen.
2. Playing on the roof of the house and street should be discouraged.
3. The flooring of the bathroom and the lavatory should not be slippery.
4. Children should be instructed to be careful in the use of instruments such as sharp knives, scissors, vegetable cutters, etc.

Postures of the Students

It is generally observed that the importance of correct postures of the students is not realised. They the affect the health, physical efficiency, mental attitude and appearance of an individual. Most of our diseases are the outcome of poor postures. A teacher can do much in the class-room and physical instruction period to prevent bad postural habits in the students. As a result of poor postures, says, Dr. Mosher, "constipation, diarrhoea, flatulence, disturbance of the circulation, nervous irritability and, most marked of all fatigue out of proportion to the effort expended, lesson the efficiency of the individual and often make life a burden." Some of the main defects of poor postures are given below:

1. They interfere in the normal working of the respiration, circulation and digestion.
2. They affect the eye-sight.
3. They spoil hand-writing because the students will not be able to hold the pen properly.
4. They lead to round shoulders and a drooping body.
5. They decrease physical efficiency and develop laziness.
6. They develop crooked bodies which are not normal it shape, and look very unpleasant.
7. They result in undesirable traits, e.g., timidness, lack of courage, etc.

Causes of Poor Postures

1. Weakness of the muscles which may be due to lack of exercise.
2. Wrong postural habits due to lack of information regarding correct positions.
3. Defective desks and seats compelling the students to stretch or cramp their bodies.
4. Wrong writing positions.
5. Wrong reading positions.
6. Defective eye-sight.
7. Defective hearing.
8. Illegible writing of the teacher on the black-board.
9. Wrong postures of the teachers leading to depressing effects on the students.

Remedial Measures

1. The students should be asked to take regular exercise to strengthen muscles.
2. Suitable furniture should be provided.
3. Good posture habits should be developed. The students should be told that the head, neck, trunk, thighs and legs are in a straight line in a good standing posture. While writing, the

students should be asked to keep their note-books at a distance of one foot. While reading, the book should be held vertically so that the top and the bottom of the book are at an equal distance from the eyes. The distance of 12 inches is an ideal one.

4. Stools should be provided for smaller children so that they may learn to sit without reclining against the chair.
5. Suitable corrective postural exercises should be recommended to the students.
6. Students having defective eye-sight and hearing should be seated on the front benches.
7. Rooms should be suitably ventilated and sufficient accommodation should be provided.
8. Bold type books should be selected.
9. The aid of the school medical officer should be sought.

Questions and Problems

A. Essay-Type Questions

1. "Physical education is not confined to the play-ground." Explain this statement and point out the aims and objectives of physical education in schools.
2. "The play-ground is the uncovered school." Elucidate this statement.
3. What are the general objectives of health education in schools? What is the scope of health education? Suggest a suitable programme of health education in school.
4. What is the importance of the medical examination of the students. How can it be made effective?

B. Short-Answer Type Questions

5. State the importance of competitions and inter-school tournaments.
6. List measures for the promotion of the health of the students.
7. Describe principles of organising physical education in schools.
8. Write notes on : (a) safety education in school (b) sanitary education in school (c) postures of the students.

23 National Policy on Education (NPE)

Background

After 1947, for the first time, a National Policy on Education was formulated in 1968. The policy guided the future development of education in India. The policy envisaged that the government of India, would also review every five years, the progress made and recommend guidelines for future development. However, a review could not take place till 1985. In 1985, it was decided to review the implementation of the 1968 policy and to formulate anew education policy. Accordingly a status paper *Challenge of Education a Policy Perspective* was issued by the Government of India. In this document, a comprehensive appraisal of the existing system of education was made. A country-wide debate took place on educational reform in the country. Finally a new National Policy on Education was formulated and approved by the Parliament in May 1986. A Programme of Action was also chalked out for the implementation of the Policy.

The implementation of the NPE was evaluated by two committees, namely the Ramamurti Committee (1990) and the Janardhana Committee (1992). As a result of the recommendation of these two committees, slight modifications were made in the NPE in 1992.

Main Features and Merits of NPE

1. *National system of education*—The NPE proposed a national system of education to provide access to education of a comparable quality to all students, to have a common educational structure with national curricular framework containing a common core.
2. *Operation Blackboard (OB)*—The policy stipulated that for the qualitative improvement of primary education, a new scheme known as Operation blackboard should be taken up.
3. *Navodaya schools*—Setting up Navodaya Vidyalays is a great landmark in the history of education in India.
4. *Vocational targets*—The policy fixed somewhat realistic targets of covering ten per cent of higher secondary students by 1990 and 25 per cent by 1995 in vocational courses.
5. *Delinking degrees from jobs*—A beginning is to be made in delinking degrees from jobs in selected areas.
6. *Performance and accountability*—Stress was laid on performance and accountability at all levels.
7. *Decentralisation of the management of education*—The policy calls for evolving a strategy of decentralisation and the creation of a spirit of autonomy for educational institutions.
8. *Indian education service*—It is envisaged that the constitution of the Indian Education Service is likely to bring about a national perspective in education.
9. *National testing service*—This is likely to be helpful in determining suitability of candidates for specified jobs and to pave the way for the emergence of norms of comparable competence across the nation.
10. *Raising resources*—The policy suggested appropriate methods of financing education. These are: (a) beneficiary communities to maintain school buildings and supplies of some consumables: (b) raising fees at the higher levels of education: (c) levying a cess or charge on user research and development agencies; and (d) affecting savings by the efficient use of facilities.

Missing Links and Limitations of the New Policy

1. *Neighbourhood school concept ignored*—The neighbourhood school concept advocated by the Kothari Commission for

eliminating the segregation that now takes place between the schools for the poor and the under-privileged classes and those for the rich and the privileged, has been completely ignored.

2. *Silent on the existence of public schools*—The NPE has evaded the issue of the 'commercialisation' of education by most of the public schools in the country.
3. *No check on the working of minority schools*—The Policy does not propose any checks to prevent the management of the public schools from exploiting the staff working there.
4. *Multiplication of institutions*—Setting up State Advisory Boards of Education, District Institutes of Education and Training and District Boards of Education is not likely to serve any useful purpose.
5. *Too much expectation from community help*—There is very little hope of obtaining community funds for educational purposes as there has developed a strong tendency on the part of the rich members of the community to contribute to political parties due to obvious reasons.
6. *No reference to basic system of education*—There is no reference to the Basic system of Education at the school stage.
7. *Working hours in schools*—For making the optimum use of human resources, increased working hours in educational institutions should have been recommended.
8. *Financial aspects not worked out*—It is very unfortunate that financial implications have not been worked out. Targets in different areas have not been fixed. Any workable document must be backed by financial resources otherwise it will remain a 'paper' document. There is no point in trying to apply one cubic inch of butter to a square mile of bread.

Suggestions for the Effective Implementation of NPE

1. Reliable and latest statistics should be obtained before planning.
2. A reasonable correct estimate of the availability of funds should be made and educational reforms planned accordingly.
3. Priorities should be determined very carefully.
4. Undue emphasis should not be laid on organising seminars.

Perhaps it would be better if funds earmarked for seminars are diverted to providing necessary equipment.

5. Funds meant for adult education programmes normally wasted on adult education centres on paper only should be used on primary education.
6. There should be no expansion of institutions like the Jawharlal Nehur University, New Delhi. Such institutions are like white elephants.
7. Vocational education should be organised meaningfully.
8. Maximum use should be made of the existing facilities in educational institutions.
9. Degrees should be delinked from jobs.
10. There should be no further expansion of professional education for a few years. The problems of the unemployed educated with professional degrees like engineering and medicine is assumed alarming proportions.
11. Education should be linked with industry.
12. Fees for higher education, should be raised considerably, However adequate provision for merit cum-means scholarship should be made.
13. All administrative posts in the Education Departments should be given to educationists and not to other cadres like the I.A.S. and P.C.S. The present practice of posting I.A.S. officers as Secretary Education and Director of Education Director of Public Instruction should be done away with.
14. Revolutionary changes are needed in the system of inspection and supervision of schools.

Important Changes Made in the Policy Formulation (1992)

NPE 1986 para 3.3—The National system of education envisages a common educational structure. The 10+2+3 structure has now been accepted in all parts of the country. Regarding the further break-up of the first 10 years efforts will be made to move towards an elementary system comprising 5 years of primary education and 3 years of upper primary, followed by 2 years of High School.

Revised NPE, 1992, para 3.3—The National System of Education envisages a common educational structure. The 10+2+3 structure has now been accepted in all parts of the country. Regarding the further break-up of the first 10 years efforts will be made to move towards an elementary system comprising 5 years of primary education and 3 years of upper primary, followed by 2 years of High School. Efforts will also be made to have the +2 stage accepted as a part of school education through out the country.

Elementary Education

NPE. 1986, para 5.5—The new thrust in elementary education will emphasise two aspects: (a) universal enrolment and universal retention of children upto 14 years of age, and (b) a substantial improvement in the quality of education.

Revised NPE, 1992, para 5.5—The new thrust in elementary education will emphasise three aspects: (a) universal access and enrolement, (b) universal retention of children upto 14 years of age; and (c) a substantial improvement in the quality of education to enable all children to achieve essential levels of learning.

A Resolve

NPE, 1986, para 5.12—The New Education Policy will give the highest priority to solving the problem of children dropping out of school and will adopt an array of menticulously formulated strategies based on micro planning, and applied at the grassroots level all over the country, to ensure children's retention at school. This effort will be fully coordinated with the network of non-formal education. It shall be ensured that all children who attain the age of about 11 years by 1990 will have had five years of schooling, or its equivalent through the non-formal stream. Likewise, by 1995 all children will be provided free and compulsory education upto 14 years of age.

Revised NPE, 1992, para 5.12—The New Educational Policy will give the highest priority to solving the problem of children dropping out of school and will adopt on array of meticulously formulated strategies based on micro planning, and applied at the grassroots level all over the country, to ensure children's retention at school. This effort will be fully coordinated with the network of non-formal education. It shall be ensured that free and compulsory education of satisfactory quality is provided to all children upto 14 years of age before we enter the twenty-first century. A national mission will be launched for the achievement of this goal.

Vocationalisation

NPE, 1986, para 5.23—It is proposed that vocational courses cover 10 per cent of higher secondary students by 1990 and 25 per cent by 1995. Steps will be taken to see that a substantial majority of the products of vocational courses are employed or become self-employed. Review of the courses offered would be regularly undertaken. Government will also review its recruitment policy to encourage diversification at the secondary level.

Revised NPE, 1992, para 5.23—It is proposed that vocational courses cover 10 per cent of higher secondary students by 1990 and 25 per cent by 2000. Steps will be taken to see that a substantial majority of the products of vocational courses are employed or become self-employed. Review of the courses offered would be regularly undertaken. Government will also review its recruitment policy to encourage diversification at the secondary level.

Ramamurti Review Committee (1990) on National Policy on Education

Appointment of the review committee—The National Front/ Janata Dal that came into power in December 1989 had mentioned in its election manifesto that the New Education Policy of 1986 as being implemented by the Central Government run by the Congress Party would be revised. Accordingly when it assumed office, it appointed on 7 May, 1990, a committee which submitted its report to the Minister of State in the Ministry of Human Resource Development on 26 December, 1990. The report was tabled in the Parliament on 9 January, 1991. The report is entitled, *Towards an Enlightened and Humane Society*.

Major Concerns of the Review Committee

1. Education should be for equity and social justice.
2. Decentralisation of educational management at all levels.
3. Establishment of a participative educational order.
4. Empowerment of work.
5. Inculcation of values for the creation of an enlightened and humane society.

Major Recommendations of the Review Committee

1. Development of a common school system.

2. Removing disparities in education.
3. Right to education to be included in the fundamental Rights.
5. Speedy promotion of women education.
6. A single stream of should education with vocational as well as non-vocational components of different mixes.
7. Reforms in the examination system.
8. Regional languages as the medium of instruction.
9. Decentralised planning and management of education.
10. Autonomy to universities and colleges.
11. Creation of work culture at all stages of education.
12. Value education.
13. Raising resources by increasing fees at the higher educational institutions.

CABE or Janardhana Reddy Committee on Policy (1992)

The CABE (Central Advisory Board of Education) Committee appointed in May 1991, submitted its report in January 1992 Shri N. Janardhana Reddy, Chief Minister and Minister of Education, Andhra Pradesh was the Chairman of this committee. The committee examined the recommendations of the Ramamurti Committee on NPE and came to the conclusion, "only a few of the recommendations of the NPERC (Ramamurti Review Committee or National Policy on Review Committee) have policy implications." Nevertheless it suggested a few modifications in the NPE which were incorporated in the Revised Policy Formulations (1992). These modifications have been described in the earlier part of this Chapter.

Important Programmes Launched after the Formulation of NPE Starting

1. Operation Blackboard for the improvement of elementary education.
2. Prescribing minimum levels of learning (MLL) at the primary stage
3. Starting of Navodaya Vidyalayas.
4. Setting up a Joint Council for Vocational Education for laying down policy guidelines.
5. Development of competency based curricular in six major vocational areas.

6. Modifications in the Apprenticeship Act, 1961.
7. Introduction of vocational courses in colleges.
8. Setting up of a Central Institution of Vocational Education at Bhopal.
9. Supply of T.V. sets and radio cum cassettes players to elementary schools.
10. Initiation of a centrally sponsored scheme for the improvement of science education.
11. Starting of a centrally sponsored scheme 'Environmental orientation to school education'.
12. Formulation of the National Curriculum for Elementary and Secondary Education by NCERT.
13. Mass orientation of teachers and training
14. Setting up District Institutes of Education and Training (DIETs).

Questions and Problems

A. Essay-Type Questions

1. Why was the NPE 1986 formulated? Evaluate its recommendations.
2. State the merits and demerits of the N.P.E.
3. Why was the NPE 1986 revised in 1992? Explain the modifications.

B. Short-Answer Type Questions

4. Why was the Ramamurti Committee appointed? What were its chief recommendations?
5. Write a short note on the Janardhana Committee (CABE Committee 1992).

24 Educational Planning in India

Meaning and Objective of Educational Planning

Planning is a rational process of setting clear objectives, choosing the most efficient and effective means for pursuing them, then following through with practical action. Educational planning is the process of shaping the system of education in accordance with the needs of a country.

The main objective of education planning is to get the most and best educational results for the effort expended and to maximise education's contribution to each individual and to the whole society.

Educational Planning in Free India

India has now a record of over four decades of planning. The plans of the Central and the State Governments and the 'public' and the 'private' sectors are coordinated and finalised after detailed discussions by the Planning Commission which is a national body. The Planning Commission draws up a long-term perspective plan and a more immediate Five-Year Plan of development. These plans are approved by the National Development Council which comprises inter alia the Prime Minister and the chief ministers of different States. The approved plan thus becomes the highest policy declaration of what is proposed to be achieved in next five years and how. The Five-Year Plan specifies the allocation for education, chalks out the policies and the programmes and sets targets of achievements.

There is a provision for a periodic appraisal of plan performance and every year 'Annual Plans' are drawn up with due modifications but within the framework of the Five-Year Plan. The first four years of independence witnessed great education expansion on a year to year budgetary planning till the birth of the National Planning Commission in 1951, the year of launching the First Five-year Plan.

Table 24.1

Financial Allocation in Plans to Different Educational Sectors

(Million Rs.)

Plan	Elementary Edn.	Sec. Edn	Adult Edn.	Hr. Edn.	Others	Techn. Edn.	Total
First Plan (1951-56)	850	200	—	140	140	200	1530
Second Plan (1956-61)	950	510	—	480	300	490	2730
Third Plan (1961-66)	2010	1030	—	870	730	1250	5890
Plan Holiday (1966-69)	750	530	—	770	370	810	3230
Fourth Plan (1969-74)	2390	1400	—	1950	1060	1060	7860
Fifth Plan (1974-79)	3170	1560	—	2050	1250	1090	9120
Sixth Plan (1980-85)	8360	5300	2240	5590	1080	2730	25300
Seventh Plan (1985-90)	28410	18320	4700	12010	1980	10830	76330
Plan Holiday (1990-92)	17290	10530	4160	5880	1180	8230	47270
Eighth Plan Out lay (1992-97)	92010	34980	18480	15160	7510	27860	196000

Source : Compiled from Five Year Plans, Planning Commission, New Delhi.

Table 24.2: **Plan Expenditure on Different Sectors of Education** *(in Percentage)*

Sector	*First Plan Expdt. 1951-56*	*Second Plan Expdt. 1956-61*	*Third Plan Expdt. 1961-66*	*Plan Holiday Expdt. 1969-74*	*Fourth Plan Expdt. 1969-74*	*Fifth Plan Expdt. 1974-79*	*Sixth Plan Expdt. 1980-85*	*Seventh Plan Expdt. 1985-80*	*1990-92 Expdt.*	*Eighth Plan Outlay 1992-97*	*Ninth Plan (1997-2002 Central Sector*	*Tenth Plan Outlay (2000-2007) Sector Central*
(1)	(2)	(3)	(4)	(5)	(6)	(7)	(8)	(9)	(10)	(11)	(12)	(13)
Elementary	58	35	34	24	50	52	32	37	37	48	66	67
Education	(870)	(950)	(2010)	(750)	(3743)	(5913)	(8414)	(28494)	(17290)	(103940)	(16396)	(287500)
Secondary	5	19	18	16	@	@	20	24	22	24	10	10
Education	(80)	(510)	(1030)	(530)			(5344)	(18315)	(10530)	(52311)	(26035)	(43250)
Adult					2	2	6	6	9	5	3	3
Education					(126)	(248)	(1533)	(4696)	(4160)	(11421)	(6304)	(12500)
Higher	8	18	15	24	25	28	21	16	12	10	10	8
Education	(120)	(480)	(870)	(770)	(1883)	(3188)	(56004)	(12011)	(5880)	(20944)	(2500)	(36070)
Others	15	10	12	11	13	9	11	3	2	3	2	2
	(230)	(300)	(730)	(370)	(936)	(1071)	(2729)	(1980)	(1180)	(7398)	(4314)	(6180)
Technical	14	18	21	25	10	9	10	14	17	10	9	10
Education	(210)	(490)	(1250)	(810)	(786)	(1015)	(2536)	(10833)	(8320)	(21987)	(23735)	(43000)
Total	100	100	100	100	100	100	100	100	100	100	100	100
	(1510)	(2730)	(5890)	(3230)	(7774)	(11435)	(26187)	(76329)	(47270)	(218001)	(249084)	(428500)

Source: Five Year Plan Documents, Planning Commission and Analysis of Budget Expenditure, Ministry of HRD.

Note: 1. Figures in parenthesis in millions of rupees.
2. Figures in Col. 2 to Col. 11 includes the share of States/UTs.
@ Included under Elementary Education.

General Observations

The percentage of expenditure on elementary education declined from 58 per cent in the First Plan to 48 per cent in the Eighth Plan. It was as low as 34 per cent in the Third Plan. On the contrary the percentage of expenditure on higher education rose from 8 per in the First Plan to 25 per cent in the Fourth Plan. It was always higher in all the Plans except in the Eighth Plan which was just on per cent lower from the First Plan. In this context it is observed that this has been the major drawback in education planning in India. Most of the expenditure on higher education is unproductive. We have created a huge army of unemployed and under-employed educational persons.

Table 24.3

Progress of Elementary Education (1950-51 to 2006-07)

Year	*No. of Pupils in Classes I-V (Lakhs)*	*Percentage thereof to Population in Age Group 6-11*	*No. of Pupils in Classes VI-VIII (Lakhs)*	*Percentage thereof to Population in Age Group 11-14*
1950-51	191.5	42.6	31.2	12.7
1960-61	349.5	62.4	67.0	22.5
1968-69	543.7	78.1	125.4	33.5
1978-79	689.6	81.6	181.6	38.0
1979-80	715.58	82.7	192.79	39.6
1982-83	795.07	86.8	236.31	45.5
1984-85	856.5	93.6	262.2	48.1
1986-87	899.9	95.96	287.8	53.14
1987-88	929.4	97.86	299.1	55.14
1988-89	957.3	99.56	309.4	56.95

(Contd.)

1989-90	973.0	99.9	322.0	59.1
1990-91	991.0	101.03	333.0	60.11
2000-01	1138	95.7	428	58.6
2006-07	1320	111.24	520	73.6

Source: *Annual Reports of the Ministry of Education/Human Resource Development, Government of India.*

Table 24.4

Progress of Secondary Education (1950-51 to 2004-2005)

Year	*No. of Pupils in Classes IX to XII (In lakhs)*	*Percentage thereof to Total Population in the Age Group 14-17*
1950-51	15	5.3
1960-61	28.9	10.6
1968-69	61.5	18.3
1978-79	84.1	18.8
1979-80	98.19	21.9
1982-83	115.88	18.6
1984-85	154.8	23.5
1986-87	155.0	22.3
1987-88	178.54	25.0
1988-89	185.24	25.3
1990-91	209.0	19.3
2000-2001	276	30.0
2006-2007	394	40.6

Source: 1. *Selected Educational Statistics 2006-2007* and Department of Education.

2. *Economic Survey 2008-2009.*

Table 24.5

Growth of Recognised Educational Institutions at the School Level

Year	*Primary Schools*	*Upper Primary (Middle Schools)*	*High/Higher Secondary School/Inter College Pre-Degree Jr. Colleges*
1950-51	2,09,671	13,596	7,416
1960-61	2,30,399	49,663	17,329
1970-71	4,08,378	90,621	37,051
1980-81	4,94,503	1,18,555	51,624
1990-91	5,58,392	1,46,636	78,619
1991-92	5,65,786	1,52,077	81,747
2000-2001	6,38,738	2,06,269	1,26,047
2006-07	7,72,568	2,88,993	1,68,900

Table 24.6

Progress of College Education (1950-51 to 2006-07)

Year	*No. of Students at the University Stage Studying in Arts Science and Commerce (In Lakh)*	*Percentage thereto Total Population in Age Group 17-23*
1950-51	3.6	0.8
1960-61	8.9	1.8
1968-69	17.0	3.3
1978-79	34.2	4.9
1988-89	34.6	3.6
1991-92	44.25	6.5
2000-2001	80.0	7.0
2006-2007	123.7	11.0

Table 24.7

Progress of Higher Education Institutions (1950-51 to 2006-07)

Year	*Colleges for General Education*	*Colleges for Professional Education*	*Universities*
1950-51	370	208	27
1960-61	967	852	45
1970-71	2,285	992	82
1980-81	3,421	1,317	110
1990-91	4,862	886*	184
1991-92	5,058	950*	196
2000-2001	7,926	2,223	254
2006-2007	11,926	5,610	371

Source: Economic Survey, 2008-2009.

* Includes only Colleges of Medicine, Engineering and Teacher Training.

Table 24.8

Number of Teachers (1950-51 to 2005-2006)

Year	*Primary Schools*	*Middle Schools*	*Secondary and Hr Secondary Schools*	*Universities, Arts and Science Colleges*
1950-51	5,37,918	85,496	1,26,504	18,648
1960-61	74,41515	3,45,228	2,96,305	41,759
1968-69	10,05,082	5,95,733	5,81,618	91,069
1978-79	12,96,639	8,25,126	8,18,507	2,49,399
1979-80	13,28,700	8,35,608	8,69,942	2,59,745
1982-83	13,89,356	8,56,389	9,93,003	3,07,242
1983-84	13,91,912	8,78,565	10,32,219	2,24,405
1984-85	14,85,305	9,27,623	10,86,574	2,02,958

(Contd.)

1986-87	15,22,108	9,79,073	11,99,367	2,21,000
1987-88	16,16,685	10,14,162	12,42,823	2,42,000
1988-89	16,03,058	10,32,534	12,35,520	2,49,000
1989-90	16,01,717	10,47,588	12,64,249	2,52,000
1990-91	16,36,898	10,59,295	12,72,502	2,56,000
1998-99	19,04,000	12,78,000	17,20,000	4,00,000
2004-05	21,61,000	15,89,000	20,83,000	4,88,000
2005-06	85,00,000	22,50,000	23,20,000	5,21,800

* Includes only Colleges of Medicine, Engineering and Teacher Training.

** Includes Deemed to be Universities and Institutions of National Importance.

Sources: 1. *Selected Educational Statistics for Different Years,* Department of Education.

2. Annual Reports of the Ministry of Education, Human Resource Development.

3. *Annual Reports of UGC.*

Table 24.9

Teacher Training/Education (1950-51 to 2006-07)

Year	*No. of Teacher Training Schools*	*No. of Teacher Training Colleges*
1950-51	782	53
1960-61	1,138	478
1968-69	231	1,377
1978-79	118	1,286
1979-80	138	1,283
1982-83	908	1,310
1983-84	914	517
1984-85	223	367
1986-87	973	462
1987-88	990	485
1988-89	992	485
1990-91	1,167	474
2000-2001	1,050	800
2004-2005	1,150	1,300
2006-07	2,300	1,500

Source: *Ibid.*

A Critical Review of Education Plans

Achievements

Explanation of educational facilities—It is generally observed that there is no parallel to expansion in the earlier history of this country and even in the contemporary world. This record would be equalled by a few countries if at all. This expansion has been shown in the tables.

Qualitative improvement programmes—Special programmes are: (a) improvement in the teaching of science; (b) curricula reforms; (c) improvement in teaching material; (d) reform in the evaluation system; and (e) experiments with new methods, techniques and procedures.

Attempts made towards equalisation of opportunities— Attempts have been made towards providing equalisation of education opportunities. Mention may be made of the following programmes— (a) free education at the primary level in all the states; (b) free education at the secondary stage in some states; (c) scholarship to meritorious students; (d) interests-free loans; (e) school meals; (f) transport facilities at some places; (g) free text books on a limited scale; (h) school uniforms at cheap rates; (i) special scholarships and grants to the underprivileged groups like the scheduled castes, the scheduled tribes; (j) special incentives towards women's education; (k) facilities for the education of handicapped children.

Defects in Educational Planning

1. Educational Planning from top to bottom and neglect of grassroots.
2. Less stress on qualitative improvement of education.
3. Educational planning not linked to economic planning.
4. Too much emphasis on degrees.
5. Lack of national policy on education till 1968.
6. Non-rational use of resources meant for education.
7. Over-dependence on foreign experts.
8. Lack of perspective planning.
9. Lopsided priorities and neglect of elementary education.
10. Too little balance between general and vocational education.
11. Absence of functional and operational educational research.

12. Planning based on inadequate and unreliable education statistics.
13. Regional disparities in the expansion of education facilities.
14. Official directed and oriented educational plans.
15. Non-coordination of agencies working in the field of education.
16. Educational planning not linked to manpower planning.

Effective Educational Planning

A review of the implementation of the educational plans highlight the need to improve the planning techniques. Some of the important measures are given here.

Estimates of availability of funds—Before taking up programmes of educational reforms, it must he ensured that sufficient funds are available. We make ambitious educational plans with the hope that requisite funds would be available from various sources.

At the last moment, when it is felt that funds are not available, plans are pruned haphazardly. A correct estimate of financial resources must be made.

The need for concentration of efforts and adoption of a selective approach—Throughout the plans, the general policy has been to do something in every sector or for every programme with the result that the meagre resources available were spread thinly over a very large area. This policy involves considerable wastage. It has, therefore, now become important to concentrate on a few crucial programmes, such as improvement of the quality of teachers, development of agricultural education, provision of good and effective primary education for all children, liquidisation of illiteracy, vocationalisation of secondary education, establishment of major universities, expansion and improvement of post-graduate education, increase in the number of scholarships and the development of about ten per cent of institutions as each stage to optimum levels of quality.

Adequate emphasis on qualitative improvement—There has been an overemphasis on the achievement of targets in enrolments and expenditure.

It is true that expansion will have to continue. But an over-emphasis on this aspect leads to the neglect of the still more important aspect of quality. Similarly and over-emphasis on expenditure targets tends to distort priorities and often leads to wastage. There is thus a need to take a more comprehensive view of the problem and to evolve a broader pattern of goals, especially those relating to qualitative improvement.

Emphasis on programmes which need talent and hard work—The emphasis on reaching expenditure targets to which a reference has been made tends to place a premium on programmes where it is easy to incur expenditure, e.g., construction of building or expansion of enrolments. This is unfortunate because there are a number of programmes which call for determined effort, organisation, talent and hard work rather than large financial investment. The following are some examples of such programmes:

— production of literature in the modern Indian languages needed for their adoption as media of education at the university stage;
— educational research;
— examination reform;
— preparation of school textbooks and teaching and learning materials;
— in service education of teachers and officers of the Education Departments;
— improving techniques of supervision;
— improving contact with the local communities and parents;
— providing enrichment programmes and guidance to gifted students and some special assistance to retarded or backward ones.

A number of instances of this type can be cited. What is important to note is that, in the existing situation where financial resources are limited, it is programmes of this type that need far greater emphasis than those which need heavy financial investment.

Pragmatic evaluation and research—Since planning is comparatively a new process and we have to evolve our own techniques, it is necessary to evaluate our programmes which will enable us to cut down costs and increase the effectiveness of the investment in education. What we would recommend is the deep involvement of universities, professional organisation, training colleges, etc., in a periodical evaluation of all major programmes included in the plans and in the development of a large-scale research programme.

Effective machinery for educational planning—The existing machinery for educational Planning leaves much to be desired. It is not adequately trained. As a matter of fact educational planning is by and large, in the hands of non-educationists who hold the top position at the Centre and in States. Educational planning must be educational and professionalised.

Different levels of priorities—Education is essentially a responsibility of the State Governments. But it is also a national concern and in certain major sectors, decisions have to be taken at the national level. This implies the need to regard education as a centre-state partnership. On the other hand, it is necessary to remember that education which concerns every parent and every family has to be taken as close to people as possible and that its administration can be best conducted by or in close association with local communities. This implies that education planning has to be decentralised to the district level and still further down to the level of each institution. The process of educational planning in a federal democracy like ours has thus to be the right blend of centralisation in the appropriate sectors, and especially in administration. Care should, however, be taken that the parts fall coherently into the totality of a broad national plan, and all discordant features and contradictions are eliminated. For this purpose, it will be necessary to devise an effective machinery of coordination. This is the direction in which administration has to strive and planning has to grow.

Manpower needs and higher education—Places in full-time institutions of secondary and higher education should be provided with due regard to manpower needs and maintenance of standards; and admissions to them should be made on the basis of an egalitarian selection.

Decentralisation of authority—Wasteful expenditure which often arises from rigidities of administrative and financial procedures should be avoided by introducing flexibility and adequate decentralisation of authority.

Questions and Problems

A. Essay-Type Questions

1. What are the objectives of educational planning in India? Give a review of the educational expansion in India from 1950-51 to 1992-93.
2. To what extent have the objectives of education planning been fulfilled in India? Are you satisfied with the results? State reasons in support of your answer.
3. Explain the achievements and failure of educational planning in India. Suggest measures for effective education planning
4. "Planning in India has been expenditure oriented". Explain this statement.

B. Short-Answer Type Questions

5. Briefly describe the financial aspects of educational planning in India.
6. List the priorities that should determine educational planning in India.

Part III

Teacher's Role, Education, Skills, Competence and Status

25 The Teacher and Society

25.1 Significance of the Teacher and the Teaching Profession

Premises and equipment are needed in the education enterprise but persons are vital to them and a teacher is the supreme factor. There is no exaggeration that a spacious building, costly equipment and sound syllabus will serve some useful purpose only when there are teachers who are fully alive to the nobility of the profession and its accompanying responsibilities. The teachers play an important role in moulding and shaping the attitudes, habits, manners and above all, the character and personality of the students. Here we quote the views of some great philosophers, statesmen and thinkers on the significance of the teacher and the teaching profession.

The Teacher is a Maker of Man

John Adams (1735-1826 second US President)

"A teacher affects eternity; he can never tell where his influence stops."

Henry Brooks Adams (1838-1918 American Man of Letters)

"I am indebted to my father for a living, but to my teacher for living well."

Alexander (355-323 B.C. The great conqueror)

"Teachers who educate children deserve more honour than parents."

Aristotle (384-322 B.C. Greek philosopher)

"The teacher is a helper and guide."

Sri Aurobindo (1872-1950 Indian seer and philosopher)

"The teacher is the Prophet of the true God and the usherer of the true kingdom of God."

John Dewey (1859-1952 A great American educator)

"Woe to the teacher who teaches one thing with the lips and carries another in his heart."

M.K. Gandhi (1869-1948 A great Indian freedom fighter, seer and an apostle of non-violence and truth)

"Like torches, a light to others; waste and destruction to themselves."

Richard Hooker (1554-1600 English theologian)

"The teacher is indeed the architect of our future. Society can neglect him at its own peril."

Zakir Hussain (1897-1969 President of India)

"They (teachers) are literally the arbiters of a nation's destiny."

Humayun Kabir (1902-1969 An Indian educator)

"If a teacher has not an ideal aim, he had better to take to shopkeeping at once, he will there, doubtless find an ideal within his capacity."

Lauri

"For him the teacher's chair became a throne."

H. Wordsworth Longfellow (1807-1882 American scholar)

"Teacher—partly doctor, partly scientist and wholly religious."

M. Montessori (1870-1952 Italian educator and originator of the Montessori System)

"We underscore that the prime task of the teacher is concerned with man-making, namely the making of the Indian of tomorrow."

National Commission (Indian) on school teachers (1983-87

"If a nations's teachers are C_3,a nation itself cannot but be C_3. And let there be no doubt about this — if we wish to be an A_1 nation, our teachers will have to be A_1.

E.A. Pires (Indian educator)

"The greatest teachers of our country have been those who have made our civilisation live."

Sarvapalli Radhakrishnan (188-1975 Indian educationist and Philosopher)

"The teacher is like the candle which lights others in consuming itself."

W.M. Ryburn (Indian educator)

"We are, however, convinced that the most important factor in the contemplated educational reconstruction is the teacher."

Secondary Education Commission (1952-53)

"He that governs well, leads the blind, but he that teaches gives him eyes."

Robert South (1634-1716, English divine)

"He (teacher) is like a lamp lighting other lamps. But a lamp cannot put light into other lamps if it does not burn and shed light."

Rabindranath Tagore (1861-1941 Indian philosopher and poet)

"If there is any profession of paramount importance, I believe it is that of the school master."

John Tyndall (1820-1893 English philosopher)

"Teacher as the 'Brahma', the 'Vishnu' and the 'Maheshwara'."

Vedic Prayer

"The teacher is the real maker of history."

A Few Epithets

H.G. Wells (1866-1946 Great historian)

"The vanity of teaching often tempteth a man to forget he is a blockhead."

Earl of Halifax (1881-1959 English statesman)

"He is awkward, and out of place, in the society of his equals. He comes like Gulliver from among his little people, and he cannot fit the stature of his understanding to others."

Charles Lamb (1775-1834 English essayist)

"The average schoolmaster is and always must be essentially an ass for how can one Imagine an intelligent man engaging in so puerile a vocation."

Henry Louis Mencken (1880-1956 American scholar)

"He who can, does. He who cannot, teaches."

George Bernard Shaw (1856-1950 English writer)

"Everybody who is incapable of learning has taken to teaching."

Oscar Wilde (1854-1900 Irish dramatist)

"He is either dead or teaching school."

25.2 Teacher's Role in Society

From the above quoted views of the eminent thinkers, it is clear that a teacher can play an important role in the progress and welfare of a society. A teacher is a member of the society. He lives and works in the society yet, in view of his special responsibilities and roles, he is expected to rise above the average member of society. His general attitude in society should be of enthusiasm and optimism. He is expected to be quite sensitive to its needs. He should be guided by the ideals of democracy, secularism and socialism. He is to be sufficiently appreciative of the changing needs and problems of society and play a dynamic and positive role.

A teacher plays his role towards society in two ways (a) inside the school by preparing students for effective citizens and (b) outside the school by assuming the role of a social worker and an agent of social change. However, his role, in the school is of vital significance.

Broad Classification of a Teacher's Role

1. Teacher as an agent of social change. (See Chapter 9)
2. Teacher's role in Community welfare. (See Chapter 10)
3. Teacher's role in elimination of social tensions and conflict. (See Chapter on Diverse Issues)
4. Teacher's role in international understanding. (See Chapter on Diverse Issues)
5. Teacher's role in pupil development. (See following pages)

Teacher's Multifarious Roles in Pupil Development

1. *Confidant*—A teacher is expected to win the confidence of the students so that they express their feelings purely, if need be in private.
2. *Democrat*—He is expected to observe democratic values so as to prepare his students for a democratic way of life.
3. *Detective*—He acts as a detective to find out the shortcomings of the students—committing of offences and law breaking tendencies also.
4. *Ego-supporter*—He is supposed to build up and maintain a healthy strong 'ego' and 'self concept' among student.
5. *Equaliser*—He should treat all students on the basis of equality. He should work for developing an egalitarian outlook in students.
6. *Facilitator of learning*—He works for the promotion of significant learning in his students.
7. *Friend and philosopher*—He must perform the role of a friend and philosopher to his students.
8. *Group leader*: As a leader of the social group in the clan, he must develop a suitable climate and cohesion.
9. *Guidance counsellor and helper*—He provides an academic career and personal guidance to his students.
10. *Initiator*—He is supposed to play the role of an initiator by exploring the new technology to the best advantage of the students and the progress of education. He should play the role of an innovator of educational ideas, practices and systems.
11. *Role model*—He is envisaged to behave in a manner whereby traits exemplified by him may be emulated by his students.
12. *Judge*—He evaluates the academic and other performance of the students in an impartial manner.
13. *Limiter or reducer of anxiety*—He can help students control their impulses and reduce anxiety about their conduct and performance in different problematic situations.
14. *Moral educator*—His important function is to inculcate the attitudes and moral values cherished by Society in the students.
15. *Parent surrogate* (parent substitute)—He can play the role of ideal parents by treating students with affection and care.

16. *Rationalist*—He should set an example of a rationalist by basing his actions on reason.
17. *Referee*—He is expected to settle disputes among students in an objective manner.
18. *Reformer*—His entire work consists of bringing about appropriate changes in his students for their full development.
19. *Resource person*—He is expected to serve as a resource person for his students as he possesses knowledge of the subject-matter and skills, better than his pupils.
20. *Secularist*—He should play the role of a secularist by having an open mind on the beliefs of students.
21. *Upholder of the norms and values*—He must present the norms and values of society in a dignified manner.

25.3 Major Functions and Responsibilities of a Teacher

Total development of the child as his primary responsibility—In the words of Dr. E.A. Pires, "he has to concern himself with the total development of the child and not only with one or two aspects. He must befriend him and help him in his emotional and social development. He must be a philosopher illumining the way of this intellectual and spiritual progress. He must be his guide in his moral and aesthetic advancement. In fact, he must be 'all things' to all his pupils— a physician concerned about their physical health, a mental hygienist leading them carefully to sound mental health, a philosopher guiding them painstakingly in their search for truth, a moralist assisting and encouraging them to acquire goodness, an artist helping them to find beauty. In fact, he must be a minister ministering to their every need. Such a ministry calls for educated service."

The following are his main functions responsibilities:

1. Character development.
2. Effective teaching learning.
3. Curriculum development and implementation.
4. Adjusting individual differences.
5. Class-room management.
6. Evaluation of pupil performance.
7. Developing good family and community relationships.

8. Total school effectiveness.
9. Professional growth and ethics.

Character development—For this, the teacher:

1. Creates an atmosphere of purposeful order, enlists pupil's assistance in orderly, friendly, courteous and co-operative inter-personal relation.
2. Develops a respect for the rights, privileges and opinions of others.
3. Creates group situations which will develop desirable leadership and followership qualities in the pupils.
4. Sets a standard of class-room and school environment behaviour which conforms to socially acceptable behaviour.
5. Directs discussion and develops understanding on moral and other ethical issues in order to develop the understanding of the reasons for ethical standard.
6. Encourages each pupil's thinking and action.

Technique of teaching—(Effective teaching) This includes—

1. Selecting materials, teaching aids and methods which will facilitate the learning process and stimulate the desire for further learning.
2. Meeting the needs, background and capacities of the children being taught.
3. Teaching by use of a suitable variety of lectures, discussions, demonstrations, visual and oral presentations, recitation, directed group effort, experimentation, special projects and field trips.
4. Analysing and evaluating the effectiveness of various teaching techniques in order to improve the learning process.
5. Endeavouring to obtain and maintain pupil interest and attention so that teaching is done in a receptive environment.
6. Endeavouring to assure that material taught is applied in such a manner so as to develop a pattern of understanding for future use in other areas.
7. Encouraging and guiding critical thinking by pupils.
8. Developing desirable work and study skills and habits.
9. Enlisting pupil participation in the lesson planning process.

10. Developing broad outlines and objectives to be attained within prescribed limits, for a subject or skill area based upon the needs and interests of a specific group of pupils.
11. Assuring that preparation adequate to assure purposeful and directed teaching precedes all actual class-room teaching.
12. Making suitable lesson plans and other necessary arrangements for substitutes.
13. Interpreting test results and relating findings to pupil progress or lack of it in order to improve the teaching and learning process.
14. Evaluating pupil performance through reports, recitations, homework and other types of assignments.
15. Reporting pupil achievement and progress to parents by means of conferences and progress reports.
16. Co-operating and enlisting the co-operation of school specialists in the process of pupil evaluation as required.

Curriculum development and implementation—This implies—

1. Participation in grade level or subject matter study of existing curricula and in the development of improved expanded curricula.
2. Determining the object, scope and methods of the grade and subjects to be taught.
3. Devising assignments, when necessary, in order to enrich the teaching programme for the pupils.
4. Correlating subject matter with the curriculum of other subjects.

Adjusting to individual differences and development levels—This calls for—

1. Drawing upon and applying the basic knowledge of the psychology of the child in order to establish readiness for learning.
2. Making an effort to know as much as possible about the background and out-of school environment of each child in order to improve the teaching learning process.
3. Developing in each pupil a sense of personal growth and value.
4. Maintaining discipline by being consistently friendly, fair and firm.

5. Handling behaviour problems in a controlled manner.

Class-room management—This means—

1. Assigning responsibility to pupils for the care and housekeeping of the class room's physical assets.
2. Developing, preparing or providing material and equipment and displaying it in a manner so as to improve the learning situation.
3. Maintaining the school-room in a healthful and safe condition, assuring proper lighting, ventilation etc.
4. Preparing and maintaining orderly and accurately all required records, such as attendance registers.

Evaluating and reporting of pupil performance—This comprises—

1. Devising and administering appropriate tests to measure the level and quality of pupil learning.
2. Interpreting test results and relating findings to pupil progress or lack of it in order to improve the teaching and learning process.
3. Evaluating pupil performances through reports, recitations, homework and other types of assignment.
4. Reporting pupil achievements and progress to parents by means of conferences and progress reports.
5. Co-operating and enlisting the co-operation of school specialist in the process of pupil evaluation as required.

Developing good family and community relations—This envisages—

1. Participating in parent-teacher and similar activities.
2. Participating in community affairs.
3. Making himself available to parents at scheduled times to discuss pupil progress and behaviour.
4. Evincing a sympathetic, helpful and understanding attitude towards parents and their childrens' schooling problems.
5. Establishing and maintaining a good relationship with parents and reporting of pupil progress, problems and needs.
6. Assuring through personal behaviour in the community that the school staff-image in the community is favourable.

Total school effectiveness—This consists of—

1. Accepting responsibility for pupil discipline throughout the school and in the interest of the school as a whole.
2. Co-operating with all co-workers and exchanging ideas in order to improve and provide a variety of approach on the teaching situation.
3. Executing all required school regulations and assignments on time.
4. Accepting one's full share of pupil activity participation; such as attending athletic contests etc.
5. Contributing constructively to committees, faculty meetings and other school system groups.
6. Taking positive steps in developing and maintaining faculty and student morale.

Professional growth and ethics—(Discussed separately)

New Demands on the Role of the Teacher

The role of the present day teacher has become very challenging, complex and multi-faceted on account of the following reasons:

First, there is the explosion of knowledge and radical changes are occurring in the content areas of all disciplines—humanities, science subjects and social sciences.

Second, the teacher has to keep in view new concepts like individualised instruction, micro-teaching, programmed learning, teaching machines and team-teaching etc.

Third, the teacher has to make the proper use of the mass media like the radio and television.

Fourth, the teacher has to handle many children who come from better socio-economic groups and family backgrounds and at times may be more informed than the teacher who often comes from a lower socio-economic moorings.

Fifth, the teacher must take into account the explosion of expectations. Students from weaker sections of the society are coming in large numbers to receive education and they have to be treated on an equal footing and given due care.

Sixth, the attitude of a teacher to life has to be democratic, secular and socialist; the ideals set forth in our constitution.

Seventh, the present teacher is supposed to have a broad view of the subjects he teaches. He cannot afford to teach his subjects in isolation.

Eighth, a teacher must adequately familiarise himself with concepts like 'Work Experience', 'Socially Useful Productive Work' and 'Community Service' etc., as these have become an integral part of the educative process.

Ninth, the present teacher is expected to be up-date and conscious of various explosions—explosion of knowledge, explosion of population, explosion of frustrations, explosion of expectations and explosion of technology, etc.

25.4 Essential Qualities and Characteristics of an Effective Teacher

Earlier we have mentioned the important roles a teacher is expected to perform. For this, he needs to posses certain qualities which can broadly be classified as under:

1. Qualities relating to professional requirements.
2. Qualities relating to character and personality.
3. Qualities relating to human relationships.
4. Qualifications relating to professional education/training.

Qualities Relating to Professional Requirements

Love of the profession—The teacher should feel the importance of his profession. He would be showing a dishonesty of purpose if once having entered it, he is engaged in other pursuits. Without an exclusive attention to his job he would fail in bringing forth a fine harvest of young men and women who are able to contribute their best for the welfare of man kind. If a teacher takes to his work just to make his living because nothing else is available he will lack the essential zeal required by the teaching profession. He must be a teacher first and a teacher last. A person who wants to join this profession must feel the call for it. "If a teacher has not an ideal aim, he had better take to shopkeeping at once, he will there doubtless find an ideal within his capacity", says Laurie. In the words of the Secondary Education Commission, "They will not look upon their work as an unpalatable means of earning a scanty living but as an avenue through which they are rendering significant social services as well as finding some measure of self-fulfillment and self-expression." Prof. Deway has said, "Every teacher should realise the dignity of his calling." William G Carr, has observed, "I wish that I could persuade every teacher to be proud of his profession. Draw yourself up to your full height, look anybody, squarely in the eyes and say, "I am a teacher."

Love for children—It has been said that if a teacher does not actually like boys and girls, he should give up teaching. He must enjoy company in groups. A good teacher feels that some sort of energy is constantly supplied by the young. "Love the child and the child will love you; hate the child and the child will hate you," is a famous maxim. One who does not like children should not stay in teaching.

Respect for the individuality of each child—A child should not be treated just like dumb driven cattle. He has his own individuality. He thinks and feels, his sense of respect should not be injured. Emerson has rightly stated, "The secret of education lies in respecting the pupil." A child wants to be heard. His opinion should not be brushed aside merely because he is a child.

Knowledge of child psychology and educational psychology—Knowledge of psychology goes a long way in providing that basic orientation towards problems of education and child development without which there would be a considerable waste of time, energy and human resources.

Mastery of the subject-matter—He must be master of his subject. Any weakness on his part will lower his prestige in the eyes of his student. K.G. Saiyidain writes, "You cannot pour out of a vessel except what you have put into it and, if a teacher is poor and shallow from within, if there is no sparking wire in him, he cannot quicken the mind or humanise the emotions of his children."

Grasp over the method—Two farmers may possess an equal amount of land and an equally great desire of good crops but the one who uses the best methods of farming will, other factors being same, get better results, Similarly, a teacher who adopts proper methods of teaching will show good results and his teaching will be more effective.

Preparation—Perhaps there is no type of work where the results of poor planning are so devastating as in teaching. Careful and systematic arrangement of the subject-matter and the classroom activities is conductive to creative discipline. A well-prepared lesson helps to overcome the feeling of nervousness and insecurity especially to summon in the first attempt at teaching. Bagley emphasises the importance of daily preparation in these words, "However able and experienced the teacher, he could never do without his preliminary preparation."

Skill in questioning—The success of a class teacher in the class also depends on the art of questioning. One who questions faultlessly, teaches effectively. With the help of right type of questions a wise teacher can lead the students from dark and unknown regions to known and bright ones.

Thirst for knowledge and experimental spirit—A teacher must refresh himself by constant reading not only about his subjects but books which touch life at every point. It would be very helpful if he would get opportunities of attending educational seminars, refresher courses and the like which enable him to get a good grip of his own thoughts.

Interest in curriculum activities—It is needless to stress the importance of co-curricular activities in the present system of education. They are equally important as the academics subjects and such a teacher can hardly afford to be indifferent to this aspect of school life.

Punctuality—We should realise that coming late to the school and going late to the class upsets the school work, causes indiscipline and undermines the tone of the school. A good teacher will make it a point to be punctual in his work. Following the teachers coming late, the students may also develop in themselves this very habit.

Professional ethics—(Separately discussed)

Use of teaching technology—(Material Aids) Various teaching aids bring clarity and vividness. It is a great asset to the teacher to narrate stories and anecdotes which appeal to children at different ages and attainment levels, Abstract words and phrases can be made clear by illustrations.

Knowledge of the aims of education—Never for a moment should the teacher forget that the aim of education is not to prepare the child for Matriculation or any other examination but to inculcate in him the quality of head, heart, hand and health.

Judicious use of praise and blame—Praise and blame are the two importance weapons in the armoury of the teacher and these should be used very judiciously. "Praise like gold and diamond owes its value to scarcity," writes Robinson Johnson. A word of praise or commendation will easily enhance the pupil's interest in any course of action. Praise, rightly employed, is forceful incentive at the disposal of the teacher. Rebukes and scoldings are to be used very sparingly, other wise they lose their value.

Awareness of the departmental rules and regulations—A teacher must keep himself fully posted with rules and regulations.

Qualities Relating to Character and Personality

Character and personality—The character and personality of the pupils cannot be developed if the teacher who is the model to be followed lacks character and personality. 'Example is better than precept' is an old saying an is absolutely true in the teaching profession. No amount of sermons from the teacher can make much headway. A teacher teaches not only by 'what he says and does' but very largely by 'what he is'. Children are imitative and suggestive by nature. They imitate the dress, voice, habits and manners of their teachers. The likes and dislikes of the teachers become their likes and desires . Children who are in the plastic period of their life are easily influenced by their teachers. The teachers should teach what they practise. Gandhi strongly denounces those teachers who teach one thing with lips and carry another in their heart. 'Man know thyself' is the advice given by Socrates in Greece and Yajnvalkya in India. The teachers must undergo an inner training. They should try to find out their own shortcomings and try to remove them. Ryburn says, 'Self analysis on the part of a teacher is a necessary equipment'. Montessori stresses that every teacher worth his salt must destroy these sins: pride, anger, sloth, sensuality, gluttony and envy. The teacher should be partly a scientist, partly a doctor and completely religious. He must acquire a moral alertness; mingling of patience, love and humility. He should always be frank, sincere and honest. Prof. Raymount urges that the teacher must avoid everything that is petty and mean. Gandhi observes, "Woe to the teacher who teaches one thing with the lips and carries another in the heart."

"While books can teach, only personality can educate," writes an eminent educationist. A good personality includes (a) appearance, (b) voice, (c) character, and (d) expression.

Missionary—Dr. E.A. Pires opines that the great teacher has the zeal of the missionary. There is a certain aptness in the analogy between a missionary and a teacher, for every true missionary is first and last a teacher. S. Balakrishan Joshi feels, "Without a band of devoted teachers who are inspired by holy zeal, an institution with the paraphernalia of modern convenience will be like beautiful corpse without spark of life, a carcass without should." According to the same author teaching is a divinely ordained mission.

Patience—He has to deal with a large number of students having low and high power of understanding. He may have to repeat his lesson many a time for the sake of the less intelligent and he should not be irritated in doing so. Some students, by nature, pick up lessons very slowly and a teacher should possess the required patience to make them understand gradually. Good habits are not formed overnight. It requires time and patience to inculcate virtues in the students.

Emotional stability—Various research studies show clearly that the emotional stability of teachers affect that of pupils. The unhappy, frustrated, dissatisfied teachers cannot help their pupils to become happy, well adjusted young people.

Good vitality—In the opinion of Arthur B. Moehlman, "Good vitality is essential to successful teaching, not only in its reflex influence upon the children but also in making possible continuity of work with the fewest possible interruptions from illness because of general fatigue."

Good memory—A teacher with a poor memory is ridiculous. It becomes easier for a teacher having a good memory to correlate many things. A good creative memory is one of the qualities that differentiates the good teacher from the mediocre.

Good voice—The voice of a teacher should be clear, moderately pitched and well-modulated. A thin low voice develops dulness and monotony in the class. A very high pitched voice or shrill must be avoided. It distracts the minds of the students and does not appeal to their aesthetic sense. Plenty of variety must be introduced in the voice. A teacher must be slow and emphatic when he is making statements he thinks worth copying. No effort should be spared to cultivate a pleasant musical tone. Anything which adds pleasure is an additional attraction for the attention and especially with children.

Humour—Dryden states, "Good humour and good nature constitute the bread of making and life."

Just and impartial—The teacher should not show undue favour to some. All should be equal in his eyes. Undue favour to some students will lead to frustration among others.

Laughter—A teacher should never make the mistake of laughing at the pupils. He should laugh with them and should also see that they laugh with him and not at him. R.R. Kumaria feels laughter is the embellishment that lends charm to the teaching profession. Humour keeps the pupils attentive. A very wise teacher once remarked, "I consider a day's teaching is wasted if we do not all have a hearty laugh." Sarcasm is to be avoided.

True to his commands—Less commands should be given to the students and when given, they must be stuck to, otherwise they lose their effectiveness.

Qualities Relating to Human Relationships

Cooperative attitude—The success of an institutions depends upon the cooperation among all. A teacher must cooperate with his colleagues, head of the insitution, parents and all others engaged in the welfare of children and other tasks.

Democratic attitude—A teacher cannot afford to be an autocarat. Present day education lays much stress on the inculcation of democratic ideals in the students. A teacher who is to show the way of democracy to the students must develop in himself a democratic attitude. His role is of a friend, philosopher and guide and not of a policeman.

Political neutrality—The students should not be exploited for political purposes. The programmes of the various political parties must be placed before them in their true perspective.

Religious tolerance—The minds of the young should not be poisoned though narrow-mindedness and bigotry. The partition of the country has shown what wrong fanaticism can do.

Self analysis on the part of the teacher—He should try to find, out his own short-comings and try to remove them. Ryburn states, "Self-analysis on the part of the teacher is a necessary equipment."

Qualifications Relating to Teaching

State Governments and departments of education of the states have prescribed minimum academic and training qualification for different categories of teachers.

Significance of Each Letter of the Word Teacher

Each letter of the word teacher signifies some traits or values to be possessed by him.

T stands for	—	Tact, Tolerance, Truth
E stands for	—	Efficiency, Ènthusiasm, Ethics, Etiquette
A stands for	—	Adaptability, Affection, Alertness
C stands for	—	Character, Clarity, Constructiveness, Creativity
H stand for	—	Hard Work, Humility, Honesty, Humour, Human Relations
E stand for	—	Eagerness, Efficiency, Emotional Stability
R stands for	—	Rationality, Relationship, Resource—fullness

The teacher should be an integration of all these.

Questions and Problems

A. Essay-Type Questions

1. Elucidate the significance of the teaching profession and the teacher.
2. State the roles played by a teacher.
3. Explain the role of the teacher in the development of the child.
4. Throw light on the qualities needed by a teacher to play his role effectively.
5. Describe the role of the teacher as:
   (i) An agent of social change and a social worker.
   (ii) Promoter of value education.
   (iii) Promoter of population education.
   (iv) Developer for values of international understanding.
   (vi) Inculcator of ideals of emotional and national integration.
6. 'A teacher is the maker of a nation'. Discuss the importance and functions of a teacher.

B. Short-Answer Type Questions

7. State the role of the teacher as a democrat.
8. What is the need for daily preparation on the part of the teacher?
9. List six most important qualities of a teacher.
10. Mention five most important functions of a teacher.

26 Teacher Education and Training

26.1 Significance, Meaning and Functions of Teacher Education

Significance of teacher education—The contention that teachers are born, not made, can be true only in a few rare cases. It is also not contended that training, by itself, is sure to make a good teacher. But it is generally observed that a teacher with training becomes more mature and confident to perform his task more efficiently. Proper education of the teacher enables him to have a knowledge of how children grow, develop and learn, how they can be taught effectively and how their inner potentialities can be brought out and developed. Teacher education is needed to kindle the imagination of the teacher and to remove the evils of the 'hit and miss' process, to accord a professional status to the teaching profession and above all to make the optimum use of the time and energy of the teacher and the taught.

It has been aptly remarked, "If you educate a boy, you educate one individual. If you educate a girl, you educate the whole family and if you educate a teacher, you educate the whole community."

The Education Commission (1964-66) said. "A sound programme of professional education of teachers is essential for the qualitative improvement of education. Investment in teacher education can yield very rich dividends because the financial resources required are small when measured against the resulting improvements in the education of millions."

The UNESCO-ILO Document on *Status of Teachers* (1967) states, "It should be recognised that the advance in education depends largely on the qualification and ability of the teaching staff in general and on the human, pedagogical and technical qualities of the individual teachers."

Meaning of Teacher Education

Dictionary of education—C.V. Good (1973), defines teacher education as "All formal and informal activities and experiences that help to qualify a person to assume the responsibility as a member of the educational profession or to discharge his responsibility most effectively."

Encyclopedia of Educational Research: (1941), Walter S. Monroe qualifies, teacher education as, "The total education experiences which contribute to the preparation of a person but the term is completely employed to designate the programme for courses and other experiences offered by an educational institute for the announced purposes of preparing persons for teaching and other educational service and for contribution to their growth in competency for such service. Such teacher education programmes are offered in teacher colleges, normal schools and colleges and universities."

Functions and Objectives of Teacher Education

As stated by Miss W. Walker in '*World Trends in Education*' (1967), "The function of teacher education is to produce good teachers. The good teacher is one who produces good results in meeting the central, presenting needs of life in whatever social context."

B.O. Smith in '*Teachers for the Real Word*' (1969) states, "If a student is to be prepared for the evolving world, then an essential attribute of effective teacher is awareness of the realities of the word."

Learning to Be (1972 UNESCO) has stated, "Pedagogical training must be geared to knowing and respecting the multiple aspects of human personality."

It has emphasised that, "what once was an art—the art of teaching—is now a science, built on firm foundations, and linked to psychology, anthropology, cybernetics, linguistics and many other disciplines."

Its recommendation Number 18 states, "Conditions in which teachers are trained should be profoundly changed so that essentially, they become educators rather than specialists in transmitting pre-established curricula; the principle of a first, accelerated training stage, followed by in-service training cycles, should be adopted."

Alvin Toffler in *Future Schools* (1973) has outlined the role of the future teacher in these words, "It is no longer sufficient for Johnny to understand the past. It is not even enough for him to understand the present, for the 'here-and-now' environment will soon vanish. Johnny must learn to anticipate the directions and rate of change....And so must Johnny's teachers."

About the professional educational status of teacher, the *International Encyclopeadia of Teaching and Teacher Education* (1987) has observed, "Enjoying the same social status and prestige as all those who eminently serve society, today's or tomorrow's teacher must be a professional, whose educational programme and level should be more and more comparable with the physician's education"

The following are the main functions and objectives of teacher education.

Better understanding of the student—Teacher training is a must as it enables the potential teacher to understand the student better. The knowledge of educational psychology helps him a lot in dealing with children scientifically. Untrained teachers not familiar with the subject may create problem children in the school.

Building confidence—Teacher training builds confidence in the potential teachers. A trained teacher can essentially face the class with confidence. He is not timid or shy. He can tackle many odd situations and he does not run away from problem situations.

Methodology of teaching—Through training, the future teacher becomes familiar with the methodology of teaching. He also gets essential knowledge of methods required for a particular subject. He teaches with a flair and not in a routine way.

Building a favourable attitude—A sort of brain wash is also done through training. It helps in building favourable attitudes towards the teaching profession. During the course of training, many doubts of the teacher trainees stand removed. It results in creation of love and respect for the teaching profession.

Familiarising with the latest in education—Teacher training programmes familiarise the future teachers with all that is latest in education. An attitude of research and experimentation is attempted to be created in them.

Familiarising with school organisation—During the course of teaching, we familiarise the teacher trainees with organisation and administration of the school. It is of immense use to them in later life.

Creating social insight—Teacher training is a must. It is required to teach the teachers to live a community life. Training is essential to create a social insight in them.

Improving standards—We are interested in raising the standards or the quality of education. A trained teacher can be a great help in improving the quality of education and also in checking wastage.

Training for democracy—Lastly, training is a must to produce teachers who can teach with zeal and zest and can strengthen the democratic set up in the country. Training is required not only with the sole aim of making one a good teacher but also making him a good citizen.

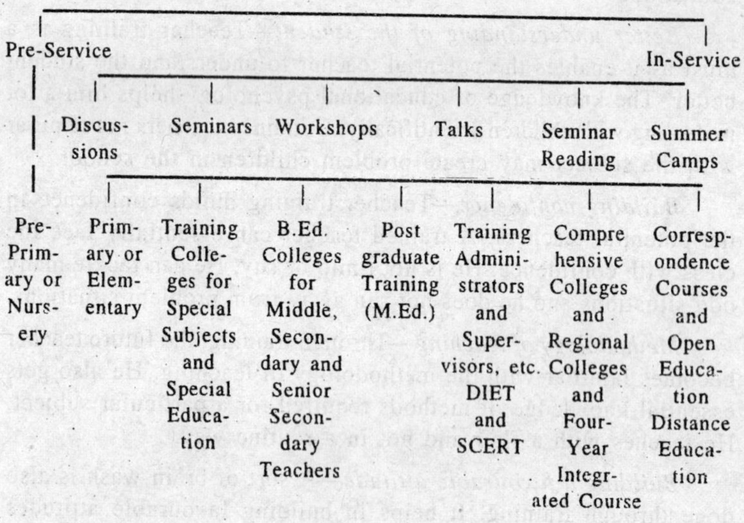

Illustration 26.1 Types of Teacher Education and Institutions

26.2 Pre-Services Teacher Education/Training Institutions

Pre-primary schools or nursery teacher institutions—Catering to the needs of teachers for Kindergarten, Bal Vihars etc., Minimum qualifications for admission to this course is secondary, higher secondary and the duration of the course is one year. Many institutions impart training for two years.

Training schools for elementary teachers—In general the course lasts for two years and the minimum qualifications for entrance is Matriculation. The present trend is to prescribe higher secondary as the minimum qualification for entrance.

Secondary training schools—These schools provide teachers for the middle and junior secondary schools. However these training schools are gradually disappearing.

Training colleges or colleges of education—The minimum qualification for entrance is graduation. The duration of the course is one year. Degrees awarded are B.T. or L.T. or B.Ed. These colleges provide teachers for secondary and senior secondary schools.

Institutes of advanced studies in education—These provide opportunities to take up Master of Education and Ph.D. Courses.

Training colleges for special subjects—These are separate classes or colleges for preparing teachers in certain subjects like physical education, home science, craft, languages etc.

Training colleges for special education—These colleges prepare teachers for teaching students with various types of handicaps—the deaf and the dumb etc.

Regional colleges of education—Another important project for teacher education in the diversified system of secondary education relates to the setting up of the Regional Colleges of Education and their attached demonstration multipurpose schools at Ajmer, Bhubaneshwar, Mysore and Bhopal. The first three were started in 1963 while the latter in 1964. These colleges are designed to represent a new enterprise in teacher education to train competent teachers and teacher educators in certain critical areas like science, technology, industrial crafts, commerce and agriculture, so that they can function in their selected subject fields, in any system of education like technical, commerce and agricultural schools, and not only in multipurpose schools. These programmes are: four-year bachelor's degree programmes in science, technology, commerce, agriculture and English; one year training programmes in science, commerce and agriculture; industrial crafts programmes of one, two and three-year duration; and two-year master's degree programme.

Comprehensive colleges—A comprehensive college of education prepares teachers for several stages of education and/or for a number of special fields. Some institutions of this type already exist in Maharashtra and have shown good results. The Education Commission recommends that a planned attempt should be made to develop more institutions of this type and add sections for training primary and/or pre-primary teachers to training colleges that now prepare teachers for secondary schools only.

Summer schools-cum correspondence courses—Four Regional Colleges of Education have been organising summer-cum-correspondence courses for teachers in-service who are untrained.

More than 12 universities in India offer pre-services education at the B.Ed. level.

In-Service Teacher Education Insitutions

State Institutes of education—A chain of State Institutes of Education for elementary school teachers was started in 1964. At present there are 30 state institutions in the country. U.P. is the only state with two such institutions; at Allahabad and Lucknow. The main purposes and functions of these institutes are to:

1. Provide various training courses for supervisors of elementary schools or elementary teacher educators.
2. Organise conferences and seminars to senior state education officers.
3. Provide, conduct and supervise extensive services to training institutions for elementary teachers.
4. Organise research in elementary education and teacher education.
5. Provide correspondence courses for teachers.
6. Assist the state departments of education in the planning and implementation of various educational plans at the elementary stage of education.

District Institutes of Education and Training (DIET)—As envisaged in the National Policy on Education, 1986, DIET's are being established in various States to organise pre-services and in-service courses for elementary teachers and for personnel working in a non-formal land adult education. It is envisaged that with the establishment of these DIET'S sub-standard institutes will be phased out. Nearly 300 DIETs are in operation.

STEI's, lASEs and CTEs—To bring about qualitative importance in teacher education, the government of India has started a scheme of strengthening about 250 Secondary Teacher Education Institutions (STEI's), the development of about 50 of them as Institutes of Advanced Studies in Education (lASEs) and the rest as Colleges of Teacher Education (CTEs).

National Council of Educational Research and training (NCERT)—NCERT is the apex organisation at the national level which is designed to undertake research and training in education at the school stage. It coordinates the entire work of in-service teacher education. It also formulates syllabi for the education/training of teachers at different levels.

National Institute of Educational Planning and Administration (NIEPA), New Delhi-NIEPA organises in-service education for educational administration, planners, and supervisors.

Table 26.1

Teachers' Education/Teacher's Training Colleges and Institutes in India (1946-47 and 2004-05)

College/Institute	*1946-47*		*2004-2005*	
	No.	*Admission Capacity*	*No.*	*Admission Capacity*
1. Normal/Basic/ Elementary Teacher Training Schools/DIETs etc.	527	33,947	2,050	2,70,000
2. Teachers Training Colleges	34	2,493	1,300	2,70,000

(Estimated)

Table 26.2

Percentage of Trained Teachers (1950-51 to 2006-2007)

	Category	*1950-51*	*2006-2007*
1.	Percentage of trained teachers in Primary/Schools Junior Basic	58.8	86.0
2.	Percentage of trained teachers in middle Schools/Senior Schools	53.3	87.0
3.	Percentage of trained teachers-in high/post basic schools	53.5	89.0
4.	Percentage of trained teachers in higher Secondary/Junior college (10+2 pattern)	—	90.0

(Estimated)

National Council of Teacher Education (NCTE)

With a view to revamping teacher education at all levels in the country, the Government of India, Ministry of Human Resource Development set up the National Council for Teacher Education in May 1973. Its important functions are:

1. To advise the Government of India on all matters concerning Teacher Education, including pre-service and in-service training, evaluation of curricula for teacher education and periodical review of progress in revising the curricula;
2. To advise the state governments on any matters referred to the council by them;
3. To review the progress of plan schemes, both central and state, concerning teacher educations;
4. To advise the government on ensuring adequate standards in teacher education;
5. Any other matter entrusted to the council by the Government of India.

The NCTE was given a statutory recognition in 1995.

26.3 Pre-Service Teacher Education/Training, in Colleges of Education

Several methods, singly or in combination as given below are followed for the section of candidates for teacher training;

1. Selection on the basis of academic qualifications.

2. Selection on the basis of an interview.
3. Selection on the basis of academic performance and interview.
4. Selection on the basis of the convenience of the selecting authorities which sometimes includes acceptance of donations and recommendations etc.
5. In a few colleges, the selection is based on (a) interest inventory (b) intelligence test (c) teaching aptitude test (d) group discussion and (e) interview.

Draw Backs in Teacher Education/Training

Several committees and commissions notably the Education Commission 1964-66 and the National Commission on Teachers 1983-85, and Challenge of Education (1985), have by and large pointed out the following drawbacks in teacher education.

1. Faulty methods of selection because of political, social and personal influences.
2. Inadequacy of one-year B.Ed. courses.
3. Lop-sided curriculum.
4. Obsolete and irrelevant methodology of teaching.
5. Neglect of study of education as a discipline.
6. Inadequate training in practical skills.
7. Insufficient time and attention paid to the actual practice teaching.
8. Isolation between the Colleges of Education and the schools.
9. Insufficient training in the art of communicating with the community.
10. Meagre training in the art of organising co-curricular activities.
11. Ineffective supervision of the teaching practice by the supervisors.
12. Faulty methods of assessment of trainees' work.
13. Under qualified teacher educators.
14. Lack of physical facilities.
15. Shorter working hours.
16. Dearth of new technology of teaching.

National Commission on School Teachers 1983-85 and Revitalisation of Teacher Education

Appointment of the National Commission on school teachers (1983-85)—The Government of India, Ministry of Education appointed the Commission on School Teachers under the Chairmanship of Prof. D.P. Chattopadhaya in 1983. The Commission went into various aspects of teacher education, status and service conditions and gave its recommendations in its report entitled *Teacher and Society.*

Main Recommendations of the National Commission on Secondary School Teacher Training

Four year training courses—The present arrangements for the training of secondary school teachers are either under one-year B.Ed. course or the four year integrated course. A four-year training course after senior secondary, or preferably a 5-year course leading to graduation and training is recommended. Each state may make a beginning during the Seventh Plan period by starting at least one four-year integrated college of education. The integrated four-year curriculum for a degree in education should consist of two elements, namely, general education and professional preparation.

General Education will include:

1. Study of language.
2. Three or four disciplines from among the subjects taught at school.
3. Seminars, projects and study visits.

Contents of professional preparation.—The professional part should consist of:

1. Study of education as a discipline including educational psychology, sociology of education and educational philosophy;
2. Practice of teaching and its content-cum-methodology; and
3. Learning a variety of skills related to the role of the teacher, including educational technology and preparation of software.

Extension of one-year B.Ed. course—The duration of the one-year B.Ed. course should be extended by two summer months ensuring an academic session of 220 days with longer working hours.

Selection of teachers for training—While selecting a teacher for training, the following factors may be taken into consideration:

1. Good physique;
2. Linguistic ability and communication skills;
3. A fair degree of general mental ability;
4. General awareness of the world;
5. A positive outlook on life; and
6. The capacity for good human relations.

The selection of trainees should be made through a combination of objective tests, rating scales, group-discussions and personnel interviews.

Recruitment first and training afterwards—The approach to recruit an nuntrained first class graduate/post graduate and then to give him on-the-job training to be followed by full training through correspondence and contact programme, could also be tried out.

Internship in place of practice teaching—The duration of the internship should not be less than four weeks in the third year and 3 weeks in the fourth year of study. During this period, stress should be laid, among other things, on black-board writing, drawing skills, making and improvising aids to learning, and using technological equipment. Participation in co-curricular activities like games, sports, music, dance and drama etc., should be obligatory.

Right tools for evaluation of pupil teacher performance—The faculty must evolve the right tools for evaluation of pupil-teacher performance in the class and also take into account such factors as attitude to work, love for children, scientific outlook etc. Self-assessment and pre-lesson and post-lesson discussion is should be encouraged.

Miscellaneous—Other recommendations included (a) modifications in teacher education curriculum, (b) teacher education cadres, (c) adequate staff for teacher training colleges, (d) teacher education to be well-versed in educational technology, (e) well-planned programmes, (f) teacher training colleges to remove their isolation, (g) training to pupil teachers in organising co-curricular activities.

Elementary teacher education—The Commission made the following recommendations:—

1. Considering that the elementary stage is so crucial the professional training of elementary school teachers should begin only after the 12th class and the training should be of at least 2 years.
2. Parallel to the four-year integrated course for the training of the secondary teacher, the possibility of a four-year training programme for the elementary teacher after class X may be explored.
3. Training curriculum for elementary teachers—The training curriculum for elementary teachers will also consist of general education and professional preparation. Sufficient emphasis needs to be given to the mastering of language and communication skills and the trainee's value orientation.

   As for professional preparation, pedagogy, practice teaching, development of skills such as story telling, recitation, writing on the black-board, use of new technology etc., are important. A greater emphasis on art, music, craft and dance is essential.
4. Practice teaching—Not less than six to eight weeks in the first year and twelve weeks in the second year should be allotted to practice teaching. The trainees may start with one or two lessons a day but should gradually be expected to stay for the whole day and take on the full responsibilities of a regular teacher. This alone will develop them in gaining needed professional competence and personal confidence.
5. Qualification for Teacher Educators—The teacher educators for the elementary training institute should be drawn primarily from the cadre of practising primary schools. The minimum qualification of the other staff should be a post-graduate degree with B.Ed. training. Their continued in-service education is equally important.

26.4 New Terminology in Teacher Education

The term 'training' is outdated and has been replaced by the term 'education'.

The degree given at the end of training course is called 'Bachelor of Education' (B.Ed.) in place of 'Bachelor in Training' (B.T.).

The term 'teacher education' has taken the place of 'teacher training.'

The term 'College of Education' has replaced the term 'Teachers' Training College.'

The 'trainee' or 'pupil teacher' has given place to 'student-teacher'.

"Teaching practice' has been substituted by 'internship'.

'Cooperating school' has taken the place of 'demonstration or practising school'.

Similarly, teachers and headmasters of the practicising school are called 'cooperating teachers' and 'cooperating headmasters'.

Terms like summer institute, seminar, conference, workshop, etc. are increasingly being used in place of refresher courses.

'Mathetic' has been gaining currency to denote the transition from teaching to learning. Mathetic may be defined as a science of learner's behaviour.

26.5 In-Service Education of Teachers

Significance of in-service education of teachers—Thomas Arnold, an eminent headmaster of Rugbly, a famous school in U.K., very rightly observed, "I prefer that any student should drink from a running stream rather than a stagnant pool."

The University Education Commission pointed out the importance of in-service education, "constant outpouring needs constant in taking; practice must be reinforced by theory and the old must be constantly tested by new."

The 'explosion of knowledge' demands that a teacher must be better informed and educated to-day than he was yesterday and will tomorrow be better educated than he is to-day.

Meaning of continuous and in-service education—The Commission on Teacher Education in USA explained this clearly: "The continued education of teachers means much more than making up defects in preparation. It means continuous growth in the capacity to teach. It means a broadened understanding of human development and human living. And now more than at any previous period in school history it means growth in one's capacity to work with others, with class-room teachers and principals in a variety of activities, with the administration, with parents and community leaders and with children of different age-groups."

The meaning of the term 'in-service education' is self explanatory. It refers to the education a teacher receives when he has entered the teaching profession after he has had his education/ training in a teacher's institute or college. It includes all the refresher courses etc. that he receives at different institutions.

Aims and objectives of In-Service teacher Education and Training (INSET)

1. To maintain the knowledge and skills of teachers.
2. To give teachers the opportunity to enlarge and improve their knowledge and educational capacities in all fields of their work.
3. To make teachers ready and able to understand and face in time new situations coming up in society and to prepare their students for the new economic, social or cultural challenges.
4. To enable teachers to gain additional qualifications and to develop their special talents and dispositions.
5. To raise the cultural and professional standard of the teaching force as a whole and strengthen its innovative vigour and creativity.

Institutions for In-service Education

1. State Institutes of Education and District Institutes of Education.
2. State Institutes of Science.
3. State Institutes of English,
4. Extension Services Department.
5. State Directorates of Education.
6. Voluntary Organisations.
7. NCERT (National Council of Educational Research and Training).
8. NCTE (National Council of Teacher Education).
9. UGC (University Grants Commission).
10. NIEPA (National Institute of Educational Planning and Administration.).
11. Professional Organisation of Teachers.
12. International Educational Organisations.

Programmes for in-service education—These include:

(a) Conferences on educational matters, (b) debates and

discussions, (c) experimenting, (d) lectures, (e) newsletters, (f) professional writings and essay competitions etc, (g) radio talks and other programmes, (h) refresher courses, (i) seminars, (j) study groups, (k) T.V. talks and other programmes.

Limitations and Shortcomings of In-service Education Programmes

The National Commission on School teachers 1983-85 pointed out the following inadequacies:

1. There is today an absence of clear-cut policies and priorities for in-service education.
2. There has been no systematic identification of needs.
3. The content and quality of programmes offered are generally poor.
4. Strategies for training are vague and half-hearted.
5. Not much emphasis appears to have been placed on solving the practical problems of teachers or meeting their educational needs.
6. In-service courses rarely result in the development of a corps of instructional material that can be used by participants and other teachers.
7. Hardly any use is made of new media and technologies.
8. Administrative support for innovations is lacking as headmasters and supervisors are not often involved in programmes where teachers being trained in the use of new methodologies.
9. The phenomenon of routine transfers finds trained personnel not placed in positions where they should use their training maximally.

Suggestions for Removing Inadequacies of In-service Teacher Education Programmes

Identification of the needs of serving teachers—In the first place, the needs of the teachers are to be identified at the institutional level and such programmes of in-service arranged as will directly meet these needs. The needs may be remedial in nature as for example updating the teacher's knowledge in mathematics or science etc., it may be necessary to find out new ways of dealing with children having multiple levels of attainment in a class. In no case in-service programmes may be thrust upon teachers, irrespective of their needs and classroom implications.

Advanced planning—Programmes should be thoroughly planned well ahead of time. We tend to be slipshod in whatever we do. To be thorough and meticulous in planning for a course being attended by a group of teachers is to show them the respect and consideration that is due to them. Papers have to be prepared by resource persons well ahead of time, reading lists and other materials mailed to participants before the course to stimulate thinking. Every detail should be attended to so that the teacher comes well prepared with the proper mind-set to benefit by the course, short or long. Conferences and workshops should be business like and the tone has to be set from the first hour eschewing all fanfare.

Selection of resource persons—In the selection of resource persons to conduct the programme, expertise and proven skills alone should matter. The system should be flexible enough to allow the co-operation of experts from various fields outside education like industry, agriculture, science, technology, management and the like. Media specialists have a particularly important role to play today. University professors, educational experts, outstanding teacher educators and teachers should also be utilised maximally as resource persons. From our dialogues with teachers in the country we are convinced that we have many dedicated teachers with excellent records of service. Their co-operation in conducting in-service programmes should be welcomed for they can give the much-needed practical wisdom in bringing about change.

Appropriate methodologies—Methodologies adopted for in-service education call for closer scrutiny. The resource persons selected should meet prior to the actual course and plan the details most thoroughly. Every course should be in the nature of a workshop demanding hard work and include the preparation of instructional and other material that can be used by the teacher when he goes back to school. No in-service course should be of such a general nature that teachers feel it is a waste of their time and energies. Practices that have been successful should be shared and classroom methodologies that have failed discussed. Attention should be given to solving the teachers' problems satisfactorily. New ideas from other countries could be evaluated and an openness of mind encouraged. The quality of inservice courses should be such as will themselves generate sustained interest for further improvement in the teachers' work.

Use of educational technology—The use of educational technology in a big way could revolutionise in-service courses. The days of lengthy lectures and note-taking thereon are over. A multi-media approach is useful. Teachers' interest could be evoked more purposefully by the use of audio and video cassettes on any subject. Extensive use needs to be made of a variety of technologies in in-service education: radio and television; film strips and the epidiascope: tape-recorder, audio and video-cassettes; the overhead projector and the 8mm or 16mm film projector and the computer. The times demand of an educated person a modicum of literacy in the technical field, in the use of his hands and the tools of technology. In these courses teachers must get acquainted with the hardware, their servicing and maintenance. These are essential skills to be learnt by every teacher and teacher educator and should not be overlooked. In organising courses with the use of media, resource persons in charge of a course should draw in media men and other entrepreneurs now available in many cities who would be only too happy to help.

Evaluation and follow up programmes—Every in-service education programme should be evaluated through checklists or questionnaires. Follow-up work is necessary.

Subject teachers' associations—As suggested by the Kothari Commission, subject teachers' associations should be formed at the city, district, state and all-India level on the different school subjects. This will stimulate initiative and experimentation and assist in the revision and upgrading of curricula through the provision of better teaching materials and the use of improved techniques of teaching and evaluation. The State Education Department should assist the subject teachers' associations to hold periodical seminars and conferences and to produce journals of their own.

Subject experts—In order to provide guidance to teachers in the techniques of teaching various subjects, subject experts should be appointed at the district level.

Teacher's centres—A teacher's centre is a meeting place for teachers. It is located in a school that has resources that it would like to share with others. At the centre, teachers may meet when free in the evenings or during weekends to borrow books, to prepare teaching aids, individually or in groups or to borrow some new materials for teaching. It is a forum where workshops of a very practical nature are organised for teachers of all faculties and of all levels; it pools the talent of all teachers of various schools who act as resource personnel for the centre's workshops and it arranges book fairs where publishers would exhibit their latest publications for sale. Since the entire initiative at the centre rests with the heads and teachers themselves, this is a move to be welcomed.

School level INSET programmes—Another mode of in-service education for teachers is the one that can be held at the instructional level. The whole staff of a school plans its in-service training after identifying its needs, drafting resource persons from within and outside the school and after preparing the necessary materials. Such orientation held voluntarily by the staff on Saturdays as is being tried with success in some private-managed schools, or during week-ends or vacations and at the commencement of school terms has much to commend itself for it is need-based, has sufficient motivation and can be evaluated continually. Needless to say it requires a committed kind of leadership on the part of the head and a congenial atmosphere of freedom of discussion in the school to enable it to become an ongoing programme.

Mobile units—It may not be possible for the teachers working in rural areas to attend in-service programmes in the cities or small suburban areas. For them mobile units of in-service education may be planned.

Motivating teachers for in-service education—It is often noticed that the teachers do not feel inspired to attend programmes of in-service education. Many of them attend these to avoid the displeasure of the officers of the education departments or to make themselves eligible for the selection grade of for crossing efficiency bars. Their response in general to such courses is not spontaneous.

The following suggestions are offered to motivate teachers to attend the in-service education programmes.

1. Teachers who attend in-service education programmes may be given some credit. For example, earned leave may be given to them on the basis of the number of days they actually spend in courses.
2. Certificates may be awarded in token of attending a course.
3. Prizes may be provided on the basis of performance in a course.

4. Programmes should be organised in such a way that these prove helpful in the daily work of the school.
5. Adequate T.A. and D.A. may be provided to the teachers.
6. Some educators are of the view that the attendance of teachers in a course should be made compulsory.
7. It is also stated in some quarters that in the absence of having attended a given number of educational programmes, the teachers may be declared ineligible for promotion. But this is going too far.
8. In the Annual Confidential Reports (A.C.R.s), mention may be made of the in-service programme attended by a teacher.

Questions and Problems

A. Essay-Type Questions

1. "Teachers are made, not born." Explain this statement.
2. Elucidate the need for pre-service teacher education. What are its limitations in the present system? How can we revamp the system of pre-service teacher education?
3. "Teachers' Training Colleges or Colleges of Education work in isolation". Suggest measures for making teacher education more effective.
4. "Professional education and general education must be integrated in teacher education programmes." Comment upon this statement and state if you favour the four-year integrated course in place of the one-year B.Ed. course.
5. "The teacher training courses as devised at present are non-functional and ineffective." Comment on this statement and suggest remedies.
6. Explain the importance of in-service programmes for teachers. What are their limitations. How would you make them effective?

B. Short-Answer Type Questions

7. Write short notes on (a) Regional Colleges of Education (b) State Institutes of Education (c) DIETS (d) NCERT.
8. Explain the concept of the four-year integrated course of teacher education.
9. How can teachers be motivated to attend in-service education programmes.
10. State the merits and demerits of correspondence courses for B.Ed.
11. Suggest measures for making practice teaching more effective.

27 Teaching Skills and Teacher Competency

27.1 Teaching as a Skill: Scientific Basis

Teaching as an Interactive Process—Teaching is an interactive process, involving four aspects: teacher, student, learning process and learning situation. The teacher creates the learning situation; The process is the interaction between the student and the teacher. The teaching and learning situation may be explained with the help of a diagram.

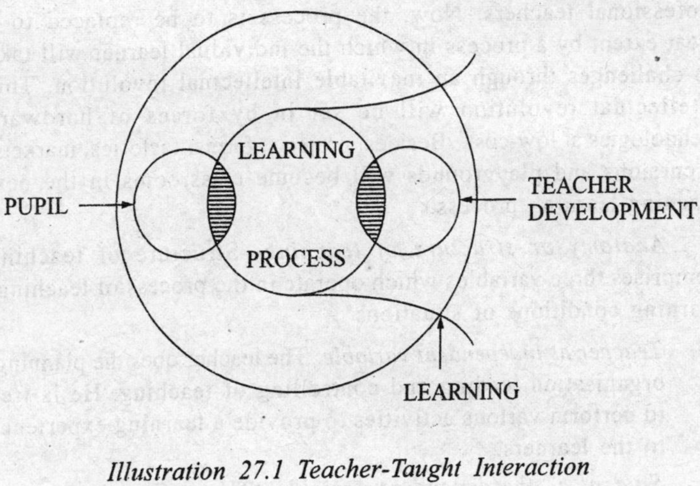

Illustration 27.1 Teacher-Taught Interaction

Scientific basis of the art of teaching—The most distinctive live feature of modern society is its science-based technology which has been making a profound impact not only on the economic and political life of a country but also on its educational system. The changes that occur as a result of this impact are broadly described as 'Modernisation'. This modernisation has affected the teaching-learning process in many ways. The recent changes in the concept of teaching-learning process have led to the development of newer areas of educational endeavour. In a traditional society the aim of teaching-learning was the preservation of the accumulated stock of knowledge. But, the main aim of teaching-learning is not the acquisition of knowledge alone. It is the awakening of curiosity, the stimulation of creativity, the development of proper interests, attitudes and values and the building of essential skills such as independent study. The teaching-learning process has to serve as a powerful instrument of social, economic and cultural transformation of the society. The teaching-learning process is conditioned by the nature and demands of society to which the learner should get adapted and attuned. One of the main aims of teaching-learning in modern society is to keep pace with the advancement of knowledge and skills. In modern society teaching-learning cannot be done passively.

For a pretty long period; the teaching-learning process has been by and large, a process dominated by the institution of professional teachers. Now, the process is to be replaced to a great extent by a process in which the individual learner will take up challenges through an inevitable intellectual revolution. This intellectual revolution will be set in by forces of hardware technologies at low-cost. Besides, projects, farms, factories, markets, excursions and playgrounds will become classrooms in the new teaching-learning process.

Anatomy or structure of teaching—Structure of teaching comprises three variables which operate in the process of teaching-learning conditions or situations.

1. *Teacher as independent variable*: The teacher does the planning, organisation leading and controlling of teaching. He is free to perform various activities to provide a learning experience to the learners.
2. *Student as the dependent variable*—The student is required to act according to the planning and organisation of the

teacher. The teaching activities of the teacher influence the learning of the students.

3. *Content and the strategy of presentation as intervening variables*: The intervening variables lead to an interaction between the teachers and the students. The content determines the mode of presentation - telling, showing and doing.

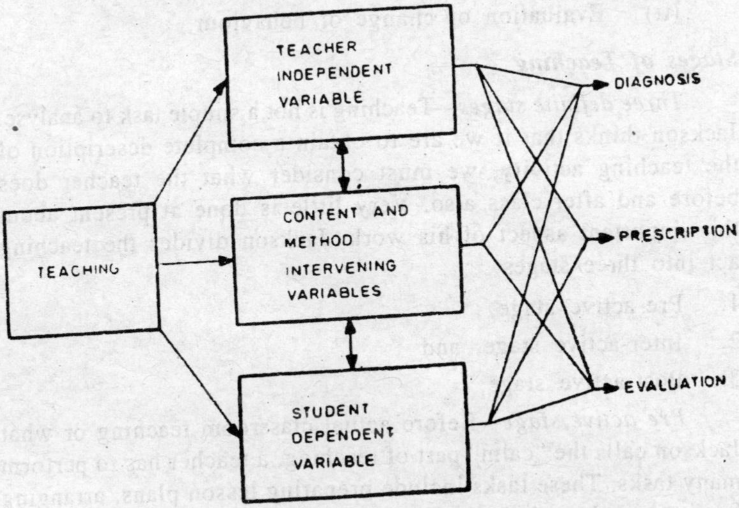

Illustration 27.2 Anatomy or Structure of Teaching

The variables perform three functions.

1. *Diagnostic function*—The teacher as an independent variable is more active and diagnoses the following:
   - (i) Entering behaviour of the students
   - (ii) Teaching problems
   - (iii) Individual variations, and
   - (iv) Content analysis in view of learning conditions.

The student as a dependent variable diagnoses on the basis of his perception for his activities and responses. In the process of interaction both teacher and the student diagnose for initiations and responses.

2. *Prescriptive function*—The main objective of this function is to bring desirable changes in the behaviour of the learner. The teacher makes efforts to organise the intervening variables in such a way so as to select teaching techniques and feedbacks

that help in the realisation of the objectives. The student helps the teacher.

3. *Evaluative functions*: This aims at examining the effectiveness of the prescriptive function. The evaluative function has two main activities:
   (i) Construction criterion test.
   (ii) Evaluation of change of behaviour.

Stages of Teaching

Three definite stages—Teaching is not a simple task to analyse. Jackson thinks that if we are to obtain a complete description of the teaching activity, we must consider what the teacher does before and after class also. Very little is done at present about this important aspect of his work. Jackson divides the teaching act into three stages:

1. Pre-active stage,
2. Inter-active stage, and
3. Post-active stage.

Pre-active stage—Before actual classroom teaching or what Jackson calls the "calm" part of teaching, a teacher has to perform many tasks. These tasks include preparing lesson plans, arranging furniture and equipment within the classroom, manning papers, studying test reports, reading sections of a textbook and thinking about the aberrant behaviour of a particular student. These activities are very crucial to the teacher's performance during regular teaching sessions.

Pre-active behaviour is, more or less, deliberative. The teacher at this stage hypothesises about the possible outcome of his action. As the teacher decides what textbooks to use or how to group the children for reading or whether to notify the students' parents of their poor performance, his behaviour is at least analysable.

At moments like this, concepts such as evaluation, production and feedback have real meaning to understand what the teacher is doing.

Inter-active stage—This is actual classroom teaching. At this stage, the teacher uses a number of strategies to achieve the goal already set. In the inter-active setting, the behaviour of the teacher is more or less spontaneous. Research suggests that things happen quickly during the teaching session. For example, the elementary teacher may change the focus of his concern as many as 1,000 times daily. Amid all this hustle and bustle the teacher often has little time to think.

The differences in the teaching behaviour with and without students are relevant for conceptualising the teaching task, to justify certain training reinforcements and to identify the criteria of good teaching.

Many teachers try to devote a little time alone with individual students but the teacher-student dialogue is usually public rather than private. When a teacher is alone with a student, he is not faced with the problem of control and management that frequently absorbs a major portion of his energies in a group setting. There is a greater sense of physical and psychological intimacy between the teacher and the student during individual sessions than when the teacher is responding to the class as a group.

The task of keeping pupils involved may entail explanation, demonstration, definition, and other logical operations that have come to be thought of as the heart of teaching.

Post-active stage.—The post-active stage arises when the teacher has left the class and thinks in retrospcet about what happened in the class.

To conclude it would be a mistake to view the teacher's behaviour during class as representing all that is involved in the complex business of teaching.

All these stages may be depicted by the following paradigm.

PREACTIVE	INTER-ACTIVE		POST ACTIVE
	LINGUISTIC Pt.→Dt→Rt	Pp→Dp→Rp	
FIXATION OF GOAL	PERFORMATIVE Pt.→Dt→Rt	Pp→Dp→Rp	→ FEED BACK
DETERMINATION OF CONTENT	EXPRESSIVE Pt.→Dt→Rt	Pp→Dp→Rp	

→BEHAVIOURAL CHANGES OR ACHIEVEMENTS

Illustration 27.3 Three Stages in the Paradigm of the Teaching Act

In the above paradigm:

1. *Pt* stands for the teacher's perception of the pupil's behaviour.
2. Dt is the teacher's diagnosis of the pupil's state of interest, readiness, knowledge etc. made by inference from the behaviour of the pupil.
3. *Rt* is the action taken by the teacher in the light of his diagnosis.
4. *Pp* is the pupil's perception of the teacher's behaviour.
5. *Dp* is the pupil's perception of the teacher's state of interest in what he is saying and as inferred from the teacher's behaviour.
6. *Rp* is the reaction of the pupil to the action of the teacher.

Each unit marked off by the double vertical line is an example of a teaching unit.

Each unit consists of teacher-pupil interaction. There are two sub-units within the teaching cycle which are divided by the single vertical line.

The sub-unit (*Pt*→*Dt*→*Rt*) is referred to as an act of teaching.

The sub-unit (*Pp*→*Dp*→*Rp*) is what we call the act of learning or taking instruction.

The act of teaching and the act of taking instruction are reciprocating acts and when performed under appropriate conditions they result in behavioural changes or achievements.

Teaching according to this paradigm implies that someone gives instruction and someone takes it.

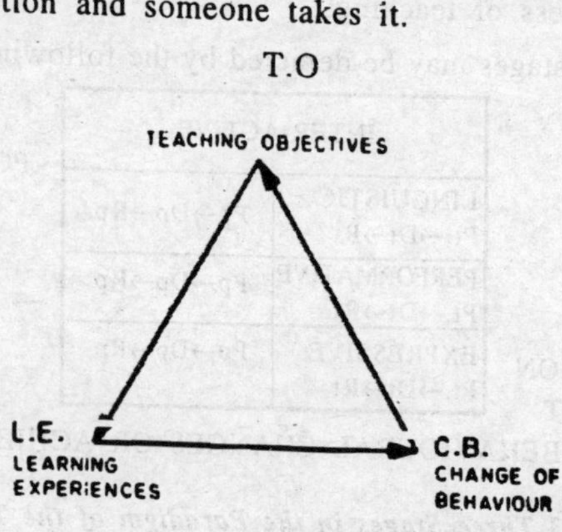

Illustration 27.4 Teaching Operations in the Preactive Stage

Operations at the preactive stage of teaching—The following operations or substages are involved (a) forming or fixing up goals, (b) taking decisions about the context, (c) managing or sequencing appropriate means and ways of presentation, (d) deciding about appropriate strategies and tactics of teaching, (e) developing teaching strategies for the specific subject matter.

Operations at the interactive stage—The interactive stage of teaching involves these operations (a) perceiving the size of the class to identify students, (b) diagnosing the achievements of the learners, (c) action or Achievement (Initiation or Response). This involves (a) Selection of stimuli, (b) presentation of the stimuli, (c) feed back of reinforcement, (d) development of strategies of teaching.

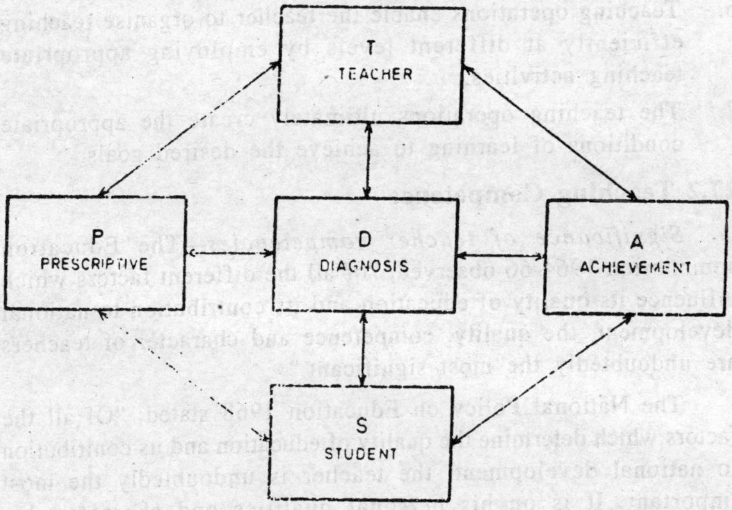

Illustration 27.5 Operation at the Interactive Stage

Operations at the post-active stage of teaching—These are (a) defining the exact dimensions of the teaching behaviour, (b) selecting appropriate teaching devices, (c) changing or improving strategies of teaching.

Importance of the Operations of Teaching

1. Teaching operations provide the scientific basis for developing effective instruction.
2. The background of the classroom teaching and interaction can be made effective through teaching operations.
3. The knowledge of teaching operations is very useful in teacher education to develop teaching skills among the student teachers. They can also overcome the limitations of the trial and error methods in solving the teaching problems.
4. The knowledge of teaching operations is useful for in-service teachers to improve their classroom efficiency.
5. The knowledge of teaching operations gives the empirical evidences about the relationships of teaching variables which in its turn will be an aid in developing the theory of teaching.
6. Teaching operations enable the teacher to organise teaching efficiently at different levels by employing appropriate teaching activities.
7. The teaching operations ultimately create the appropriate conditions of learning to achieve the desired goals.

27.2 Teaching Competence

Significance of teacher competencies—The Education commission 1964-66 observed, "of all the different factors which influence its quality of education and its contribution to national development, the quality, competence and character of teachers are undoubtedly the most significant."

The National Policy on Education 1968 stated, "Of all the factors which determine the quality of education and its contribution to national development, the teacher is undoubtedly the most important. It is on his personal qualities and character, his educational qualifications and professional competence that the success of all educational endeavour must ultimately depend."

The National Commission on Teachers II 1983-85 noted: "In the eyes of the community recognition of professional competency and increase in emoluments and benefits were the most salient factors that were expected to enhance the teacher's status." The commission further noted "Professional competence having an edge over the economic factor" was necessary to improve the status of the teacher.

Meaning of Teacher Competence

Modern thought and scientific technological advancements have given an orientation to teacher competence. New concepts like Performance-Based Teacher Education (PBTE), Competence-Based Teacher Education (CBTE) and File-Based Teaching Education (FBTE) are becoming popular in the field of educational literature.

The Commonwealth report (1974) explains teacher competency, "In order to be competent the teacher must have a knowledge of child development, of the material to be taught and suitable methods; his skills must enable him to teach, advise and guide his pupils, community and culture with which he is involved; his attitudes should be positive without being aggressive, so that his example is likely to be followed as he transmits explicitly, and implicitly the national aims and moral and social values.

According to Karl Massanari, "Competence-Based Education or Performance-Based Teacher Education has the potential to revolutionise the entire field of educational personnel development through its emphasis on clearly stated role derived objectives, the individualisation and personalisation of instruction, a field-centred approach, prespecified performance, mastery level and modes of assessment."

In the words of Murthy and Lulla, "Competence-Based Teacher Education is that type of professional education of classroom teachers that takes the pre-determined competence of teaching behaviours as the base of teacher education programmes."

Teaching competencies: general and specific—David G.Rayns, in *Characteristics of Teacher* (1969) described the two types of teacher competencies, "Teaching is complex and many-sided, demanding a variety of human traits and abilities. These may be grouped in two major categories—first those involving the teacher's mental abilities and skills, his understandings of psychological and educational principles and his knowledge of general and specific subject-matter to be taught and second those qualities stemming from the teacher's personality, his interests, attitudes and beliefs, his behaviour in working relationships with pupils and other individuals and the like."

A to Z of Teaching competencies

'A' is for *alertness.*

'B' is for *business like* attitude—to keep busy in worthwhile tasks.

'C' is for *clarity* and *cooperative* teaching-learning.

'D' is for *devotion* and *discovery.*

'E' is for *enthusiasm, expecting* children to learn, and *evaluation.*

'F' is for *feedback* for the guidance of the learner and the teacher himself.

'G' is for *goal setting* and achieving.

'H' is for *hard work, honest* work, *humility* and *humour.*

'I' is for *involvement* of children.

'J' is for *judicious* attitude and *just* action.

'K' is for *knowledge* of the students, subject matter and oneself.

'L' is for *linking learning* with daily experiences and life.

'M' is for motivation.

'N' is for *need-based* learning.

'O' is for *objectivity* and providing *out of classroom* learning experiences.

'P' is for *practice* and *praising* children when needed.

'Q' is for *quiz-organising* for monitoring learning progress

'R' is for *relationships* and *review.*

'S' is for *stimulation.*

'T' is for *tolerance* and *the technology* of teaching-learning.

'U' is for *unbiased* attitude and *unexpected* encounters and situations.

'V' is for *a variety* of learning experience.

'W' is for *warmth* and *wisdom.*

'X' is for *x-ray* of the learning process.

'Y' is for *yearning* and eagerness.

'Z' is for *Zeal.*

27.3 Technical Skills of Teaching

Meaning and nature of technical skills—Technical skills of teaching are specific aspects of the teaching behaviour that are considered to be particularly effectively in facilitating desired learning in students.

Allen and Ryan point out in '*Microteaching*' (1969) that the first technical skill used in the microteaching clinic at Stanford University was "how to begin a lesson." Subsequently many other skills were added and a list developed which included the following skills:

1. *Stimulate variation*—Using stimulating material and variation, in movement, gestures, interaction techniques and sensory channels in order to alleviate boredom and inattentiveness.
2. *Set induction*—Preparing students for a lesson by clarifying its goals, relating to the students prior knowledge and skills, by using analogies, demonstrations, and passing stimulating problems.
3. *Closure*—Assisting students to establish links between new and past knowledge by reviewing and applying material to familiar and new examples, cases and situations.
4. *Silence and non-verbal cues*—Reducing reliance at teacher talk by encouraging teachers in the proper use of pauses and in the effective use of facial expression, body movement, head movement and gestures.
5. *Reinforcing students participation*—Encouraging students to respond through the use of praise and acceptance as well as non-verbal use such as nodding and smiling.
6. *Fluency in asking questions*—Elimination of unnecessary repetitions of questions.
7. *Probing questions*—Skills in framing questions which lead students to elaborate on, or raise the level of their responses.
8. *Higher order questions*—Questions which elicit student responses that require a higher intellectual level from students instead of responses that involve only fact stating or descriptions.
9. *Divergent questions*—Questions which elicit student responses that are unconventional, imaginative and cannot be judged simply to be correct or incorrect.

10. *Recognising attendance behaviour*—Ability to judge while teaching how much interest the students are taking in the lesson.
11. *Illustration and use of visuals*—Ability to illustrate so as to capture the attention of the students.
12. *Lecturing*—Ability to explain the subject matter.
13. *Planned repetition*—Ability to focus attention of the students on some focal points.
14. *Completeness of communication*—Ability to communicate with students.

Desirable Teaching Skills for Different Stages of a Lesson

While talking of teaching skills, it must be remembered that there is no water tight compartment as regards skills at different stages. These are classified for the sake of convenience, otherwise they are interrelated. A particular skill cannot be confined to one teaching stage only.

1. Teaching Skills at the Planning Stage

- (i) Writing instructional objectives.
- (ii) Selecting the content.
- (iii) Organising the content.
- (iv) Selection of audio-visual aids and their procurement.

2. Introductory Stage Skills

- (i) Creating set induction—preparing the minds of the students.
- (ii) Introducing the lessons.

3. Presentation Stage Skills

- (i) Questioning Skills.
  - (a) structuring classroom questions.
  - (b) fluency in asking questions.
  - (c) probing question.
  - (d) question delivery and distribution.
  - (e) higher order questions.
  - (f) divergent questions.
  - (g) management of answers.

(ii) Presentation Skills
 (a) pacing of the lesson.
 (b) lecturing.
 (c) illustrating with examples.
 (d) demonstrating.
 (e) explaining.
 (f) discussing.

(iii) Audio-Visual Aid Skills
 (a) using teaching aids.
 (b) using blackboard.
 (c) using maps.
 (d) stimulous variation.
 (e) silence and non-verbal cues.
 (f) reinforcement.

(iv) Managerial Skills.
 (a) promoting pupil involvement and participation.
 (b) recognising attending behaviour.
 (c) class management.

4. Closing Stage Skills

(i) Planned recapitulation.
(ii) Evaluating pupil progress.
(iii) Diagnosing learning difficulties of the pupils and taking remedial measures.
(iv) Giving assignments.

Seven-fold classification of technical skills—An Australian team of authors (Turney et al. 1973) developed a system of classifying teaching skills under which the following seven categories emerged:

1. *Motivational skills*—Including reinforcing student behaviour, varying the stimulus, set induction, encouraging student involvement, accepting, and supporting student feelings, displaying warmth and enthusiasm and recognising and meeting student's needs.
2. *Presentation and communication skills*—Including explaining, dramatising, reading, using audio-visual aids, closure, using

silence, encouraging student feed back, clarity, expressiveness, pacing and planned repetition.

3. *Questioning skills*—Including refocusing and redirecting, probing, high level questions, convergent and divergent questions, stimulating student initiative.
4. *Skills of small group and individual instruction*—Organising small group work, developing independent learning, counselling, encouraging cooperative activity and student to student interaction.
5. *Developing student thinking*—Such as fostering inquiry learning, guiding discovery, developing concepts, using stimulation, role playing to stimulate thought, developing student problem solving skills, encouraging students to evaluate and make judgements and developing critical thinking.
6. *Evaluative skills*—Including recognising and assessing students progress, diagnosing learning difficulties, providing remedial techniques, encouraging self-evaluation and handling evaluative discussions.
7. *Classroom management and discipline*—Including recognising attending and non-attending behaviour, supervising class group work, encouraging task-oriented behaviour, giving directions and coping with multiple issues.

Who, Whom, Why Where, What, How and When of Teaching

To play his role competently, a teacher is expected to understand the significance of the following:

1. *Who is to teach*—The teacher is to teach and he must understand himself thoroughly—his strengths and weaknesses—and strive to present a reasonably good model before his students.
2. *Whom to teach*—The child is to be taught. Therefore, a teacher should understand him thoroughly - his abilities, aptitudes, attitudes, manners and temperaments and accordingly cater to the individual differences of students.
3. *Why to Teach*—The teacher should always keep in view that the aim of education is to develop harmonious personalities, who are culturally refined, emotionally stable, ethically sound, mentally alert, morally upright, physically strong, socially efficient and spiritually enlightened. He should not forget

even for a moment that the traditional 3 R's have been replaced by 7 R's, that is, reading, writing, arithmetic (representing various disciplines), rights, responsibilities, relationships and recreation.

4. *Where to teach*—The teacher ought not to visualise the school to be merely a place of importing information but a place where men of tomorrow are trained to take their place as enlightened citizens in the society and contribute to national development.
5. *What to teach*—The teacher must have mastery over the subject he teaches.
6. *How to teach*—The teacher must use new teaching-learning technology to make his teaching effective and inspirational.
7. *When to teach*—Appropriate steps need to be taken by the teacher to develop motivation of the student in the entire work.

Questions and Problems

A. Essay-Type Questions

1. Discuss teaching as an interactive process.
2. Elucidate the scientific basis of the art of teaching with the help of illustrations.
3. What is the significance of teaching competencies? How can these be developed?
4. Name the most important skills needed by a teacher. State their significance.
5. "Teaching competence is broad based." Explain.

B. Short-Answer Type Questions

6. State the various phases or stages of education.
7. Describe the various operations in teaching.

28 Teacher Education and Micro Teaching

Micro Teaching—A Recent Concept

Micro teaching has been described as an important innovation in teacher education. It is not a gimmick or a fad. It faces a real situation with the minimum risk for the pupil teacher and the pupil. The term micro teaching was first coined by A.W. Dwight Allen of the Stanford University in 1963. A number of experiments have been conducted in many institutions in the USA, UK and the Netherlands. In India, too, a number of institutions have started work in the area of micro-teaching in recent years. The Lever Halme Trust gave a five-year grant to the Stirling University in the UK for its work on micro-teaching. Work is being done at the Exeter University by E.C. Wragg. A lot of work in this field has been done at the Purdue University by Dr. Joe E Shivley, Aderehen P. Wan Mondtrans and Chery L. Read. A comprehensive bibliography on micro-teaching has been prepared by W. Raymond Mc Aleese of the University of Aberdeen and Derick Unwin of the University of Ulster. Perlberg Arye and David C. Oberiant of the Department of General Engineering, University of Illinois, have used micro-teaching techniques to improve engineering instruction.

A survey was conducted in the US recently, on the use of microteaching in teacher education programmes. It was found that about 150 of the 440 NCATE-accredited colleges and universities were using micro teaching in the secondary education programmes and about 50 reported the beginning of its use in in-service programmes.

Meaning of micro teaching—Micro teaching is a training procedure aimed at simplifying the complexities of the regular teaching process. In a micro-teaching procedure the trainee is engaged in a scaled-down teaching situation. It is scaled down in terms of class size, since the trainee is teaching small groups of four to six pupils. The lesson is scaled down in length of class-time and is reduced to five or ten minutes. It is also scaled down in terms of teaching tasks. These tasks may include (a) the practising and mastering of a specific teaching skill such as lecturing, (b) questioning, or leading a discussion, (c) mastering of specific teaching strategies, (d) flexibility, (e) instructional decision-making, (f) alternative uses of specific curricula, (g) instructional materials and classroom management.

The short lesson is recorded on an audio or video-tape recorder and the trainee gets to hear and see himself immediately after the lesson. The pupils who attend the lesson are asked to fill in rating questionnaires evaluating specific aspects of the lesson. The trainee's own analysis of the lesson based on the authentic feedback from the tape together with the pupils reaction and a supervisor's analysis and suggestions, assists the trainee in restructuring the lesson, which he then immediately reteaches to a new group of pupils. Further assessment by the 'learners' and the supervisor leads to further improvements when he teaches again, either immediately or after several days. This micro-teaching sequence is practised usually in a micro-teaching laboratory in a teacher-training institution, or an in-service training programme in regular schools.

Definitions of Micro Teaching

D.W. Allen (1968) defines micro teaching as "a scaled down teaching encounter in class, size and time."

In the words of Allen and Eve (1986), "Micro teaching is a system of controlled practice that makes it possible to concentrate on specific teaching behaviour and to practise teaching under controlled conditions."

According to M.B. Buch (1948) Micro-teaching is "a teacher education technique which allows teachers to apply well defined teaching skills to a carefully prepared lesson in a planned series of five to ten minutes encounters with a small group of real classroom students, often with an opportunity to observe the performance on video-tape"

Cliff and others (1976) have defined it "a teacher training procedure which reduces the teaching situation to a simpler and more controlled encounter achieved by limiting the practice to a specific skill and reducing teaching time and class size."

According to the *Encylopaedia of Education*, (1971) edited by L.C. Deighton, "Micro teaching is a real, constructed, scaled down teaching encounter which is used for teacher training, curriculum development and research.

Mc Allese and Unwin (1970) write, "The term micro teaching is most often applied to the use of closed Circuit Television (CCTV) to give immediate feed back of a trainee teacher's performance in a simplified environment."

B.K. Passi (1976) states, "It is a training technique which requires pupil teachers to teach a single concept using specified teaching skills to a small number of pupils in a short duration of time."

David B. Young defines micro-teaching as, "a device which provides the novice and experienced teachers alike, new opportunities to improve teaching."

Basic principles of micro-teaching—The following are the basic principles of micro-teaching.

1. Principle of enforcement—feed-back and reteaching make teaching perfect.
2. Principle of practice and drill—like surgery, teaching also is a complex skill which needs constant drill and practice. Micro-teaching affords practice in each small task or skill and thereby the pupil-teacher gains mastery.
3. The Principle of continuity—micro-teaching is a continuous process; teaching-feedback-reteaching-feedback till perfection is attained.
4. Principle of microscopic supervision—The supervisor has an observation schedule which he fills up while supervising and

makes an assessment on a rating scale. The supervisor sees through the lesson all important points, paying full attention to one point at a time.

Operations and steps in micro teaching—Micro teaching involves various operations for its success. These operations are detailed below:

1. A particular skill in terms of teaching behaviour is defined to trainees for providing the knowledge and awareness of teaching skills.
2. The skill is demonstrated by the expert or shown through videotape or film to the teacher trainee.
3. The student-teacher plans a short lesson in which he practises the particular skill.
4. The student-teacher teaches the lesson to a small group of pupils.
5. This skill teaching by the student-teacher is observed by the supervisor or peers on video-tape or audio-tape.
6. Teaching is followed by discussions to provide the feed-back.
7. The trainee is shown the video-tape or audio-tape to observe his own teaching activities.
8. The awareness of his own teaching performance provides the reinforcement to the pupil teacher.
9. The student-teacher replans the lesson in the light of the discussion to practise the same more effectively.
10. The revised lesson is retaught to a different group of same class for the same duration to practise the same skill.
11. The re-teaching is followed by discussions, suggestions and encouragement to the teacher on his performance. In this way feedback is again provided to the trainee.
12. The 'teach-reteach' cycle is followed till a desired level of the skill is achieved.

Three Phases of Micro-Teaching Procedure

Clift and others mention three phases of a teaching procedure:

Knowledge acquisition phase—It involves two major activities:

(i) Observing a demonstration skill, and

(ii) Analysing and discussing the demonstration.

2. *Skill acquisition phase*—The following activities are performed in the sequence given below:
   (i) Preparing a micro-lesson.
   (ii) Practising teaching skill, and
   (iii) Evaluating performance.
3. *Transfer phase*—After acquiring skills in the second phase, the trainees are provided an opportunity to use the skill in normal classroom teaching.

Strategy and standard procedure of micro-planning—The following points may be stated:

1. Orientation lectures to be given by the supervisor on each teaching skill.
2. Model presentation of each skill by the supervisor.
3. Discussion on the presentation with the pupil-teachers.
4. Preparation of a time-schedule of micro-lesson for each pupil-teacher by the supervisor.
5. Delivery of the lesson under controlled conditions by the pupil-teacher.
6. Supervision of the lesson by the supervisor.
7. Video-taping of the lesson, or lesson to be televised through closed-circuit television (CCTV).
8. Discussion about the lesson with the supervisor.
9. Again preparation of the lesson after the feedback.
10. Teaching the same lesson to another small group of students by the pupil-teacher.
11. Again discussion with the supervisor and feedback.

Five R's of micro-teaching—The pupil teacher tries to complete the following 5 R's in micro-teaching.

1. Recording,
2. Reviewing,
3. Responding,
4. Refining, and
5. Reading.

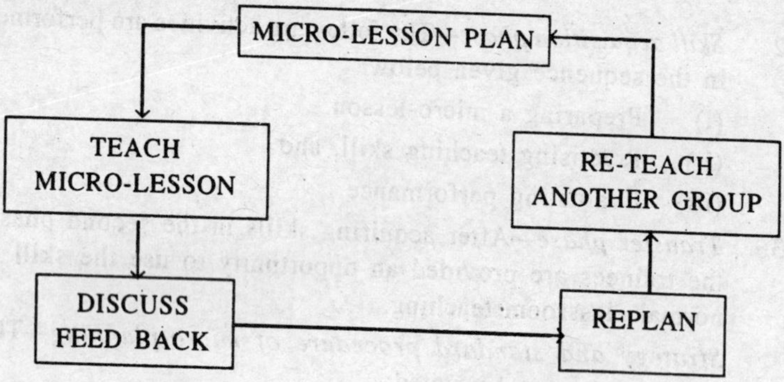

Illustration 28.2.-Micro Teaching Cycle

1. Time:	Teach	6 mts
	Feedback	6 mts
	Replan	12 mts
	Re-teach	6 mts
	Feedback	6 mts
2. Number of students		10
3. Supervisor(s)		1 or 2
4. Feedback by supervisor(s)		

Generally seven steps are followed: (a) orientation involving basis of micro-teaching, (b) discussion on teaching skills, (c) presentation of model lessons, (d) preparation of micro-lesson plan, (e) micro-teaching setting, (f) simulated condition (student-teachers act as pupils), (g) practice of teaching skills, (h) observation of teaching skills, (i) feed back, (j) teaching time (7 to 10 minutes for each skill)

Micro teaching flow chart—The procedure of micro-teaching in the Tokyo Institute of Technology may be briefly described by using the flow chart.

Three volunteers from the participants play the teacher's roles in front of the VTR camera and the other participants play the pupil's roles. After discussing how the teaching behaviours should be improved, three volunteers teach the other participants again. A comparison is made between these two teaching traits in each teacher on the evaluation sheet.

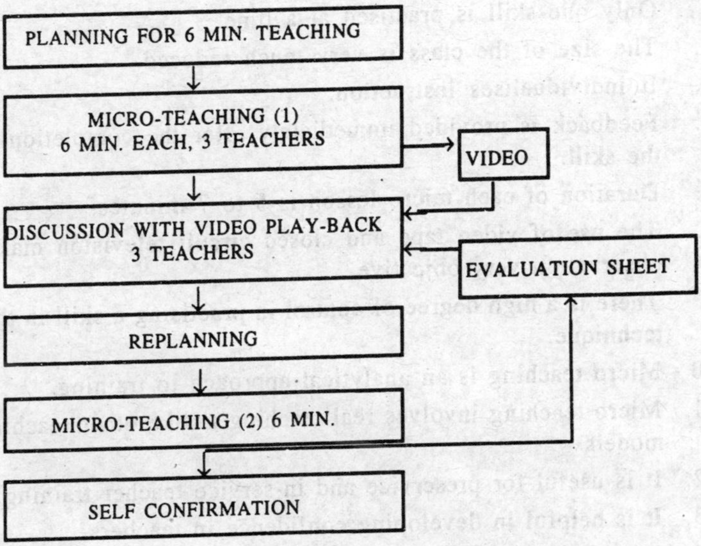

Illustration 28.2 Micro Teaching Flow Chart

Role of the supervisor in micro-teaching—A supervisor plays a leading role in micro-teaching. He helps pupil teachers in relating components skills of teaching to both the theory underlying the skills and to the practical conditions of the classroom. The supervisor has to provide continuous consultation so that he can help the trainee transfer the skill learnt in a micro-teaching setting to the actual classroom. First of all he gives a demonstration of a particular skill. Thereafter he prepares a special schedule of micro-teaching lessons in the practising schools. He supervises the lesson and discusses the lesson with the pupil teacher in a group where other pupil teachers are present. He completes the evaluation schedule and gives the feedback. The supervisor has to work very hard to be a model for the pupil teachers.

Evaluation of Micro-Teaching

Chief Merits of Micro Teaching

1. Micro teaching lessens the complexities of normal classroom teaching.
2. A single concept is taken up at a time.

3 Only one skill is practised at a time.
4. The size of the class is very much reduced.
5. It individualises instruction.
6. Feedback is provided immediately after the completion of the skill.
7. Duration of each micro lesson is 5 to 7 minutes.
8. The use of video tape and closed circuit television makes observation very objective.
9. There is a high degree of control in practising a skill in this technique.
10. Micro teaching is an analytical approach to training.
11. Micro teaching involves real teaching unlike other teaching models.
12. It is useful for preservice and in-service teacher training.
13. It is helpful in developing confidence in teachers.
14. It helps in sorting out problems relating to classroom teaching.
15. Close supervision is possible in this technique.
16. Micro teaching can be carried on in real classroom situations or in simulated conditions.

Critics of Micro Teaching

Like other innovations micro-teaching too has critics. Earl Seidman has raised the point that "much emphasis is placed on training in teaching skills which presupposes the idea that the teacher's role is to control the students and to direct the class ... if we treat our interns mechanistically, how will they treat their students?" Noam Chomsky, a scientific linguist at the Massachussetts Institute of Technology, has also questioned such a Skinnerian type of training, which is appropriate only to industrial workers who need to develop complex technical skills. Chomsky asks, "Is growing up and learning no more than the shaping of behaviour? If that is what education is all about, authoritarian figures shaping people, then may be we don't need it." Other critics of micro-teaching claim that while teaching a micro-class the teacher does not encounter the regular management problems common in large classes. It requires very competent and fully trained supervisors. It involves a lot of time.

Micro Teaching in India

A number of educational institutions have started work in the area of micro-teaching. D.D. Tiwari was the first to take up this work in 1967 at the Government Central Pedagogical Institute at Allahabad. This was followed by G.B. Shah who tried an experiment in micro-teaching with the help of a tape-recorder in the Faculty of Education and Psychology, Baroda in 1970. Other names in the field are R.R. Chandasama, L.P. Singh, N.S. Sarkar and N. Pangotra. A major break-through was made at the Technical Teachers Training Institute, Madras where a studio for educational television programme was set up in which micro-teaching was introduced to train technical teachers. A major contribution to micro-teaching as a teaching device was made in 1974 at the Technical Teacher's Training Institute, Chandigarh under the guidance of Dr. N.L. Dosajh. The Institute has published a number of research papers in the area of micro-teaching. The Royal Netherlands government provided a closed circuit television to this Institute. The Technical Teachers Training Institute Calcutta, started micro-teaching with the help of an audiotape.

Perhaps the first book on micro-teaching in India was written by Dr. N.L. Dosajh under the caption '*Modification of Teacher Behaviour through Micro-Teaching* (1977)'

Apparatus needed in micro-teaching—Micro-teaching can be conducted with or without closed circuit television.

The following apparatus may be considered sufficient for a simple type of micro-teaching:

1. Video on camera preferably with a zoom lens and tripod.
2. Video tape-recorders.
3. Two monitors.
4. Recording tapes.
5. Two clocks, a dozen lamps, about 100 yards of wire and switchgear.

Questions and Problems

A. Essay-Type Questions

1. Explain the meaning of micro teaching. State its merits and limitations.
2. "In spite of the fact that micro teaching is a powerful technique in the training of teachers, it is not generally used in the colleges of education in India." Comment upon this statement and state under what circumstances it can be used in India.
3. "Micro teaching is a scaled down encounter." Discuss this statement and point out the nature, characteristics and scope of micro-teaching.

B. Short-Answer Type Questions

4. State the basic principles and steps of micro teaching.
5. List the components of micro-teaching.
6. What are the 5 R's of microteaching?

29 Status and Code of Ethics for Teachers

29.1 Significance of Teacher Status

The National Policy on Education 1986 rightly points out, "The status of the teacher reflects the socio cultural ethos of a society. It is said that no people can rise above the level of its teachers."

The Programme of Action 1986 states, "The status of teachers has had a direct bearing on the quality of education and many of the ills of the latter can be ascribed to the indifferent manner in which society has looked upon the teacher and the manner in which many teachers have performed their functions."

The National Commission on School Teachers 1983-85 notes, "The status of the teacher, his professional competence and his welfare are all bound to his environment of work. If it is congenial, he would know that society values his activities and he could be proud of his role and therefore, he would strive to be worthy of it."

Meaning and factors determining the state of teachers—The Inter Governmental Conference on the status of the teacher held at Paris on October 5, 1966 stated the meaning of the term status. "The term 'status' as used in relation to teachers means both the standing or regard accorded to them as evidenced by the level of appreciation of the importance of their functions and of their competence in performing it, and the working conditions, remuneration and other material benefits accorded them relative to other professions."

The International Conference on Education convened by UNESCO at Geneva in 1975 observed, "It should be recognised that the social and economic status of teachers and the level of appreciation of their role are important for the quantitative and qualitative development of education. The National Commission on School Teachers (Chattopadhyaya Commission) observed, "the teacher's status is a complex sociological concept and can mean different things in different cultural contexts. In some countries a teacher's status is letermined by the teacher's freedom from religion and political restrictions, in some countries he derives his status from the "control of professional standards." In many countries it is the good salary and salary scales which confer status. Some of the other factors that will influence the status of the teacher are the sex of the teacher, the social class of the pupils, the subjects taught and the qualifications of the teachers.

A publication of the NCERT entitled *Status of Teacher in India (1993)* states, "status is generally defined as standing, esteem or prestige accorded by society to people in a profession. The word 'status' as used in relation to teachers means both standing and regard accorded to them, as evidenced by the level of appreciation of the importance of their functions and of their competence in performing it and the working and service conditions, remuneration and other material benefits accorded to them. Status can be studied only in relation to its environment and changes in society."

Dimensions of status—The following are the various indicators and dimensions of the status of teachers:-

1. Academic and professional requirements of or entry into the teaching profession.
2. Financial and other benefits.
3. Professional responsibilities assumed.
4. Forms and measures of public recognition of teachers.

The status of teachers may be seen from other aspects as mentioned below:

1. Academic status—minimum educational and professional qualifications necessary to enter the teaching profession.

2. Economic status—salaries, selection grade, various allowances and benefits etc.
3. Political status—importance attached to teachers in the selection of candidates for contesting elections.
4. Professional status—representation of teachers in different academic and professional committees and boards.
5. Social status—public recognition of the services rendered by teachers.

Teacher's low and shadowed position and status—The National Commission on Teacher—1 (School Teachers) examined the status and working conditions of the teachers and observed, "That our teachers do not enjoy a high social status is no secret; every commission before and after independence has bemoaned the fact. University Education regretted that school teaching was a much 'denigrated profession' while Mudaliar and his team (Secondary Education Commission) expressed their dissatisfaction in no uncertain terms that the social status given to the school teacher in the country was unsatisfactory, as also his salary and other conditions of service. In our own survey nearly 82 per cent of primary schools who responded to the question regretted that the teacher in our society to-day does not receive adequate respect and recognition. An equally high proportion of secondary teachers (83.3 per cent) felt like-wise. The response of teacher's organisation was understandably even more pessimistic: 97 per cent finding the present position of teachers entirely unsatisfactory and unacceptable."

The National Commission for Teachers further noted, "Because of low teacher status a growing number of teachers and parents are turning away from the idea of accepting teaching as an attractive career for their wards. Some recent studies have produced objective data."

Prof. R.P. Singh in his publication entitled *The Teacher in India* described the 'diminitive' role of the teacher as, "The halo and power of a teacher of pre-printing days is gone. A teacher has diminishing teaching value; and in keeping kids busy elsewhere, he is a very helpful tool. Beyond this he has no power, no control, and therefore no status."

Contributory factors for low status—The National Commission on Teachers—II (Higher Education) found the following reasons:-

1. Low salary and service conditions.
2. Lack of recognition by the government.
3. Lack of devotion to work.
4. Lack of integrity.
5. Lack of sense of pride.
6. Low level of efficiency.
7. Low level of scholarship.
8. Inadequate pedagogic skill.

B.J. Biddle in an article in *The Encyclopedia of Teaching and Teacher Education (1987)* lists the following reasons for the relatively low prestige of teachers, (a) prevalence of women in the teaching profession, (b) lack of specificity, in the role expected of teachers, (c) teachers working with the young, (d) devaluation of the knowledge deemed necessary to teach well, (e) the large number of persons presently employed or available for employment as teachers and others.

Measures for Improving the Status of the Teacher

William Carr, Secretary General of the World Confederation of Organisations of the Teaching Profession listed the following.

1. The higher the public respect for the school, the better the status of the teachers. It is bad for teachers to be under paid; it is even worse for education to be undervalued;
2. The better the payment and security of the teacher, the better their status;
3. The better the preparation and in service education of teachers, the better the status;
4. The greater the skill of the teacher in the classroom, the better the status;
5. The more united the profession, the better the status of the members.

The National Commission for School Teachers very emphatically stated, "Their (teachers) new sense of commitment and effective linkage between their work and the attainment of national goals and purposes, will restore in full measure the reverence that traditionally was given to the teacher. Status by reason of a title or position will become increasingly difficult to come by.

Status, in other words, will have to be earned, by the teacher, as by any other professional worker. It may be recalled that the 'Guru' never demanded reverence but the 'Shisya', his parents and the adult community gladly and gratefully professed it to the teacher. So must the new teacher earn status through achievement. The closer the teacher is able to link himself and his vocation with the mission of the nation, the more relevant he will become and the more revered by students, parents and society."

The Commission also suggested the following measures for refurbishing the image of the teacher.

1. Invitation of teachers to important public functions and according then a higher precedence on such occasions.
2. Associating teachers and teachers' organisations with policy-making decisions for educational planning and administration.
3. Associating teachers and teachers organisations with planning and execution of local and community development programmes, for which they have been consistently pressing and rightly so, for many years.

Payscale: The commission recommended the following pay scale:

Table 29.1

Composite Running Pay Scale (Excluding all allowances) for School Teachers Rs 500—3950

Post	*Pay at the entry point*	*Presumed Age of Entry*	*Retire-ment Age*	*Expec-ted ye-ears of Service*	*Expe-cted max-imum*
1. Primary school teacher	500	25	60	35	1600
2. T.G.T. Head-master Primary	700	25	60	35	2100
3. P.G.T. Head-master (Middle)	1000	25	60	35	2600

Contd.

4. Headmaster (Secondary)	1200	30	60	30	2600
5. Dy. Inspector of Schools	1200	30	60	30	2600
6. Head (senior Secondary)	1600	35	60	25	2900
7. Inspector of Schools	1850	40	60	20	2900
8. Deputy Director of Education	2350	40	60	20	3575
9. Joint Director of Education	2600	45	60	15	3575
10. Director of Education	3200	50	60	10	3950

The National Commission on Teachers II (Higher Education) viewed the following factors necessary to improve teacher's status;

1. Professional competence
2. Increase in emoluments
3. Recognition to the profession—nominating a teacher to various committees

While discussing the role and the status of teachers, two factors are generally missed today. First, a teacher in earlier times combined the functions of the 'guru' or 'preceptor' and the teacher. He guided his students in spiritual matters also. Secondly, an individual received his education from one or a few teachers only. Now a days, a student before obtaining his M.A. degree, receives his education from more than a dozen teachers. Naturally, therefore, the modern teacher proportionately gets recognition and respect.

29.2 Code of Conduct for Teachers

Commitment to the teaching profession—The concept of professional ethics may be summed up in the words of Laurie, "If a teacher has not an ideal aim he had better take to shop keeping at once, he will there doubtless find an ideal within his capacity." The Secondary Education commission 1952-53 has stated, "They (teachers) will not look upon their work as an unpalatable means of carrying a scanty living but as an avenue through which they are rendering significant social services as well as finding some measure of self-fulfillment and self-expression." The National Commission for School Teachers recommended that "the Ministry of Education (Now called the Ministry of Human Resource Development) in concert with the State Governments, should take immediate steps to prepare a code of conduct for teachers. The code should be prepared in consultation with the teachers' organisations and the formulation must be done at the national level. Its preparation at the national level is important as that alone would be consistent with the dignity, unity and integrity of the teaching profession and make the code equally applicable to all teachers throughout this land." The commission, however, at the same time cautioned, "If the political leadership wants to implement a national code for teachers, it will first have to create a work climate in which, not only teachers but every other category of worker feels motivated to do his duty conscientiously, to work hard and to give of his best. If such a climate is created, we feel that not only the teachers but the entire nation can be relied upon to support the measure enthusiastically."

The National Commission for Teachers—Higher Education 1983-85 stressed the necessity of professional ethics and values.

1. As a man devoted to learning, to the pursuit of truth in his creative endeavours, and hence being in a position to see faster than many others—as a social critic, the teacher has to struggle for the propagation of values. Therefore, we believe that teachers should be the first to introspect, and scrutinise their own value system so as to raise it to the highest moral standard.
2. We would like to say unambiguously that no profession and no service can survive without its do's and don'ts.
3. We would urge the teaching community to apply a worthy criteria of performance to itself so that it earns the most honourable place in the society.

A Few Elements/Provision of the Code

1. A teacher shall cooperate with and secure the cooperation of other persons in all activities which aim at the improvement of the moral, mental and physical well-being of pupils.

2. A teacher shall not exploit school influence for private gain.
3. A teacher shall have an exemplary moral conduct.
4. A teacher shall be temperate and sober in his habits. He would avoid smoking, chewing of betel leaves and such other undesirable habits in the presence of students within the precincts of the school.
5. A teacher shall take pride in his calling and try to promote the dignity and solidarity of his profession.
6. A teacher shall be punctual in his work.
7. A teacher shall keep himself abreast of the latest developments in educational thought and practices.
8. A teacher shall maintain right ethical behaviour in relations parents, and the community:
9. A teacher shall not prescribe or recommend books on some consideration.
10. A teacher shall not indulge in tuitions etc.

Questions and Problems

A. Essay-Type Questions

1. Write an essay on the role and status of the teacher in the Indian society.
2. Explain the meaning of the concept of status of teachers. What are the factors on which it depends. State measures for according a reasonable status to the teachers.
3. "Status will have to be earned by the teachers themselves." Elucidate this statement.
4. Do you think that of late there has been an erosion in the status of the teacher? Give reasons in support of your answer.
5. Explain the significance of the code of conduct of the teachers. What are the chief elements of the code of conduct?

B. Short-Answer Type Questions

6. State briefly the impact of the status of the teacher on the role of the teachers.
7. Describe briefly various dimensions of the status of the teacher.
8. Write a note on the 'shadowed' status of the teachers.

Part IV

Diverse Issues

30 Diverse Issues

30.1 Education and Employment

Alarming situation regarding unemployed educated persons—The need for a regular and dependable job or a vocation or gainful employment can hardly be disputed. A job gives money which in turn gives one purchasing power. It also helps in the country's economic prosperity. But in spite of the best efforts of the government, the spectre of unemployment is haunting the land and its grimness is increasing day-by-day.

The problem of unemployed matriculates is very serious. Next come the arts, science and commerce graduates and post-graduates. Surveys conducted reveal large scale dissatisfaction among the educated employed with their jobs because of unsatisfactory earnings. There is maladjustment between the demand and supply of different categories of people, especially at the lower levels. Unemployment among the technically trained is comparatively a recent phenomenon.

The total number of people registered, with the Employment Exchanges as on 30 March, 1993 was 36 million. On 31 December, 1989, this figures stood at 32.14 million (matric and above 19.14 million and below matric including illiterate 13 million. At the end of March, 1994, this figure stood at 36.04 million. About 68 per cent of these were in rural areas and 32 in urban areas. (Reply in Parliament on 12 August, 1994).

In April 1993, there were 31,700 doctors and 95,600 engineers whose names figured on the Registers of the Employment Exchanges in the country.

Causes of unemployment and inadequacy of the educational system (Including University Education).

1. Education is not related to the needs of the employment situation.
2. The educational system is by and large a continuation of the old system designed for the needs of a colonial regime and requires considerable re-orientation to fulfil the demands of economic and social development.
3. The allocation of employment intensive programmes like elementary education, buildings for schools, primary health centres have not been adequate.
4. Micro-planning has remained a very neglected aspect in the educational and economic planning in India.
5. From the point of view of employment as from that of social and political development, elementary education has not received due attention. The largest ejection from the education system into the world of work takes place at the elementary stage and hardly anything is done to prepare the pupils to fight under-employment.
6. There is very little information with regard to job satisfaction. No cumulative cards are kept. Facilities for educational and vocational guidance are very meagre.
7. Courses are largely academic and do not fit the students for the large diversity of middle level jobs.
8. In rural areas education alienates the educated persons from their environment.
9. Courses of universities and colleges are unrelated to the realities of the world of work. There is preponderance of arts courses and inadequate emphasis on science and technology.
10. Vocational and professional education is not adequately geared to the needs of agriculture, industry and commerce because of inadequate linkages with the employment system.
11. Apart from the question of insufficient and distorted priorities in education, insufficient attention is paid to the building up of those basic attitudes, skills and personality traits which

are essential pre-requisites for employment creation. These basic qualities are industriousness, respect for manual work, initiative, resourcefulness, an enquiring mind and anad venturous spirit, power of observation, an eye for detail and manipulative skill. They are largely a function of methodology and need to be inculcated from the very beginning of the child's life.

12. In addition to the maladjustment between demand and supply there is the general tendency of the education and employment systems to stand part. The result is that there is very little cooperation coming forth from the industry in the practical training of technical personnel.
13. The educational system does not lend the assistance of functional literacy to the extension agencies.
14. There is the general absence of a system of life-long training and retraining.

Specific Responsibility of Education Towards Employment

The specific responsibility of education towards employment situation is three-fold:

1. Education and employment preparation.
2. Education and employment adaptation.
3. Education and creation of employment to some extent.

Future Strategy of Educational Development

Education and Overall Development—The education system must lend support to the overall strategy of the development of a country. The following are the major steps to be taken to interlink development, employment and education:

1. A major support that education can give to the overall strategy of development, especially in rural areas is to improve the technology of existing crafts without destroying their decentralised and employment intensive character.
2. The second major support that education can give to the overall strategy is to impart population education at all appropriate stages.
3. The education of girls should be given very high priority.

Education for work—Another essential function which education has to perform is to prepare those students who leave at various stages to join the world of work.

Estimate of manpower skills—To provide needed trained and skilled manpower for technical and administrative jobs, the following measures seem to be very essential:

1. Existing shortage and surplus of skilled manpower in each major sector of the economy must be estimated.
2. Total availability of unskilled labour force should be found out.
3. Reasonable demands for different types of skilled manpower in all the sectors of the economy must be estimated.

On the basis of these estimates, the future policy for education should be outlined for a period of at least ten years.

Education in the rural sector—The education system should be capable of providing an adequate knowledge of recent scientific and technical advancement to the adults of the rural areas. It should aim at providing a framework conducive to increasing rural productivity. It should also act as a powerful instrument against the problem of unemployment.

More emphasis on elementary education—Overall main emphasis should be on elementary education rather than higher education. Elementary education should contain preliminary knowledge of social science and small-scale industries.

Promotion of adult education—It should be designed in such a manner that it is helpful to improve general village welfare through improved community schemes.

Promotion of professional education—In the field of higher education investments should be made in professional education including scientific, engineering, medical and high level training institutions rather than in the costly system of academic education producing graduates and post-graduates in various fields of social science and humanities. In the immediate future the main emphasis will be on job-oriented facilities which directly help to improve the standard of living of the masses—the final goal of all developmental efforts.

In short, it may be stressed that for the present, the provision of agricultural extension training in agricultural science, mechanical and technical skills, training in supervisory and administrative skills should be given first priority so that it can contribute to fulfil the manpower requirement of economic development. Such an investment in the educational field will have the shortest possible payback period and thus have a high rate of return to the economy.

Delinking of the academic degree from the job—There has been an endless talk of 'job-oriented education' and 'vocationalisation' but nothing much has happened in practice. A realistic vocationalisation at this stage could reduce the intractability of the unemployment problem and keep the enrolment in colleges and universities within manageable limits.

Promotion of right attitudes—Socially relevant skills and capacities must be carefully spelled out and conditions for their inculcation and acquisition created.

30.2 Education of the Deprived Sections (OBCs)

Introduction—Gross inequalities arise from differences in home environments. These inequalities are obviously the most difficult to overcome and here progress essentially depends on the general improvement in the standard of living of the population. But something could be done by giving special attention in educational institutions to the children coming from deprived groups.

These groups can be classified in a number of ways, for instance, those suffering from cultural deprivation, economic deprivation, political deprivation and social deprivation. The traditional method of classification is in terms of Scheduled Castes, Scheduled Tribes and Other Backward Classes. People belonging to remote hilly areas, forest areas, desert areas and Slum areas etc. are also classified as such. The entire tribal population comes under the category of deprived sections.

Sometimes women are also included in the category of deprived group. The handicapped children may also be placed in this category.

Constitutional Provisions Regarding Deprived Sections

Art.15. Prohibition of Discrimination on grounds of religion, race, caste, sex or place of birth.

Subsection (4). It states "Nothing in this article or in clause (2) of Article 29 shall prevent the state from making any special provision for the advancement of any socially and educationally backward classes of citizens or for the scheduled castes and scheduled Tribes."

Art. 46. It states "The state shall promote with special care the educational and economic interests of the weaker sections of the people, and in particular, of the scheduled castes and scheduled tribes and shall protect them from social injustice and all forms of exploitation."

Art. 338. It makes provision for the appointment of a special officer for SCs and STs.

Art 340. It envisages the appointment of the commission to investigate the conditions of the backward classes.

Present State of Education of SCs and STs

Table 30.1

Literacy Rates 2001 Census

	Item	*Persons*	*Males*	*Females*
1.	General	65.38	75.85	54.41
2.	Scheduled Castes	54.69	66.64	41.90
3.	Scheduled Tribes	47.10	59.17	34.76

Source: *2001 Census.*

Table 30.2

Gross Enrolment Ratios (2006-2007)

Items	*Classes I-V (6 to 11 years)*			*Classes VI to VIII (11 to 14 years)*		
	Persons	*Boys*	*Girls*	*Persons*	*Boys*	*Girls*
1. General	111.29	114.4	107.8	73.6	77.4	69.5
2. Scheduled Castes	102.4	103.6	100.5	72.5	73.6	70.3
3. Scheduled Tribes	99.7	112.7	100.2	68.0	73.9	62.0

Source : *Economic Survey 2008-2009.*

Table 30.3

Drop-out Rates (2004-2005)

S.No	*Item*	*Classes I to V Total*	*I to VIII Total*	*I to X Total*
1.	General	29.0	50.84	61.92
2.	Scheduled	34.2	57.3	77.3
3.	Scheduled Tribes	42.3	65.9	79

Source: *Educational Statistics, 2004-05 Department of Education, MHRD.*

General Conclusions

1. Literacy rates of STs are extremely low.
2. Enrolment position of SCs and STs at the primary stage is quite favourable.
3. Enrolement position in classes Vl to VIII cannot be considered satisfactory.
4. Drop-out rates are very alarming.

Promotion of Education among the Deprived Sections

The Education Commission 1964-66 in chapter VI entitled 'Equalisation of Educational Opportunity and Social Change' very aptly observed, "one of the important social objectives of education is to equalise opportunity, enabling the backward or under-privileged classes and individuals to use education as a lever for the improvement of their conditions. Every society that values social justice and is anxious to improve the lot of the common man and cultivate all available talent must ensure progressive equality of opportunity to all sections of the population. This is the only guarantee for the Building up of an egalitarian and humane society in which the exploitation of the weak is minimised". The Commission further stated, "The education of the backward classes in general and the tribal people in particular is a major programme of equalisation and of social and national integration. No expenditure is too great for this purpose." Alas! We have not paid heed to those words of wisdom. Non-implementation of this vital recommendation has led to disintegrative tendencies, hatred and strife.

The National Policy on Education, 1968, 1986 and modified Policy Formulation 1992—all stress upon speedy action for the promotion of education of the deprived sections.

Measures for the Promotion of Education of the Deprived Sections*

Preparatory classes and compensatory instruction—Many children belonging to the Scheduled Castes and Scheduled Tribes come from a comparatively poor environment. They may not be neat or smart. Their usage of standard language may be poor. Their vocabulary is under-developed as compared to their peers. They may not have formed the initial mathematical concepts. On the other hand they may be more enthusiastic to act. Because of the lack of a congenial home environment, these children may not be in a position to complete their home assignments. Their parents are usually employed as landless labour or in other manual or agrarian activities. Therefore, such children are not able to conceptualise their future as educated persons.

There is the need to conduct some preparatory classes for children coming from the Scheduled Castes and Scheduled Tribes. The primary objective of conducting such classes is to raise the school entry ability level of such children. This is also helpful in having a somewhat homogeneous group in the class. The classes may be conducted two to three weeks in advance of the general admissions. Classes may be conducted on healthy habits, personal and environmental cleanliness, eating habits etc. The children may also be helped in improving the pronunciation of the words and picking up standard language. For this, they may be motivated to participate in discussions, recitation and story-telling etc. Initial concepts of mathematics may also be introduced.

Remedial instruction—Students coming from Scheduled Castes and Scheduled Tribes are also likely to be deficient in the scholastic areas. The school may provide some remedial education programmes. Adoption of instructional strategies, such as peer group learning, monitorial assistance, diagnostic testing and tutoring would help to improve the educational levels of these learners.

Provision of outdoor games and activities, co-curricular and work experience activities will also help in the retention of such

* See Chapter 19 also

children in the schools and create an interest in them for continued schooling.

Role of the teachers—The teachers can play an important role in developing a favourable school climate conducive to the educational progress of Scheduled Castes and Scheduled Tribes. Some suggestions in this regard are given here.

1. The teacher's own example in his behaviour towards students belonging to these castes is the most effective and powerful way to build up a congenial climate.
2. The school staff should ensure non-discrimination between the children of Scheduled Castes, Scheduled Tribes and other communities.
3. The school staff should avoid the use of the caste names or derogatory words while calling roll calls or naming children.
4. Teachers should provide equal opportunities to all the children to participate in the curricular and co-curricular activities of the school, including games.
5. Frequent meetings between the staff, school teachers and parents of Scheduled Castes and Scheduled Tribes children should be arranged. The details of the schemes for promoting education amongst Scheduled Castes and Scheduled Tribes should be explained to the parents at these meetings. It should be impressed upon them that they must continue the education of their children.
6. Special attention should be paid to motivating parents to educate girls.
7. Teachers should suggest to illiterate parents the advantages gained by attending functional literacy classes in the centre.

Other Measures

These include:

1. A standing Committee of the Central Advisory Board of Education (CABE) under the Chairmanship of Minister of Human Resource Development may be constituted to monitor and review implementation of all educational programmes for the deprived sections.
2. Incentive schemes in operation for the promotion of the education of the deprived sections may be evaluated and appropriate strategies evolved in the light of such studies.

3. In the curriculum, suitable changes should be made which reflect the contribution of the deprived sections in the national development. The curriculum should include the salient features of the culture of these groups.
4. Recruitment of teachers to the prescribed percentage should be ensured.

30.3 Environmental Education

Meaning of environment—Whatever is present around the living beings and above the land, on the surface of the earth and under the earth is environment in its broader sense. According to Douglass and Holland, "Environment is a word which describes, in the aggregate, all external forces, influences and conditions which affect the life, nature, behaviour and the growth, development and maturation of living organism". In the words of Wordsworth, "The environment is everything that affects the individual except his genes."

Environment covers all the outside factors that have acted on the individual since he began life.

Broadly speaking following are the two types of environment:

1. Natural environment related to nature.
2. Social environment related to society.

Pollution of environment—In his attempt to produce goods for his own comforts and luxuries, man has been destroying his environment. He has opened industries without a thought for air and water pollution caused by the indiscriminate discharge of wastes and land dereliction caused by despoiling forests. Man, in doing so has inevitably jumped towards environmental pollution and crisis. Now the time has come when he should be careful. In this context, the need for environmental education, assumes special significance. Man has to improve the environment for the survival and welfare of his species.

Pollution of Environment and Major Environment Factors and Problems Needing Environmental Education

1. *Macro Kind*
   (i) Soil erosion.
   (ii) Extinction of wild life.
   (iii) Deforestation.

(iv) Lack of water.

(v) Energy crisis and related issues.

2. *Micro Kind*

(i) Poor health and sanitation.

(ii) Inadequate housing.

(iii) Population growth.

Global ecology—Global ecology is fast deteriorating due to unrestrained mechanisation.

Specific Examples of Environmental Pollution and Problems

1. Silent valley Hydro-electric project which threatens to destroy the ecology the of the tropical rain forest in Kerala.
2. Air pollution has crossed the safety limit at Chembur and Lalbang in Greater Bombay and in many other big towns.
3. Danger of National Lake being dried up in 90 years if the present rate of silting is not arrested.
4. Sewage threat to major rivers.
5. Dangers of chimney smoke to the poor and deprived.
6. Dying forests.
7. Danger to the Taj.

Meaning of environmental education—Environmental education implies establishing an ecological equilibrium which implies proper use and conservation of resources and also control of environment pollution. Environmental education is a process of recognising values and clarifying concepts relating to the environment and its problems. The aim is to develop skills and attitudes necessary to understand the environment. Environmental education has been described as education for the environment, education about the environment and education through the environment.

Objectives of environmental education—Environmental education is designed to open our eyes to the havoc we have brought on ourselves. Environmental education should enable to people to learn how hazardous environmental pollution, population explosion and resource depletion can be. The best place to start such learning is in school.

Environmental education aims at developing awareness and knowledge about environmental issues and helping individuals to develop proper attitudes and skills in this regard and also enlisting their participation in protecting the environment.

Organisation of Environmental Education

1. Environmental education should be integrated into the whole system of format education at all levels;
2. It should be interdisciplinary in nature;
3. It should adopt a holistic perspective which will examine the ecological, social, cultural and other aspects of particular problems;
4. It should be centred on practical problems related to real life; and
5. It should aim at building up a sense of values.

Role of the Teacher for Better Environment

Traditionally a teacher has been regarded as an agent of social change and modernisation. He has been called the 'maker of history', 'the builder of the nation' and the social engineer. Children and especially children in the plastic period of their life emulate their teachers and draw inspiration from them. A teacher, therefore, can play an important role in promoting environmental awareness and understanding among his students. The following are the different methods in this regard:

1. He should set up healthy examples before the students.
2. He should impart information regarding environmental pollutants.
3. He should acquaint students with the techniques of preventing pollution.
4. He can arrange declamation contents, essay writings, poetical recitations, dramas etc.
5. Educational excursions could be arranged to arouse a love for nature.
6. Tree plantation functions can be organised.
7. Cleanliness drives are also very useful.
8. Poster competitions can be held.

History of Environmental Education

One of the landmarks in the history of environmental education is the 1972 Stockholm Conference on Human Environment, organised by UNESCO. This was followed by the International Environmental Education Workshops in Belgrade, Yugoslavia in October, 1975. The Belgrade Workshop was followed by Regional workshops. Environmental education is concerned with the improvement of all ecological relationship. Including the relationship of humanity with nature and people with each other.

Centrally Sponsored Scheme of Environmental Education

A centrally sponsored scheme of Environmental Orientation to School Education has been started with effect from 1989-90 year under which 100 per cent financial assistance is provided to States/UTs and voluntary organisations working in the field of environment education. Various programmes aimed at creating environmental consciousness among the students and the community are organised on a project basis in selected areas comprising homogenous ecological conditions. The project activities include a review of curriculum, preparation of revised textbooks, curricular and extra curricular materials, preparation of general informative books/brochures/posters/audio-visual materials, adoption of monuments by schools for study and upkeep, study of ecological problems in the neighbourhood, participation in conservation projects, etc. The setting up of school nurseries is being taken as one of the preferred activities with the help of the State Departments of Environment and Forests and the National Wastelands Development board.

Role of Voluntary Organisations and Pressure Groups in Environmental Education

Under the above mentioned scheme, voluntary organisations are provided assistance to undertake experimental and innovative programmes aimed at integrating educational programmes in schools with local environmental conditions. The scheme also envisages assistance to the NCERT during the Eighth Plan for organising workshops etc. Some of the proposals sanctioned for voluntary organisations are as undmer:

1. Uttarkhand Seva Nidhi, Almora for environmental orientation to elementary education in the Kumaon and Garhwal region of Uttar Pradesh.
2. Sanchal Foundation, New Delhi for a project on social imperatives of development which seeks to establish a linkage between the natural disasters and environmental degradation.

3. Centre of Environment Education (CEE) Ahmedabad to act as a nodal agency for involving NGOs (Non-Government Organisations) working in the area of environment education to take up locale-specific activities in a cluster of schools around which programmes would be designed and implemented with the national and state level perspectives. The full intent of environmental education will not be achieved because the environmental concerns are locale-specific and therefore, do not admit a global solution. These efforts, therefore, need to be supplemented by more intensive locale specific efforts.

Movements like 'Chipko', started by Sunder Lal Bahuguna are very helpful in providing environmental education. It raises a protest against the indiscriminate felling of trees and construction of dams at the cost of environmental safety. These movements draw the attention of the people to the tragedy that may fall upon us if we do not hear the call of nature. All help should be given to these programmes.

So far about 60 projects have been sanctioned in 25 states and UTs. Twenty voluntary organisations are involved in the scheme.

30.4 Moral and Religious Education

Need for the Teaching of Moral and Spiritual Values

We have to lay special stress on the teaching of moral and spiritual values. Moral values particularly refer to the conduct of man towards man in the various situations in which human beings come together in the home, in social and economic fields, and in the life of the outside world generally. It is essential that from the earliest childhood, moral values should be inculcated in us. We have to influence the home first. We fear that our homes are not what they ought to be. Habits, both of mind and body, formed in the early years at home, persist and influence our life afterwards. Good manners are a very important part of moral education. It is not unusual that when a people attain freedom suddenly, after long years of bondage, they are inclined to become self-willed, arrogant and inconsiderate. In such situations good manners are easily set aside and young people tend to express the first flush of freedom in licence and rowdyism.

The importance of good manners cannot be overstressed. Good manners will impose a proper restraint on us and remove harshness in our words and rudeness in our behaviour. Good manners verily are like the oil that helps keep the machine of human society running smoothly. We have been losing our manners rather rapidly and it is necessary that we should recover them. Good manners should be sedulously inculcated and teachers must give instruction in this to all students at all times, both by examples and by precept. We must be constantly be told that what hurts us, hurts others also and we must behave towards others as we want others to behave towards us.

Then there is a great deal of talk of corruption and dishonesty in our official and business life. It is the students of today who are to be incharge of the various departments of life tomorrow; if they learn what real integrity is in their early years, they are not likely to go very wrong later on. Every effort must, therefore, be made to teach students true moral values from the earliest stage of their educational life.

Moral development is an important dimension of the education of the child. The National Policy on Education, 1986 expressed a great concern over the erosion of moral values. It strongly emphasised that the curriculum should be readjusted in such a way as to make education a forceful tool for the cultivation of moral and social values.

Meaning of moral development—Behaviour which relates to honesty, integrity, truthfulness, righteousness and self-control including right attitude to sex is that which concerns our moral life.

'*Psychology of the Child and Curriculum*' Published by NCERT in 1983 has listed the following important moral qualities which need to be developed in children:

1. Honesty in words and deeds
2. Truthfulness
3. Self-respect and so desire to respect others
4. Righteousness
5. Self control
6. Duty consciousness
7. Compassion.

Broadly speaking every religion has four aspects:

1. Personality of the founder-dealing with the greatness and holiness of the founder. (Hinduism has no founder as such).
2. Genesis—seeking to give an account of the creator and the universe created by Him.
3. Rituals—prescribing some outward forms which the followers should accept and follow.
4. Ethical or moral code—telling what is right and what is wrong—code of behaviour and conduct.

Swami Vivekananda declared emphatically, "unselfishness is the test of religion. He who has more of this unselfishness is nearer to Shiva. And if a man is selfish even though he has visited all the temples and painted himself like a leopard, he is still further off from Shiva."

Being moral and being religious are not synonymous expressions. Being moral refers to being able to understand the principles of right and wrong and act in the right way. Being religious refers to having a belief in the supernatural powers of God. It also refers to performing a certain type of worship. It is not logically necessary for a moral person to go to a place of worship and have faith in religion. One could be moral without committing oneself to any religious faith. A religious person may not necessarily be a moral person. Saints and Seers have always stressed the importance of moral values and consequently of a clean life - life free from selfishness and greed.

Methods of Imparting Moral Education

There are two important methods of imparting moral education—the direct method and the indirect method.

The direct method of moral education refers to deliberate and systematic attempts by the teacher to teach morality as a subject. It includes regular classroom instruction and discussion.

The indirect method of moral education implies morality through doing good acts, and learning moral values through participation in social service activities. It also implies emphasising moral values during the course of teaching various subjects.

Role of the School and the Teacher

A school can play a very important role in the moral development of children. The most important agent in the school is obviously the teacher. It has been stressed again and again that nothing can be more effective and helpful in moulding the child's moral behaviour than the teacher' own moral behaviour.

Through the organisation of various curricular and co-curricular activities, teachers can foster among children various moral qualities. In the teaching of different subjects like languages and social studies etc., teachers can stress moral qualities.

The teacher should establish an maintain clear standards of behaviour and encourage his pupils to behave towards himself, towards one another, and towards the whole community in an orderly and considerate way. Every school demands a certain standard of behaviour form its pupils. The teacher should develop a rational acceptance of these standards in his pupils and also the ability to discriminate right from the wrong.

To conclude, Maharshi Aurobindo's message should be kept in mind by every teacher. "The attempt to make boys moral... by the teaching of moral ... textbooks is a vanity and delusion, precisely because the heart is not the mind and to instruct the mind does not necessarily improve the heart".

30.5 Value Education

Definition and meaning of a value—According to John Dewey (1948), "to value means to prize, to esteem, to appraise to estimate. It means the act of cherishing something, holding it dear and also the act of passing judgement upon the nature and amounts of values as compared with something else."

E.S. Brightman (1978) has stated, "in the most elementary sense, value means whatever in actually liked, 'prized, esteemed desired, approved or enjoyed by anyone at a time"

M.S. Cuber (1962) says, "values are the ideas and beliefs which people cherish. These ideas contain or express the judgement which people have, of the relative importance of things."

Dictionary of Education (1959) defines values, "as the things in which people are interested—things they want to desire to be or become; feel as obligatory, worship or enjoy."

Educators and thinkers differ regarding the precise meaning of the term 'value'. Nevertheless, there is no doubt that values guide our behaviour and conduct, set goals and determine actions 'towards different events, objects and situations. They are the moving spirit in our lives. The following are some of the important definitions of a value.

T.W. Hipple (1969) holds, "values are conscious or unconscious motivators and justifiers of the actions and judgements."

M.P. Hung (1975) perceives values, "as a judgement concerning the worth of an object, person, group or situation. Value judgement contains evaluative rating terms, such as good, bad, moral, immoral, beautiful, ugly etc.

B. Elizabeth Hurlock has said, "values are concepts heavily weighted with emotions."

Kane (1962) says, "values are the ideals, beliefs or norms which a society or the large majority of a society's members hold."

A.K.C. Ottaway (1955) observes, "values stand for ideas men live for."

D.H. Parker thinks, "values belong wholly to the inner world of the mind. The satisfaction of desire is the real value, the thing that serves is only an instrument. A value is always an experience, never a thing or an object.'

T. Parson (1960) points out, "value is an element of a shared symbolic system which serves a criterion or standard for selection among the alternatives of orientation which are intrinsically open in a situation."

M.T. Ramji (1986) writes, "A value is what is desired or what is sought."

I.A. Spaulding (1963) perceives values in terms of "involvement among the components of a limited closed system which are essential for the inteigration of the system as constituted at the given time."

A. Zaleznik and D. David (1964) consider values "as the ideas in the mind of men comparable to norms in that they specify how people should behave. Values also attach degrees of goodness to aetivities and relationships"

In short values stand for ideals men live for. they are part and parcel of the philosophy of a nation and that of its educational system. They are the guiding principles of life.

Values may be operationally conceived as those guiding principles of life which are conducive to one's physical and mental health as well as to social adjustment and welfare.

Classification of Values

Strictly speaking there are no hard and fast rules to classify values as they are closely interlinked and interrelated.

Values are individual as well as social. Individual values refer to the good of oneself and social values refer, to the good of others. They may be classified into three categories biological values, intrinsic values and instrumental values or as instrumental values and terminal values. Plato classified values into three categories—Truth, Goodness and Beauty.

Eight-fold Classification of Values

Aesthetic	—	appreciation of beauty and joy
Emotional	—	courage, endurance, friendliness, harmony and heroism
Material	—	love of money, pleasure of life
Mental	—	impartiality and perseverance
Moral	—	benevolence, gratitude honesty
Physical	—	beauty, truth, grace, health and strength
Social	—	civic sense, cooperation, courtesy, devotion to duty
Spiritual	—	meditation, pursuit of ultimate reality.

Basic Human Values

S.J. Dackawish (1959) refers to the following 12 basic values—(a) love for people (b) respect for dignity (c) interactional skills (d) happiness (e) mentality (f) integrity (g) humility (h) religion (i) impulse control (j) sobriety (k) genuineness (l) fairness.

A conference organised by the Central Board of Secondary Education in 1986 listed 50 values.

An NCERT publication *Documents on Social Moral and Spiritual Values* (1979) lists 84 values.

Sources of values—Values derive their origin from a variety of sources: Literature, philosophy, religion, science, social customs and the constitution. As far as schools are concerned, they must give due importance to the values enshrined in our constitution.

Erosion of Values

It is said about the principal of a college maintained by a religious and a social organisation that he was so particular about values of public and social morality that he never used his office pen for writing a personal letter. This was honesty, observed scrupulously. The principal faithfully followed the shining example of Chanakya, the great administrator, economist, statesman and the Prime Minister of King Chandragupta Maurya.

According to the highest value system, even the use of an office pin for personal benefit is a corrupt act. But then who cares for such things!

Unfortunately, after independence, the value system that Gandhi and his devoted followers had so laboriously built started crumbling gradually. There is little exaggeration in the statement that there is a 'corruption explosion' and 'erosion of values'. The malady of a gradual erosion of moral and social values is so deep rooted in our economic, political and social life (religious life may also be included) that on numerous occasions, even the actions of those who could be emulated, become questionable. Planning for a 'clean life, clean politics and 'clean administration' is the need of the hour.

Value Education and School Situational Dimensions

Valued-oriented school education (1973)—a publication of the NCERT, lists the following situational dimensions of the value-oriented education:-

1. To understand the rights and duties of citizenship as envisaged in the Indian Constitution.
2. To realise the importance of morality which is essential for the stability and progress of society. It includes the norms of conduct as (a) respect and obedience (b) affection and consideration for others (c) discipline and civic sense (d) honesty in work and dealing with others (e) cooperation and observance of proper manners.

3. To understand the criteria which make an action moral (related to the social aspect)
4. To practise values such as courage, truth, universal love, dignity of manual labour, service, cleanliness, purity, courtesy, peace and joy.

Suggestive activities are: (1) community prayer programmes (2) health and cleanliness activities (3) classroom teaching (4) productive manual work-oriented activities (5) activities for training in citizenship and other cultural and recreational activities and social service activities.

A Few Examples of Human Values as Contained in Various Religions

Buddhism: One should make good men one's closest friends.

Confucianism: Friendship and brotherhood are the cardinal virtues.

Hinduism: The good man makes no distinction between friend and foe, brother and stranger but regards them all with impartiality.

Islam: All men are brothers and should live as such.

Jainism: Treat all men as brothers at all times.

Judaism: God has made all men brothers and they should live together as brothers at all times.

Sikhism: Get together, my brethren. And remove all misunderstanding through regard for each other.

Duty

Buddhism: One should be faithful to one's duty at all times.

Christianity: One has a duty to God and duties towards one's fellows.

Confucianism: The wise man makes duty his aim at all times.

Hinduism: Never falter in doing your duty.

Islam: All men who do their duty will receive a fitting reward from the Lord.

Jainism: It is the duty of all to be impartial.

Value-Oriented Programmes

Activity programme to develop values—The following are the important activities to be undertaken in the school in this regard:

1. Community prayer in the school.
2. Cleanliness programme in the school.
3. Community service programmes.
4. Social service programmes in fairs and festivals.
5. First-aid programmes.
6. Celebration of national days and festivals.
7. Dramas, etc. depicting values.
8. Organisation of a school panchayat or parliament.

Talks—Emphasis should be laid on the unity of all religions, harmony among communities and national integration.

Personal examples—The most important aspect of the programme is that the teachers should set examples of good conduct and behaviour which the students may imbibe in themselves.

Lastly, it may be observed that a special responsibility for creating a value-oriented environment lies on the V.I.P's, leaders of all shades and all those people who matter in different walks of life. In fact, by and large, these are the people responsible for the erosion of values. they must set the highest standards of ethical morality.

30.6 Population Education

Problem of 3 P's—Population, poverty and pollution (environmental degradation—brushing aside moral degradation or moral pollution) have close linkages and the quest for food, education, health and work for all will remain illusory unless success is achieved in limiting the growth of population.

Our population has already crossed the 100 crore mark and by the year 2010, a population of over 120 crore seems inevitable. The data made available by the Census of India, 2001, conducted in February-March 2001 would go a long way in the social-economic development of the country.

Literacy and education are the two most important indicators of development of a nation. Higher levels of literacy and education act as a catalyst for cultural, economic, political and social development.

The literacy rates obtained at the Census give a reflection of the government policies and programmes.

With a population of 102.7 crore on 1 March 2001, India's share in the world population increased to 16.87 per cent from 15.2 per cent in 1981.

Table 30.4

Census of India 2001: Population and Literacy at a Glance

Population	Total	1,027,015,247	
	Male	531,277,078	
	Female	495,738,169	
Decadal Population		**Absolute**	**Percentage**
Growth 1991-2001	Total	180,627,359	21.34
	Male	91,944,020	20.79
	Female	88,683,339	21.79
Density of Population (per sq. km.)			324
Sex Ratio (females per 1,000 males)			933
Population in the Age Group 0-6		**Absolute**	**Percentage to Total Population**
	Total	157,863,145	15.42
	Male	81,911,041	15.47
	Female	75,952,104	15.36
Literates		**Absolute**	**Percentage to Total Population**
	Total	566,714,995	65.38
	Male	339,969,048	75.85
	Female	226,745,947	54.16

Source: *Census 2001.*

It is of interest to not that every 10 years we add to our population the equivalent of two Britains, three Frances, five Canadas or half to the U.S.A.

On an average we add about 180 million people every year.

Table 30.5

Population of Some Select Countries 2006

S.No	*Country*	*Population*	*S.No*	*Country*	*Population*
1.	China	1316 million	2.	India	1100 million
3.	U.S.A.	298 million	4.	Indonesia	222 million
5.	Pakistan	157 million	6.	Japan	128 million
7.	Bangladesh	141 million	8.	Germany	83 million
9.	U.K.	65 million	10.	France	61 million
11.	Sweden	9.0 million	12.	Switzerland	7 million

Source: *The State of World's Children 2008.*

Table 30.6

Population of States/Union Territory by Sex

Sl. No.	India/State/ Union Territory	Total Population Persons	Males	Females
	INDIA	**1,027,015,247**	**531,277,078**	**495,738,169**
1.	Andaman & Nicobar Is.	356,265	192,985	163,28
2.	Andhra Pradesh	75,727,541	38,286,811	37,440,730
3.	Arunachal Pradesh	1,091,117	573,951	517,16
4.	Assam	26,638,407	13,787,799	12,850,608
5.	Bihar	82,878,796	43,153,964	39,724,832
6.	Chandigarh	900,914	508,224	392,69
7.	Chhattisgarh	20,795,956	10,452,426	10,323,530
8.	Dadra & Nagar Haveli	220,451	121,731	98,72
9.	Daman & Diu	158.059	92,478	65,58
10.	Delhi	13,782,976	7,570,890	6,212,086
11.	Goa	1,343,998	685,617	658,38
12.	Gujarat	50,596,992	26,344,053	24,252,939
13.	Haryana	21,082,989	11,327,658	9,755,331
14.	Himachal Pradesh	6,077,248	3,085,256	2,991,992
15.	Jammu & Kashmir	10,069,917	5,300,574	4,769,434
16.	Jharkhand	26,909,428	13,861,277	13,048,151
17.	Karnataka	52,733,958	26.856,343	25,877,615
18.	Kerala	31,838,619	15,468,664	16,369,955
19.	Lakshadweep	60,595	31,118	29,47
20.	Madhya Pradesh	60.385,118	31,456,873	28, 928,245
21.	Maharashtra	96,752,247	50,334,270	46,417,977
22.	Manipur	2,388,634	1,207,338	1,181,296
23.	Meghalay	2,306,069	1,167,840	1,138,229
24.	Mizoram	891,058	459,783	431,27
25.	Nagaland	1,988,636	1,041,686	94,695
26.	Orissa	36,706,920	18,612,340	18,094,580
27.	Pondicherry	973,829	486,705	487,12
28.	Punjab	24,289,296	12,963,362	11,325,934
29.	Rajasthan	56,473,122	29,381,657	27,091,46
30.	Sikkim	540,493	288,217	252,27
31.	Tamil Nadu	62,110,839	31,268,654	30,842,18
32.	Tripura	3,191,168	1,636,138	1.555,03
33.	Uttar Pradesh	166,052,859	87,466,301	78,586,55
34.	Uttaranchal	8,479,562	4,316,401	4,163,16
35.	West Bengal	80,221.171	41,487,694	38,733,47

1. The Population of India includes the estimated population of entire Kachchh district, Morvi, Maliya-Mayana and Wankaner Talukas of Rajkot district, Jodiya taluka of Jamanagar district of Gujarat state and entire Kinnam district of Himachal Pradesh where population enumeration of Census of India, 2001 could not be conducted due natural calamities.

Table 30.7: **Five States with Maximum and Minimum Population (2001)**

Sl. No.	*States with Maximum Population*		*Sl. No.*	*States with Minimum Population*	
	State	*Population*		*State*	*Population*
1.	Uttar Pradesh	166,052,859	1.	Sikkim	540,493
2.	Maharashtra	96,752,247	2.	Mizoram	891,058
3.	Bihar	82,878,796	3.	Arunachal Pradesh	1,091,117
4.	West Bengal	80,221,171	4.	Goa	1,343,998
5.	Andhra Pradesh	75,727,541	5.	Nagaland	1,988,636

General Implications of Overpopulation of India

The general implications of overpopulation of India may be summed up as (a) poverty, (b) increased pressure on land, (c) pollution, (d) unemployment, (e) undernourishment, (f) unhygienic living conditions of the general public, (g) slums, (h) unsatisfactory economy of the country, and (i) heavy imports of some essential commodities.

Educational Problems and Difficulties on account of Overpopulation

1. Unwieldy classes at all levels.
2. Poor buildings, furniture and equipment for the growing enrolment.
3. Lack of general amenities in educational institutions.
4. Poor quality of education.
5. Student absenteeism from schools.
6. High rate of drop-outs, stagnation and wastage.
7. Unemployment among the educated.

Meaning of population education—A UNESCO Regional Seminar on Population and Family Life Education held at Bangkok in 1970 defined population education as "an educational programme which provides for a study of the population situation in the family, community, nation and the world with the purpose of developing in the students rational and responsible attitudes and behaviour towards that situation."

Objectives of Population Education

1. To develop among the students a keen insight into the inter-relationship between population change and the process of socio-economic development vis-a-vis the individual, the family, the society, the nation and the world.
2. To create among the students and teachers an awareness about the population situation in the country and the strategies adopted to meet this critical situation.

3. To create an awareness among children that the present population explosion in our country is due to a steady birth rate as against a rapidly falling death rate over the past few decades.
4. To develop desirable attitudes and behaviour in the students and the teachers as well as in the community at large towards the population issues so as to enable them to arrive at a rational decision about the quality of life that suits them best.
5. To impress upon the children that the use of science and technology has helped us in bringing down the death rate and that the same can help us in bringing down the birth rate as well.
6. To help children realise the socio-economic burden involved in bringing up large families usually resulting in the deterioration in the quality of living.
7. To provide population education its rightful place in the curriculum of the formal as well as the non-formal programme of education.

Scope of population education—Population education included the following:

1. Basic instruction in population dynamics—pattern of population growth.
2. Development of basic understanding of the process of human reproduction.
3. Understanding of health problems associated with child bearing.
4. Appreciation of the relationship between the quality of life of a family and its size.
5. Appreciation of the significance of population characteristics and policies for social and economic development.
6. Familiarity with the population policies and family planning programmes of one's own country.

Population education is not sex education—In the words of D. Gopal Rao, the differences is shown in the following words, "The need for population education mainly arose because of the consequences of the imbalance between the population and world resources. Family life education in the west grew out of the growing evidence of the disintegration of the family, whereas sex education developed as a reaction to an increase in general diseases and out of wedlock pregnancies."

Secondly in sex education, the stress is on the individual whereas in population education, it is the interaction between the individual, family and society.

Problems of imparting population education—Some of the major problems of population education are:

1. Confusion in concept.
2. Shortage of teachers who can impart population education effectively.
3. Prejudice of parents.
4. Lack of suitable planning.
5. Lack of co-ordination among various agencies working in the field of family planning, welfare and education.

Proposed Measures for Popularising Population Education

Population Education not a Separate Subject

Population education is not to be introduced as a separate subject. It has got to be integrated with other subjects; all teachers are expected to be involved in the population programme. Already a good deal of material exists in various school subjects. The only need is to focus attention on the existing material and to present it in such a manner that it attracts the attention of the learners. A large number of activities and projects can also be undertaken in the population education programme. The following examples will illustrate the scope of population education in different subjects.

Languages—Material in the form of stories, essays, blank verses etc. can be incorporated in the language textbooks in the mother tongue, regional language, Hindi and English.

Social studies—Statistics on population education, material on the impact of population explosion on social-economic development of the nation should find place in the social studies.

Mathematics—Problems relating to population growth in reproduction, family planning etc. can studied in science and health education.

Role of the Teachers in Learning Exercises for Population Education

1. Children may compare two families; one with an earning member and five dependants and the other with two earning members and only two dependant young children.
2. They may draw pictures of average Japanese and Indian family and compare them in terms of their size and living conditions or standards of living.
3. Children may collect census figures for their village or town for the past few decades and draw a graph showing the increase or decrease in population.
4. Children may also collect figures of school enrolment for the past few years to draw their inference.
5. Children may collect figures about area and population of countries like Canada, China, United States of America, Brazil, Australia and India and compare them in terms of population, area and average density of population.
6. Similar exercises can be done for a few states in India, such as, Kerala, West Bengal, Bihar, Uttar Pradesh, Tamil Nadu and Rajasthan. They may arrange them as per average density of population.
7. Presenting two or three imaginary monthly budgets of people drawn from lower middle class families with somewhat equal incomes but with varying family size (children can also be asked to collect data).
8. Working out per head income of families with equal income but varying sizes.
9. Finding out broadly the food requirements of our country after 30 years. Holding debates and discussions on how and at what cost can this be achieved.
10. Finding out how additional primary teachers would be required if every year an additional 10 million students join the primary school.
11. Finding out if the population remains steady and no new class is required to be opened in their schools, how can the amount which was otherwise spent on new classes be spent under the new situation.
12. Finding out the total number of doctors we would need in a district if there would be one doctor for every 500 people.

13. Finding out what happens when one new job is created in the school or a village. Also finding out what happens when a person loses his job against his wish.
14. Comparing life in various respects in two families, one with a working woman and the other only a house wife.
15. Finding out the advantages for a family when the mother is educated and that the size of the family is small.
16. Comparing the standards of living in advanced and developing countries. Finding out probable causes that account for vast differences between the two.
17. Children may collect information on four or five families they know in regard to their basic needs of food, clothing, shelter.

(**Note** : Exercises could be graded according to the standard/class. Illustrative aids may be used.)

Population Education Project in India

Realising the potential of education in tackling the problems of growing rate of population; A Population Education Programme was launched with effect from April 1980. The underlying object of the programme is to create in the younger generation, an adequate awareness of the population problems and realisation in this regard of its responsibilities towards the nation.

The Population Education Programme is a plan scheme in the Central Sector of Ministry of Human Resource Development, Government of India. It has been developed in collaboration with the United Nations Funds for Population Active (UNFPA) and with the active involvement of the Ministry of Health and Family Welfare which is the model Ministry of Population Education.

Since the begining of the project in 1980, over 400 booklets/ leaflets, etc. on population education have been brought out in 17 languages of India. Eight types of print visual materials have also been developed. These are: charts, calendars, albums, paintings, picture books, posters, flash charts and wall newspapers.

So far about 12 lakh key resource persons, teacher educations and elementary and secondary teachers have been trained in various programmes of population education.

30.7 Education for Emotional Integration

Meaning and significance of emotional integration—Emotional integration, national integration, national unity, nationalism, patriotism and social integration, by and large, connote the same meaning. The following words of wisdom of the first Prime Minister of India Jawaharlal Nehru, truly reflect the significance and meaning of emotional integration, " In India, the first essential is the maintenance of the unity of the country, not merely a political unity, but a unity of 'mind and heart', which discards the urges which separate and disunite and which breaks down the barriers, which are raised in the name of religion or between state and state or in any other form. It is of the first importance that we should not lose ourselves in the passion and prejudice of the moment. National integration and cohesion is a matter of vital importance to-day. It is the base of all other activities which we try to further."

National integration implies:

A strong feeling of brotherhood in the hearts of all citizens.
A feeling of cohesion.
A feeling of harmony.
A feeling of loyalty to the country.
A feeling of patriotism.
A feeling of oneness.
A feeling of solidarity for the country.
A feeling of tolerance-tolerance of other's beliefs etc.
A feeling of unity of the country.

Why emotional integration—India is a land of so many castes, creeds, faiths and languages etc. As observed by Rabindranath Tagore, "Indian culture is a full-bloomed lotus in whose every petal flows the culture of different types of ardour; if one of the petals is distorted or remains underdeveloped, the beauty of the flower gets impaired." Pt. Nehru has observed, "we should not become parochial, narrow-minded, provincial, communal and caste-minded because we have a great mission to perform. Let us, the citizens of the Republic of India, stand up straight, with straight backs and look up at the skies, keeping our feet firmly planted on the ground and bring about this synthesis, this integration of the Indian People. Political integration has already taken place to some extent, but what I am after is something much deeper than that—emotional integration of the Indian people so that we might be welded into one, and made into one strong national unit, maintaining at the same time all our wonderful diversity."

The Emotional Integration Committee (1961-62) has felt, "one of the hardest problems before us to-day is the building up of a national mind by curbing the religious, linguistic and communal conflicts which tend to disunite us."

It is a matter of great concern that the situation to-day is no better than it was in 1962. In fact it tends to worsen.

Hindrances in emotional integration—Among the chief hindrances in the promotion of ideals of emotional integration, mention may be made of the following: (a) castism (b) classism (c) linguism (d) localism (e) narrow political loyalties and over ambitiousness (f) provincialism (g) regionalism (h) religious fanaticism (i) sectorianism (j) kelfishness (self over society/nation) and (k) untouchability.

The Education Commission 1964-66 pointed out, "The old values which held society together, have been disappearing and as there is no effective programme to replace them by a new sense of social responsibility, innumerable signs of social disorganisation as evident everywhere are continually on the increase. These include strikes, increasing lawlessness, and a disregard for public property, corruption of public life and communal tensions and troubles."

Education and Promotion of Ideals of Emotional Integration

Dr. Radhakrishnan has very clearly stated the role of education in emotional integration as, "If India is to remain free, united and democratic, education should train people for unity and not localism, for democracy and not dictatorship." He further observed, "National integration cannot be built by brick and mortar, it cannot be built by chisel or hammer. It has to grow silently in the minds and hearts of man. The only process is the process of education."

Regarding the role of education, the Emotional Integration Committee (1961) remarked, "Education can play a vital role in strengthening emotional integration. It is felt that education should not only aim at imparting knowledge but should develop all aspects of a student's personality. It should broaden the outlook, foster a feeling of oneness and nationalism and a spirit of sacrifice and tolerance so that narrow group interests are submerged in the larger interests of the country."

Ways and Means of Promoting Emotional Integration: Committee on Emotional Integration

With a view to examining the role of education in emotional integration, the Ministry of Education, Government of India, appointed a committee under the chairmanship of Dr. Sampurnan and in 1961 the committee examined the various facts of education in the promotion of ideals of emotional integration among the students and made the following recommendations:

1. Reorienting the school curriculum to suit the needs of secular India.
2. Organisation of co-curricular activities like the observation and celebration of common festivals and events of national importance, educational tours etc.
3. Emphasising the aspects of the common culture and cementing factors in the teaching of social studies.
4. Recreation of books including material on national feelings.
5. Following an appropriate language policy—use of international numerals and teaching of Hindi in the Non-Hindi areas in the regional script.
6. Having common uniform for school children in the whole of India.
7. Singing of the National Anthem in unison in a disciplined way by children.
8. Showing reverence to the National flag.
9. Celebrating national days.
10. Holding special talks on the unity and oneness of the country.
11. Organising open air dramas.
12. Conducting students exchange and tours.
13. Associating students with school improvement programmes.
14. Admissions to educational institutions on the basis of merits and means and on the basis of caste.
15. Awarding scholarships on the basis of means and merits.
16. Publishing suitable handbooks for teachers
17. Instituting all India awards for the best general essay on different states in India;

18. Producing educational and travel documentaries on various aspects of Indian scenery, flora and fauna.
19. Undertaking school projects on 'Know Your Country and States',
20. Exchanging professors of universities.
21. Setting up an All India Youth Council for co-ordinating youth programmes.
22. Withdrawing recognitions to institutions where divisive tendencies are encouraged.
23. Taking pledges as given below:-

"India is my country, all Indians are my brothers and sisters.

"I love my country, and I am proud of its rich and varied heritage. I shall always strive to be worthy of it.

"I shall give my parents, teachers and all elders respect and treat everyone with courtesy. I shall be kind to animals.

"To my country and my people, I pledge my devotion. In their well-being and prosperity alone lies my happiness."

Recent Educational Programmes for National Integration

1. Setting up of the National Integration Council.
2. Setting up of National Integration Samitis in universities and colleges for the purpose of promoting mutual understanding and appreciation among persons coming from different parts of India. At present there are 105 samitis functioning in the country.
3. Formation of committees composed of members drawn from various fields of national life to act as spearheads for a mass movement in the cause of national integration.
4. Survey of textbooks and elimination of biased and prejudiced material leading to hatred among different communities.
5. Establishing planning foums for disseminating information.
6. Organisation of writers' camps.
7. National integration inter-state student-teacher camps.
8. Celebration of centenaries.
9. Implementing a uniform pattern of education 10+2

Community singing—A national integration project—A national movement has been launched by the Ministry of Human Resource

Development for the promotion of community singing. NCERT has been organising community singing camps for music and musically inclined teachers drawn from different states and Union Territories of the country. Under the scheme every trained teacher is given an illustrated book entitled, 'Let's sing together'. A recorded cassette containing 15 songs in different Indian languages and a tape-recorder in also given to each teacher.

National Policy on Education 1986 and 1992 on National Integration—The National policy envisages suitable steps to foster among students an understanding of the diverse cultural and social systems of people living in different parts of the country. The National System provides for a common core including the history of the Indian freedom movement, the constitutional obligations and other content essential to nurture national identity. These elements cut across subject areas and are designed to promote values such as India's common cultural heritage, egalitarianism, democracy and secularism, equality of the sexes, protection of the environment, removal of social barriers, etc.

Role of the Teachers in Emotional Integration

The entire programme of emotional integration through education primarily depends upon the teachers. In this context, the following are their specific roles:

1. Setting ideal examples of emotional integration through their personal behaviour, ways of thinking and doing things.
2. Presenting historical facts in an impartial manner.
3. Appreciating deeds of honesty and patriotism of great persons belonging to all communities.
4. Emphasising the need for unity in all allied lessons.
5. In Geography, explaining the importance of interdependence of different regions and states.
6. Inculcating a rational attitude.
7. Organising camps, educational tours and exercursions.
8. According equal treatment to all students irrespective of caste or colour etc.

Emotional Integration—A Challenge

"The emotional integration of the Indian people is a challenge that cannot be ignored. Clarity and compassion must be practised if they are not to remain catchwords and empty phrases. Integration touches all points of national life and depends, in the final analysis, on the type of education given to our young people in schools and colleges."

30.8 Education for International Understanding

Indian tradition of universalism and world peace—The following two great Vedic sayings reflect our Indian seers' great breadth of vision and liberal universalism:

'*Mata bhoomihi putro aham prithivya*'. The whole world is our motherland, we are all children of the earth.

'*Ekam brahma viprah bahuda vadanti.*'

God is one, but wise men call Him by different names.

Another example. *Vasudev Kutumbhakam.* The world is a family.

One of the most famous Vedic prayers runs like:

'*Sarve bhavantu sukhinah, sarve santu niramayah,*

Sarve bhadrani pashantu, ma kaschitdukha bhagabhvet'

Let all be happy, let all be healthy,

Let all be gentle, let none have sorrow.

Again according to Indian tradition '*Sakal bhumi gopal ki*'

The entire world is ours.

The Indian seers have also said:

'*Ano bhadra kratu viswatah*'

Let noble thoughts come from all sides.

Meaning of International Understanding

Dr. Walter H.C. Lewis, a former deputy director general of UNESCO in his address to the American Association of Teacher Education in Chicago in 1956 stated, "... International understanding is the ability to observe critically and objectively and appraise the conduct of men everywhere to each other, irrespective of the nationality or culture to which they may belong. To do this one must be able to detach oneself from one's own particular cultural and national prejudices—and to observe men of all nationalities, cultures and races on equally important varieties of human beings inhabiting this earth."

Kenworthy S. Leonard thinks that education for international understanding would, "help children to understand the pride of all peoples for their own group and to develop respect for their feelings. Social scientists call the feeling 'empathy' and consider it among the important attributes to develop."

Why International Understanding!

More interdependence and intimate relationship in the world of today—"Modern scientific means of rapid communications—the radio, the television and telephone—have conquered both space and time. K.G. Saiyidain rightly remarked, "A war starts in Europe and three million people die of famine in Bengal and millions more find themselves up-rooted from their homeland, cut off from their national occupation and deprived of all that makes life pleasant, gracious and meaningful."

In the words of P.E. James, "an industrial society by its essential nature, is global in its scope and international in its needs. If it is to survive it must draw upon all the world's resources and all the world's people must share its benefits. Our way of living is dependent on the co-ordinated economic activities of distant people. This is the concept of one world—of one community of interdependent peoples."

Democratic ideals—'One world', 'one state' has taken the place of the slogan 'my country, right or wrong'. People have begun to realise that all men are equal and all the nations should strive for the betterment of humanity so that all individuals get adequate opportunities to grow and develop.

Longing for world prosperity—The Vedic hymns speak of a world in which all people had a prosperous and happy life. India, true to her ancient traditions, rightly works for international understanding.

The Panchatantra states, "It is the thought of little-minded persons to inquire whether a man is one of ourselves or an alien."

Wrong emphasis on 'my country, right or wrong'—The Secondary Education Commission Report observes, "There is no other more dangerous maxim in the world of today than, 'My country, right or wrong'. The whole world is now so intimately interrelated that no nation can or dare live alone and the development of a sense of world citizenship. In a very real sense, therefore, patriotism is not enough, and it must be supplemented by a lively realisation of the fact that we are all members of one world and must be prepared mentally and emotionally, to discharge the responsibilities which such a membership implies." Nationalism should not degenerate into nationalistic jingoism.

Adjustment of human consciousness—Dr. Radhakrishnan states, "We need today an adjustment of the human consciousness to the nuclear age in which we live. It is now conceivable that the human race may put an end to itself by nuclear warfare or preparations for it. This, if it happens, will be the result of the failure of man's consciousness to adjust itself to the technological revolution."

Progress in art and literature—K.G. Saiyidain writes, "There can neither be health, nor economic prosperity, nor the leisured pursuit of art and literature and culture in a world, that is either plunged in or over-shadowed by war."

Obstructions in the Way of International Understanding

1. Physical barriers. People of different countries live in isolation.
2. Political barriers. Narrow nationalism affecting understanding between nations and nations.
3. Economic barriers. Restrictions on international trade, foreign exchange and currency.
4. Religious barriers. Religious barriers leading to prejudices.
5. Linguistic barriers. Differences of language not allowing people of different linguistic groups to come closer.
6. Psychological barriers. Frustration and fear born of ignorance, selfishness and hostility leading to aggression and war.
7. Educational barriers. Teaching of social studies leading to narrow nationalism and narrow loyalties.

Role of Education in International Understanding and Peace

The UNESCO has very aptly observed in its Preamble, "Since war begin in the minds of men, it is in the minds of men that the defences of peace must be constructed." Education is the best means of constructing defences of peace in the minds of growing children.

The signatories to the United Nations Charter have pledged "to live together in peace with one another as good neighbours, to take effective measures for the removal of areas of differences and to develop friendly relations among nations." It is understood that these ends cannot be achieved without education. This point is made explicit in the Universal Declaration of Human Rights in which it is declared—

"Education shall promote understanding, tolerance and friendship among all nations, racial or religious groups and shall further the activities of the United Nations in the maintenance of peace."

One of the resolutions of UNESCO reads, "Member states of UNESCO in accepting its constitution have agreed that the purpose of the organisation is to contribute to peace and security by promoting collaboration among the nations through education, science and culture in order to promote a universal respect for justice, for the rule of law, for the human rights and fundamental freedoms."

Dr. Radhakrishnan has rightly stated, "There is nothing national with regard to education. The different countries are provinces of a common republic of culture. There is no such thing as Proletarian mathematics or Nazi chemistry or Jewish physics. Culture is international and science is cosmopolitan in its essence and reality."

Functions and Implications of a Programme for International Understanding

Our school programmes for international understanding should enable an individual:

1. To know and understand how people of other lanas live.
2. To recognise the common humanity which underlines all differences in culture.
3. To work for a fair and just world.
4. To maintain an interest in world affairs.
5. To recognise the importance of solving world problems according to democratic practices.
6. To appreciate the contribution of all peoples to the world citizenship.
7. To combine the love of one's country with a broad social consciousness towards an inter-dependent community of nations.

8. To understand the economic, cultural and the like factors which make the world an inter-dependent community of nations.
9. To respect the dignity and worth of man by giving him equality of rights and opportunities.
10. To take the world as one unit.
11. To realise that truth always triumphs and leads to human progress and prosperity.
12. To believe in the common values and goals for the world community.
13. To understand that victories of peace are greater than the victories of war.

Ways and Means of Creating World Understanding

Teaching for world understanding should pervade the whole educational programme—the attitudes of the members of the staff, curricular and co-curricular activities and experiences, of the school. We have to fashion and plan our teaching and learning process in a way that the children can grow with world-mindedness.

Proper interpretation of history—K.G. Saiyidain has said very lucidly that we should reorient our history teaching towards a higher and nobler objective and should bring through it re-education of people's ideas and emotions. The following points may be observed while teaching history:—

1. The history of the countries should be taught objectively.
2. History should be taught with a cultural bias.
3. The impact of technological and scientific techniques on the lives of the different countries of the world should be stressed in the teaching of history.
4. The interdependence of the different countries of the world should be explained in concrete terms.
5. Selected stories from great personalities of the world like Gandhi, Christ, Mohammed, Buddha, Alfred. etc., should be included.
6. Nothing should figure in the textbook of history which may tend to spoil international harmony.
7. Students should be told more and more about international agencies like the UNO and the UNESCO.

Geography—This enables an individual to have a vivid concept of the global scenario in which he can see all parts in terms of the whole and his own country in inter-relationships. The students learn concretely how they depend upon others for the enrichment and happiness of their life. They come to know how geographical situations have affected the environment and the course of history of different countries of the world. They are given a sense of space and location as affecting human actions.

Civics—A survey of certain countries' government, economics, technology, family system, etc., would develop in children "an acceptance of differences and an appreciation of the reasons for culture diversity." The students come to know that the modern civilisation is the result of the cumulative and cooperative effort of many people rather than the product of the genius of one people.

Science and its social implications—Students should be told how scientific discoveries could be made use of for the betterment of human civilisation and how natural resources could be taught for the betterment of the world as a whole. We should stress that the great scientists like Copernicus, Galileo, Newton, Jagdish Chandra Bose etc., belong to the entire world and that they did not work for any particular country.

Philosophy—This also brings forth the fact that human behaviour everywhere is guided by similar innate tendencies.

Psychology—It proves that human behaviour everywhere is guided by similar innate tendencies.

Music—In learning the words and tunes of songs from other countries young children begin to have a sense of the variety or differences in traditional songs and folk music.

Drawing, painting, modelling, handicrafts—These subjects represent the unity of human feeling and thought.

It has been observed in a pamphlet on 'Education for International Understanding' that "a planned programme involving several subjects probably has the most impact and is likely to have the greatest effect in orienting the whole life of a school towards a world outlook."

Co-curricular Activities

Teachers Role in International Understanding

Teachers can develop attitudes favourable to international understanding among their students. Regarding the role of the teacher, C.F. Strong has observed, "he and the curriculum represent two vital formative factors for translating the aims and ideas of education into practice."

Helping students understand the value of international understanding of the curriculum—While teaching various subjects the teachers should concentrate in helping students build up proper behaviour patterns and psychological dispositions impressing upon their minds that barriers of race, colour and distance do not stand in the way of uniting the peoples of different countries

Objective and impartial in their treatment—They should avoid indoctrinating the mind of the pupils. They should be impartial and highly objective in interpreting or describing facts. They should not be propagandists.

They should impress upon the students that, 'man' remains 'man' first and then he can be called a Jew, an Englishman, a German, Russian, Indian and American.

They should impress upon the students that there is no special merit or value in being born in one part or the other.

Well-informed about world situations—They should be well informed about the contemporary world, science and its historical back ground, and concerned about improving the conditions of people everywhere and try to make students well informed.

Activities in the school—They should organise the following kinds of activities in the school to develop an international outlook in the students:

1. UN societies and international clubs.
2. Celebration of social days for heroes of peace and great men of all nations.
3. Enact plays to showing the horrors of war.
4. Encourage student to collect stamps pen-friendships between children of different countries.
5. Debates, lectures and discussions on the working of the U.N.O.

Teacher's role in understanding the child—A UNESCO publication reads as follows, "We hold that in a very real sense, 'wars begin in the minds of men,' that war is a mental disorder strictly analogous with the psychological disease it sometimes causes. Therefore, we regard it as matter of first importance for social and international living that educators should be more concerned with the child, and the healthy development of his body and mind, Than with the contents of the various' subjects which go to make a school curricula."

Faith and enthusiasm for the value of international understanding—Teachers should have faith and enthusiasm for the value of international understanding and co-operation and should possess the equipment to infuse this spirit in the minds of their students.

We may close the topic with a quotation from Leonard S. Kenworthy that "a world-minded teacher is an integrated individual, skilled in the art and science of human relations and conscious of the wide variety of behaviour patterns in the world to which he may have to adjust—an intelligent participant in efforts to improve his own community and nation, mindful of their relationships to the world community, clear in his mind about the goals of education for international understanding."

United Nation Educational Scientific and Cultural Organisation (UNESCO)

UNESCO is one of the specialised agencies of the United Nations. It came into being in 1945. The opening sentence of the constitution of UNESCO is, "since wars begin in the minds of men, it is in the minds of men that the defences of peace must be constructed."

Aims of UNESCO

Article I of UNESCO's constitution states, "The purpose of the organisation is to contribute to peace and security by promoting a collaboration among the nations through education, science and culture in order to further universal respect for the role of law and for human rights and fundamental freedoms which are affirmed for the people of the world, without distinction of race, sex, language or religion, by the character of the United Nations." To achieve this broad aim, three main fields of work are prescribed. The first is to "collaborate in the work of advancing the mutual knowledge and understanding of peoples, through all means of mass communication" and "to work towards the promotion of the free flow of ideas by word and image." The second is to "give a fresh impulse to popular education and to the spread of culture." Finally, UNESCO is to "maintain, increase and diffuse knowledge" by various means, including the conservation of the world's inheritance of learning and culture and the encouragement of co-operation between countries in all branches of intellectual activity.

Programmes of UNESCO

1. It tries to rehabilitate devastated countries culturally.
2. It strives for world peace by taking the following steps:
   - (i) International exchange of teachers and students in order to remove racial prejudice.
   - (ii) The organisation of international camps where students of different nations will meet each other and exchange their views.
   - (iii) Organising tours of foreign countries so as to bring about understanding and goodwill.
   - (iv) Organisation of study circles with a view to studying the needs of other nations.
   - (v) Writing of history books with an international outlook.
   - (vi) Establishment of an international university so as to discuss the common problems of all the nations.
   - (vii) The establishment of an International Civil Service in due course that its employees may render service to the entire universe.
   - (viii) Reorganisation of the press, the radio and the cinema for international welfare.
   - (ix) The reduction of illiteracy especially in backward countries.
   - (x) Translating literary classics and significant contemporary works.
   - (xi) Organising art exhibitions.
   - (xii) Expansion of libraries and museums.
   - (xiii) Fostering international understanding through the improvement of curricula and experimental activities in teacher training institutions.

International Commission for Cooperation with UNESCO

UNESCO has been carrying on its activities through the National Commissions of its state members. The government of India also established the National Commission in 1949. The Commission performs the following activities:.

1. Dissemination of information about the UNESCO and other countries.
2. Celebration of UN Day, Human Rights Day and International literacy year, centenaries, year book, etc.
3. Exchange of persons.
4. Liaison with states and universities.
5. Relations with other national commissions.
6. Publications.
7. Associated school projects.
8. UNESCO International coupon scheme for assisting the import of books.
9. Assisting Indian experts to find UNESCO jobs.
10. UNESCO Clubs.

UNESCO associated school project—There are now over 1,000 schools and teacher training colleges in 61 countries participating in this programme. In 1953 when India joined the programme it started with six institutions which later increased to 37. These schools work on three main themes: (*a*) teaching about the United Nations and its specialised agencies, (*b*) teaching about Human Rights and Fundamental Freedom, and (*c*) teaching about other countries.

UNESCO clubs—The Indian National Commission for UNESCO has been encouraging the establishment of UNESCO clubs/cultural organisations in India to function as the main clearing house to disseminate information about the purpose and programmes of UNESCO, to enlist the support of individuals or groups interested in the fields of education, science, culture and mass communication and to promote and popularise the work of UNESCO.

At present we have about 285 UNESCO clubs/centre is which are functioning at different places in India. Sponsoring and setting up of these centres is a significant trend in the efforts of the Indian National Commission for UNESCO to obtain the support of the maximum number of agencies for the Programme of UNESCO.

30.9 Decentralised Management of Education 1993 (Veerapa Moily Report)

Appointment of the committee—The 73rd and the 74th constitution amendment envisages states will establish a three-tier system of panchayats and municipalities respectively with adequate powers, responsibilities and finances. It is also envisaged that the Panchayat Raj/Municipal bodies have an important role to play in the reconstruction of the education system. To make a detailed analysis of the issue, in July 1993 the Central Advisory Board of Education (CABE), set up a committee under the Chairmanship of Shri M. Veerapa Moily, the Chief Minister of Karnataka, to formulate guidelines on decentralised management.

Major Recommendations of the Committee

1. There should be a panchayat standing committee on education (PEC) at the panchayat level.
2. The PEC should be given statutory powers.
3. The role of the PEC may include generation and sustenance of awareness among the village community. It will also exercise suspervison over early childhood care and education, non-formal education, primary education and adult education programmes in its jurisdiction.
4. The Zilla Parishad may setup its standing Committee on Education as a statutory body.

30.10 Learning without Burden, 1993 (Yash Pal Committee Report)

Background—During the past two decades concern regarding the academic burden on school children and the unsatisfactory quality of learning has been voiced time and again in our country. The question has been discussed extensively by several committees and groups. A new curriculum was introduced in the wake of the implementation of the NPE. With a view to have a fresh look at the problems of education, particularly with regard to the problem of academic burden on students, the Ministry of Human Resource Development, Government of India set up a National Advisory Committee in March 1992 which submitted its recommendations in July 1993. Professor Yash Pal, former chairman U.G.C. was the chairman of this committee.

Major Recommendations of the Committee

1. There is no justification for torturing young children by compelling them to carry heavy bags of books everyday to school.
2. Textbooks should be treated as school property and thus there should be no need for children to purchase the books individually and carry them daily to homes.
3. A separate time-table for the assignment of home work and the use of textbooks be prepared by the school and be known to the children in advance.
4. In the primary classes, children should not be given any homework, save for extension and exploration in the home environment.
5. In the upper primary and seconday classes, homework, where necessary, should be non-textual.
6. An attempt should be made to reduce the existing norms of teacher pupil ratio from 1 : 40 to 1 : 30.
7. Greater use of the electronic media should be made for the creation of a child-centred social ethos in the country.
8. A project team with a number of sub-groups be set up in each state to examine the syllabi and textbooks for all school classes.

30.11 Education for the Twenty-first Century

Appointment of the International Commission on Education for the Twenty-first Century—The report entitled '*Learning the Treasure Within*' (1996) prepared by the ICE set up by UNESCO in 1993 seeks to answer the question 'How to plan for education in the twenty-first century?' The report of the Commission which was chaired by former European Commission President Jacques Delors is the outcome of a worldwide process of consultation and analysis over a period of three years. The Commission included 15 experts from different countries. (Maharaja) Karan Singh from India also served as a member of the Commission.

Expected Scenario of the 21st Century—The Commission visualised the scenario of the 21st century as under:

1. From the local community to a world society.
2. From social cohesion to democratic participation.
3. From economic growth to human development.

Role of Education in the Coming Scenario

Education is expected to be re-engineered as follows:

(i) Education Policy must be sufficiently diversified and must be so designed as not to become another contributory cause of social exclusion.

(ii) The socialization of individuals must not conflict with personal development. It is therefore, necessary to work towards a system that strives to combine the virtues of integration with respect for individual rights.

(iii) Education cannot, on its own, solve the problems raised by the severance (when this happens) of social ties. It can, however, be expected to help to foster the desire to live together, which is a basic component of social cohesion and national identity.

(iv) Schools cannot succeed in this task unless they make their own contribution to the advancement and integration of minority groups by mobilizing those concerned while showing due regard for their personality.

(v) Democracy appears to be progressing, taking forms and passing through stages that fit the situation in each country. Its vitality is nevertheless, constantly threatened. Education for conscious and active citizenship must begin at school.

(vi) Democratic participation is, so to say, a matter of good citizenship, but it can be encouraged or stimulated by instruction and practices adapted to a media and information society. What is needed is to provide reference points and aids to interpretation, so as to strengthen the faculties of understanding and judgement.

(vii) It is the role of education to provide children and adults with the cultural background that will enable them, as far as possible, to make sense of the changes taking place. This presupposes that they are capable of sorting the mass of information so as to interpret it more effectively and place events in a historical perspective.

The Four Pillars of Education—Education throughout life is based on four pillars: learning to know, learning to do, learning to live together and learning to be.

Learning to know, by combining a sufficiently broad general knowledge with the opportunity to work in depth on a small number of subjects. This also means learning to learn, so as to benefit from the opportunities education provides throughout life.

Learning to do, in order to acquire not only an occupational skill but also, more broadly, the competence to deal with many situations and work in teams. It also means learning to do in the context of young peoples' various social and work experiences which may be informal, as a result of the local or national context, or formal, involving courses, alternating study and work.

Learning to live together, by developing an understanding of other people and an appreciation of interdependence — carrying out joint projects and learning to manage conflicts — in a spirit of respect for the values of pluralism, mutual understanding and peace.

Learning to be, so as to develop better one's personality and be able to act with ever greater autonomy, judgement and personal responsibility. In that connection, education must not disregard any aspect of a person's potential: memory, reasoning, aesthetic sense, physical capacities and communication skills.

Role of Formal Education and Learning Throughout Life—Formal Education Systems tend to emphasize the acquisition of knowledge to the detriment of other types of learning; but it is vital now to conceive education in a more encompassing fashion. Such a vision should inform and guide future educational reforms and policies, in relation both to contents and methods.

The concept of learning throughout life is the key that gives access to the twenty-first century. It goes beyond the traditional distinction between initial and continuing education. It links up with another concept often put forward, that of the learning society, in which everything affords an opportunity of learning and fulfilling one's potential.

In its new guise, continuing education is seen as going far beyond what is already practised, particularly in the developed countries, i.e. upgrading, with refresher training, retraining and conversion or promotion courses for adults. It should open up opportunities for learning for all, for many different purposes, offering them a second or third chance, satisfying their desire for knowledge and beauty or their desire to surpass themselves, or making it possible to broaden and deepen strictly vocational forms of training, including practical training.

In short, 'learning throughout life' must take advantage of all the opportunities offered by society.

Directions

1. *From Basic Education to University*

(i) A requirement valid for all countries, albeit in various forms and with different types of content — the strengthening of basic education: hence the emphasis on primary education and its traditional basic programmes — reading, writing, arithmetic — but also on the ability to express oneself in a language that lends itself to dialogue and understanding.

(ii) The need, which will be still greater tomorrow, for receptivity to science and the world of science, which opens the door to the twenty-first century with its scientific and technological upheavals.

(iii) The adaptation of basic education to specific contexts, the most deprived countries contexts, the most deprived countries as well as the most deprived section of the population, starting out with the facts of everyday life, which affords opportunities for understanding natural phenomena and for different forms of socialization.

(iv) The pressing needs of literacy work and basic education for adults are to be kept in mind.

(v) In all cases, emphasis is to be placed on pupil-teacher relations since the most advanced technologies can be no more than a back-up to the relationship (transmission, dialogue and confrontation) between teacher and pupil.

(vi) Secondary education must be rethought in this general context of learning throughout life. The key principle is to arrange for a variety of individual paths through schooling, without ever closing the door on the possibility of a subsequent return to the education system.

(vii) Debates on selection and guidance would be greatly clarified if this principle was fully applied. Everyone would then feel that whatever the choice made or the courses followed in adolescene, no doors would ever be closed in the future, including the doors of the school itself. Equality of opportunity would then really mean what it says.

(viii) Universities should be central to the higher level of the system, even if, as is the case in many countries, there are other, non-university establishments of higher education.

(ix) Universities would have vested in them four key functions:

(a) To prepare students for research and teaching.

(b) To provide highly specialized training courses adapted to the needs of economic and social life.

(c) To be open to all, so as to cater to the many aspects of lifelong education in the widest sense.

(d) International co-operation.

(x) The universities should also be able to speak out on ethical and social problems as entirely independent and fully responsible institutions exercising a kind of intellectual authority that society needs to help it to reflect, understand and act.

(xi) The diversity of secondary schooling and the possibilities afforded by universities should provide a valid answer to the challenges of mass education by dispelling the obsession with a one-and-only educational 'king's highway'. Combined with more widespread application of the practice of alternating periods of education with periods of work, these approaches can provide effective tools for fighting against school failure. The extension of learning throughout life will require consideration of new procedures for certification that take account of acquired competences.

2. Teachers in Search of New Perspectives

(a) While the psychological and material situation of teachers differs greatly from country to country, an upgrading of their status is essential if 'learning throughout life' is to fulfil the central function assigned to it by the Commission in the advancement of our societies and the strengthening of mutual understanding among peoples. Their position as master or mistress in the classroom should be recognized by society and they should be given the necessary authority and suitable resources.

(b) The concept of learning throughout life leads straight on to a learning society, a society that offers many and varied opportunities of learning, both at school and in economic, social and cultural life, whence the need for more collaboration and partnerships with families, industry and business, voluntary associations, people active in cultural life, etc.

(c) Teachers are also concerned with the imperative requirement to update knowledge and skills. Their professional lives should be so methodical as to accommodate the opportunity, or even the obligation, for them to become more proficient in their art and to benefit from periods of experience in various spheres of economic, social and cultural life. Such possibilities are usually provided for in the many forms of study leave or sabbatical leave. These formula, suitably adapted, should be extended to all teachers.

(d) Even though teaching is essentially a solitary activity, in the sense that each teacher is faced with his or her own responsibilities and professional duties, team work is essential, particularly at the secondary level, in order to improve the quality of education and adapt it more closely to

(e) The Commission stresses the importance of exchanges of teachers and partnerships between institutions in different countries. As is confirmed by current activities, such exchanges and partnerships provide an essential added value not only for the quality of education but also for a greater receptivity to other cultures, civilizations and experiences.

(f) All these lines of emphasis should be the subject of a dialogue, or even of contracts, with teachers' organizations which go beyond the purely corporatist nature of such forms of collaboration; over and above their aims of defending the moral and material interests of their members, teachers' organizations have built up a fund of experience which they are willing to make available to policy-makers.

3. Choices for Education: the Political Factor

Choosing a type of education means choosing a type of society. In all countries, such choices call for extensive public debate, based on an accurate evaluation of education systems. The Commission invites the political authorities to encourage such debate, in order to reach a democratic consensus, this being the best route to success for educational reform strategies.

4. International Co-operation: Educating the Global Village

The need for international co-operation-which itself has to be radically re-thought-is also felt in the field of education. This is an issue not only for education policy-makers and the teaching profession but for all who play an active part in community life.

Questions and Problems

A. Essay-Type Questions

1. "National integration is vital for India's Survival." Explain briefly what educational programmes you suggest to bring about emotional and national integration?
2. State the disruptive forces which are striking at the roots of emotional integration. How can their effects be counteracted through education?
3. What is the meaning of the concept of international understanding? How can education help in educating for international understanding?
4. What is the role of education in the promotion of values of international understanding. State how teachers can play an effective role in the context.
5. "My country right or wrong". Explain this briefly and point out the role of education in developing international understanding.
6. Write an essay on the language problem of India.
7. Explain the main features of the three language formula. Are you in its favour? State reasons in support of your answer.
8. State the magnitude of the problem of unemployment and especially of the educated unemployed. What are its contributory factors? State measures for solving this problem.
9. How do we categorise deprived sections? Suggest measures for the speedy promotion of their education.
10. What is the meaning of environment and its pollution? State the role of education in improving environment.
11. What is environmental education? What are its objectives? Elucidate the role of the teacher in environmental education.
12. "Morality is caught and not taught." Explain the significance of this statement and suggest a suitable programme of moral education.
13. What is value education? How can it be organised in school?

14. Explain the relationship between moral education and religious education.
15. What are the educational implications of population explosion? Give the meaning of population education. How can it be imparted effectively in schools?
16. State the role of a teacher in moral education, environmental education and population education.

B. Short-Answer Type Questions

17. Briefly describe the role of pressure groups and voluntary organisations in environmental education and protection.
18. List a few values which are common to all religions.
19. Classify values.
20. Population education is not family planning and sex education. Explain this statement.
21. List a few activities related to population education.
22. Write notes on (i) Learning without burden (heavy school bag); (ii) Decentralised management of education.
23. Why was the Samparnanand Committee appointed? Describe its recommendations.
24. State the type of education needed to meet the challenges of the 21st century.

Part V

Recent Developments in Education

31 Census of India 2001: Literacy and Education

31.1 Introduction

The data made available by the Census of India 2001. conducted in Feb.-Mar., 2001 would go a long way in the Socio-Economic development of the country. Here our scope is limited to literacy and education.

Literacy and education are the two most important indicators of development of a nation. Higher levels of literacy and education act as a catalyst for cultural, economic, political and social development.

The Literacy rates obtained at the census give a reflection of the government policies and programmes. Table 31.1 provides comparative data on literacy since independence.

Table 31.1

Literacy Rate in India (1951 to 2001)

Census Year	*Persons*	*Males*	*Females*	*Male-female gap in literacy rate*
1	2	3	4	5
1951	18.33	27.16	8.86	18.30
1961	28.30	40.40	15.35	25.05
1971	34.45	45.96	21.98	23.98
1981	43.57	56.38	29.76	26.62
1991	52.21	64.13	39.29	24.84
2001	65.38	75.85	54.16	21.69

Notes :

1. Literacy rates for 1951, 1961 and 1971 Censuses relate to population aged five years and above. The rates for the 1981, 1991 and 2001 Census relate to the population aged seven years and above.
2. The 1981 literacy rates exclude Assam where the 1981 Census could not be conducted. The 1991 Census Literacy rates exclude Jammu & Kashmir where the 1991 Census could not be conducted due to disturbed conditions.
3. The 2001 Census, literacy rates exclude entire Kachchh district, Morvi, Maliya-Miyana and Wankaner talukas of Rajkot district, Jodiya taluka of Jamnagar district of Gujarat State and entire Kinnaur district of Himachal Pradesh where population enumeration of Census of India, 2001, could not be conducted due to natural calamities.

The literacy rates for the country as a whole in 2001 work out to 65.38 per cent for the population aged seven years and over. The corresponding figures for the males and females are 75.85 and 54.16 per cent respectively. Thus three-fourth of the males and more than half of the females aged seven years and above are literate in the country to-day. However, this figure is far below the several countries which have nearly 98 per cent literacy.

The literacy rates in Table 31.1 for the 1951, 1961 and 1971 Census relate to the population aged five years and above, those for the 1981, 1991 and 2001 relate to the population seven years and above.

As compared with the literacy rated of 1991 there has been a jump of 13.7 per cent points from 52.21 to 65.38 in 2001.

While male literacy rates increased by 11.72 per cent (from 64.13 to 75.85), female literacy rates increased by 14.87 (from 39.29 to 54.16 per cent) during the period 1991 to 2001. Nevertheless there is still a gap of 21.69 per cent between the literacy rates of male and females.

Table 31.2 presents the number of literates and illiterates among population aged 7 years and above the their difference between 1991 and 2001. The total number of illiterates has come down from 328,167,228 in 1991 to 296,208,952.

Table 31.2

Number of Literates and Illiterates Among Population Aged 7 Years and above and their Change—India: 1991 to 2001

Literates/Illiterates	*Persons*	*Males*	*Females*
Literates			
1991	358,402,626	228,983,134	129,419,492
2001	562,010,743	336,969,695	25,041,048
Increase in 2001over 1991	203,608,117	107,986,561	95,621,556
Illiterates			
1991	328,187,288	128,099,211	200,068,077
2001	296,208,952	106,654,066	189,554,886
Decrease in 2001 over 1991	31,958,336	21,445,145	10,513,191

Notes:

1. To make the data comparable shown against literates for the 1991 and 2001, the corresponding figures for Jammu and Kasmir have not been included in both the years as the data for 1991 Census for Jammu and Kashmir is not available because the 1991 Census could not be conducted in this state due to disturbed conditions.
2. To make the date comparable the figures of literates and illiterates shown against 1991 and 2001 do not include the figures for entire district of Kachchh, Morvi, Maliya-Miyana and Wankaner talukas of Rajkot district, Jodiya taluka of Jamnagar district of Gujarat State of entire Kinnaur district of Himachal Pradesh where population enumeration of Census of India 2001, could not be conducted due to natural calamities.

Table 31.3

State and Union Territory Statewise Literacy Rates and Percentage Increase During 1991-2001

State	*Literacy Rates*		*% Increase*
	1991	*2001*	
1. A&N Islands	73.02	81.18	8.16
2. Andhra Pradesh	44.09	61.11	17.02
3. Arunachal Pradesh	41.59	54.74	13.15

(*Contd.*)

4.	Assam	52.89	64.28	11.39
5.	Bihar	38.48	47.53	9.05
6.	Chandigarh	75.51	81.76	6.25
7.	Chhattisgarh	—	65.18	—
8.	Dadra & N. Haveli	40.71	60.03	19.32
9.	Daman & Diu	71.20	81.09	9.89
10.	Delhi	75.29	81.82	6.53
11.	Goa	75.51	82.32	6.81
12.	Gujarat	61.29	69.97	8.68
13.	Haryana	55.85	68.59	12.74
14.	Himachal Pradesh	63.86	77.13	13.27
15.	Jammu & Kashmir	—	54.46	—
16.	Jharkhand		54.13	—
17.	Karnataka	56.04	67.04	11.00
18.	Kerala	89.81	90.92	1.11
19.	Lakshadweep	81.78	87.52	5.74
20.	Madhya Pradesh	44.20	64.11	19.91
21.	Maharashtra	64.87	77.27	12.40
22.	Manipur	59.89	68.87	8.98
23.	Meghalaya	49.10	63.31	14.21
24.	Mizoram	82.27	88.49	6.22
25.	Nagaland	61.65	67.11	5.46
26.	Orissa	49.09	63.61	1452
27.	Pondicherry	74.74	81.49	6.75
28.	Punjab	58.51	69.95	11.44
29.	Rajasthan	38.55	61.03	22.48
30.	Sikkim	56.94	69.68	12.74
31.	Tamil Nadu	62.66	73.47	10.81
32.	Tripura	60.44	73.66	13.22
33.	Uttar Pradesh	41.60	57.36	15.76
34.	Uttaranchal	—	72.28	—
35.	West Bengal	57.70	69.22	11.52
	INDIA	52.21	65.38	13.17

Table 31.4

Literacy Rates in States and Union Territories by Sex and Rank (2001)

Rank	Persons		Males		Females	
	India/States/Union Territories*	Literacy rate	India/States/Union Territories*	Literacy rate	India/States/Union Territories*	Literacy rate
1	2	3	4	5	6	7
1.	Kerala	90.92	Kerala	94.20	Kerala	87.86
2.	Mizoram	88.49	Lakshadweep*	93.15	Mizoram	86.13
3.	Lakshadweep*	87.32	Mizoram	90.69	Lakshadweep*	81.56
4.	Goa	82.32	Pondicherry*	88.89	Chandigarh*	76.65
5.	Delhi*	81.82	Goa	88.88	Goa	75.51
6.	Chandigarh*	81.76	Daman & Diu*	88.40	A&N Islands*	75.29
7.	Pondicherry*	81.49	Delhi*	87.37	Delhi*	75.00
8.	A & N Islands*	81.18	Maharashtra	86.27	Pondicherry*	7413
9.	Daman & Diu	81.09	A & N Island*	8607	Daman & Diu*	70.37
10.	Maharashtra	77.27	Himachal Pradesh	86.02	Himachal Pradesh	68.08
11.	Himachal Pradesh	77.13	Chandigarh*	85.65	Maharashtra	67.51
12.	Tripura	73.66	Uttaranchal	84.01	Tripura	65.41
13.	Tamil Nadu	73.47	Tamil Nadu	82.33	Tamil Nadu	64.55
14.	Uttaranchal	72.28	Tripura	81.47	Punjab	63.55
15.	Gujarat	69,97	Gujarat	80.50	Nagaland	61.92

(*Contd.*)

16.	Punjab	69.95	Haryana	79.25	Sikkim	61.46
17.	Sikkim	69.68	Manipur	77.87	Meghalaya	60.41
18.	West Bengal	69.22	Chhattisgarh	77.86	Uttaranchal	60.26
19.	Manipur	68.87	West Bengal	77.58	West Bengal	60.22
20.	Haryana	68.87	Madhya Pradesh	76.80	Manipur	59.70
21.	Nagaland	67.11	Sikkim	76.73	Gujarat	58.60
22.	Karnataka	67.04	Rajasthan	76.46	Karnataka	57.45
	INDIA[1]	65.38	Karnataka	76.46	Haryana	56.31
23.	Chhattisgarh	65.18	Orissa	75.95	Assam	56.03
24.	Assam	64.28	INDIA	75.85	INDIA	54.16
25.	Madhya Pradesh	64.11	Punjab	75.63	Chhattisgarh	52.40
26.	Orissa	63.61	Dadra & Nagar Haveli*	73.32	Andhra Pradesh	51.17
27.	Meghalaya	63.31	Assam	71.93	Orissa	50.97
28.	Andhra Pradesh	61.11	Nagaland	71.77	Madhya Pradesh	50.28
29.	Rajasthan	61.03	Andhra Pradesh	70.85	Rajasthan	44.34
30.	Dadra & Nagar Haveli	60.03	Uttar Pradesh	70.23	Arunachal Pradesh	44.24
31.	Uttar Pradesh	57.36	Jharkhand	67.94	Dadra & Nagar Haveli*	42.99
32.	Arunachal Pradesh	54.74	Meghalaya	66.14	Uttar Pradesh	42.98
33.	Jammu & Kashmir	54.46	Jammu & Kashmir	65.75	Jammu & Kashmir	41.82
34.	Jharkhand	54.13	Arunachal Pradesh	64.07	Jharkhand	39.38
35.	Bihar	47.53	Bihar	60.32	Bihar	33.57

Note:

1. The Literacy rates for India have been worked out by excluding entire Kachchh district, Morvi, Maliya-Miyana land Wankaner talukas or Rajkot district, Jodiya taluka of Jamnagar district of Gujarat State and entire Kinnaur district of Himachal Pradesh.

32 Cultural, Educational and Socio-Economic Profile of North-Eastern Region

Chief Characteristics of North-Eastern Region

The North-Eastern Region of India comprises the seven sister states Arunachal Pradesh, Assam, Manipur, Meghalaya, Mizoram, Nagaland and Tripura. Focusing on the North-East Region, it is observed that barring Assam, most of the states are late comers in the process of development as they were created subsequent to the first decade of planning. Nagaland was created in 1963; Manipur, Meghalaya and Tripura in 1972; Arunachal Pradesh and Mizoram in 1987. On account of geographical and political reasons, this region is considered one of the most sensitive regions of India.

At the time of independence in 1947, almost the entire North-East was in the Assam Province and administered from its capital at Shillong.

The North-Eastern region is endowed with rich natural resources. It is, however, economically backward with intra-regional disparities in levels of development. The states of the region have several common characteristics like physical, social and cultural patterns including also areas of tribal concentration, hill areas and chronically flood affected areas. Other characteristics are: high rurality, agricultural predominance, industrial backwardness and presence of a very high proportion of unorganised labour. Physiographically, the region is not a homogeneous unit at all and about 60 per cent of it is mountainous, 13 per cent plateaus and 27 per cent plains.

The seven sister states of North-East spread over 2,55,153 sq.km (12 per cent of the total land surface of India) had a population of about 39 million in 2001. The region has boundaries with Bangladesh, Myanmar, Tibet and China. The influx of Bangladeshi immigrants into this region has led to serious demographic and electoral imbalance.

Currently this region is going through a transition involving a quantum jump over many intermediate stages of its historical and socio-political evolution. The jump is from subsistence economy to the high grade competitive consumerism, from ethnic tribal loyalties to modern bourgeois democracy based on adult and universal franchise, from tribal chieftainship to semicapitalist state and from isolated hamlet and village economy to high velocity market forces.

THE NORTH-EASTERN COUNCIL

The North-Eastern Council established in the year 1971 is an apex body under the special provision of the Indian Parliament. It looks after the problems of development in this relatively sensitive region and has a crucial role to play in bringing diverse nationalities together and inspire them to participate in the national main stream.

The constitution of North-Eastern Council clearly recognizes its integrated regional development approach through regional planning and development of economic infrastructure such as interstate roads, extension of railways into interior areas, power supply, flood control measures, upgradtion of production technology, jhum cultivation control, settled cultivation and forest conservation etc.

The Council consists of the heads of states, namely the governors of the seven political units of the region and the Chief Ministers of all the seven states. The Council is an advisory body and it serves as an institutional mechanism of cooperation and coordination among different political units of the region.

EDUCATIONAL POLICY BEFORE INDEPENDENCE

Till towards the end of the 19th century, the educational policy in the hills was dominated and guided by the missionaries. In fact, for all practical purposes, education was in the hands of missionaries. The government took no educational measures. Textbooks on Vernacular subjects in the schools in the Khasi and Jaintia Hills were mostly written and published by the missionaries of the Welsh Mission and contained several lessons on Christanity and western culture. There were some lessons which decried other religious faiths. Books in Khasi written by Khasi nationalists containing lessons on Khasi culture were secluded from the prescribed curriculum. The Headmaster of the Government Boy's High School–the only High school for the hill boys from all the then hill districts of the then Province of Assam was invariably a Welsh missionary of the Welsh Mission.

Following are the significant landmarks in education from 1835 to 1947 :

1. As in the rest of the country, system of education as advocated by Lord Macaulay in 1835 bacame the corner stone of the educational policy. Macaulay advocated the supremacy of English and the European knowledge.
2. The Despatch of 1854 popularly known as Wood's Despatch after the name of Charles Wood, the President of the Board of Control, became a landmark in the history of education in India. It was made very clear that the object of education was the diffusion of European knowledge.
3. The establishment of Universities in the 1857 was the third landmark in the English system of education in India.
4. The Hunter Commission of 1882 anticipated a diversified instruction at the secondary stage of education.
5. The University Commission 1902 stipulated that the secondary schools had to be recognised by the universities.
6. Gokhale's resolution (1913-14) on compulsory primary education was rejected in the Imperial Council but it focused on primary education.
7. The Sadler Commission or the Calcutta University Commission (1917) made a very comprehensive study of education from the secondary stage to the university.
8. The Hartog Committee Report (1929) defined the concept of wastage and stagnation in primary education and suggested remedies.
9. Abbot Wood Report (1936-37) made recommendations on general and technical education.
10. The Wardha Report on Basic Education (1937) worked out the details of the education system as advocated by Gandhiji.
11. The Sargent Report (1944) prepared a plan for the post-war educational development in India.

It is believed by several thinkers that the introduction of the English language led to the opening of the doors of the West to the East. At the same time it is held by several scholars that the English system of education led to a vast army of educated unemployed people in India.

The Progress of States of the North-Eastern Region in Education

Literacy. Mizroram has the highest literacy rate (88.49) and Arunachal Pradesh the least (54.74). Of course out of 7 states, 5 have higher literacy rate than the national average. In female literacy rate, 6 states are above the national average.

Significantly, in the case of literacy among the Scheduled Tribes, all the 7 states higher ranks than the national average.

Tribal women literacy. It is of interest to observe the Mizoram records the highest percentage of literacy among tribal women in the country, (78.70%), followed by Lakshadweep (71.72%). The male literacy rate in Mizoram (86.66%) is about 8% higher than the female literacy rate, This difference is about 10% in the case of Kerala. Female literacy rate among Scheduled Tribes in States of Andhra Pradesh, Bihar, Madhya Pradesh, Orissa, Rajasthan and Uttar Pradesh among others is below 20 per cent. (1991 figures)

Enrolment ratios. Enrolment ratios at the primary stage (class I-V) are higher in six states out of seven in the North-East region, than the national average. In the case of enrolment of girls at this stage, all the 7 states record higher enrolment that the national average. At the middle stage (classes VI-VIII), all states are above the national average. (Table 32.3)

Enrolment ratios of students belonging to Scheduled Tribes at the primary stage are higher than the overall enrolment ratios at the national level.

Drop-out rates. Baring Nagaland, drop-out rates in other states at the primary stage are lower than the national average. At the middle stage, excepting Nagaland and Meghalaya all the other 5 states, show lower figures than the national average. Overall drop-out rates for classes I to X, reflect the same pattern.

Teacher-Pupil ratio. Teacher-pupil ratio is quite favourable at all the school stages in the North-East region as compared with the All India level.

Trained Teachers. As regards trained teachers situation in NER is very depressing. At the primary stage, it varies from 19 per cent to 38 per cent (National Average 90 per cent). Likewise at the middle, high and higher secondary stages, situation is quite alarming.

Expenditure on Education. The per capita budgeted expenditure, barring Assam, is higher in all the States than the national level.

Number of Educational Institution. Table 32.2 reflects the member of educational institutions from the primary to the university stage in all the 7 states in the region.

Demographic Date. The most notable feature is the predominance of the Scheduled Tribe population in the region. The population of STs is as high as 95 per cent in Mizoram. It exceeds 85 per cent in Meghalaya and Nagaland. Assam is the only exception with about 12 per cent STs population

Primary Schools in Rural Habitation. The percentage of rural habitations served by primary (77.87), Assam (88.64), Meghalaya (87.97), Tripura (85.00) and Sikkim (83.44).

Single Teacher School. The percentage of single teacher primary schools is higher than national average of 20.12 Arunachal Pradesh (45.46), Assam (20.90) and Meghalaya (37.13).

Drinking Water and other Facilities. The percentage of total schools having drinking water facilities in rural areas is lower than the national average of 47.98, in all the seven states. The percentage of total schools having toilets in rural areas is lower than the national average of 12.76, Assam (4.02), Meghalaya (5.47), Nagaland (10.84) and Tripura (8.57).

The percentage of total schools having separate toilets for girls is lower than the national average of 6.43, in Arunachal Pradesh (5.57), Assam (1.35), Meghalaya (2.38) and Tripura (2.30).

Technical Education. The Central Government has set up an IIT at Guwahati, one Regional engineering College at Silchar and the North-Eastern Regional Institute of Science and Technology (NERIST) at Itanagar as joint ventures. Besides this, about 600 seats at the degree level and 300 seats at the diploma level have been reserved in various engineering colleges and polytechnics in India for the students of the North-Eastern States.

Table 32.1

Literacy Rates in North-Eastern Region (2001)

S.No.	*State*	*Total*	*Male*	*Female*
1.	Arunachal Pradesh	54.74	64.07	44.24
2.	Assam	64.28	71.93	56.03
3.	Manipur	68.87	77.87	59.70
4.	Meghalaya	63.31	66.14	60.41
5.	Mizoram	88.49	90.69	86.13
6.	Nagaland	67.11	77.77	61.92
7.	Tripura	73.66	81.47	65.41
	INDIA	65.38	75.85	54.16

Table 32.2

Number of Recognised Educational Institutions in North-Eastern Region (2004-2005)

S.No.	*State*	*Primary/ Junior Basic Schools*	*Middle/ Senior Basic Schools*	*High/ Hr. Sec/ Interme-diate/ Pre-Degree Jr. Colleges*	*Colleges for General Education*	*Colleges for Professi-onal Education*	*Universities/ Deemed Universities/ Institutes of National Importance*
1.	Arunachal Pradesh	1371	495	214	9	1	2
2.	Assam	30068	8143	5374	341	45	13
3.	Manipur	2552	831	706	60	10	2
4.	Meghalaya	5851	1759	711	49	5	1
5.	Mizoram	1481	939	512	29	1	1
6.	Nagaland	1520	480	379	42	3	1
7.	Tripura	1776	1001	652	15	6	1
INDIA	7675210	274731	152043	12751	5179	—	350

Table 32.3

Gross Enrolment Ratio in Classes I-V and VI-VIII and I-VIII in North Eastern Region Vis-a-Vis all India (2004-05)

S.No.	States/ Unlon Territorries	2004-2005								
		Classes I-V (6-11 yrs)			*Classes VI-VIII (11-14 yrs)*			*Classes I-VIII (6-14 yrs)*		
		Boys	*Girls*	*Total*	*Boys*	*Girls*		*Boys*	*Girls*	*Total*
1	2	3	4	5	6	7	8	9	10	11
1.	Andhra Pradesh	96.05	97.40	96.71	73.73	69.68	71.76	87.32	86.64	86.99
2.	Arunachal Pradesh	129.95	115.90	123.12	81.75	69.16	75.53	113.47	99.63	106.70
3.	Assam	105.59	104.80	105.20	72.05	67.22	69.70	92.99	90.81	91.92
4.	Manipur	154.41	148.88	151.69	97.72	91.53	94.69	132.45	126.75	129.65
5.	Meghalaya	145.34	149.95	147.62	72.08	80.96	76.45	118.78	125.17	121.93
6.	Mizoram	132.25	122.71	127.53	82.19	81.33	81.77	112.47	106.47	109.51
7.	Nagaland	88.68	87.15	87.94	55.68	55.50	55.60	76.23	75.26	75.76
8.	Tripura	133.67	128.26	131.03	80.65	75.55	78.16	112.14	106.92	109.59
	INDIA	110.70	104.67	107.80	74.30	65.13	69.93	96.91	89.87	93.54

Source: Selected Educational Statistics, 2004-05, Ministry of Human Resource Development, Government of India.

33 Recent Developments and Initiatives in Education in India

I. Modification in the National Policy on Education (1992)

Reasons for the Modification of 1986 NPE

It was stipulated in the NPE (1986) that the implementation of the policy would be reviewed every five years. Accordingly to NPE was modified in 1992 and the Programme of Action 1992 was formulated for its implementation.

MAJOR ORIGINAL PROVISIONS AND REVISED POLICY CHANGES

National System on Education (1986)

NPE 1986 Para 3.3

The National System on Education envisages a common educational structure. The 10+2+3 structure has now been accepted in all parts of the country. Regarding the further break-up of the first 10 years efforts will be made to mover towards an elementary system comprising 5 years of primary education and 3 years of upper primary, followed by 2 years of High School.

Revised NPE, 1992, Para 3.3

The National System of Education envisages a common educational structure. The 10+2+3 structure has now been accepted in all parts of the country. Regarding the further break-up of the first 10 years efforts will be made to mover towards an elementary system comprising 5 years of primary education and 3 years of upper primary, followed by

2 years of High School. Efforts will also be made to have the +2 stage accepted as a part of school education throughout the country.

Elementary Education

NPE, 1986, Para 5.5

The new thrust in elementary education will emphasise two aspects: (i) universal enrolment and universal retention of children up to 14 years of age, and (ii) a substantial improvement in the quality of education.

Revised NPE, 1992, Para 5.5

The new thrust in elementary education will emphasise two aspects: (i) universal access and enrolment, (ii) universal retention of children up to 14 years of age; and (iii) a substantial improvement in the quality of education to enable all children to achieve essential levels of learning.

A Resolve

NPE, 1986, Para 5.12

The New Educational Policy will give the highest priority to solving the problem of children dropping out of school and will adopt an array of meticulously formulated strategies based on micro-planning, and applied at the grassroots level all over the country, to ensure children's retention at school. This effort will be fully coordinated with the network of non-formal education. It shall be ensured that all children who attain the age of about 11 years by 1990 will have had five years of schooling, or its equivalent through the non-formal stream. Likewise, by 1995 all children will be provided free and compulsory education up to 14 years of age.

Revised NPE, 1992, Para 5.12

The New Educational Policy will give the highest priority to solving the problem of children dropping out of school and will adopt an array of meticulously formulated strategies based on micro-planning, and applied at the grassroots level all over the country, to ensure children's retention at school. This effort will be fully coordinated with the network of non-formal education. It shall be ensured that free and compulsory education of satisfactory quality is provided to all children up to 14 years of age before we enter the twenty-first century. A national mission will be launched for this purpose.

Vocationalisation

NPE, 1986, Para 5.23

It is proposed that vocational courses cover 10 per cent of higher secondary students by 1990 and 25 per cent by 1995. Steps will be taken to see that a substantial majority of the products of vocational courses are employed or become self-employed. Review of the course offered would be regularly undertaken. Government will also review its recruitment policy to encourage diversification at the secondary level.

Revised NPE, 1992, Para 5.23

It is proposed that vocational courses cover 10 per cent of higher secondary students by 1995 and 25 per cent by 2000. Steps will be taken to see that a substantial majority of the products of vocational courses are employed or become self-employed. Review of courses offered would be regularly undertaken. Government will also review its recruitment policy to encourage diversification at the secondary level.

II. Elementary Education

Following are the major initiations in this regard:

1. Amendment in the constitution.
2. Sarva Shiksha Abhiyan (SSA)
3. Mid-day Meal Scheme/National Programme of Nutritional Support to Primary Education (NPNSPE).
4. Education guarantee scheme and Alternative and Innovative Education (ECG and AGE).
5. District Primary Education Programme (DPEP).
6. Mahila Samakhya Scheme (MSS)
7. Prarambhik Shiksha Kosh.
8. Kasturba Gandhi Balika Vidyalaya Scheme (KCBVS).

1. Amendment in the Constitution

The constitution of India which came into force on January 26, 1950, envisaged that by 1960 all children would be provided free and compulsory education until they complete the age of Fourteen years. However, in spite of vigorous efforts, the target could not be achieved. It great concern was expressed in several quarters. The Apex Court also showed great concern. It observed in one of its judgements that right to education may be included in the category of Fundamental Right.

Accordingly, the Parliament made the following amendments, in the constitution in 2002.

(1) A new Article 21 A was inserted to provide for free and compulsory education to all children of the age of 6-14 years in such a manner as the State, by law determine.

(2) A new change (k) in Article 51 A relating to 'Fundamental Duties was included. It shall be the duty of every citizen who is a parent or guardian to provide opportunities for education to his child, or as the case be a ward between the age of 6-14 years.

2. Sarva Shiksha Abhiyan (SSA)

Objective the scheme was launched in 2001 with the objective of providing useful and relevant elementary education for all children in the 6-14 age group by 2010 *Targets*. The targets of the SSA are as under:

(1) All children in the age group 6-14 to be in School/Education Guarantee Scheme (EGS) Cente/Bridge course by 2005.

(2) Bridge all gender and social category gaps at the primary stage by 2007 and at the elementary stage by 2010.

(3) Universal retention by 2010.

(4) Focus on elementary education of satisfactory quality with emphasis on education for life.

Special Focus

The programme covers the entire country with special focus on educational needs of girls, SCs/STs and other children in difficult circumstances. The programme seeks to open new schools in those place which do not have schooling facilities and strengthen existing school infrastructure through provision of additional class rooms, toilets, drinking water, maintenance grant and school improvement grant. SSA has a special focus on girls and children of weaker sections. A number of initiatives, including distribution of free textbooks, targeting these children is under the programme. The SSA also seeks to provide computer education even in the rural areas.

Financial Assistance

It is a centrally sponsored scheme. The assistance under the programme of Sarva Shiksha Abhiyan was on a 85 : 15 sharing arrangement during the Ninth Plan, 75 : 25 sharing arrangement during the Tenth Plan and 50 : 50 sharing thereafter between the Central Government and the State Government except for 8 NE states, where 15 per cent of the state there met by Ministry of DONER far the two years 2005-06 and 2006-07.

Coverage

Since the inception of the scheme nearly 1.81 lakh new schools had been opened upto the financial year 2006-07. About 1,47,000 new school building and 650000 additional classrooms were constructed.

Nearly 8.14 lakh teachers were appointed during the period 2001 and 2007.

In the Eleventh Five year, a provision for B 27,900 was made for SSA.

Impact on Enrolment

SSA has succeeded in bringing about a huge reduction in the number of out of school children from 320 lakh in 2001-02 to about 70 lakh in March 2007. The enrolment of girls during the same period increased by 19.2 per cent a primary level and 15 per cent at upper primary level, sixty-seven lakh children are presently enrolled in flexible alternative schools that provide access in small, remote habitations and for specific groups of children like working children, children who migrate seasonally with families, urban deprived children etc.

3. Education Guarantee Scheme and Alternative and Innovative Education

Education Guarantee Scheme and Alternative and Innovative Education (EGS and AIE) is an important component of Sarva Shiksha Abhiyan (SSA) to bring out-of-school children in the fold of Elementary Education. The scheme envisages that child-wise planning is undertaken for each out-of-school children.

EGS addresses the inaccessible habitation where there is no formal school within the radius of one km and at least 15-25 children of 6-14 years age group who are not going to school are available. In exceptional cases remote habitations in hilly areas even for 20 children an EGS school can be opened.

Alternative Education interventions for specific categories of very deprived children e.g., child labour, street chiidren, migrating children, working children, children living in difficult circumstances and older children in the 9+ age group especially adolescent girls are being supported under EGS and AIE all over the country.

A sizeable number of out-of school children are in the habitations where schooling facility is available but these children either did not join the school or dropped out before completing their schooling. These children may not fit into the rigid formal system. To bring such children back to school; back to school camp and Bridge Courses strategies have been implemented. Bridge courses and Back to school camps can be residential or non-residential depending upon the need of children.

During 2006-07 the EGS/AIE component helped to provide elementary education to 103.82 lakh children, i.e., 47.71 lakh children who were living in non-accessible habitations were provided elementary education through 1 lakh EGS centres and 31.92 lakh children not going to school were brought into Bridge Courses/Schools camps.

4. Mid-Day Meal Scheme or National Programme of Nutritional Support to Elementary Education (NPNSPE)

Background

With a view to enhancing enrolment, retention and attendance and simultaneously improving nutritional levels among children, the National Programme of Nutritional Support to Primary Education (NP-NSPE) was launched as a Centrally Sponsored Scheme on 15th August 1995, initially in 2408 blocks in the country. By the year 1997-98 the NP-NSPE was introduced in all blocks of the country. It was further extended in 2002 to cover not only children in classes I-V of government, government aided and local body schools, but also children studying in EGS and AI centres.

Objectives

The objectives of the mid-day meal scheme are:

(i) Improving the nutritional status of children in classes I-V in Government, Local Body and Government aided schools, and EGS and AIE centres.

(ii) Encouraging poor children, belonging to disadvantaged sections, to attend school more regularly and help them concentrate on classroom activities.

(iii) Providing nutritional support to children of primary stage in drought affected areas during summer vacation.

Programme Intervention and Coverage

To achieve the above objectives a cooked mid-day meal with nutritional content as shown in column 3 of the table below will be provided to all children studying in classes I-V.

Nutritional Content	*Norm as per NP-NSPE, 2004*	*Revised Norm as per NP-NSPE, 2006*
Calorie	300	450
Protein	8-12	12
Micronutrients	Not Prescribed	Adequate quantities of micronutrients like iron, folic acid, vitamin-A etc.

Components of the revised scheme

The revised scheme provided for the following components:

(i) Supply of free food grains (wheat/rice) @ 100 grams per child per School Day from the nearest FCI godown.

(ii) Reimbursement of the actual cost incurred in transportation of food grains from nearest FCI godown to the Primary. School subject to the following ceiling:

(a) Rs. 100 per Quintal for 11 special category States, viz., Arunachal Pradesh, Assam, Meghalaya, Mizoram, Manipur, Nagaland, Tripura, Sikkim, J & K, Himachal Pradesh and Uttrakhand, and

(b) Rs. 75 per quintal for all other States and UTs.

(iii) Provision of assistance for cooking cost at the following rates:

(a) States in North Eastern Region: @ Rs. 1.80 per child per school day, provided the State Govt. contributes a minimum of 20-paise.

(b) For other States & UTs: @ Rs. 1.50 per child per school day provided the State Govt./UT Admn. contributesa minimum of 50 Paise. State Government/UT Administrations are required to provide the above minimum contribution in order to be eligible or the enhanced rate of Central assistance mentioned above.

(iv) Provision of assistance for cooked Mid-Day Meal during summer vacations to school children in areas declared by State Governments as "drought-affected".

(v) Provision of assistance to construct kitchen-*cum* store in a phased manner up to a maximum of Rs. 60,000 per unit. However, as allocations under MDMS for construction of kitchen-*cum*-store for all schools in next 2-3 years may not be adequate. States would be expected to proactively pursue convergence with other development programmes for this purpose.

(vi) Provision of assistance in a phased manner for provisioning and replacement of *kitchen devices* at an average cost of Rs. 5,000 per school. States/UTs Administration will have the flexibility to incur expenditure on the items listed below on the basis of the actual requirements of the school (provided that the overall average for the State/UT administration remains Rs. 5,000 per school).

(a) Cooking devices (Stove, Chulha etc.)

(b) Containers for stroage of food grains and other ingredients.

(c) Utensils for cooking and serving.

(vii) provision of assistance to States/UTs for *Management, Monitoring & Evaluation* (*MME*) at the rate of 1.8% of total assistance on (a) free food grains, (b) transport cost, and (c) cooking cost. Another 0.2% of the above amount will be utilised at the Central Government for management, monitoring and evaluation.

Monitoring Mechanism

The Department of School Education and Literacy Ministry of Human Rosource Development has prescribed a comprehensive and elaborate mechanism for monitoring and supervising this scheme. It includes the following:

(1) Local level monitoring by Village Education Committees (VECS) and Parent Teacher Associations (PTAS) etc.

(2) Display of Information under Right to Information Act.

(3) Inspection by State Government Officers.

(4) Responsibility of Food Corporation of India.

(5) Submission of Periodic Returns.

5. District Primary Education Programme (DPEP)

The centrally sponsored scheme of district primary Education is an externally aided project. The central government meets 85 per cent of the project cost and the remaining 15 per cent is shared by the concerned state government.

Objectives of the Programme

DPEP adopts a holistic approach to universalise access, retention and improve learning achievement and to reduce disparities among social groups. Adopting an 'area-specific approach' with district as the unit of planning, the key strategies of the programme have been to retain the sensitivity to local conditions and ensuring full participation of the community. It also seeks to strengthen the capacity of national, state and district institutions and organisations for planning, management and professional support in the field of primary education.

Components of the Programme

The programme components include construction of classrooms and new schools, opening of Non-formal/Alternative Schooling Centres, appointment of new setting up early childhood education centres, strengthening of State Countries of Educational Research and Training (SCERTs)/District Institute of Educational Training (DIETs), setting up of Block Resource Centres/Cluster Resource Centres, teacher training, development of Teaching Learning material Research based interventions, special interventions for promoting education of disadvantaged groups, girls, SC, ST, etc., initiatives for providing integrated education to disabled children and distance education for teacher training have also been incorporated in the DPEP scheme.

Investment Per District

Under the Programme parameters, investment per district is limited to Rs. 40 crore over a project period of 5-7 years. There is ceiling of 33.3 per cent on civil works component and 6 per cent on management cost. The remaining amount is required to be spent on quality improvement activities.

Coverage

DPEP at its peak was in operation in 273 districts in 18 states. However, with the progressive closure of the programme it exists only in 123 districts.

Major Achievements of DPEP: (i) DPEP has so far opened more than 1,60,000 new schools, including almost 84,000 alternative schooling (AS) centres. The AS centres cover nearly 3.5 million children, while another two lakh children are covered by Bridge Courses of different types, (ii) The school infrastructure created under DPEP include 52.758 school buildings, 58,604 additional classrooms, 16,619 resource centres,

29, 307 repair works, 64,592 toilets, and 24,909 drinking water facilities, (iii) The Gross Enrolment Ratio (GER) for Phase-I states was around 93 to 95 per cent for the last three years. (iv) The enrolment of girls has shown significant improvement. In DPEP-I districts, the share of girls enrolment in relation to total enrolment has increased from 48 per cent to 49 per cent, while this increase in the subsequent phases of DPEP districts has been from 46 per cent to 47 per cent; (v) The total number of differently-abled children enrolled is now more than 4,20,203 which represents almost 76 per cent of the nearly 5,53,844 differently-abled children identified in the DPEP States; (vi) Village Education Committees/ School Management Committees have been set up in almost all project villages/habitations/schools, (vii) About 1,77,000 teachers, including para-teachers/Shiksha Karmis have been appointed; (viii) About 3,380 resource centres at block level and 29,725 centres at cluster level have been set-up for providing academic support and teacher training facilities.

6. Mahila Samakhya Scheme

Empowerment of Women

Pursuant to the objectives of the NPE, 1986, the Mahila Samakhya Scheme was started in 1989 to translate the goals enshrined in the NPE into a concrete programme for the education and empowerment 61 women in rural areas particularly those from socially and economically marginalised groups. The MS scheme recognises the centrality of education in empowering women to achieve equality. The Mahila Sanghas or women's collectives at the village level provide the women a space to meet, reflect, ask questions and articulate their thoughts and needs and make informed choices.

The Mahila Sanghas though various programmes and awareness campaigns have brought about a change in the outlook of rural women and the effects can how be seen in various facets of life at home within the family, the community and at the block and panchayat levels. The programme has also focussed on awareness of the need to educate the children, especially girls, to give the equal status and opportunities which has resulted in a direct impact on enrolment and retention of girls in schools.

Coverage

The Mahila Samakhya Scheme is currently being implemented in nine States viz., Andhra Pradesh, Assam, Bihar, Jharkhand, Karnataka, Kerala, Gujarat, Utter Pradesh and Uttrakhand spread over 83 districts and covering more than 21,000 villages. From the 2008-09 financial year the programme is being extended to two new States i.e., Madhya Pradesh and Chhatisagarh.

7. **Praramabhik Shiksha Kosh (PSK)**

The fund was created in 2004 to help finance governments commitment to quality primary education. The funds available in PSK are utilised exclusively for SSA and MDM scheme.

III. Quality Improvement in Schools

The following schemes are in operation:

(1) Vocationalisation of Education

(2) Improvement of Science Education

(3) International Science Olympiads.

(4) Environmental Orientation to School Education.

(5) Educational Technology

(6) Introduction of Yoga in Schools

(7) Navodaya/Schools Vidyalaya

(8) Integrated Education for Disabled Children (IEDC)

1. Vocationalisation of Education

The scheme was introduced in 1988 with the following objectives:

(1) To enhance individual employability

(2) To reduce the mismatch between demand and supply of skilled manpower.

(3) To provide an alternative for those pursuing higher education without particular interest or purpose.

A joint council for Vocational Education (JCVE) was set up in April 1990 for policy formulation and coordination at the national level.

In 1993, Pandit Sundar lal Sharma Central Institute of Vocational Education (SSCIVE) was set up at Bhopal to provide technical and academic support to the programme in the country. Nearly 60 vocational courses have been notified under the apprenticeship Act.

About 6800 schools with 195600 sections provide for vocational courses. The enrolment capacity is nearly 98,000 students.

2. Improvement of Science Education in Schools

To improve the quality of science education and to promote the scientific temper as envisaged in the National Policy on Education, 1986, a Centrally Sponsorted Scheme; "Improvement of Science Education in Schools" was initiated during 1987-88. Under the scheme financial assistance was being provided to States/UTs and voluntary agencies. While voluntary agencies were provided assistance for conducting experimental and innovative programmes States/Union Territories were assisted for provision of science kits to Upper Primary Schools, setting up of upgradation of science laboratories in Secondary/Senior Secondary Schools, Library facilities in Secondary/Senior Secondary Schools and Training of Science and Mathematics teachers.

3. International Science Olympiads

With an aim to identify and nurture talents in Mathematics, Physics.

Chemistry and Biology at school level, and International Mathematical Olympiad (IMO), International Physics Olympiad (IPhO), International Chemistry Olympiad (IChO) and International Biology Olympiad (IBO) are held every year. India has been participating country in these Olympiads since 1989, 1998, 1999 and 2000, respectively. Each participating country is required to send a team comprising not more than 6 secondary students contestants to IMO. 5 secondary student contestants at IPhO, 4 contestants to IChO and 4 contestants to IBO apart from a Team Leader and a Deputy Team Leader. Since 2002 Indian team is also participating in international Olympiad in informatics.

As per the exiting financial pattern, the host country pay, for the boarding and lodging and transportation of teams during their stay in the nest country, while the international travel cost is borne by the participating countries. The Indian teams in the last Olympiads were jointly sponsored by the Department of Secondary and Bhabha Centre for Science Education (HBCSE)/Bangalore Association for Science Education (BASE)/Indian Association for Research in Computing Science (IARCS) and Central Board of Secondary Education (CBSE). The cost of international travel is paid by the Department of Secondary and Higher Education while all other expenses on selection of students internal travel incidental borne by NBHM/HBCSE/IARCS.

At IChO-2005 held at Taipei, Taiwan during July 2005 the Indian team won two gold and three bronze medals. At IChO-2006 held at

Gyeongsangbuk, Korea from July 2-12, 2006 and Indian team won one gold, two silver and one bronze medals. In the IMO-2006 held at Lublijana, Slovenia from July 6-18, 2006 the Indian team won five bronze medals and one honourable mention. At IBO-2006 held at Jordoba. Argentina from July 9-16, 2006 the Indian team won three silver and a bronze medal.

4. Environmental Orientation to School Education

The National Policy on Education (NPE)-1986 provides that the protection of environment is a value which , along with certain other values, must form an integral part of curricula at all stages of education. To operationalise this noble objective, the mind and intellect of the students must be sensitised to the hazards inherent in nature upsetting the ecological balance in nature. This step inculcates awareness and respect among students for basic concepts relating to the conservation of environment.

To this end, a Centrally Sponsored Scheme "Environment Orientation to School Education" was initiated in 1988-89. The scheme envisages assistance to voluntary agencies for conduct of experimental and innovative programmes aimed at promoting integration of educational programmes in school with local environmental conditions. During the year 2006-07, voluntary organisations were provided financial assistance to the extent of Rs. 90 lakh for undertaking innovative and experimental projects in the field of environmental education.

5. Educational Technology

Six autonomous State Institutes of Educational Technology (SIET) have been set up in Uttar Pradesh, Bihar, Orissa, Maharashtra, Gujarat and Andhra Pradesh.

6. Introduction of Yoga in Schools

Introduction of Yoga in schools was launched as a Centrally Sponsored Scheme during 1989-90 to provide financial assistance to States/Union Territories/Non-Governmental Organisations. It aimed at giving central assistance for training and research, enrichment of library and construction/expansion of hostels for teacher trainees. It was being implemented through the concerned Departments of Education of States/UTs. It was transferred to NCERT w.e.f. April 2007.

7. Navodaya Vidyalaya Schools

The National Policy on Educationn-1986 envisaged setting up of model school, one in each district of the Country. Accordingly a scheme was formulated under which it was decided to set up co-educational residential schools (now called Jawahar Navodaya Vidyalayas).

Navodaya Vidyalayas are fully residential co-educational institutions providing education up to senior secondary stage. The scheme, which started with only two schools on experimental basis in 1985-86, has grown to 565 schools (as on 31 March 2007) covering as many districts in 34 States UTs with over 1.93 lakh students on rolls as on 31 March 2007. More than 30,000 new students are admitted every year.

The Vidyalayas envisaged a new style of growth with identification and development of talented, bright and gifted children predominantly from rural areas who may otherwise be denied good educational opportunities. Efforts are made to ensure that at least 33 per cent of the students enrolled are girls.

Migration is a unique feature of Navodaya Vidyalaya scheme whereby 30 per cent of students of Class IX from a Vidyalaya located in Hindi speaking area spend one academic year in a Vidyalaya located in Non-Hindi speaking area and *vice-versa* to promote national integration through understanding of the diversity and plurality of country's people, their language and culture.

8. Integrated Education for Disabled Children (IEDC)

The scheme introduced in 1974 was revised in 1992. It provides educational opportunities for disabled children in common schools to facilitate their integration and ultimate retention in the general school system. Under IEDC, 100 per cent assistance is being provided under various components for education of children suffering from mild to moderate disabilities in common schools. The components include educational aids supporting equipments, salaries for special teachers and facilities for children with disability.

By the end of 2005, a total of approximately 2 lakh disabled children had been covered.

IV. Girl's Education

1. National Programme for Education of Girls at Elementary Educational Level (NPEGEL)

The programme is aimed at enhancing girl's education by providing additional support for development of 'model giri child friendly school' in every cluster with more intense community mobilisation and supervision of girls enrolment in schools. Under NPEGEL, nearly 35250 model schools have been opened in addition to supporting 25,540 Early Childhood Care and Education (ECCE) centres. Besides 24,389 additional classrooms have been constructed Nearly 1.85 lakh teachers have been given training on gender sensitization. Remedial teaching has also been provided to 9.67 lakh girls.

2. Kasturba Gandhi Balika Vidyalaya (KGBV) Scheme

The KGBV scheme was launched in July 2004 for setting up residential schools upper primary level for girls belonging to predominantly to the SC, ST, OBC and minority commities. It ran as a separate scheme for two years but was merged with SSA w.e.f. April 1, 2007. As on October 31, 2007, nearly 1,560 KGBVs were in existence and about 1,10,00 girls (26 per cent SC, 33 per cent ST, 26 per cent OBC, 11 per cent BPL-Below Poverty Line and 5 per cent minority girls) were enrolled in them.

V. National Literacy Mission (NLM)

Target: The National Literacy Mission set up in May 1988 aims to attain a sustainable threshold level of 75 per cent literacy by 2007 by imparting functional literacy to non-literates in the age group of 15-35 years, which is the productive and reproductive age group and constitutes a major segment of the work force. Apart from predetermined levels of reading, writing and numeracy with comprehension, functional literacy includes imbibing values of national integration, conservation of environment women's equality, observance of small family norms, etc. Literacy, as enunciated in NLM, is not an end in itself but has to be an active and potent instrument of change ensuring achievement of these social objectives and creation of a learning society.

Special Interventions for Female Literacy: As per Census, 2001, 47 districts in the country have a female literacy rate below 30 per cent. Hence, dealing with low female literacy is of immense concern to the National Literacy Mission and it was decided to target the 47 low female literacy districts for improvement. As most of the these districts are concentrated in the States of Utter Pradesh, Bihar, Orissa and Jharkhand, special innovative programmes have been taken up in these districts for promoting female literacy.

Nine districts in Orissa, which have low female literacy rates, have been covered under Special Project for Accelerated Female Literacy Programme.

Projects for Residual Illiteracy: Although the Total Literacy Campaigns took the form of mass movement and spread throughout the country in many cases a number of campaigns stagnated due to natural calamites, lack of political will, etc. Despite success of literacy phase, there are still pockets of residual illiteracy and low female literacy. To tackle this problem, Projects for Residual Illiteracy (PRI) have been taken up in 9 Districts of Rajasthan covering about 6.60 lakh learners, 10 districts of Andhra Pradesh covering 22.81 lakh learners, 7 districts of Bihar, covering 12.54 lakh learners, 14 districts of Karnataka covering 27.35 lakh learners, 12 districts of Madhya Pradesh covering 7.01 lakh learners, 3 districts of Tripura covering 1.38 lakh learners, 3 district of Jharkhand covering 3.01 lakh learners and 18 districts of Utter Pradesh covering 36.11 lakh learners, 4 districts of Mizoram covering 0.45 lakh learners, and West Bengal covering 29.54 lakh learners.

Special Literacy Drive: The Council of the NLMA in its meeting held in April 2005 identified 150 districts which have the lowest literacy rates in the country for launching a special literacy drive, with special focus on the minority groups, persons belonging to scheduled castes, scheduled tribes, women and other backward sections of the society by drawing up implementation strategies suited to the specific needs of the groups, sections of the society or region. So far, 134 districts in the States of Arunachal Pradesh (7), Andhra Pradesh (8), Bihar (31), Chhatisgarh (2), Jammu and Kashmir (8), Rajasthan (10), Jharkhand (12), Karnataka (2), Madhya Pradesh (9), Meghalaya (3), Nagaland (2) Orissa (8), Punjab (1), Utter Pradesh (27) and West Bengal (4) have been covered under the Special Literacy Drive.

Jan Shikshan Sansthan: The objective of the Jan Shikshan Sansthan (JSS) is educational, vocational and occupational development of the socio-economically backward and educationally disadvantaged groups of urban/rural population particularly neo-literates, semi-literates, SCs, STs, women and girls, slum dwellers, migrant workers etc. At Present, there are 172 JSSs in the Country. Jan Shikshan Sansthans run a number of vocational programmes with varying duration of different skills. More than 250 types of courses and activities are offered by these institutions. The trandes/courses for which training is imparted include cutting, tailoring & dress making; knitting and embroidery; beauty culture and health care; handicrafts; art, drawing and painting repair of electrical software, etc.

VI. Restructuring Teacher Education

Launching of the Scheme

The Scheme was launched in 1987-88 with the following components:

1. Establishment of District Institute of Education & Training (DIETs) by upgradation of existing Elementary Teacher Education Institutions (ETEIs) wherever possible, and establishment of new DIET where necessary.

   Upgradation of selected Secondary Teacher Education Institutions (STETIs) into:
2. (a) College of Teacher Education (CTEs) and

   (b) Institutes of Advanced Study in Education (IASEs).
3. Strengthening of State Council of Educational Research and Training (SCERTs).

Revision of the Scheme

The Scheme was revised in 2003 and the revised guidelines were issued in January 2004 the main objectives of the Teacher Education Scheme are as follows:

1. Speedy completion of DIET/CTE/IASE/SCERT projects sanctioned but not completed up to the end of the IX Plan period.
2. Making DIETs, IASEs sanctioned (and SCERTs strengthened) up to the IX Plan period, optimally functional and operational.
3. Sanction and implementation of fresh DIET/CTE/IASE/SCERT projects to the extent necessary.
4. Improvement in the quality of programmes to be undertaken by DIETs, etc. especially those of pre-service and in-service training, so as to enable them to effectively play their nodal role of improving quality of elementary and secondary education in their respective jurisdiction, as measured in terms of levels of learner achievements.

Criteria for Setting up DIET

Criteria for setting up of DIETs/District Resource Centre (DRC) are:

1. One DIET for each district having a minimum of 2,500 teachers. If there is an existing Government ETEI in the district, it would be upgraded into a DIET. If no Government ETEI exists in the district, a new institution (DIET) will be established.
2. District Resource Centres in districts with less than 2,500 teachers. If a Government ETEI exists in the district, it would be upgraded into a DRC. Otherwise, a new DRC would be established in which case it would not conduct pre-service course.
3. If in a district with more than 2,500 teachers, State Government wishes to establish a DRC in preference to a DIET, it would be able to do so.

There are nearly 570 DIETs and 31 IASEs.

New Norms for Teacher Education Institution: The NITE was issued now norms and standards for various teacher training programmes like CEd, D.Ed, B.Ed. DP.Ed. and MP.Ed. The objective is to improve the quality of teacher education programmes and to strengthen. The infrastructural and the facilities in teacher training institutes.

VII. Expenditure on Education

The allocation for education has over the years, increased significantly. The Plan outlay on education increased from Rs. 151.20 crore in the First Five-Year Plan to Rs. 43,825 crore in the Tenth Five-Year Plan (2002-2007).

The outlay for Education in the Tenth Five-Year Plan of Rs. 43,825 crore was higher than the Ninth Plan outlay of Rs. 24,908.38 crore by 1.76 times. Rs. 30,000 crore had been provided for the Department of Elementary Education and Literacy and Rs. 13,825 crore for the Department of Secondary and Higher Education. The expenditure during the plan periods on the different sectors of education is in Table 33.1.

Table 33.1

Plan Expenditure on Different Sectors of Education

Sector	*First Plan Expdt. 1951-56*	*Second Plan Expdt. 1956-61*	*Third Plan Expdt. 1961-66*	*Plan Holiday Expdt. 1966-69*	*Fourth Plan Expdt. 1969-74*	*Fifth Plan Expdt. 1974-79*	*Sixth Plan Expdt. 1980-85*	*Seventh Plan Expdt. 1985-90*	*1990-92 Expdt.*	*Eighth Plan Expdt. 1992-97*	*Ninth Plan Expdt. (1997-02) (Central Sector)*	*Tenth Plan Outlay (2002-07) (Central Sector)*
(1)	(2)	(3)	(4)	(5)	(6)	(7)	(8)	(9)	(10)	(11)	(12)	(13)
Elementary Education	58 (870)	35 (950)	34 (2010)	24 (750)	50 (3743)	52 (5913)	32 (8414)	37 (28494)	37 (17290)	48 (103940)	65.7 (145233)	65.6 (287500)
Secondary Education	5 (83)	19 (510)	18 (1030)	16 (530)	@	@	20 (5344)	24 (18315)	22 (10530)	24 (52311)	10.5 (23227)	9.9 (43250)
Adult Education					2 (126)	2 (248)	6 (1533)	6 (4696)	9 (4160)	5 (11421)	2.4 (5204)	2.9 (12500)
Higher Education	8 (117)	18 (480)	15 (870)	24 (770)	25 (1883)	28 (3188)	21 (5604)	16 (12011)	12 (5880)	10 (20944)	10.3 (22709)	9.5 (41765)
Others	15 (227)	10 (300)	12 (730)	11 (370)	13 (936)	9 (1071)	11 (2729)	3 (1980)	2 (1180)	3 (7398)	1.6 (3492)	1.4 (6235)
Technical Education	14 (215)	18 (490)	21 (1250)	25 (810)	10 (786)	9 (1015)	10 (2563)	14 (10833)	17 (8230)	10 (21987)	9.5 (21095)	10.7 (47000)
Total	100 (1512)	100 (2730)	100 (5890)	100 (3230)	100 (7474)	100 (11435)	100 (26187)	100 (76329)	100 (47270)	100 (218001)	100 (220960)	100 (438250)

Source: Five-Year Plan Documents, Planning Commission and Analysis of Budget Expenditure, Ministry of HRD.

Notes: 1. Figures in parenthesis in millions of rupees.

2. Figures in Col. 2 to Col. 11 includes the share of States/UTs.

@ Included under Elementary Education.

VIII. Education in the Eleventh Five Year Plan (2007-2012)

Introduction

The Eleventh Five Year Plan Approved by the National Developmental Council on December 19, 2007 was released by the Prime Minister of India on June 28, 2008. The Plan reaffirms the vital role of the education sector. On account of the focus on education in the Eleventh Plan, the Prime Minister called this plan a 'National Education Plan'.

1. Goals, Targets and Strategies in Elementary Education

(1) Restructuring SSA

Nearly 7.1. million children being out of school and over 50 per cent dropping out at elementary level are matters of serious concern. SSA would, therefore, be reoriented to meet the challenges of equity, retention, and high-quality education. It is necessary to consider passing appropriate legislation for this purpose. SSA would be restructured into a National Mission for Quality Elementary Education to ensure minimum norms and standards for schools (both government and private). It would address access, quality, and equity holistically though a systems approach.

(2) Grading of Schools

The substantial step up in the Eleventh Plan outlay in the Central sector would increasingly be invested in improving quality of elementary education, recruiting additional teachers (particularly science and mathematics), seeking technology upgradation including ICT in schools, and Technical Assistance (TA) including the educationally fragile States. The issue of poor performing schools would be addressed by grading schools through a composite index and by providing TA.

(3) Universal Enrolment

There will be universal enrolment of 6-14 age group children including the hard to reach segment.

Eliminating Dropout: Dropout at the primary level would be eliminated and at the upper primary level reduced from over 50 per cent to 20 per cent by 2011-12.

2. Secondary Education Scheme for Universal Access and Quality at the Secondary Stage (SUCCESS)

The erstwhile schemes of ICT in schools, girls child incentive, IEDC, VE, etc. will be subsumed under a new umbrella CSS named SUCCESS. The principal objectives of SUCCESS will be (i) universalizing access with major reduction in gender, social and regional gaps in enrolment, dropout, and retention and (ii) improving quality with focus on Science and Maths. Specific interventions will include:

- Setting up 6000 high quality Model Schools at block level to serve as benchmark for excellence in secondary schooling.
- Upgrading 15000 existing primary schools to secondary schools.
- Increasing the intake capacity of about 44000 existing secondary schools.
- Strengthening infrastructure in existing schools with 3.43 lakh additional classrooms and additional 5.14 lakh teachers.
- Encouraging establishment of good quality schools in deficient areas in both public and more in PPP (Private-Public Partnership) mode.
- Expansion of KVs and NVs in underserved areas.
- 100 per cent trained teachers in all schools and reaching PTR (Pupil Teacher Ratio) of 25 : 1 by 2011-12.
- Revamped ICT in secondary and higher secondary schools.

Bridging Social Disparities

In order to bridge social gaps in secondary education in respect of SCs, STs, minorities, and OBCs, the Eleventh Plan will address specific areas including (i) upgradation of elementary schools to secondary schools in geographic concentration areas of relevant social groups, (ii) supply of free uniforms text books, footwear, (iii) supply of bicycle/wheelchairs, (iv) hostels for boy and girls, (v) stipends to the deserving children, (vi) support to all Madrasa for adoption of general curriculum of States, (vii) pre-matric and post-matric scholarships, (viii) special remedial coaching within/outside school for weakened students, and (ix) an area-intensive approach with community participation.

3. Education for Girls

Most of the States implement incentive schemes for education of girls, but generally with very limited coverage. Measures will be undertaken to overcome obstacles to girls' education posed by factors such as poverty, domestic/sibling responsibilities, girl child labour, low preference to girls' education, preference to marriage over the education of girls, etc. A Girl Child Incentive Scheme will be launched on a pilot basis in the selected EBBs. On the basis of quick evaluation, its expansion will be considered in the Eleventh Plan period. The merger of all girl child incentives schemes will be ensured.

4. Vocational Education

Greater emphasis will be placed on the services sector and, therefore, on soft skills, computer literacy, and flexi-time. There will also be emphasis on development of generic and multiple skills so that persons may respond to changes in technology and market demands. Generic skills that cut across a number of occupations would enable an individual to transfer from one field to another during his/her working life. Other features will include compulsory partnership with employers who could provide trainers and arrange for internships, give advice on curricula, and participate in assessment and certification.

5. Teacher Education

The Eleventh Plan would be a Quality Plan in respect of the education sector. The following specific programmes are proposed to be taken up in teacher education during the Eleventh Plan.

- Strengthening Teacher Education by (i) developing Teacher Education Information Base in Public Domain, (ii) creating additional support systems in the field, and (iii) strengthening academic capacity.
- Continuation of existing scheme relating to SCERTs.
- Continuation of support to IASEs and CTEs.
- Conducting training of Educational Administrators including Head Teachers.
- Introducing substitute/stipend scheme for enabling teachers and educational administrators to enhance their academic qualifications.
- Continuation of support to DIETs.
- Augmenting Teacher Education capacity in SC/ST and minority areas.
- Professional Development of teacher through training programmes.

- Professional Development of Teacher Educators through Refresher Courses and Fellowship programmes.
- Support to NGOs.
- Technology in Teacher Education.
- Integrating Elementary Teacher Education with Higher Education.

6. Higher Education Quality improvement

Quality improvement in higher education will be brought about through restructuring academic programmes to ensure their relevance to modern market demands; domestic and global linkages with employers and external advisory resource support groups and tracer studies; greater emphasis on recruitment of adequate and good quality teachers; complete revamping of teaching/learning methods by shifting from traditional repetitive experiments to open-ended design-oriented work for encouraging invention and innovation; compulsory interactive seminar-tutorials, broadening the content of Science and engineering programmes to strengthen fundamental concepts, improving learning opportunities and conditions by updating text books and learning material; and improving self-directed learning with modern aids and development of IT network.

7. Adult Education

Targets

(1) Achieving 80% literacy rate

(2) Reducing gender gap in literacy to 10 per cent

(3) Extending coverage of NLM programmes to 35^{+} age group.

Special Focus Areas

(a) Special focus to be on SCs, STs, minorties and rural women.

(b) Focus also on low literacy states, tribal areas and adolescents.

34 Overview of Development of Education in India

1. Primary Education

The 86th Constitutional Amendment Act; 2002 led to insertion of a new Article 21-A in Part III of the Constitution that made Free and Compulsory Education to all children of 6 to 14 years of age a Fundamental Right. The Compulsory Education Act in this regard was passed by the Parliament in 2009.

The progress made in some of the important primary education schemes is given below:

1. *Sarva Shiksha Abhiyan:* SSA is being implemented in partnership with State Governments to address the needs of children in age group of 6-14 years. The achievements of SSA till December 2008 are opening of 2,76,903 new schools, construction of 2,25,383 school buildings, construction of 9,18,981 additional classrooms, 1,82,019 drinking water facilities, construction of 2,51,023 toilets, supply of free textbooks to 8.40 crore children, appointment of 9.66 lakh teachers and in-service training for 23.82 lakh teachers. There has been a significant reduction in the number of out-of-school children on account of SSA interventions.
2. *National Programme for Education of Girls at Elementary Education:* NPEGEL is being implemented in educationally backward blocks (EBBs) where the level of rural female literacy is less than the national average and the gender gap is more than the national average and blocks having at least 5 per cent SC/ST population with SC/ST female literacy below 10 per cent. It is also being implemented in select urban slums. About 3,286 educationally backward blocks are covered under the

scheme in 25 states. Under NPEGEL, 39,852 model schools have been opened in addition to supporting 11,261 Early Childhood Care and Education (ECCE) centres. Besides, 27,282 additional classrooms have been constructed, and 2,11,215 teachers have been given training on gender sensitization. Remedial teaching has also been provided to 11,44,370 girls apart from holding bridge courses covering 89,462 girls and additional incentives like uniforms etc. to about 1,60,73,048 girls (up to January 31, 2009).

3. *National Programme of Mid-Day Meals in Schools:* The programme provides a mid-day meal of 450 calories and 12 grams of protein to children at the primary stage. For children at the upper primary stage, the nutritional value is fixed at 700 calories and 20 grams of protein. Adequate quantities of micro-nutrients like iron, folic acid and vitamin-A are also recommended under the programme. Since April 1, 2008, it covers all children studying in government, local body and government-aided primary and upper primary schools and the Education Guarantee Scheme/ Alternative & Innovative Education centres of all areas across the country. During 2008-09, 11.74 crore children (8.24 crore of primary stage, i.e. Class I-V and 3.50 crore of upper primary stage i.e. Class VI-VIII) were to be benefitted under the scheme. The scheme was provided an outlay of Rs. 8,000 crore in the interim budget for 2009-10 compared to the same level of allocation in 2008-09.
4. *Kasturba Gandhi Balika Vidyalaya:* KGBV: scheme was launched in July 2004 for setting up residential schools at upper primary level for girls belonging predominantly to SC, ST, OBC and minority communities. The KGBV scheme was merged With the Sarva Shiksha Abhiyan (SSA) as of April 1, 2007. 2,573 KGBVs were sanctioned by Government of India up to March 31, 2009. As on March 31, 2009, 2,460 KGBVs are reported to be functional (i.e. 95.61 per cent) in the states and 2,15,269 girls enroled in them - 53,503 SC girls (24.85 per cent); 74,487 ST girls (34.60 per cent); 54,201 OBC girls (25.18 per cent); 18,647 BPL girls (8.66 per cent), and 14,431 minority girls (6.7 per cent).

II. Secondary Education

Secondary education serves as a bridge between primary and higher education and prepares young persons between the age group of 14-18 years for entry into higher education and work. The number of secondary and higher secondary schools has increased from 7,416 in 1950-51 to 1 ,68,900 in 2006-07. Total enrolment in secondary and higher secondary stage has increased correspondingly from 1.5 million in 1950-51 to 39.44 million in 2006-07. Gross Enrolment Ratio (GER), which shows total enrolment in secondary stage (9th-12th) as a percentage of total population in the relevant age-group has also increased steadily from 19.3 in 1990-91 to 40.62 in 2006-07. GER for Class IX-X (14-16 years) was 52.26 and for Class XI-XII (16-18 years) was 28.54 in 2006-07. Important Government initiatives for providing enhanced access to secondary education during the year were:

- A comprehensive Centrally-sponsored scheme called Rashtriya Madhyamik Shiksha Abhiyan was launched in 2008-09 with the objective to universalize access to and to improve quality of secondary education.
- Government of India has launched a Centrally-sponsored scheme called the National Means-cum-Merit Scholarship Scheme to award 1 ,00,000 scholarships each year, under which each student will be given Rs. 6,000 per annum (Rs. 500 per month) for study in Class IX to XII. To fund this scheme, a corpus of Rs. 750 crore has already been created with the State Bank of India in 2008-09 and a like amount would be added to this corpus fund every year over the next three years.
- First phase of a new Centrally-sponsored scheme to establish one high quality model school in each block of the country to serve as schools of excellence has been launched from 2008-09.
- The Government of India has launched a Centrally-sponsored scheme called "Incentive to Girls for Secondary Education" in June 2008. According to the scheme, a sum of Rs. 3,000 will be deposited in the name of eligible girl as fixed deposit and she would be entitled to withdraw it along with interest thereon on reaching 18 years of age. The scheme will cover (i) All eligible girls belonging to SC/ST communities, who pass Class VIII and (ii) All girls who pass Class VIII examination from Kasturba Gandhi Balika Vidyalayas (irrespective of whether they belong to SC/ST) and enrol in Class IX in Government, Government-aided and local body schools.
- A new Centrally-sponsored scheme to set up girls' hostels in about 3,500 educationally backward blocks has been launched in 2008-09. Under this scheme, priority will be given to girls belonging to SC/ST/OBC/minority communities.

- Setting up of 20 Navodaya Vidyalayas which are residential schools meant primarily for meritorious rural children in districts having a large concentration of Scheduled Castes and Scheduled Tribes has been sanctioned. Ten schools will be set up in districts having a large concentration of Scheduled Castes and the remaining 10 in districts having large concentration of Scheduled Tribes.

III. Higher and Technical Education

There has been a significant growth in higher education. According to the University Grants Commission (UGC), enrolment in various courses at all levels in universities/colleges and other institutions of higher education in 2006-07 was 11.61 million as compared to 11.34 million in the previous year. Out of this, the number of women students were 4.70 million constituting 40.55 per cent. There has also been a significant expansion of Central institutions of higher education in recent years. Recent expansion of higher educational institutions includes the following:

1. An ordinance has been promulgated under Article 123 of the Constitution for establishment of 15 Central Universities including the conversion of three State Universities into Central Universities – one in each such state which does not have a Central University, except Goa, which has not been included at the request of the State Government.
2. Six new Indian Institutes of Technology (IITs), one each in Bihar, Andhra Pradesh, Rajasthan, Orissa, Gujarat and Punjab have been set up during 2008-09.
3. One new Indian Institute of Management (IIM) namely the Rajiv Gandhi Indian Institute of Management (RGIIM) at Shillong in Meghalaya started functioning from the academic session 2008-09.
4. Two new Indian Institutes of Science Education & Research (IISERs) have been set up at Bhopal and Thiruvananthapuram which started functioning with the academic session 2008-09.
5. Two new Schools of Planning & Architecture (SPAs) have been set up in Bhopal in Madhya Pradesh and Vijayawada in Andhra Pradesh. Classes started from the academic session 2008-09 in temporary premises.

6. One new Central university, namely Indira Gandhi National Tribal University at Amarkantak in Madhya Pradesh started functioning in 2008-2009.
7. A new Scholarship Scheme has been started to cover top 2 per cent of the student population of Class XII (equally divided between boys and girls on the basis of Class XII results) by providing them with scholarship of Rs. 1,000 per month for 10 months in a year for the first three years of undergraduate level studies and Rs. 2,000 per month for 10 months in a year for subsequent 2 years.
8. Central Institute of Classical Tamil started functioning during 2008-09.
9. To encourage research, the amount of fellowships under Junior Research Fellowships has been enhanced by about 50 per cent.

IV. Reforms in education

Government policies have been focusing on providing quality education and upgrading skills. However, further reforms are needed in the education sector where both the Central and State Governments are involved (Box).

Box: Educational reforms: Some issues

Education in India comes under the concurrent list and thus both the Central and State Governments are involved leading to multiple controls and regulations by the governments and statutory bodies. There is an urgent need for replacement of bureaucratic controls in education by professional regulators along with private-public partnership to ensure universal primary education. Competition in tertiary and secondary education is also equally essential. Rating the quantity of educational institutions and all education service providers (private and public) may be helpful. Entry of registered societies (non-profit) and publicly listed (education) companies in all fields of education, subject to the regulatory framework which ensures quality and reasonable pricing may be encouraged. Government's higher education funds should be focused on promoting scientific and technical education and encouraging R & D in all subjects. Education societies acquiring land at concessional rates or other assistance from the government should pass on the benefits to the students. There is a mad rush for higher education

(Contd.)

at prestigious institutions like IIT's and IIMs. A large number of private coaching institutions are thriving on this phenomenon. Parents are incurring huge expenditure on their children to get coaching from the tutorial colleges to compete for engineering or management entrance examination. At the same time, there is heavy pressure on children which may adversely affect their physical and mental development. There is a need to streamline the admission procedure to such institutions while at the same time ensuring that quality of student intake does not suffer. Intake should be based on entrance examination which tests the aptitude to grasp knowledge and not the knowledge itself. Besides, the number of institutions could be increased through entry of private players while ensuring that they are professionally regulated so that their curriculums/ degrees are internationally accepted.

Source: *Economic Survey 2008-2009.*

The Rights of Children to Free and Compulsory Education. Act, 2009 (35 of 2009)

Brief History of Legislation

When the Constitution of India was framed, there was no Article relating to Right to Education. Article 45 was introduced under Part IV **'Directive Principles of State Policy'.** The Article **stated— 'Provision for free and compulsory education for children';** The state shall endeavour to provide within a period of ten years from the commencement of this Constitution, for free and compulsory education for all children until they complete the age of fourteen years'.

Vigorous efforts were made to implement the Article 45 but results were not satisfactory. From time to time great concerns were expressed in official and non-official circles on this. The target date of 1960 went on changing from year to year. The Government of India in 2001 initiated the Sarv Shiksha Abhiyan'.

The Supreme Court of India while hearing a case pertaining to education advised the Government of India to enact a suitable Legislation for Universalization of Elementary Education (UEE). Accordingly the Constitution of India was amended by 'The Constitution (Eighty Sixth Amendment) Act 2002. The amendment included the following provisions:

(a) **Insertion of new article** 21A.— After article 21 of the constitution, the following article shall be inserted namely:

"21A. Right to Education.—The state shall provide free and compulsory education to all children of the age of six to fourteen years in a manner as the state may by law determine".

(b) **Substitution of New Article for Article 45**—For Article 45 of the constitution, the following article shall be substituted, namely:

"45. Provision for early childhood care and education to children below the age of six years.—The state shall endeavour to provide early childhood care and education for all children until they complete the age of six years".

(c) **Amendment of Article 51** A.—In Article 51A of the constitution, after clause(j), the following clause shall be added namely:

"(k) Who is a parent or guardian to provide opportunities for education to his child or ward, as the case may be, between the age of six and fourteen years".

The Right of children for free and compulsory education Bill having been passed by both Houses of parliament received the assent of the president on 26th August 2009. It came in the Statue Book as 'The Rights Of Children To Free And Compulsory Education Act 2009 (35 of 2009)'.

Significance of the Act

In several educational quarters the Education Act has been hailed as a great landmark legislation in the history of education in India. It is expected that its implementation will provide not only for free and compulsory education to every child between the age of 6 and 14 years of age but also help in raising standard of education. However, there are sceptics who do not find any weight in such arguments. It is true that the Act has raised high hopes but if past performance in free and compulsory education is any indicator it does not inspire much.

As a matter of fact every state has its own Education Act, Code which includes almost these provisions contained in the present Act. Nevertheless there is one major difference. Now it is backed by an Act of the Parliament. The Present Act specifies the duties of various stake holders in education i.e., the Central Government, The State Government, Local Authorities, the parents and Teachers, etc.

It appears a detailed mechanism will have to be worked out to demare clearly the role of various authorities. From the contents of the Act, one is inclined to get the impression, that it will lead to more litigation and may become a haven for the legal community.

The Act comprising seven chapters gives out the specific rights of the child as also the duties of various agencies involved in the imparting of education to the child.

Main Provisions of the Act

- Provision of free and compulsory elementary education (class I to VIII) to every child.
- Ensuring availability of a neighbourhood school.
- Ensuring that the children belonging to weaker section are not discriminated against and prevented from pursuing and completing elementary eduction on any grounds;
- Providing infrastructure including school building, teaching staff and learning equipment;
- Providing special training facility.
- Ensuring and monitoring admission, attendance and completion of elementary education by every child;
- Ensuring good quality elementary education conforming to the standards and norms specified in the Schedule; (given separately).
- Ensuring timely prescribing of curriculum and courses of study for elementary education.
- Providing training facility for teachers.
- Charging of no capitation fee.
- No screening procedure for admission.
- No denial for admission.
- No holding back in the same class.
- No expulsion.
- No physical punishment to the child.
- No mental harassment of the child.
- Appropriate condition of service teachers.
- Constituting managing committee for every school.
- Suitable pupils teachers ratio.
- Filling of vacancy of teachers in time.

- Prohibition of deployment of teachers for non-education purposes.
- Prohibition of tuition by teachers.
- Monitoring child's right to education.
- Updating of curriculum from time to time and continuous and comprehensive evaluation.
- Constitution of National and State Advisory Councils.

Appendix: Major Educational Statistics: INDIA (2004-05)

S.No	State/UT		GER	Drop-out	PTR		Schools per lakh population		Lakh of population per institution		
		Literacy 2001	Classes (I-VIII)	Classes (I-X)	Primary	UP	Elem.	Sec./ Hr Sec	University	College	Technical
1	2	3	4	5	6	7	8	9	10	11	12
1.	Andhra Pradesh	60.5	86.99	63.69	33	31	99	22	31.6	0.59	1.97
2.	Arunachal Pradesh	54.3	106.70	70.79	34	30	163	19	11.4	1.14	5.70
3.	Assam	63.3	91.92	74.96	42	16	137	19	46.5	0.88	25.34
4.	Bihar	47.0	65.16	83.06	104	75	57	4	46.2	1.18	43.87
5.	Chhattisgarh	64.7	112.63	0.00	48	46	203	12	43.8	1.03	18.25
6.	Goa	82.0	106.04	40.65	21	17	76	31	14.1	0.61	1.57
7.	Gujarat	69.1	101.70	59.29	35	39	73	14	26.6	1.05	5.55
8.	Haryana	67.9	80.01	32.48	44	30	63	23	24.9	1.35	2.20
9.	Himachal Pradesh	76.5	108.74	6.98	24	30	212	37	9	0.71	7.00
10.	Jammu & Kashmir	55.5	74.45	53.75	34	16	153	13	11.8	2.12	6.64
11.	Jharkhand	53.6	75.82	0.00	81	61	76	4	35.5	2.43	18.93
12.	Karnataka	66.6	98.76	59.38	26	37	97	21	20.3	0.59	1.84
13.	Kerala	90.9	95.35	7.15	28	27	30	16	40.9	1.76	2.68
14.	Madhya Pradesh	63.7	114.09	64.70	43	30	205	13	30.5	0.84	6.15
15.	Maharashtra	76.9	105.70	54.16	37	37	67	18	24.8	0.84	2.99
16.	Manipur	70.5	129.65	43.02	30	20	150	31	11.25	0.39	11.25

1	2	3	4	5	6	7	8	9	10	11	12
17.	Meghalaya	62.6	121.93	79.15	44	16	317	29	24.1	0.45	24.1
18.	Mizoram	88.8	109.51	66.95	17	8	263	56	9.2	0.35	4.60
19.	Nagaland	66.6	75.76	97.29	19	16	97	18	20.7	0.56	6.90
20.	Orissa	63.1	108.47	64.42	53	44	162	23	25.4	0.54	7.05
21.	Punjab	69.7	72.57	44.06	43	19	62	16	28.2	1.20	5.52
22.	Rajasthan	60.4	102.67	73.87	49	34	137	17	24	0.98	10.71
23.	Sikkim	68.8	111.49	82.30	22	25	155	29	2.8	2.8	1.87
24.	Tamil Nadu	73.5	113.96	55.19	33	41	63	14	16.4	1.44	1.51
25.	Tripura	73.2	109.59	73.36	54	15	84	20	33.2	2.37	16.6
26.	Uttar Pradesh	56.3	87.04	43.77	58	35	95	7	45.2	1.75	11.76
27.	Uttranchal	71.6	106.39	0.00	25	18	207	21	9.9	1.04	4.46
28.	West Bengal	68.6	94.67	78.03	54	44	63	10	34.7	2.23	8.86
29.	Andaman & Nicobar Islands	81.3	107.97	36.97	20	18	69	24		1.3	1.95
30.	Chandigarh	81.9	71.87	16.73	41	29	3	12	3.33	0.83	3.33
31.	Dadra & Nagar Haveli	57.6	113.70	67.06	62	43	91	9			2.39
32.	Daman & Diu	78.2	128.85	43.43	43	29	40	15		1.9	1.90
33.	Delhi	81.7	91.84	46.92	40	26	20	11	1	2.4	3.69
34.	Lakshadweep	86.7	58.75	18.88	21	16	38	16			
35.	Pondicherry	81.2	121.34	16.89	24	21	45	22	10.1	0.92	1.01
	India	64.8	93.54	61.92	46	35	97	14	27.4	1.04	4.36

Note: GER: Gross Enrolment Ratio; PTR: Pupil Teacher Ratio; UP; Upper Primary.

Source: Selected Educational Statistics, 2004-05.

Index